Create GUI Applications with Python & Qt6
The hands-on guide to making apps with Python

Martin Fitzpatrick

Version 2.0, 2022-07-25

Table of Contents

Introduction

If you want to create GUI applications with Python it can be tricky to know where to start. There are a lot of new concepts you need to understand to get *anything* to work. But, like any coding problem, the first step is learning to approach the problem in the right way. In this book I take from the basic principles of GUI development to creating your own, fully functional, desktop apps with PyQt6.

The first edition of this book was released in 2016. Since then it has been updated 14 times, adding and expanding chapters in response to reader feedback. There are more PyQt resources available now than when I started, but there is still a shortage of in-depth, practical guides to building complete apps. This book fills that gap!

The book is formatted as a series of chapters exploring different aspects of PyQt6 in turn. They are arranged to put the simpler chapters toward the beginning, but if you have specific requirements for your project, don't be afraid to jump around. Each chapter will guide you through learning the fundamental concepts before taking you through a series of coding examples to gradually explore and learn how to apply the ideas yourself.

You can download source code and resources for all examples in this book from http://www.pythonguis.com/d/pyqt6-source.zip

It is not possible to give you a *complete* overview of the entire Qt ecosystem in a book of this size, so there are links to external resources — both on the pythonguis.com website and elsewhere. If you find yourself thinking "I wonder if I can do *that*?" the best thing you can do is put this book down, then *go and find out!* Just keep regular backups of your code along the way so you always have something to come back to if you royally mess it up.

Throughout this book there are boxes like this, giving info, tips and warnings. All of them can be safely skipped over if you are in a hurry, but reading them will give you a deeper and more rounded knowledge of the Qt framework.

1. A *very* brief history of the GUI

The **Graphical User Interface** has a long and venerable history dating back as far as the 1960s. Stanford's NLS (oN-Line System) introduced the mouse and windows concepts, first demonstrated publicly in 1968. This was followed by the Xerox PARC Smalltalk system GUI 1973, which is the foundation of most modern general purpose GUIs.

These early systems already had many of the features we take for granted in modern desktop GUIs, including windows, menus, radio buttons, check boxes and icons. This combination of features gave us the early acronym used for these types of interfaces: WIMP (windows, icons, menus, pointing device — a mouse).

In 1979 the first commercial system featuring a GUI was released — the PERQ workstation. This spurred a number of other GUI efforts including, notably, the Apple Lisa (1983), which added the concept of the menu bar and window controls, as well as other systems from Atari (GEM) and Amiga. On UNIX, the X Window System emerged in 1984 while the first version of Windows for PC was released in 1985.

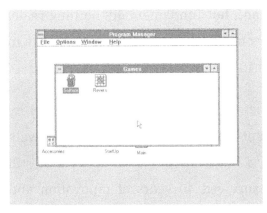
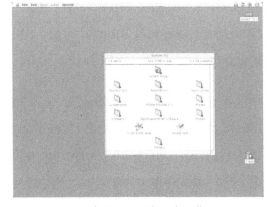

Microsoft Windows 3.1   Apple System 7 (Emulated)

Figure 1. The desktop on Microsoft Windows 3.1 (1992) and Apple System 7 (1991)

Early GUIs were not the instant hit you might think, due to the lack of compatible software at launch and expensive hardware requirements — particularly for home users. However, slowly, but steadily, the GUI paradigm become the preferred way to interact with computers and the WIMP metaphor became firmly established as the standard. That's not to say there haven't been *attempts* to replace the WIMP metaphor on the desktop. Microsoft Bob (1995), for example, was Microsoft's much maligned attempt to replace the desktop with a house.

Figure 2. Microsoft Bob — Discarding the desktop metaphor for a cartoon house.

There has been no shortage of user interfaces hailed as *revolutionary* in their time, from the launch of Windows 95 (1995) through to Mac OS X (2001), GNOME Shell (2011) and Windows 10 (2015). Each of these overhauled the UI of their respective systems, often with much fanfare, but fundamentally nothing really changed. These user interfaces are still very much WIMP systems and function in much the same way as GUIs have since the 1980s.

When the revolution came, it was mobile — the mouse has been replaced by touch, and windows by full-screen apps. But even in a world where we all walk around with smartphones in our pocket, a huge amount of daily work is still done on desktop computers. WIMP has survived 40 years of innovation and looks to survive many more.

2. A bit about Qt

Qt is a free and open-source *widget toolkit* for creating cross-platform GUI applications, allowing applications to target multiple platforms from Windows, macOS, Linux and Android with a single codebase. But Qt is *much more* than a widget toolkit and features built in support for multimedia, databases, vector graphics and MVC interfaces, it is more accurate to think of it as an application development *framework*.

Qt was started by Eirik Chambe-Eng and Haavard Nord in 1991, founding the first Qt company *Trolltech* in 1994. Qt is currently developed by *The Qt Company* and continues to be regularly updated, adding features and extending mobile and cross-platform support.

Qt and PyQt6

PyQt6 is a Python *binding* of the Qt toolkit, developed by *Riverbank Computing*. When you write applications using PyQt6 what you are *really* doing is writing applications in Qt. The PyQt6 library is actually a wrapper around the C++ Qt library, which makes it possible to use it in Python.

Because this is a Python interface to a C++ library, the naming conventions used within PyQt6 do not adhere to PEP8 standards. For example, functions and variables are named using `mixedCase` rather than `snake_case`. Whether you adhere to this standard in your own applications is entirely up to you, however I find it helpful to continue to follow Python standards for my own code, to help clarify where the PyQt6 code ends and your own begins.

Lastly, while there is PyQt6 specific documentation available, you will often find yourself reading the Qt documentation itself as it is more complete. If you need advice on converting Qt C++ code to Python, take a look at Translating C++ Examples to Python.

Updates & Additional Resources

This book is regularly updated. If you bought this book from me directly you'll receive automatic digital updates as they are released. If you bought the book elsewhere, send your receipt to **register@pythonguis.com** to get the latest digital edition & register for future updates.

You may also be interested in joining my **Python GUI Academy** where there are video tutorials covering the topics in this book & beyond.

Join me at **academy.pythonguis.com**

Basic PyQt6 Features

It's time to take your first steps in creating GUI applications with PyQt6!

In this chapter you will be introduced to the basics of PyQt6 that are the foundations of any application you create. We will develop a simple windowed application on your desktop. We'll add widgets, arrange them using layouts and connect these widgets to functions, allowing you to trigger application behavior from your GUI.

Use the provided code as your guide, but always feel free to experiment. That's the best way to learn how things work.

 Before you get started, you need a working installation of PyQt6. If you don't have one yet, check out Installing PyQt6.

 Don't forget to download the source code that accompanies this book from http://www.pythonguis.com/d/pyqt6-source.zip

3. My first Application

Let's create our first application! To start create a new Python file — you can call it whatever you like (e.g. myapp.py) and save it somewhere accessible. We'll write our simple app in this file.

 We'll be editing within this file as we go along, and you may want to come back to earlier versions of your code, so remember to keep regular backups.

Creating your App

The source code for your very first application is shown below. Type it in verbatim, and be careful not to make mistakes. If you do mess up, Python will let you know what's wrong. If you don't feel like typing it all in, the file is included in the source code with this book.

Listing 1. basic/creating_a_window_1.py

```python
from PyQt6.QtWidgets import QApplication, QWidget

# Only needed for access to command line arguments
import sys

# You need one (and only one) QApplication instance per application.
# Pass in sys.argv to allow command line arguments for your app.
# If you know you won't use command line arguments QApplication([])
# works too.
app = QApplication(sys.argv)

# Create a Qt widget, which will be our window.
window = QWidget()
window.show()  # IMPORTANT!!!!! Windows are hidden by default.

# Start the event loop.
app.exec()


# Your application won't reach here until you exit and the event
# loop has stopped.
```

First, launch your application. You can run it from the command line like any other Python script, for example —

```
python MyApp.py
```

Or, for Python 3 —

```
python3 MyApp.py
```

From now on, you'll see the following box as a hint to run your application and test it out, along with an indication of what you'll see.

🚀 Run it! You will now see your window. Qt automatically creates a window with the normal window decorations and you can drag it around and resize it like any window.

What you'll see will depend on what platform you're running this example on. The image below shows the window as displayed on Windows, macOS and Linux (Ubuntu).

Figure 3. Our window, as seen on Windows, macOS and Linux.

Stepping through the code

Let's step through the code line by line, so we understand exactly what is happening.

First, we import the PyQt6 classes that we need for the application. Here we're importing QApplication, the application handler and QWidget, a basic *empty* GUI widget, both from the QtWidgets module.

```
from PyQt6.QtWidgets import QApplication, QWidget
```

The main modules for Qt are QtWidgets, QtGui and QtCore.

 You could use from <module> import * but this kind of global import is generally frowned upon in Python, so we'll avoid it here.

Next we create an instance of QApplication, passing in sys.arg, which is Python list containing the command line arguments passed to the application.

```
app = QApplication(sys.argv)
```

If you know you won't be using command line arguments to control Qt you can pass in an empty list instead, e.g.

```
app = QApplication([])
```

Next we create an instance of a QWidget using the variable name window.

```
window = QWidget()
window.show()
```

In Qt *all* top level widgets are windows — that is, they don't have a *parent* and are not nested within another widget or layout. This means you can technically create a window using any widget you like.

I can't see my window!

Widgets *without a parent* are invisible by default. So, after creating the window object, we must **always** call .show() to make it visible. You can remove the .show() and run the app, but you'll have no way to quit it!

What is a window?

- Holds the user-interface of your application
- Every application needs at least one (...but can have more)
- Application will (by default) exit when last window is closed

Finally, we call app.exec() to start up the event loop.

What's the event loop?

Before getting the window on the screen, there are a few key concepts to introduce about how applications are organised in the Qt world. If you're already familiar with event loops you can safely skip to the next section.

The core of every Qt Application is the `QApplication` class. Every application needs one — and only one — `QApplication` object to function. This object holds the **event loop** of your application — the core loop which governs all user interaction with the GUI.

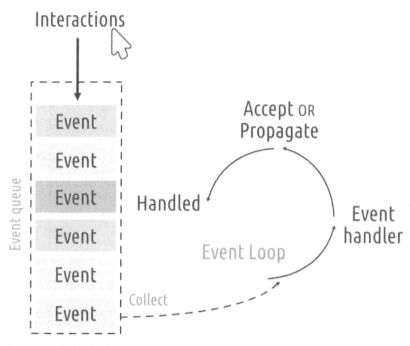

Figure 4. The event loop in Qt.

Each interaction with your application — whether a press of a key, click of a mouse, or mouse movement — generates an *event* which is placed on the *event queue*. In the event loop, the queue is checked on each iteration and if a waiting event is found, the event and control is passed to the specific *event handler* for the event. The event handler deals with the event, then passes control back to the event loop to wait for more events. There is only **one** running event loop per application.

The QApplication *class*

- QApplication holds the Qt event loop

- One QApplication instance required

- Your application sits waiting in the event loop until an action is taken

- There is only **one** event loop at any time

QMainWindow

As we discovered in the last part, in Qt *any* widgets can be windows. For example, if you replace QtWidget with QPushButton. In the example below, you would get a window with a single push-able button in it.

Listing 2. basic/creating_a_window_2.py

```python
import sys

from PyQt6.QtWidgets import QApplication, QPushButton

app = QApplication(sys.argv)

window = QPushButton("Push Me")
window.show()

app.exec()
```

This is neat, but not really very *useful* — it's rare that you need a UI that consists of only a single control! But, as we'll discover later, the ability to nest widgets within other widgets using *layouts* means you can construct complex UIs inside an empty QWidget.

But, Qt already has a solution for you — the QMainWindow. This is a pre-made widget which provides a lot of standard window features you'll make use of in your apps, including toolbars, menus, a statusbar, dockable widgets and more. We'll look at these advanced features later, but for now, we'll add a simple empty

`QMainWindow` to our application.

Listing 3. basic/creating_a_window_3.py

```
from PyQt6.QtWidgets import QApplication, QMainWindow

import sys


app = QApplication(sys.argv)

window = QMainWindow()
window.show()  # IMPORTANT!!!!! Windows are hidden by default.

# Start the event loop.
app.exec()
```

🚀 **Run it!** You will now see your main window. It looks exactly the same as before!

So our `QMainWindow` isn't very interesting at the moment. We can fix that by adding some content. If you want to create a custom window, the best approach is to subclass `QMainWindow` and then include the setup for the window in the `__init__` block. This allows the window behavior to be self contained. We can add our own subclass of `QMainWindow` — call it `MainWindow` to keep things simple.

Listing 4. basic/creating_a_window_4.py

```python
import sys

from PyQt6.QtCore import QSize, Qt
from PyQt6.QtWidgets import (
    QApplication,
    QMainWindow,
    QPushButton,
)  ①


# Subclass QMainWindow to customize your application's main window
class MainWindow(QMainWindow):
    def __init__(self):
        super().__init__()  ②

        self.setWindowTitle("My App")

        button = QPushButton("Press Me!")

        # Set the central widget of the Window.
        self.setCentralWidget(button)  ③


app = QApplication(sys.argv)

window = MainWindow()
window.show()

app.exec()
```

① Common Qt widgets are always imported from the QtWidgets namespace.

② We must always call the __init__ method of the super() class.

③ Use .setCentralWidget to place a widget in the QMainWindow.

 When you subclass a Qt class you must **always** call the super __init__ function to allow Qt to set up the object.

15

In our `__init__` block we first use `.setWindowTitle()` to change the title of our main window. Then we add our first widget — a `QPushButton` — to the middle of the window. This is one of the basic widgets available in Qt. When creating the button you can pass in the text that you want the button to display.

Finally, we call `.setCentralWidget()` on the window. This is a `QMainWindow` specific function that allows you to set the widget that goes in the middle of the window.

🚀 **Run it!** You will now see your window again, but this time with the `QPushButton` widget in the middle. Pressing the button will do nothing, we'll sort that next.

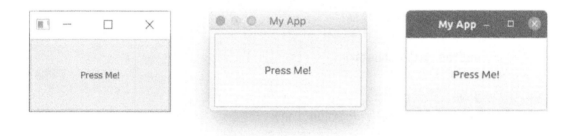

Figure 5. Our `QMainWindow` with a single `QPushButton` on Windows, macOS and Linux.

Hungry for widgets?

We'll cover more widgets in detail shortly but if you're impatient and would like to jump ahead you can take a look at the QWidget documentation [https://doc.qt.io/qt-6/widget-classes.html# basic-widget-classes]. Try adding the different widgets to your window!

Sizing windows and widgets

The window is currently freely resizable — if you grab any corner with your mouse you can drag and resize it to any size you want. While it's good to let your users resize your applications, sometimes you may want to place restrictions on minimum or maximum sizes, or lock a window to a fixed size.

In Qt sizes are defined using a QSize object. This accepts *width* and *height* parameters in that order. For example, the following will create a *fixed size* window of 400x300 pixels.

Listing 5. basic/creating_a_window_end.py

```python
import sys

from PyQt6.QtCore import QSize, Qt
from PyQt6.QtWidgets import QApplication, QMainWindow, QPushButton


# Subclass QMainWindow to customize your application's main window
class MainWindow(QMainWindow):
    def __init__(self):
        super().__init__()

        self.setWindowTitle("My App")

        button = QPushButton("Press Me!")

        self.setFixedSize(QSize(400, 300))   ①

        # Set the central widget of the Window.
        self.setCentralWidget(button)


app = QApplication(sys.argv)

window = MainWindow()
window.show()

app.exec()
```

① Setting the size of the window.

🚀 **Run it!** You will see a fixed size window — try and resize it, it won't work.

Figure 6. Our fixed-size window, notice that the maximize control is disabled on Windows & Linux. On macOS you can maximize the app to fill the screen, but the central widget will not resize.

As well as `.setFixedSize()` you can also call `.setMinimumSize()` and `.setMaximumSize()` to set the minimum and maximum sizes respectively. Experiment with this yourself!

 You can use these size methods on *any* widget.

In this section we've covered the `QApplication` class, the `QMainWindow` class, the event loop and experimented with adding a simple widget to a window. In the next section we'll take a look at the mechanisms Qt provides for widgets and windows to communicate with one another and your own code.

 Save a copy of your file as `myapp.py` as we'll need it again later.

4. Signals & Slots

So far we've created a window and added a simple *push button* widget to it, but the button doesn't do anything. That's not very useful at all—when you create GUI applications you typically want them to do something! What we need is a way to connect the action of *pressing the button* to making something happen. In Qt, this is provided by *signals* and *slots*.

Signals are notifications emitted by widgets when *something* happens. That something can be any number of things, from pressing a button, to the text of an input box changing, to the text of the window changing. Many signals are initiated by user action, but this is not a rule.

In addition to notifying about something happening, signals can also send data to provide additional context about what happened.

 You can also create your own custom signals, which we'll explore later in Extending Signals.

Slots is the name Qt uses for the receivers of signals. In Python any function (or method) in your application can be used as a slot—simply by connecting the signal to it. If the signal sends data, then the receiving function will receive that data too. Many Qt widgets also have their own built-in slots, meaning you can hook Qt widgets together directly.

Let's take a look at the basics of Qt signals and how you can use them to hook widgets up to make things happen in your apps.

 Load up a fresh copy of `myapp.py` and save it under a new name for this section.

QPushButton **Signals**

Our simple application currently has a `QMainWindow` with a `QPushButton` set as the central widget. Let's start by hooking up this button to a custom Python method. Here we create a simple custom slot named the_button_was_clicked which accepts the clicked signal from the QPushButton.

Listing 6. basic/signals_and_slots_1.py

```python
from PyQt6.QtWidgets import (
    QApplication,
    QMainWindow,
    QPushButton,
)  ①

import sys


class MainWindow(QMainWindow):
    def __init__(self):
        super().__init__()  ②

        self.setWindowTitle("My App")

        button = QPushButton("Press Me!")
        button.setCheckable(True)
        button.clicked.connect(self.the_button_was_clicked)

        # Set the central widget of the Window.
        self.setCentralWidget(button)

    def the_button_was_clicked(self):
        print("Clicked!")


app = QApplication(sys.argv)

window = MainWindow()
window.show()

app.exec()
```

🚀 **Run it!** If you click the button you'll see the text "Clicked!" on the console.

Console output

Receiving data

That's a good start! We've heard already that signals can also send *data* to provide more information about what has just happened. The `.clicked` signal is no exception, also providing a *checked* (or toggled) state for the button. For normal buttons this is always `False`, so our first slot ignored this data. However, we can make our button *checkable* and see the effect.

In the following example, we add a second slot which outputs the *checkstate*.

Listing 7. basic/signals_and_slots_1b.py

```python
import sys

from PyQt6.QtWidgets import (
    QApplication,
    QMainWindow,
    QPushButton,
)   ①


class MainWindow(QMainWindow):
    def __init__(self):
        super().__init__()   ②

        self.setWindowTitle("My App")

        button = QPushButton("Press Me!")
        button.setCheckable(True)
        button.clicked.connect(self.the_button_was_clicked)
        button.clicked.connect(self.the_button_was_toggled)

        # Set the central widget of the Window.
        self.setCentralWidget(button)

    def the_button_was_clicked(self):
        print("Clicked!")

    def the_button_was_toggled(self, checked):
        print("Checked?", checked)


app = QApplication(sys.argv)

window = MainWindow()
window.show()

app.exec()
```

🚀 Run it! If you press the button you'll see it highlighted as *checked*. Press it again to release it. Look for the *check state* in the console.

```
Clicked!
Checked? True
Clicked!
Checked? False
Clicked!
Checked? True
Clicked!
Checked? False
Clicked!
Checked? True
```

You can connect as many slots to a signal as you like and can respond to different versions of signals at the same time on your slots.

Storing data

Often it is useful to store the current *state* of a widget in a Python variable. This allows you to work with the values like any other Python variable and without accessing the original widget. You can either store these values as individual variables or use a dictionary if you prefer. In the next example we store the *checked* value of our button in a variable called `button_is_checked` on `self`.

Listing 8. basic/signals_and_slots_1c.py

```python
class MainWindow(QMainWindow):
    def __init__(self):
        super().__init__()

        self.button_is_checked = True   ①

        self.setWindowTitle("My App")

        button = QPushButton("Press Me!")
        button.setCheckable(True)
        button.clicked.connect(self.the_button_was_toggled)
        button.setChecked(self.button_is_checked)   ②

        # Set the central widget of the Window.
        self.setCentralWidget(button)

    def the_button_was_toggled(self, checked):
        self.button_is_checked = checked   ③

        print(self.button_is_checked)
```

① Set the default value for our variable.

② Use the default value to set the initial state of the widget.

③ When the widget state changes, update the variable to match.

You can use this same pattern with any PyQt6 widgets. If a widget does not provide a signal that sends the current state, you will need to retrieve the value from the widget directly in your handler. For example, here we're checking the checked state in a *pressed* handler.

Listing 9. basic/signals_and slots_1d.py

```
class MainWindow(QMainWindow):
    def __init__(self):
        super().__init__()

        self.button_is_checked = True

        self.setWindowTitle("My App")

        self.button = QPushButton("Press Me!")   ①
        self.button.setCheckable(True)
        self.button.released.connect(
            self.the_button_was_released
        )  ②
        self.button.setChecked(self.button_is_checked)

        # Set the central widget of the Window.
        self.setCentralWidget(self.button)

    def the_button_was_released(self):
        self.button_is_checked = self.button.isChecked()   ③

        print(self.button_is_checked)
```

① We need to keep a reference to the button on self so we can access it in our slot.

② The *released* signal fires when the button is released, but does not send the check state.

③ .isChecked() returns the check state of the button.

Changing the interface

So far we've seen how to accept signals and print output to the console. But how about making something happen in the interface when we click the button? Let's update our slot method to modify the button, changing the text and disabling the button so it is no longer clickable. We'll also remove the *checkable* state for now.

Listing 10. basic/signals_and_slots_2.py

```python
from PyQt6.QtWidgets import QApplication, QMainWindow, QPushButton

import sys


class MainWindow(QMainWindow):
    def __init__(self):
        super().__init__()

        self.setWindowTitle("My App")

        self.button = QPushButton("Press Me!")   ①
        self.button.clicked.connect(self.the_button_was_clicked)

        # Set the central widget of the Window.
        self.setCentralWidget(self.button)

    def the_button_was_clicked(self):
        self.button.setText("You already clicked me.")   ②
        self.button.setEnabled(False)   ③

        # Also change the window title.
        self.setWindowTitle("My Oneshot App")


app = QApplication(sys.argv)

window = MainWindow()
window.show()

app.exec()
```

① We need to be able to access the `button` in our `the_button_was_clicked` method, so we keep a reference to it on `self`.

② You can change the text of a button by passing a `str` to `.setText()`.

③ To disable a button call `.setEnabled()` with `False`.

🚀 Run it! If you click the button the text will change and the button will become unclickable.

You're not restricted to changing the button that triggers the signal, you can do *anything you want* in your slot methods. For example, try adding the following line to `the_button_was_clicked` method to also change the window title.

```
self.setWindowTitle("A new window title")
```

Most widgets have their own signals and the QMainWindow we're using for our window is no exception.

In the following more complex example, we connect the `.windowTitleChanged` signal on the QMainWindow to a custom slot method `the_window_title_changed`. This slot also receives the new window title.

Listing 11. basic/signals_and_slots_3.py

```
from PyQt6.QtWidgets import QApplication, QMainWindow, QPushButton

import sys
from random import choice

window_titles = [    ①
    "My App",
    "My App",
    "Still My App",
    "Still My App",
    "What on earth",
    "What on earth",
    "This is surprising",
    "This is surprising",
    "Something went wrong",
]


class MainWindow(QMainWindow):
```

```
    def __init__(self):
        super().__init__()

        self.n_times_clicked = 0

        self.setWindowTitle("My App")

        self.button = QPushButton("Press Me!")
        self.button.clicked.connect(self.the_button_was_clicked)

        self.windowTitleChanged.connect(
            self.the_window_title_changed
        )  ②

        # Set the central widget of the Window.
        self.setCentralWidget(self.button)

    def the_button_was_clicked(self):
        print("Clicked.")
        new_window_title = choice(window_titles)
        print("Setting title:  %s" % new_window_title)
        self.setWindowTitle(new_window_title)  ③

    def the_window_title_changed(self, window_title):
        print("Window title changed: %s" % window_title)  ④

        if window_title == "Something went wrong":
            self.button.setDisabled(True)


app = QApplication(sys.argv)

window = MainWindow()
window.show()

app.exec()
```

① A list of window titles we'll select from using `random.choice()`.

② Hook up our custom slot method `the_window_title_changed` to the windows `.windowTitleChanged` signal.

③ Set the window title to the new title.

④ If the new window title equals "Something went wrong" disable the button.

🚀 **Run it!** Click the button repeatedly until the title changes to "Something went wrong" and the button will become disabled.

There are a few things to notice in this example.

Firstly, the `windowTitleChanged` signal is not *always* emitted when setting the window title. The signal only fires if the new title is a *change* from the previous one. If you set the same title multiple times, the signal will only be fired the first time.

It is important to double-check the conditions under which signals fire, to avoid being surprised when using them in your app.

Secondly, notice how we are able to *chain* things together using signals. One thing happening — a button press — can trigger multiple other things to happen in turn. These subsequent effects do not need to know *what* caused them, but simply follow as a consequence of simple rules. This *decoupling* of effects from what triggered them is one of the key considerations when building GUI applications. We'll come back to this throughout the book!

In this section we've covered signals and slots. We've demonstrated some simple signals and how to use them to pass data and state around your application. Next we'll look at the widgets which Qt provides for use in your applications — together with the signals they provide.

Connecting widgets together directly

So far we've seen examples of connecting widget signals to Python methods. When a signal is fired from the widget, our Python method is called and receives the data from the signal. But you don't *always* need to use a Python function to handle signals — you can also connect Qt widgets directly to one another.

In the following example, we add a QLineEdit widget and a QLabel to the window. In the __init__ for the window we connect our line edit .textChanged signal to the .setText method on the QLabel. Now any time the text changes in the QLineEdit the QLabel will receive that text to it's .setText method.

Listing 12. basic/signals_and_slots_4.py

```python
from PyQt6.QtWidgets import (
    QApplication,
    QMainWindow,
    QLabel,
    QLineEdit,
    QVBoxLayout,
    QWidget,
)

import sys


class MainWindow(QMainWindow):
    def __init__(self):
        super().__init__()

        self.setWindowTitle("My App")

        self.label = QLabel()

        self.input = QLineEdit()
        self.input.textChanged.connect(self.label.setText)   ①

        layout = QVBoxLayout()   ②
        layout.addWidget(self.input)
        layout.addWidget(self.label)

        container = QWidget()
        container.setLayout(layout)

        # Set the central widget of the Window.
        self.setCentralWidget(container)


app = QApplication(sys.argv)

window = MainWindow()
window.show()

app.exec()
```

① Note that to connect the input to the label, the input and label must both be defined.

② This code adds the two widgets to a layout, and sets that on the window. We'll cover this in detail in the following chapters, you can ignore it for now.

🚀 **Run it!** Type some text in the upper box, and you'll see it appear immediately on the label.

Figure 7. Any text typed in the input immediately appears on the label

Most Qt widgets have *slots* available, to which you can connect any signal that emits the same *type* that it accepts. The widget documentation has the slots for each widget listed under "Public Slots". For example, see QLabel [https://doc.qt.io/qt-6/qlabel.html#public-slots].

5. Widgets

In Qt *widget* is the name given to a component of the UI that the user can interact with. User interfaces are made up of multiple widgets, arranged within the window. Qt comes with a large selection of widgets available, and even allows you to create your own custom widgets.

In the code examples for the book there is a file `basic/widgets_list.py` which you can run to display a collection of widgets in a window. It uses a few complex tricks which we'll cover later, so don't worry about the code just now.

🚀 **Run it!** You will see a window with multiple, interactive, widgets.

Figure 8. The example widgets app shown on Windows, macOS and Linux (Ubuntu).

The widgets shown in the example are given below, from top to bottom.

Widget	What it does
QCheckbox	A checkbox
QComboBox	A dropdown list box
QDateEdit	For editing dates
QDateTimeEdit	For editing dates and datetimes
QDial	Rotatable dial
QDoubleSpinbox	A number spinner for floats
QFontComboBox	A list of fonts
QLCDNumber	A quite ugly LCD display
QLabel	Just a label, not interactive
QLineEdit	Enter a line of text
QProgressBar	A progress bar
QPushButton	A button
QRadioButton	A group with only one active choice
QSlider	A slider
QSpinBox	An integer spinner
QTimeEdit	For editing times

There are far more widgets than this, but they don't fit so well! For a full list see the Qt documentation [https://doc.qt.io/qt-6/qtwidgets-module.html]. Here we're going to take a closer look at some of the most useful.

 Load up a fresh copy of myapp.py and save it under a new name for this section.

QLabel

We'll start the tour with QLabel, arguably one of the simplest widgets available in the Qt toolbox. This is a simple one-line piece of text that you can position in your application. You can set the text by passing in a string as you create it —

```
widget = QLabel("Hello")
```

Or, by using the .setText() method —

```
widget = QLabel("1") # The label is created with the text 1
widget.setText("2")  # The label now shows 2
```

You can also adjust font parameters, such as the size or alignment of text in the widget.

Listing 13. basic/widgets_1.py

```python
import sys

from PyQt6.QtCore import Qt
from PyQt6.QtWidgets import QApplication, QLabel, QMainWindow


class MainWindow(QMainWindow):
    def __init__(self):
        super().__init__()

        self.setWindowTitle("My App")

        widget = QLabel("Hello")
        font = widget.font()   ①
        font.setPointSize(30)
        widget.setFont(font)
        widget.setAlignment(
            Qt.AlignmentFlag.AlignHCenter
            | Qt.AlignmentFlag.AlignVCenter
        )   ②

        self.setCentralWidget(widget)


app = QApplication(sys.argv)

window = MainWindow()
window.show()

app.exec()
```

① We get the *current* font, using `<widget>.font()`, modify it and then apply it
   back. This ensures the font face remains in keeping with the system font style.

② The alignment is specified by using a flag from the `Qt.` namespace.

🚀 **Run it!** Adjust the font parameters and see the effect.

 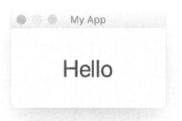 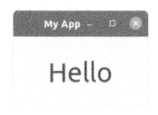

Figure 9. A `QLabel` *on Windows, macOS and Ubuntu*

 The Qt namespace (`Qt.`) is full of all sorts of attributes that you can use to customize and control Qt widgets. We'll cover that in detail later in Enums & the Qt Namespace.

The flags available for horizontal alignment are —

Flag	Behavior
`Qt.AlignmentFlag.AlignLeft`	Aligns with the left edge.
`Qt.AlignmentFlag.AlignRight`	Aligns with the right edge.
`Qt.AlignmentFlag.AlignHCenter`	Centers horizontally in the available space.
`Qt.AlignmentFlag.AlignJustify`	Justifies the text in the available space.

The flags available for vertical alignment are —

Flag	Behavior
`Qt.AlignmentFlag.AlignTop`	Aligns with the top.
`Qt.AlignmentFlag.AlignBottom`	Aligns with the bottom.
`Qt.AlignmentFlag.AlignVCenter`	Centers vertically in the available space.

You can combine flags together using pipes (|), however note that you can only use one vertical or horizontal alignment flag at a time.

```
align_top_left = Qt.AlignmentFlag.AlignLeft | Qt.AlignmentFlag
.AlignTop
```

🚀 Run it! Try combining the different alignment flags and seeing the effect on text position.

Qt Flags

Note that you use an **OR** pipe (|) to combine the two flags by convention. The flags are non-overlapping *bitmasks*. e.g. `Qt.AlignmentFlag.AlignLeft` has the binary value `0b0001`, while `Qt.AlignmentFlag.AlignBottom` is `0b0100`. By ORing together we get the value `0b0101` representing 'bottom left'.

We'll take a more detailed look at the `Qt` namespace and Qt flags later in Enums & the Qt Namespace.

Finally, there is also a shorthand flag that centers in both directions simultaneously —

Flag	Behavior
`Qt.AlignmentFlag.AlignCenter`	Centers horizontally **and** vertically

Weirdly, you can also use `QLabel` to display an image using the `.setPixmap()` method. This accepts an *pixmap* (a pixel array), which you can create by passing an image filename to `QPixmap`. In the example files provided with this book you can find a file `otje.jpg` which you can display in your window as follows:

Listing 14. basic/widgets_2a.py

```python
import sys

from PyQt6.QtGui import QPixmap
from PyQt6.QtWidgets import QApplication, QLabel, QMainWindow


class MainWindow(QMainWindow):
    def __init__(self):
        super().__init__()

        self.setWindowTitle("My App")

        widget = QLabel("Hello")
        widget.setPixmap(QPixmap("otje.jpg"))

        self.setCentralWidget(widget)


app = QApplication(sys.argv)

window = MainWindow()
window.show()

app.exec()
```

Figure 10. Otje the cat. What a lovely face.

Run it! Resize the window, and the image will be surrounded by empty space.

 Don't see the image? Keep reading!

In the example above, we've given the name of the file to load using just the filename `otje.jpg`. This means that the file will be loaded from the *current folder* when the app is run. However, the current folder *isn't* necessarily the folder the script is in — you can run a script from anywhere.

If you change to the folder above `cd ..` and run the script again the file will not be found and the image will not load. Oh dear.

Figure 11. Otje the cat has vanished.

 This is also a common problem when running scripts from IDEs which set the paths based on the active project.

To fix this we can get the path of the *current script file* and use that to determine the folder the script is in. Since our image is stored in the same folder (or in a folder relative to this location) that also gets us the location of the file.

The `file` built-in variable gives us the path of the current file. The `os.dirname()` function gets the folder (or *directory* name) from that path, and then we use `os.path.join` to build the new path for the file.

Listing 15. basic/widgets_2b.py

```python
import os
import sys

from PyQt6.QtGui import QPixmap
from PyQt6.QtWidgets import QApplication, QLabel, QMainWindow

basedir = os.path.dirname(__file__)
print("Current working folder:", os.getcwd())   ①
print("Paths are relative to:", basedir)   ②


class MainWindow(QMainWindow):
    def __init__(self):
        super().__init__()

        self.setWindowTitle("My App")

        widget = QLabel("Hello")
        widget.setPixmap(QPixmap(os.path.join(basedir, "otje.jpg")))

        self.setCentralWidget(widget)


app = QApplication(sys.argv)

window = MainWindow()
window.show()

app.exec()
```

① Current working directory.

② Our base path (relative to this file).

Don't worry if you don't understand this completely yet, we'll go into more detail later.

If you run this now, the image will appear as expected — no matter where you run the script from. The script will also output the path (and current working directory) to help debug issues. Keep this in mind when loading *any* external files from your apps. For a more in depth look at dealing with paths for data files see Working with Relative Paths.

By default the image scales while maintaining its aspect ratio. If you want it to stretch and scale to fit the window completely you can set `.setScaledContents(True)` on the `QLabel`.

Modify the code to add `.setScaledContents(True)` to the label —

Listing 16. basic/widgets_2b.py

```
widget.setPixmap(QPixmap(os.path.join(basedir, "otje.jpg")))
widget.setScaledContents(True)
```

🚀 **Run it!** Resize the window and the picture will deform to fit.

Figure 12. Showing a pixmap with `QLabel` on Windows, macOS and Ubuntu

QCheckBox

The next widget to look at is QCheckBox which, as the name suggests, presents a checkable box to the user. However, as with all Qt widgets there are a number of configurable options to change the widget behaviors.

Listing 17. basic/widgets_3.py

```python
import sys

from PyQt6.QtCore import Qt
from PyQt6.QtWidgets import QApplication, QCheckBox, QMainWindow


class MainWindow(QMainWindow):
    def __init__(self):
        super().__init__()

        self.setWindowTitle("My App")

        widget = QCheckBox("This is a checkbox")
        widget.setCheckState(Qt.CheckState.Checked)

        # For tristate: widget.setCheckState(Qt.PartiallyChecked)
        # Or: widget.setTristate(True)
        widget.stateChanged.connect(self.show_state)

        self.setCentralWidget(widget)

    def show_state(self, s):
        print(Qt.CheckState(s) == Qt.CheckState.Checked)
        print(s)


app = QApplication(sys.argv)

window = MainWindow()
window.show()

app.exec()
```

🚀 **Run it!** You'll see a checkbox with label text.

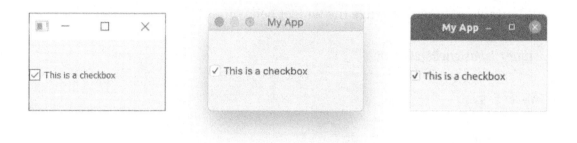

Figure 13. `QCheckBox` *on Windows, macOS and Ubuntu*

You can set a checkbox state programmatically using `.setChecked` or `.setCheckState`. The former accepts either `True` or `False` representing checked or unchecked respectively. However, with `.setCheckState` you also specify a *partially* checked state using a `Qt.` namespace flag —

Flag	Behavior
`Qt.CheckState.Checked`	Item is checked
`Qt.CheckState.Unchecked`	Item is unchecked
`Qt.CheckState.PartiallyChecked`	Item is partially checked

A checkbox that supports a partially-checked (`Qt.CheckState.PartiallyChecked`) state is commonly referred to as 'tri-state', that is being neither on nor off. A checkbox in this state is commonly shown as a greyed out checkbox, and is commonly used in hierarchical checkbox arrangements where sub-items are linked to parent checkboxes.

If you set the value to `Qt.CheckState.PartiallyChecked` the checkbox will become tri-state — that is have *three* possible states. You can also set a checkbox to be tri-state without setting the current state to partially checked by using `.setTristate(True)`

You may notice that when the script is running the current state number is displayed as an `int` with checked = 2, unchecked = 0, and partially checked = 1. You don't need to remember these values — they are just the internal value of these respective flags. You can test state using `state == Qt.CheckState.Checked`.

QComboBox

The QComboBox is a drop down list, closed by default with an arrow to open it. You can select a single item from the list, with the currently selected item being shown as a label on the widget. The combo box is suited to selection of a choice from a long list of options.

 You have probably seen the combo box used for selection of font faces, or size, in word processing applications. Although Qt actually provides a specific font-selection combo box as QFontComboBox.

You can add items to a QComboBox by passing a list of strings to .addItems(). Items will be added in the order they are provided.

Listing 18. basic/widgets_4.py

```python
import sys

from PyQt6.QtCore import Qt
from PyQt6.QtWidgets import QApplication, QComboBox, QMainWindow


class MainWindow(QMainWindow):
    def __init__(self):
        super().__init__()

        self.setWindowTitle("My App")

        widget = QComboBox()
        widget.addItems(["One", "Two", "Three"])

        widget.currentIndexChanged.connect(self.index_changed)
        widget.currentTextChanged.connect(self.text_changed)

        self.setCentralWidget(widget)

    def index_changed(self, i):  # i is an int
        print(i)

    def text_changed(self, s):  # s is a str
        print(s)


app = QApplication(sys.argv)

window = MainWindow()
window.show()

app.exec()
```

🚀 **Run it!** You'll see a combo box with 3 entries. Select one and it will be shown in the box.

 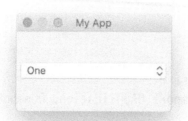 

Figure 14. QComboBox *on Windows, macOS and Ubuntu*

The .currentIndexChanged signal is triggered when the currently selected item is updated, by default passing the index of the selected item in the list. There is also a .currentTextChanged signal which instead provides the label of the currently selected item, which is often more useful.

QComboBox can also be editable, allowing users to enter values not currently in the list and either have them inserted, or simply used as a value. To make the box editable:

```
widget.setEditable(True)
```

You can also set a flag to determine how the insert is handled. These flags are stored on the QComboBox class itself and are listed below —

Flag	Behavior
QComboBox.InsertPolicy.NoInsert	No insert
QComboBox.InsertPolicy.InsertAtTop	Insert as first item
QComboBox.InsertPolicy.InsertAtCurrent	Replace currently selected item
QComboBox.InsertPolicy.InsertAtBottom	Insert after last item
QComboBox.InsertPolicy.InsertAfterCurrent	Insert after current item

Flag	Behavior
`QComboBox.InsertPolicy.InsertBeforeCurrent`	Insert before current item
`QComboBox.InsertPolicy.InsertAlphabetically`	Insert in alphabetical order

To use these, apply the flag as follows:

```
widget.setInsertPolicy(QComboBox.InsertPolicy.InsertAlphabetically)
```

You can also limit the number of items allowed in the box by using `.setMaxCount`, e.g.

```
widget.setMaxCount(10)
```

QListWidget

Next up is QListWidget. This widget is similar to QComboBox, except options are presented as a scrollable list of items. It also supports selection of multiple items at once. A QListWidget offers an currentItemChanged signal which sends the QListItem (the element of the list widget), and a currentTextChanged signal which sends the text of the current item.

Listing 19. basic/widgets_5.py

```python
import sys

from PyQt6.QtWidgets import QApplication, QListWidget, QMainWindow


class MainWindow(QMainWindow):
    def __init__(self):
        super().__init__()

        self.setWindowTitle("My App")

        widget = QListWidget()
        widget.addItems(["One", "Two", "Three"])

        widget.currentItemChanged.connect(self.index_changed)
        widget.currentTextChanged.connect(self.text_changed)

        self.setCentralWidget(widget)

    def index_changed(self, i):  # Not an index, i is a QListItem
        print(i.text())

    def text_changed(self, s):  # s is a str
        print(s)


app = QApplication(sys.argv)

window = MainWindow()
window.show()

app.exec()
```

🚀 **Run it!** You'll see the same three items, now in a list. The selected item (if any) is highlighted.

Figure 15. A QListWidget *on Windows, macOS and Ubuntu*

QLineEdit

The QLineEdit widget is a simple single-line text editing box, into which users can type input. These are used for form fields, or settings where there is no restricted list of valid inputs. For example, when entering an email address, or computer name.

Listing 20. basic/widgets_6.py

```python
import sys

from PyQt6.QtCore import Qt
from PyQt6.QtWidgets import QApplication, QLineEdit, QMainWindow


class MainWindow(QMainWindow):
    def __init__(self):
        super().__init__()

        self.setWindowTitle("My App")

        widget = QLineEdit()
        widget.setMaxLength(10)
        widget.setPlaceholderText("Enter your text")

        # widget.setReadOnly(True) # uncomment this to make readonly

        widget.returnPressed.connect(self.return_pressed)
        widget.selectionChanged.connect(self.selection_changed)
        widget.textChanged.connect(self.text_changed)
        widget.textEdited.connect(self.text_edited)

        self.setCentralWidget(widget)

    def return_pressed(self):
        print("Return pressed!")
        self.centralWidget().setText("BOOM!")

    def selection_changed(self):
        print("Selection changed")
        print(self.centralWidget().selectedText())
```

```
    def text_changed(self, s):
        print("Text changed...")
        print(s)

    def text_edited(self, s):
        print("Text edited...")
        print(s)


app = QApplication(sys.argv)

window = MainWindow()
window.show()

app.exec()
```

🚀 **Run it!** You'll see a simple text entry box, with a hint.

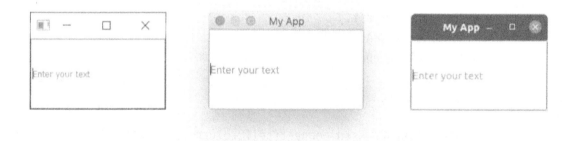

Figure 16. QLineEdit *on Windows, macOS and Ubuntu*

As demonstrated in the above code, you can set a maximum length for the text field by using .setMaxLength. Placeholder text, which is text shown until something is entered by the user can be added using .setPlaceholderText.

The QLineEdit has a number of signals available for different editing events including when return is pressed (by the user), when the user selection is changed. There are also two edit signals, one for when the text in the box has been edited and one for when it has been changed. The distinction here is

54

between user edits and programmatic changes. The textEdited signal is only sent when the user edits text.

Additionally, it is possible to perform input validation using an *input mask* to define which characters are supported and where. This can be applied to the field as follows:

```
widget.setInputMask('000.000.000.000;_')
```

The above would allow a series of 3-digit numbers separated with periods, and could therefore be used to validate IPv4 addresses.

QSpinBox **and** QDoubleSpinBox

QSpinBox provides a small numerical input box with arrows to increase and decrease the value. QSpinBox supports integers, while the related widget QDoubleSpinBox supports floats.

 A double or *double float* is a C++ type which is equivalent to Python's own float type, hence the name of this widget.

Listing 21. basic/widgets_7.py

```python
import sys

from PyQt6.QtWidgets import QApplication, QMainWindow, QSpinBox


class MainWindow(QMainWindow):
    def __init__(self):
        super().__init__()

        self.setWindowTitle("My App")

        widget = QSpinBox()
        # Or: widget = QDoubleSpinBox()

        widget.setMinimum(-10)
        widget.setMaximum(3)
        # Or: widget.setRange(-10,3)

        widget.setPrefix("$")
        widget.setSuffix("c")
        widget.setSingleStep(3)  # Or e.g. 0.5 for QDoubleSpinBox
        widget.valueChanged.connect(self.value_changed)
        widget.textChanged.connect(self.value_changed_str)

        self.setCentralWidget(widget)

    def value_changed(self, i):
        print(i)

    def value_changed_str(self, s):
        print(s)


app = QApplication(sys.argv)

window = MainWindow()
window.show()

app.exec()
```

🚀 **Run it!** You'll see a numeric entry box. The value shows pre and post fix units, and is limited to the range +3 to -10.

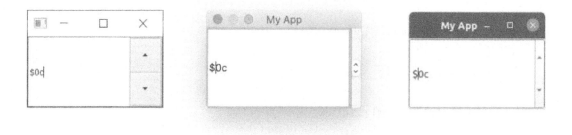

Figure 17. QSpinBox *on Windows, macOS and Ubuntu*

The demonstration code above shows the various features that are available for the widget.

To set the range of acceptable values you can use setMinimum and setMaximum, or alternatively use setRange to set both simultaneously. Annotation of value types is supported with both prefixes and suffixes that can be added to the number, e.g. for currency markers or units using .setPrefix and .setSuffix respectively.

Clicking on the up and down arrows on the widget will increase or decrease the value in the widget by an amount, which can be set using .setSingleStep. Note that this has no effect on the values that are acceptable to the widget.

Both QSpinBox and QDoubleSpinBox have a .valueChanged signal which fires whenever their value is altered. The .valueChanged signal sends the numeric value (either an int or a float) while there is a separate .textChanged signal which sends the value as a string, including both the prefix and suffix characters.

QSlider

QSlider provides a slide-bar widget, which functions internally much like a QDoubleSpinBox. Rather than display the current value numerically, it is represented by the position of the slider handle along the length of the widget. This is often useful when providing adjustment between two extremes, but where absolute accuracy is not required. The most common use of this type of widget is for volume controls.

There is an additional .sliderMoved signal that is triggered whenever the slider moves position and a .sliderPressed signal that emits whenever the slider is clicked.

Listing 22. basic/widgets_8.py

```python
import sys

from PyQt6.QtCore import Qt
from PyQt6.QtWidgets import QApplication, QMainWindow, QSlider


class MainWindow(QMainWindow):
    def __init__(self):
        super().__init__()

        self.setWindowTitle("My App")

        widget = QSlider()

        widget.setMinimum(-10)
        widget.setMaximum(3)
        # Or: widget.setRange(-10,3)

        widget.setSingleStep(3)

        widget.valueChanged.connect(self.value_changed)
        widget.sliderMoved.connect(self.slider_position)
        widget.sliderPressed.connect(self.slider_pressed)
        widget.sliderReleased.connect(self.slider_released)
```

```
            self.setCentralWidget(widget)

    def value_changed(self, i):
        print(i)

    def slider_position(self, p):
        print("position", p)

    def slider_pressed(self):
        print("Pressed!")

    def slider_released(self):
        print("Released")


app = QApplication(sys.argv)

window = MainWindow()
window.show()

app.exec()
```

🚀 **Run it!** You'll see a slider widget. Drag the slider to change the value.

Figure 18. QSlider *on Windows, macOS and Ubuntu. On Windows the handle expands to the size of the widget.*

You can also construct a slider with a vertical or horizontal orientation by passing the orientation in as you create it. The orientation flags are defined in the Qt. namespace. For example —

```
widget.QSlider(Qt.Orientiation.Vertical)
```

Or —

```
widget.QSlider(Qt.Orientiation.Horizontal)
```

QDial

Finally, the QDial is a rotatable widget that functions just like the slider, but appears as an analogue dial. This looks nice, but from a UI perspective is not particularly user friendly. However, they are often used in audio applications as representation of real-world analogue dials.

Listing 23. basic/widgets_9.py

```python
import sys

from PyQt6.QtCore import Qt
from PyQt6.QtWidgets import QApplication, QDial, QMainWindow


class MainWindow(QMainWindow):
    def __init__(self):
        super().__init__()

        self.setWindowTitle("My App")

        widget = QDial()
        widget.setRange(-10, 100)
        widget.setSingleStep(1)

        widget.valueChanged.connect(self.value_changed)
        widget.sliderMoved.connect(self.slider_position)
        widget.sliderPressed.connect(self.slider_pressed)
        widget.sliderReleased.connect(self.slider_released)

        self.setCentralWidget(widget)

    def value_changed(self, i):
        print(i)

    def slider_position(self, p):
        print("position", p)

    def slider_pressed(self):
        print("Pressed!")
```

```
    def slider_released(self):
        print("Released")


app = QApplication(sys.argv)

window = MainWindow()
window.show()

app.exec()
```

🚀 **Run it!** You'll see a dial, rotate it to select a number from the range.

Figure 19. QDial *on Windows, macOS and Ubuntu*

The signals are the same as for QSlider and retain the same names (e.g. .sliderMoved).

This concludes our brief tour through the Qt widgets available in PyQt6. To see the full list of available widgets, including all their signals and attributes, take a look at the Qt documentation [https://doc.qt.io/qt-6/].

QWidget

There is a QWidget in our demo, but you can't see it. We previously used QWidget in our first example to create an empty window. But QWidget can also be used as a *container* for other widgets, together with Layouts, to construct windows or compound widgets. We'll cover Creating Custom Widgets in more detail later.

Keep QWidget in mind, as you'll be seeing a lot of it!

6. Layouts

So far we've successfully created a window and we've added a widget to it. However, you will usually want to add more than one widget to a window, and have some control over where the widgets you add end up. To arrange widgets together in Qt we use *layouts*. There are 4 basic layouts available in Qt, which are listed in the following table.

Layout	Behavior
QHBoxLayout	Linear horizontal layout
QVBoxLayout	Linear vertical layout
QGridLayout	In indexable grid XxY
QStackedLayout	Stacked (z) in front of one another

There are three 2-dimensional layouts available in Qt. The QVBoxLayout, QHBoxLayout and QGridLayout. In addition there is also QStackedLayout which allows you to place widgets one on top of the other within the same space, yet showing only one widget at a time.

In this chapter we'll go through each of these layouts in turn, showing how we can use them to position widgets in our applications.

Qt Designer

You can actually design and lay out your interface graphically using the Qt Designer, which we will cover later. Here we're using code, as it's simpler to understand and experiment with the underlying system.

Placeholder widget

 Load up a fresh copy of myapp.py and save it under a new name for this section.

To make it easier to visualize the layouts, we'll first create a simple custom widget that displays a solid color of our choosing. This will help to distinguish widgets that we add to the layout. Create a new file in the same folder as your script named layout_colorwidget.py and add the following code. We'll import this into our app in the next example.

Listing 24. basic/layout_colorwidget.py

```
from PyQt6.QtGui import QColor, QPalette
from PyQt6.QtWidgets import QWidget


class Color(QWidget):
    def __init__(self, color):
        super().__init__()
        self.setAutoFillBackground(True)

        palette = self.palette()
        palette.setColor(QPalette.ColorRole.Window, QColor(color))
        self.setPalette(palette)
```

In this code we subclass QWidget to create our own custom widget Color. We accept a single parameter when creating the widget — color (a str). We first set .setAutoFillBackground to True to tell the widget to automatically fill it's background with the window color. Next we change the widget's QPalette.Window color to a new QColor described by the value color we provided. Finally we apply this palette back to the widget. The end result is a widget that is filled with a solid color, that we specify when we create it.

If you find the above confusing, don't worry too much! We cover Creating Custom Widgets and Palettes in detail later. For now it's sufficient that you understand that you can create a solid-filled red widget by with the following code —

```
Color('red')
```

First let's test our new `Color` widget by using it to fill the entire window in a single color. Once it's complete we can add it to the main window using `.setCentralWidget` and we get a solid red window.

Listing 25. basic/layout_1.py

```
import sys

from PyQt6.QtCore import Qt
from PyQt6.QtWidgets import QApplication, QMainWindow

from layout_colorwidget import Color


class MainWindow(QMainWindow):
    def __init__(self):
        super().__init__()

        self.setWindowTitle("My App")

        widget = Color("red")
        self.setCentralWidget(widget)


app = QApplication(sys.argv)

window = MainWindow()
window.show()

app.exec()
```

🚀 **Run it!** The window will appear, filled completely with the color red. Notice how the widget expands to fill all the available space.

Figure 20. Our Color *widget, filled with solid red color.*

Next we'll look at each of the available Qt layouts in turn. Note that to add our layouts to the window we will need a dummy QWidget to hold the layout.

QVBoxLayout **vertically arranged widgets**

With QVBoxLayout you arrange widgets one above the other linearly. Adding a widget adds it to the bottom of the column.

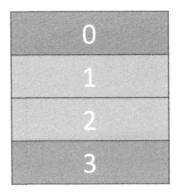

Figure 21. A QVBoxLayout, filled from top to bottom.

Lets add our widget to a layout. Note that in order to add a layout to the QMainWindow we need to apply it to a dummy QWidget. This allows us to then use .setCentralWidget to apply the widget (and the layout) to the window. Our colored widgets will arrange themselves in the layout, contained within the QWidget in the window. First we just add the red widget as before.

Listing 26. basic/layout_2a.py

```python
import sys

from PyQt6.QtCore import Qt
from PyQt6.QtWidgets import (
    QApplication,
    QMainWindow,
    QVBoxLayout,
    QWidget,
)

from layout_colorwidget import Color


class MainWindow(QMainWindow):
    def __init__(self):
        super().__init__()

        self.setWindowTitle("My App")

        layout = QVBoxLayout()

        layout.addWidget(Color("red"))

        widget = QWidget()
        widget.setLayout(layout)
        self.setCentralWidget(widget)


app = QApplication(sys.argv)

window = MainWindow()
window.show()

app.exec()
```

🚀 **Run it!** Notice the border now visible around the red widget. This is the layout spacing — we'll see how to adjust that later.

Figure 22. Our `Color` *widget, in a layout.*

Next add a few more colored widgets to the layout:

Listing 27. basic/layout_2b.py

```python
import sys

from PyQt6.QtCore import Qt
from PyQt6.QtWidgets import (
    QApplication,
    QMainWindow,
    QVBoxLayout,
    QWidget,
)

from layout_colorwidget import Color


class MainWindow(QMainWindow):
    def __init__(self):
        super().__init__()

        self.setWindowTitle("My App")

        layout = QVBoxLayout()

        layout.addWidget(Color("red"))
        layout.addWidget(Color("green"))
        layout.addWidget(Color("blue"))

        widget = QWidget()
        widget.setLayout(layout)
        self.setCentralWidget(widget)


app = QApplication(sys.argv)

window = MainWindow()
window.show()

app.exec()
```

As we add widgets they line themselves up vertically in the order they are added.

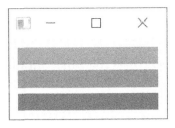

Figure 23. Three Color *widgets arranged vertically in a* QVBoxLayout.

QHBoxLayout **horizontally arranged widgets**

QHBoxLayout is the same, except moving horizontally. Adding a widget adds it to the right hand side.

Figure 24. A QHBoxLayout, filled from left to right.

To use it we can simply change the QVBoxLayout to a QHBoxLayout. The boxes now flow left to right.

Listing 28. basic/layout_3.py

```python
import sys

from PyQt6.QtCore import Qt
from PyQt6.QtWidgets import (
    QApplication,
    QHBoxLayout,
    QLabel,
    QMainWindow,
    QWidget,
)

from layout_colorwidget import Color


class MainWindow(QMainWindow):
    def __init__(self):
        super().__init__()

        self.setWindowTitle("My App")

        layout = QHBoxLayout()

        layout.addWidget(Color("red"))
        layout.addWidget(Color("green"))
        layout.addWidget(Color("blue"))

        widget = QWidget()
        widget.setLayout(layout)
        self.setCentralWidget(widget)


app = QApplication(sys.argv)

window = MainWindow()
window.show()

app.exec()
```

⚓ Run it! The widgets should arrange themselves horizontally.

Figure 25. Three Color *widgets arranged horizontally in a* QHBoxLayout.

Nesting layouts

For more complex layouts you can nest layouts inside one another using .addLayout on a layout. Below we add a QVBoxLayout into the main QHBoxLayout. If we add some widgets to the QVBoxLayout, they'll be arranged vertically in the first slot of the parent layout.

Listing 29. basic/layout_4.py

```python
import sys

from PyQt6.QtCore import Qt
from PyQt6.QtWidgets import (
    QApplication,
    QHBoxLayout,
    QLabel,
    QMainWindow,
    QVBoxLayout,
    QWidget,
)

from layout_colorwidget import Color


class MainWindow(QMainWindow):
    def __init__(self):
        super().__init__()

        self.setWindowTitle("My App")

        layout1 = QHBoxLayout()
        layout2 = QVBoxLayout()
        layout3 = QVBoxLayout()

        layout2.addWidget(Color("red"))
        layout2.addWidget(Color("yellow"))
        layout2.addWidget(Color("purple"))

        layout1.addLayout(layout2)

        layout1.addWidget(Color("green"))
```

```
            layout3.addWidget(Color("red"))
            layout3.addWidget(Color("purple"))

            layout1.addLayout(layout3)

            widget = QWidget()
            widget.setLayout(layout1)
            self.setCentralWidget(widget)


app = QApplication(sys.argv)

window = MainWindow()
window.show()

app.exec()
```

🚀 **Run it!** The widgets should arrange themselves in 3 columns horizontally, with the first column also containing 3 widgets stacked vertically. Experiment!

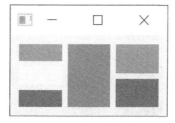

Figure 26. Nested QHBoxLayout *and* QVBoxLayout *layouts.*

You can set the spacing around the layout using .setContentMargins or set the spacing between elements using .setSpacing.

```
layout1.setContentsMargins(0,0,0,0)
layout1.setSpacing(20)
```

The following code shows the combination of nested widgets and layout margins and spacing.

Listing 30. basic/layout 5.py

```python
import sys

from PyQt6.QtCore import Qt
from PyQt6.QtWidgets import (
    QApplication,
    QHBoxLayout,
    QLabel,
    QMainWindow,
    QVBoxLayout,
    QWidget,
)

from layout_colorwidget import Color


class MainWindow(QMainWindow):
    def __init__(self):
        super().__init__()

        self.setWindowTitle("My App")

        layout1 = QHBoxLayout()
        layout2 = QVBoxLayout()
        layout3 = QVBoxLayout()

        layout1.setContentsMargins(0, 0, 0, 0)
        layout1.setSpacing(20)

        layout2.addWidget(Color("red"))
        layout2.addWidget(Color("yellow"))
        layout2.addWidget(Color("purple"))

        layout1.addLayout(layout2)

        layout1.addWidget(Color("green"))

        layout3.addWidget(Color("red"))
        layout3.addWidget(Color("purple"))

        layout1.addLayout(layout3)
```

```
            widget = QWidget()
            widget.setLayout(layout1)
            self.setCentralWidget(widget)


app = QApplication(sys.argv)

window = MainWindow()
window.show()

app.exec()
```

🚀 **Run it!** You should see the effects of spacing and margins. Experiment with the numbers until you get a feel for them.

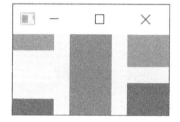

Figure 27. Nested QHBoxLayout *and* QVBoxLayout *layouts with spacing and margins around the widgets.*

QGridLayout **widgets arranged in a grid**

As useful as they are, if you try and use QVBoxLayout and QHBoxLayout for laying out multiple elements, e.g. for a form, you'll find it very difficult to ensure differently sized widgets line up. The solution to this is QGridLayout.

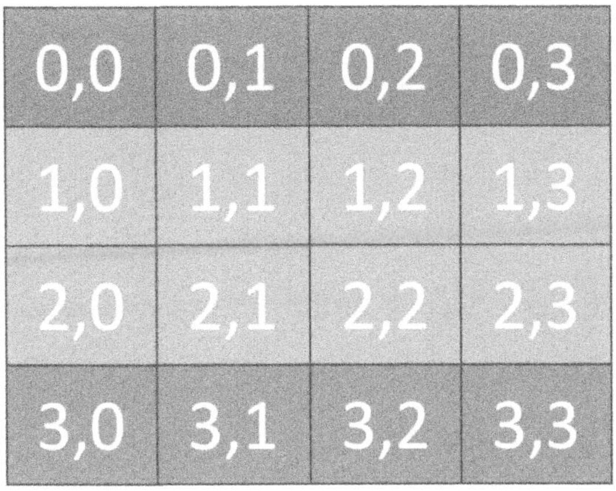

Figure 28. A QGridLayout showing the grid positions for each location.

QGridLayout allows you to position items specifically in a grid. You specify row and column positions for each widget. You can skip elements, and they will be left empty.

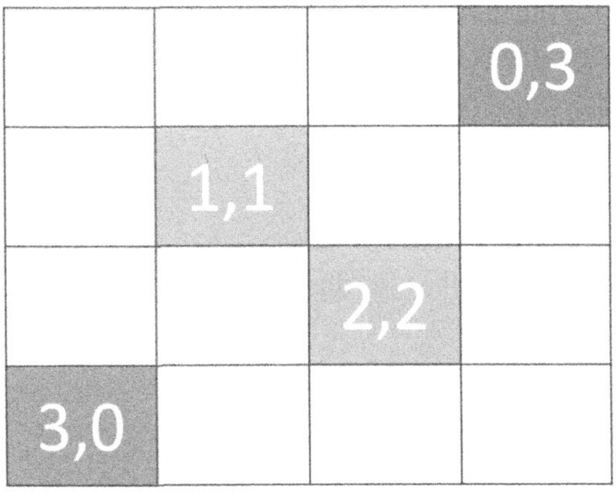

Figure 29. A QGridLayout with unfilled slots.

Listing 31. basic/layout_6.py

```python
import sys

from PyQt6.QtCore import Qt
from PyQt6.QtWidgets import (
    QApplication,
    QGridLayout,
    QLabel,
    QMainWindow,
    QWidget,
)

from layout_colorwidget import Color


class MainWindow(QMainWindow):
    def __init__(self):
        super().__init__()

        self.setWindowTitle("My App")

        layout = QGridLayout()

        layout.addWidget(Color("red"), 0, 0)
        layout.addWidget(Color("green"), 1, 0)
        layout.addWidget(Color("blue"), 1, 1)
        layout.addWidget(Color("purple"), 2, 1)

        widget = QWidget()
        widget.setLayout(layout)
        self.setCentralWidget(widget)


app = QApplication(sys.argv)

window = MainWindow()
window.show()

app.exec()
```

🚀 **Run it!** You should see the widgets arranged in a grid, aligned despite missing entries.

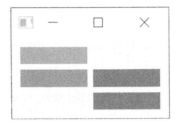

Figure 30. Four `Color` *widgets in a* `QGridLayout`.

QStackedLayout multiple widgets in the same space

The final layout we'll cover is the QStackedLayout. As described, this layout allows you to position elements directly in front of one another. You can then select which widget you want to show. You could use this for drawing layers in a graphics application, or for imitating a tabbed interface. Note there is also QStackedWidget which is a container widget that works in exactly the same way. This is useful if you want to add a stack directly to a QMainWindow with .setCentralWidget.

Figure 31. QStackedLayout — in use only the uppermost widget is visible, which is by default the first widget added to the layout.

Figure 32. QStackedLayout, with the 2nd (1) widget selected and brought to the front.

Listing 32. basic/layout_7.py

```python
import sys

from PyQt6.QtCore import Qt
from PyQt6.QtWidgets import (
    QApplication,
    QLabel,
    QMainWindow,
    QStackedLayout,
    QWidget,
)

from layout_colorwidget import Color


class MainWindow(QMainWindow):
    def __init__(self):
        super().__init__()

        self.setWindowTitle("My App")

        layout = QStackedLayout()

        layout.addWidget(Color("red"))
        layout.addWidget(Color("green"))
        layout.addWidget(Color("blue"))
        layout.addWidget(Color("yellow"))

        layout.setCurrentIndex(3)

        widget = QWidget()
        widget.setLayout(layout)
        self.setCentralWidget(widget)


app = QApplication(sys.argv)

window = MainWindow()
window.show()

app.exec()
```

🚀 **Run it!** You will see only the last widget you added.

Figure 33. A stack widget, showing one widget only (the last-added widget).

QStackedWidget is how tabbed views in applications work. Only one view ('tab') is visible at any one time. You can control which widget to show at any time by using .setCurrentIndex() or .setCurrentWidget() to set the item by either the index (in order the widgets were added) or by the widget itself.

Below is a short demo using QStackedLayout in combination with QButton to provide a tab-like interface to an application —

Listing 33. basic/layout_8.py

```python
import sys

from PyQt6.QtCore import Qt
from PyQt6.QtWidgets import (
    QApplication,
    QHBoxLayout,
    QLabel,
    QMainWindow,
    QPushButton,
    QStackedLayout,
    QVBoxLayout,
    QWidget,
)

from layout_colorwidget import Color


class MainWindow(QMainWindow):
    def __init__(self):
```

```python
        super().__init__()

        self.setWindowTitle("My App")

        pagelayout = QVBoxLayout()
        button_layout = QHBoxLayout()
        self.stacklayout = QStackedLayout()

        pagelayout.addLayout(button_layout)
        pagelayout.addLayout(self.stacklayout)

        btn = QPushButton("red")
        btn.pressed.connect(self.activate_tab_1)
        button_layout.addWidget(btn)
        self.stacklayout.addWidget(Color("red"))

        btn = QPushButton("green")
        btn.pressed.connect(self.activate_tab_2)
        button_layout.addWidget(btn)
        self.stacklayout.addWidget(Color("green"))

        btn = QPushButton("yellow")
        btn.pressed.connect(self.activate_tab_3)
        button_layout.addWidget(btn)
        self.stacklayout.addWidget(Color("yellow"))

        widget = QWidget()
        widget.setLayout(pagelayout)
        self.setCentralWidget(widget)

    def activate_tab_1(self):
        self.stacklayout.setCurrentIndex(0)

    def activate_tab_2(self):
        self.stacklayout.setCurrentIndex(1)

    def activate_tab_3(self):
        self.stacklayout.setCurrentIndex(2)


app = QApplication(sys.argv)

window = MainWindow()
```

```
window.show()

app.exec()
```

🚀 **Run it!** You'll can now change the visible widget with the button.

Figure 34. A stack widget, with buttons to control the active widget.

Helpfully, Qt provides a built-in tab widget that provides this kind of layout out of the box - although it's actually a widget, not a layout. Below the tab demo is recreated using QTabWidget —

Listing 34. basic/layout_9.py

```python
import sys

from PyQt6.QtCore import Qt
from PyQt6.QtWidgets import (
    QApplication,
    QLabel,
    QMainWindow,
    QPushButton,
    QTabWidget,
    QWidget,
)

from layout_colorwidget import Color


class MainWindow(QMainWindow):
    def __init__(self):
        super().__init__()

        self.setWindowTitle("My App")

        tabs = QTabWidget()
        tabs.setTabPosition(QTabWidget.TabPosition.West)
        tabs.setMovable(True)

        for n, color in enumerate(["red", "green", "blue",
"yellow"]):
            tabs.addTab(Color(color), color)

        self.setCentralWidget(tabs)


app = QApplication(sys.argv)

window = MainWindow()
window.show()

app.exec()
```

As you can see, it's a little more straightforward — and a bit more attractive! You can set the position of the tabs using the cardinal directions and toggle whether tabs are moveable with .setMoveable.

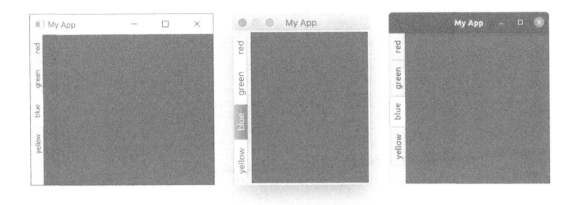

Figure 35. The QTabWidget *containing our widgets, with tabs shown on the left (West). Screenshots show Windows, macOS and Ubuntu appearance.*

You'll notice that the macOS tab bar looks quite different from the others — by default on macOS tabs take on a *pill* or *bubble* style. On macOS this is typically used for tabbed configuration panels. For documents, you can turn on *document mode* to give slimline tabs similar to what you see on other platforms. This option has no effect on other platforms.

Listing 35. basic/layout_9b.py

```
tabs = QTabWidget()
tabs.setDocumentMode(True)
```

Figure 36. QTabWidget *with document mode set to* True *on macOS.*

7. Actions, Toolbars & Menus

Next we'll look at some of the common user interface elements, that you've probably seen in many other applications — toolbars and menus. We'll also explore the neat system Qt provides for minimising the duplication between different UI areas — QAction.

Toolbars

One of the most commonly seen user interface elements is the toolbar. Toolbars are bars of icons and/or text used to perform common tasks within an application, for which accessing via a menu would be cumbersome. They are one of the most common UI features seen in many applications. While some complex applications, particularly in the Microsoft Office suite, have migrated to contextual 'ribbon' interfaces, the standard toolbar is sufficient for the majority of applications you will create.

Figure 37. Standard GUI elements - The toolbar

Qt toolbars support display of icons, text, and can also contain any standard Qt widget. However, for buttons the best approach is to make use of the QAction system to place buttons on the toolbar.

Let's start by adding a toolbar to our application.

 Load up a fresh copy of myapp.py and save it under a new name for this section.

In Qt toolbars are created from the QToolBar class. To start you create an instance of the class and then call .addToolbar on the QMainWindow. Passing a string in as the first parameter to QToolBar sets the toolbar's name, which will be used to identify the toolbar in the UI.

Listing 36. basic/toolbars_and_menus_1.py

```python
class MainWindow(QMainWindow):
    def __init__(self):
        super().__init__()

        self.setWindowTitle("My App")

        label = QLabel("Hello!")
        label.setAlignment(Qt.AlignmentFlag.AlignCenter)

        self.setCentralWidget(label)

        toolbar = QToolBar("My main toolbar")
        self.addToolBar(toolbar)

    def onMyToolBarButtonClick(self, s):
        print("click", s)
```

🚀 **Run it!** You'll see a thin grey bar at the top of the window. This is your toolbar. Right click and click the name to toggle it off.

Figure 38. A window with a toolbar.

I can't get my toolbar back!?

Unfortunately once you remove a toolbar there is now no place to right click to re-add it. So as a general rule you want to either keep one toolbar un-removeable, or provide an alternative interface to turn toolbars on and off.

Let's make the toolbar a bit more interesting. We could just add a QButton widget, but there is a better approach in Qt that gets you some cool features — and that is via QAction. QAction is a class that provides a way to describe abstract user interfaces. What this means in English, is that you can define multiple interface elements within a single object, unified by the effect that interacting with that element has. For example, it is common to have functions that are represented in the toolbar but also the menu — think of something like Edit→Cut which is present both in the Edit menu but also on the toolbar as a pair of scissors, and also through the keyboard shortcut Ctrl-X (Cmd-X on macOS).

Without QAction you would have to define this in multiple places. But with QAction you can define a single QAction, defining the triggered action, and then add this action to both the menu and the toolbar. Each QAction has names, status messages, icons and signals that you can connect to (and much more).

See the code below for how to add your first QAction.

Listing 37. basic/toolbars_and_menus_2.py

```python
class MainWindow(QMainWindow):
    def __init__(self):
        super().__init__()

        self.setWindowTitle("My App")

        label = QLabel("Hello!")
        label.setAlignment(Qt.AlignmentFlag.AlignCenter)

        self.setCentralWidget(label)

        toolbar = QToolBar("My main toolbar")
        self.addToolBar(toolbar)

        button_action = QAction("Your button", self)
        button_action.setStatusTip("This is your button")
        button_action.triggered.connect(self.onMyToolBarButtonClick)
        toolbar.addAction(button_action)

    def onMyToolBarButtonClick(self, s):
        print("click", s)
```

To start with we create the function that will accept the signal from the QAction so we can see if it is working. Next we define the QAction itself. When creating the instance we can pass a label for the action and/or an icon. You must also pass in any QObject to act as the parent for the action — here we're passing self as a reference to our main window. Strangely for QAction the parent element is passed in as the final parameter.

Next, we can opt to set a status tip — this text will be displayed on the status bar once we have one. Finally we connect the .triggered signal to the custom function. This signal will fire whenever the QAction is 'triggered' (or activated).

🚀 **Run it!** You should see your button with the label that you have defined. Click on it and the our custom function will emit "click" and the status of the button.

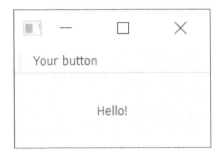

Figure 39. Toolbar showing our QAction *button.*

Why is the signal always false?

The signal passed indicates whether the action is **checked**, and since our button is not checkable — just clickable — it is always false. This is just like the QPushButton we saw earlier.

Let's add a statusbar.

We create a status bar object by calling QStatusBar and passing the result into .setStatusBar. Since we don't need to change the statusBar settings we can just pass it in as we create it. We can create and define the status bar in a single line:

Listing 38. basic/toolbars_and_menus_3.py

```python
class MainWindow(QMainWindow):
    def __init__(self):
        super().__init__()

        self.setWindowTitle("My App")

        label = QLabel("Hello!")
        label.setAlignment(Qt.AlignmentFlag.AlignCenter)

        self.setCentralWidget(label)

        toolbar = QToolBar("My main toolbar")
        self.addToolBar(toolbar)

        button_action = QAction("Your button", self)
        button_action.setStatusTip("This is your button")
        button_action.triggered.connect(self.onMyToolBarButtonClick)
        toolbar.addAction(button_action)

        self.setStatusBar(QStatusBar(self))

    def onMyToolBarButtonClick(self, s):
        print("click", s)
```

🚀 **Run it!** Hover your mouse over the toolbar button and you will see the status text appear in the status bar at the bottom of the window.

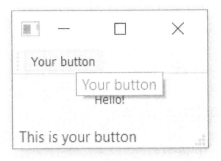

Figure 40. Status bar text is updated as we hover our actions.

Next we're going to turn our QAction toggleable — so clicking will turn it on, clicking again will turn it off. To do this, we simple call setCheckable(True) on the QAction object.

Listing 39. basic/toolbars_and_menus_4.py

```python
class MainWindow(QMainWindow):
    def __init__(self):
        super().__init__()

        self.setWindowTitle("My App")

        label = QLabel("Hello!")
        label.setAlignment(Qt.AlignmentFlag.AlignCenter)

        self.setCentralWidget(label)

        toolbar = QToolBar("My main toolbar")
        self.addToolBar(toolbar)

        button_action = QAction("Your button", self)
        button_action.setStatusTip("This is your button")
        button_action.triggered.connect(self.onMyToolBarButtonClick)
        button_action.setCheckable(True)
        toolbar.addAction(button_action)

        self.setStatusBar(QStatusBar(self))

    def onMyToolBarButtonClick(self, s):
        print("click", s)
```

🚀 **Run it!** Click on the button to see it toggle from checked to unchecked state. Note that custom slot function we create now alternates outputting True and False.

Figure 41. The toolbar button toggled on.

The `.toggled` *signal*

There is also a `.toggled` signal, which only emits a signal when the button is toggled. But the effect is identical so it is mostly pointless.

Things look pretty boring right now, so let's add an icon to our button. For this I recommend the fugue icon set [http://p.yusukekamiyamane.com/] by designer Yusuke Kamiyamane. It's a great set of beautiful 16x16 icons that can give your apps a nice professional look. It is freely available with only attribution required when you distribute your application — although I am sure the designer would appreciate a contribution too if you are able.

Figure 42. Fugue Icon Set — Yusuke Kamiyamane

Select an image from the set (in the examples here I've selected the file `bug.png`) and copy it into the same folder as your source code. We can create a `QIcon` object by passing the path of the file to the class. We're loading the icon using the `basedir` technique we learnt in the Widgets chapter. This ensures the file can be found no matter where you run the script from. Finally, to add the icon to the `QAction` (and therefore the button) we simply pass it in as the first parameter when creating the `QAction`.

You also need to let the toolbar know how large your icons are, otherwise your icon will be surrounded by a lot of padding. You can do this by calling `.setIconSize()` with a `QSize` object.

Listing 40. basic/toolbars_and_menus_5.py

```python
import os
import sys

from PyQt6.QtCore import QSize, Qt
from PyQt6.QtGui import QAction, QIcon
from PyQt6.QtWidgets import (
    QApplication,
    QLabel,
    QMainWindow,
    QStatusBar,
    QToolBar,
)

basedir = os.path.dirname(__file__)

# tag::MainWindow[]
class MainWindow(QMainWindow):
    def __init__(self):
        super().__init__()

        self.setWindowTitle("My App")

        label = QLabel("Hello!")
        label.setAlignment(Qt.AlignmentFlag.AlignCenter)

        self.setCentralWidget(label)

        toolbar = QToolBar("My main toolbar")
        toolbar.setIconSize(QSize(16, 16))
        self.addToolBar(toolbar)

        button_action = QAction(
            QIcon(os.path.join(basedir, "bug.png")),
            "Your button",
            self,
        )
```

```
            button_action.setStatusTip("This is your button")
            button_action.triggered.connect(self.onMyToolBarButtonClick)
            button_action.setCheckable(True)
            toolbar.addAction(button_action)

            self.setStatusBar(QStatusBar(self))

        def onMyToolBarButtonClick(self, s):
            print("click", s)


# end::MainWindow[]


app = QApplication(sys.argv)

window = MainWindow()
window.show()

app.exec()
```

🚀 **Run it!** The QAction is now represented by an icon. Everything should function exactly as it did before.

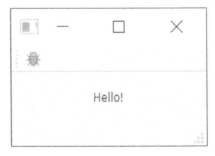

Figure 43. Our action button with an icon.

Note that Qt uses your operating system default settings to determine whether to show an icon, text or an icon and text in the toolbar. But you can override this by using `.setToolButtonStyle`. This slot accepts any of the following flags from the `Qt.` namespace:

Flag	Behavior
`Qt.ToolButtonStyle.ToolButtonIconOnly`	Icon only, no text
`Qt.ToolButtonStyle.ToolButtonTextOnly`	Text only, no icon
`Qt.ToolButtonStyle.ToolButtonTextBesideIcon`	Icon and text, with text beside the icon
`Qt.ToolButtonStyle.ToolButtonTextUnderIcon`	Icon and text, with text under the icon
`Qt.ToolButtonStyle.ToolButtonFollowStyle`	Follow the host desktop style

Which style should I use?

The default value is `Qt.ToolButtonStyle.ToolButtonFollowStyle`, meaning that your application will default to following the standard/global setting for the desktop on which the application runs. This is generally recommended to make your application feel as **native** as possible.

Next we'll add a few more bits and bobs to the toolbar. We'll add a second button and a checkbox widget. As mentioned you can literally put any widget in here, so feel free to go crazy.

Listing 41. basic/toolbars_and_menus_6.py

```python
class MainWindow(QMainWindow):
    def __init__(self):
        super().__init__()

        self.setWindowTitle("My App")

        label = QLabel("Hello!")
        label.setAlignment(Qt.AlignmentFlag.AlignCenter)

        self.setCentralWidget(label)

        toolbar = QToolBar("My main toolbar")
```

```python
        toolbar.setIconSize(QSize(16, 16))
        self.addToolBar(toolbar)

        button_action = QAction(
            QIcon(os.path.join(basedir, "bug.png")),
            "Your button",
            self,
        )
        button_action.setStatusTip("This is your button")
        button_action.triggered.connect(self.onMyToolBarButtonClick)
        button_action.setCheckable(True)
        toolbar.addAction(button_action)

        toolbar.addSeparator()

        button_action2 = QAction(
            QIcon(os.path.join(basedir, "bug.png")),
            "Your button2",
            self,
        )
        button_action2.setStatusTip("This is your button2")
        button_action2.triggered.connect(self.onMyToolBarButtonClick)
        button_action2.setCheckable(True)
        toolbar.addAction(button_action2)

        toolbar.addWidget(QLabel("Hello"))
        toolbar.addWidget(QCheckBox())

        self.setStatusBar(QStatusBar(self))

    def onMyToolBarButtonClick(self, s):
        print("click", s)
```

🚀 **Run it!** Now you see multiple buttons and a checkbox.

Figure 44. Toolbar with an action and two widgets.

Menus

Menus are another standard component of UIs. Typically they are on the top of the window, or the top of a screen on macOS. They allow access to all standard application functions. A few standard menus exist — for example File, Edit, Help. Menus can be nested to create hierarchical trees of functions and they often support and display keyboard shortcuts for fast access to their functions.

Figure 45. Standard GUI elements - Menus

To create a menu, we create a menubar we call .menuBar() on the QMainWindow. We add a menu on our menu bar by calling .addMenu(), passing in the name of the menu. I've called it '&File'. The ampersand defines a quick key to jump to this menu when pressing Alt.

Quick Keys on macOS

This won't be visible on macOS. Note that this is different from a keyboard shortcut — we'll cover that shortly.

This is where the power of actions comes in to play. We can reuse the already existing QAction to add the same function to the menu. To add an action you call .addAction passing in one of our defined actions.

Listing 42. basic/toolbars_and_menus_7.py

```python
class MainWindow(QMainWindow):
    def __init__(self):
        super().__init__()

        self.setWindowTitle("My App")

        label = QLabel("Hello!")
        label.setAlignment(Qt.AlignmentFlag.AlignCenter)

        self.setCentralWidget(label)

        toolbar = QToolBar("My main toolbar")
        toolbar.setIconSize(QSize(16, 16))
        self.addToolBar(toolbar)

        button_action = QAction(
            QIcon(os.path.join(basedir, "bug.png")),
            "&Your button",
            self,
        )
        button_action.setStatusTip("This is your button")
        button_action.triggered.connect(self.onMyToolBarButtonClick)
        button_action.setCheckable(True)
        toolbar.addAction(button_action)

        toolbar.addSeparator()

        button_action2 = QAction(
            QIcon(os.path.join(basedir, "bug.png")),
            "Your &button2",
```

```
            self,
        )
        button_action2.setStatusTip("This is your button2")
        button_action2.triggered.connect(self.onMyToolBarButtonClick)
        button_action2.setCheckable(True)
        toolbar.addAction(button_action2)

        toolbar.addWidget(QLabel("Hello"))
        toolbar.addWidget(QCheckBox())

        self.setStatusBar(QStatusBar(self))

        menu = self.menuBar()

        file_menu = menu.addMenu("&File")
        file_menu.addAction(button_action)

    def onMyToolBarButtonClick(self, s):
        print("click", s)
```

Click the item in the menu and you will notice that it is toggleable — it inherits the features of the QAction.

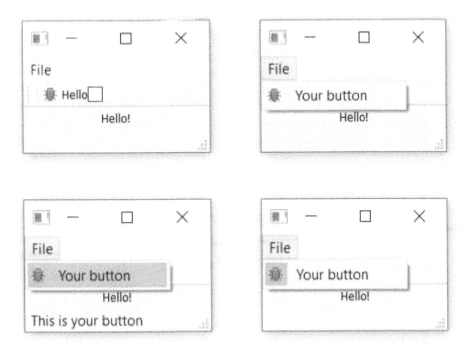

Figure 46. Menu shown on the window — on macOS this will be at the top of the screen.

Let's add some more things to the menu. Here we'll add a separator to the menu, which will appear as a horizontal line in the menu, and then add the second QAction we created.

Listing 43. basic/toolbars_and_menus_8.py

```python
class MainWindow(QMainWindow):
    def __init__(self):
        super().__init__()

        self.setWindowTitle("My App")

        label = QLabel("Hello!")
        label.setAlignment(Qt.AlignmentFlag.AlignCenter)

        self.setCentralWidget(label)

        toolbar = QToolBar("My main toolbar")
        toolbar.setIconSize(QSize(16, 16))
        self.addToolBar(toolbar)
```

```python
        button_action = QAction(
            QIcon(os.path.join(basedir, "bug.png")),
            "&Your button",
            self,
        )
        button_action.setStatusTip("This is your button")
        button_action.triggered.connect(self.onMyToolBarButtonClick)
        button_action.setCheckable(True)
        toolbar.addAction(button_action)

        toolbar.addSeparator()

        button_action2 = QAction(
            QIcon(os.path.join(basedir, "bug.png")),
            "Your &button2",
            self,
        )
        button_action2.setStatusTip("This is your button2")
        button_action2.triggered.connect(self.onMyToolBarButtonClick)
        button_action2.setCheckable(True)
        toolbar.addAction(button_action2)

        toolbar.addWidget(QLabel("Hello"))
        toolbar.addWidget(QCheckBox())

        self.setStatusBar(QStatusBar(self))

        menu = self.menuBar()

        file_menu = menu.addMenu("&File")
        file_menu.addAction(button_action)
        file_menu.addSeparator()
        file_menu.addAction(button_action2)

    def onMyToolBarButtonClick(self, s):
        print("click", s)
```

🚀 **Run it!** You should see two menu items with a line between them.

Figure 47. Our actions showing in the menu.

You can also use ampersand to add *accelerator keys* to the menu to allow a single key to be used to jump to a menu item when it is open. Again this doesn't work on macOS.

To add a submenu, you simply create a new menu by calling addMenu() on the parent menu. You can then add actions to it as normal. For example:

Listing 44. basic/toolbars_and_menus_9.py

```python
class MainWindow(QMainWindow):
    def __init__(self):
        super().__init__()

        self.setWindowTitle("My App")

        label = QLabel("Hello!")
        label.setAlignment(Qt.AlignmentFlag.AlignCenter)

        self.setCentralWidget(label)

        toolbar = QToolBar("My main toolbar")
        toolbar.setIconSize(QSize(16, 16))
        self.addToolBar(toolbar)

        button_action = QAction(
            QIcon(os.path.join(basedir, "bug.png")),
            "&Your button",
            self,
```

```
        )
        button_action.setStatusTip("This is your button")
        button_action.triggered.connect(self.onMyToolBarButtonClick)
        button_action.setCheckable(True)
        toolbar.addAction(button_action)

        toolbar.addSeparator()

        button_action2 = QAction(
            QIcon(os.path.join(basedir, "bug.png")),
            "Your &button2",
            self,
        )
        button_action2.setStatusTip("This is your button2")
        button_action2.triggered.connect(self.onMyToolBarButtonClick)
        button_action2.setCheckable(True)
        toolbar.addAction(button_action2)

        toolbar.addWidget(QLabel("Hello"))
        toolbar.addWidget(QCheckBox())

        self.setStatusBar(QStatusBar(self))

        menu = self.menuBar()

        file_menu = menu.addMenu("&File")
        file_menu.addAction(button_action)
        file_menu.addSeparator()

        file_submenu = file_menu.addMenu("Submenu")
        file_submenu.addAction(button_action2)

    def onMyToolBarButtonClick(self, s):
        print("click", s)
```

If you run the example now, and hover your mouse over the *Submenu* entry in the File menu, you'll see a single-entry submenu appear containing our 2nd action. You can continue to add entries to this submenu, the same way you did for the top level menu.

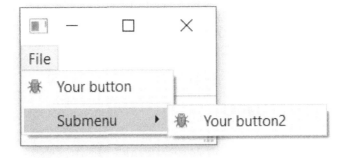

Figure 48. Submenu nested in the File menu.

Finally we'll add a keyboard shortcut to the QAction. You define a keyboard shortcut by passing setKeySequence() and passing in the key sequence. Any defined key sequences will appear in the menu.

Hidden shortcuts

Note that the keyboard shortcut is associated with the QAction and will still work whether or not the QAction is added to a menu or a toolbar.

Key sequences can be defined in multiple ways - either by passing as text, using key names from the Qt namespace, or using the defined key sequences from the Qt namespace. Use the latter wherever you can to ensure compliance with the operating system standards.

The completed code, showing the toolbar buttons and menus is shown below.

Listing 45. basic/toolbars_and_menus_end.py

```python
class MainWindow(QMainWindow):
    def __init__(self):
        super().__init__()

        self.setWindowTitle("My App")

        label = QLabel("Hello!")
```

```python
        # The `Qt` namespace has a lot of attributes to customize
        # widgets. See: https://doc.qt.io/qt-5/qt.html
        label.setAlignment(Qt.AlignmentFlag.AlignCenter)

        # Set the central widget of the Window. Widget will expand
        # to take up all the space in the window by default.
        self.setCentralWidget(label)

        toolbar = QToolBar("My main toolbar")
        toolbar.setIconSize(QSize(16, 16))
        self.addToolBar(toolbar)

        button_action = QAction(
            QIcon(os.path.join(basedir, "bug.png")),
            "&Your button",
            self,
        )
        button_action.setStatusTip("This is your button")
        button_action.triggered.connect(self.onMyToolBarButtonClick)
        button_action.setCheckable(True)
        # You can enter keyboard shortcuts using key names (e.g.
Ctrl+p)
        # Qt.namespace identifiers (e.g. Qt.CTRL + Qt.Key_P)
        # or system agnostic identifiers (e.g. QKeySequence.Print)
        button_action.setShortcut(QKeySequence("Ctrl+p"))
        toolbar.addAction(button_action)

        toolbar.addSeparator()

        button_action2 = QAction(
            QIcon(os.path.join(basedir, "bug.png")),
            "Your &button2",
            self,
        )
        button_action2.setStatusTip("This is your button2")
        button_action2.triggered.connect(self.onMyToolBarButtonClick)
        button_action2.setCheckable(True)
        toolbar.addAction(button_action)

        toolbar.addWidget(QLabel("Hello"))
        toolbar.addWidget(QCheckBox())
```

```python
        self.setStatusBar(QStatusBar(self))

        menu = self.menuBar()

        file_menu = menu.addMenu("&File")
        file_menu.addAction(button_action)

        file_menu.addSeparator()

        file_submenu = file_menu.addMenu("Submenu")

        file_submenu.addAction(button_action2)

    def onMyToolBarButtonClick(self, s):
        print("click", s)
```

Organising Menus & Toolbars

If your users can't find your application's actions, they can't use your app to it's full potential. Making actions discoverable is key to creating a user-friendly application. It is a common mistake to try and address this by adding actions *everywhere* and end up overwhelming and confusing your users.

File menu sections in Qt Creator, notice common actions are at the top, less common further down.

Place *common* and *necessary* actions first, making sure they are easy to find and recall. Think of the **File › New** in most editing applications. Quickly accessible at the top of the File menu and bound with a simple keyboard shortcut **Ctrl + N** . If **New document...** was accessible through **File › Common operations › File operations › Active document › New** or the shortcut **Ctrl + Alt + J** users would have a much harder time finding it.

If you hid **File › Save** away like this, your users would be less likely to save their work & more likely to lose it — literally and figuratively! Look at existing applications you have on your computer to get inspiration. But keep a critical eye, there is plenty of poorly designed software out there.

Use *logical groups* in menus & toolbars to make it easier to find something. It is easier to find something among a small number of alternatives, than in a long list.

Grouped toolbars in Qt Designer.

Avoid replicating actions in multiple menus, as this will make their purpose ambiguous — "do these do the same thing?" — even if they have an identical label. Lastly, don't be tempted to simplify menus by hiding/removing entries dynamically. This leads to confusion as users hunt for something that doesn't exist "...it was here a minute ago". Different states should be indicated by disabling menu items or using separate windows, clearly distinguishable interface modes or dialogs.

DO Organize your menus into a hierarchy & group actions logically.
DO Replicate the *most common* functions onto your toolbars.
DO Disable items in menus when they can't be used.
DON'T Add the same action to multiple menus.
DON'T Add all your menu actions onto the toolbar.
DON'T Use different names or icons for the same action in different places.
DON'T Remove items from your menus — disable them instead.

8. Dialogs

Dialogs are useful GUI components that allow you to *communicate* with the user (hence the name dialog). They are commonly used for file Open/Save, settings, preferences, or for functions that do not fit into the main UI of the application. They are small modal (or *blocking*) windows that sit in front of the main application until they are dismissed. Qt actually provides a number of 'special' dialogs for the most common use-cases, allowing you to provide a platform-native experience for a better user experience.

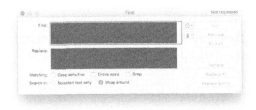

Figure 49. Standard GUI features — A search dialog

Figure 50. Standard GUI features — A file Open dialog

In Qt dialog boxes are handled by the QDialog class. To create a new dialog box simply create a new object of QDialog type passing in a parent widget, e.g. QMainWindow, as its parent.

Let's create our own QDialog. We'll start with a simple skeleton app with a button to press hooked up to a slot method.

Listing 46. basic/dialogs_start.py

```python
import sys

from PyQt6.QtWidgets import QApplication, QMainWindow, QPushButton


class MainWindow(QMainWindow):
    def __init__(self):
        super().__init__()

        self.setWindowTitle("My App")

        button = QPushButton("Press me for a dialog!")
        button.clicked.connect(self.button_clicked)
        self.setCentralWidget(button)

    def button_clicked(self, s):
        print("click", s)


app = QApplication(sys.argv)

window = MainWindow()
window.show()

app.exec()
```

In the slot `button_clicked` (which receives the signal from the button press) we create the dialog instance, passing our `QMainWindow` instance as a parent. This will make the dialog a *modal window* of `QMainWindow`. This means the dialog will completely block interaction with the parent window.

Listing 47. basic/dialogs_1.py

```python
import sys

from PyQt6.QtWidgets import (
    QApplication,
    QDialog,
    QMainWindow,
    QPushButton,
)


class MainWindow(QMainWindow):
    def __init__(self):
        super().__init__()

        self.setWindowTitle("My App")

        button = QPushButton("Press me for a dialog!")
        button.clicked.connect(self.button_clicked)
        self.setCentralWidget(button)

    def button_clicked(self, s):
        print("click", s)

        dlg = QDialog(self)
        dlg.setWindowTitle("?")
        dlg.exec()


app = QApplication(sys.argv)

window = MainWindow()
window.show()

app.exec()
```

🚀 **Run it!** Click the button and you'll see an empty dialog appear.

Once we have created the dialog, we start it using exec() — just like we did for

`QApplication` to create the main event loop of our application. That's not a coincidence: when you *exec* the `QDialog` an entirely new event loop — specific for the dialog — is created.

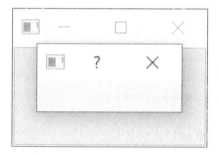

Figure 51. Our empty dialog overlaying the window.

Like our very first window, this isn't very interesting. Let's fix that by adding a dialog title and a set of OK and Cancel buttons to allow the user to *accept* or *reject* the modal.

To customize the `QDialog` we can subclass it.

Listing 48. basic/dialogs_2a py

```
class CustomDialog(QDialog):
    def __init__(self):
        super().__init__()

        self.setWindowTitle("HELLO!")

        buttons = (
            QDialogButtonBox.StandardButton.Ok
            | QDialogButtonBox.StandardButton.Cancel
        )

        self.buttonBox = QDialogButtonBox(buttons)
        self.buttonBox.accepted.connect(self.accept)
        self.buttonBox.rejected.connect(self.reject)

        self.layout = QVBoxLayout()
        message = QLabel("Something happened, is that OK?")
        self.layout.addWidget(message)
        self.layout.addWidget(self.buttonBox)
        self.setLayout(self.layout)
```

In the above code, we first create our subclass of QDialog which we've called
CustomDialog. As for the QMainWindow we apply our customizations in the class
__init__ block so our customizations are applied as the object is created. First we
set a title for the QDialog using .setWindowTitle(), exactly the same way we did
for our main window.

The next block of code is concerned with creating and displaying the dialog
buttons. This is probably a bit more involved than you were expecting. However,
this is due to Qt's flexibility in handling dialog button positioning on different
platforms.

Easy way out?

You could of course choose to ignore this and use a standard QButton in a layout, but the approach outlined here ensures that your dialog respects the host desktop standards (OK on left vs. right for example). Messing around with these behaviors can be incredibly annoying to your users, so I wouldn't recommend it.

The first step in creating a dialog button box is to define the buttons you want to show, using namespace attributes from QDialogButtonBox. The full list of buttons available is below:

Table 1. QDialogButtonBox *available button types.*

Button types

QDialogButtonBox.Ok	QDialogButtonBox.Open
QDialogButtonBox.Save	QDialogButtonBox.SaveAll
QDialogButtonBox.Cancel	QDialogButtonBox.Close
QDialogButtonBox.Discard	QDialogButtonBox.Apply
QDialogButtonBox.Reset	QDialogButtonBox.RestoreDefaults
QDialogButtonBox.Yes	QDialogButtonBox.YesToAll
QDialogButtonBox.No	QDialogButtonBox.NoToAll
QDialogButtonBox.Abort	QDialogButtonBox.Retry
QDialogButtonBox.Ignore	QDialogButtonBox.Help
QDialogButtonBox.NoButton	

These should be sufficient to create any dialog box you can think of. You can construct a line of multiple buttons by OR-ing them together using a pipe (|). Qt will handle the order automatically, according to platform standards. For example, to show an OK and a Cancel button we used:

```
buttons = QDialogButtonBox.Ok | QDialogButtonBox.Cancel
```

The variable buttons now contains an integer value representing those two buttons. Next, we must create the QDialogButtonBox instance to hold the buttons. The flag for the buttons to display is passed in as the first parameter.

To make the buttons have any effect, you must connect the correct QDialogButtonBox signals to the slots on the dialog. In our case we've connected the .accepted and .rejected signals from the QDialogButtonBox to the handlers for .accept() and .reject() on our subclass of QDialog.

Lastly, to make the QDialogButtonBox appear in our dialog box we must add it to the dialog layout. So, as for the main window we create a layout, and add our

QDialogButtonBox to it (QDialogButtonBox is a widget), and then set that layout on our dialog.

Finally, we launch the CustomDialog in our MainWindow.button_clicked slot.

Listing 49. basic/dialogs_2a.py

```python
def button_clicked(self, s):
    print("click", s)

    dlg = CustomDialog()
    if dlg.exec():
        print("Success!")
    else:
        print("Cancel!")
```

🚀 **Run it!** Click to launch the dialog and you will see a dialog box with buttons in it.

Figure 52. Our dialog with a label and buttons.

When you click the button to launch the dialog, you may notice that it appears away from the parent window — probably in the center of the screen. Normally you want dialogs to appear over their launching window to make them easier for users to find. To do this we need to give Qt a **parent** for the dialog. If we pass our main window as the parent, Qt will position the new dialog so that the center of the dialog aligns with the center of the window.

We can modify our CustomDialog class to accept a parent parameter.

Listing 50. basic/dialogs_2b.py

```python
class CustomDialog(QDialog):
    def __init__(self, parent=None):    ①
        super().__init__(parent)

        self.setWindowTitle("HELLO!")

        buttons = (
            QDialogButtonBox.StandardButton.Ok
            | QDialogButtonBox.StandardButton.Cancel
        )

        self.buttonBox = QDialogButtonBox(buttons)
        self.buttonBox.accepted.connect(self.accept)
        self.buttonBox.rejected.connect(self.reject)

        self.layout = QVBoxLayout()
        message = QLabel("Something happened, is that OK?")
        self.layout.addWidget(message)
        self.layout.addWidget(self.buttonBox)
        self.setLayout(self.layout)
```

① We set a default value of None so we can omit the parent if we wish.

Then, when we create our instance of CustomDialog we can pass the main window in as a parameter. In our button_clicked method, self is our main window object.

Listing 51. basic/dialogs_2b.py

```python
    def button_clicked(self, s):
        print("click", s)

        dlg = CustomDialog(self)
        if dlg.exec():
            print("Success!")
        else:
            print("Cancel!")
```

🚀 **Run it!** Click to launch the dialog and you should see the dialog pop up right in the middle of the parent window.

Figure 53. Our dialog, centered over the parent window.

Congratulations! You've created your first dialog box. Of course, you can continue to add any other content to the dialog box that you like. Simply insert it into the layout as normal.

There are many common dialogs that are needed in most applications. While you *can* construct these dialogs yourself, Qt also provides a number of built-in dialogs which you can use instead. These dialogs take care of a lot of the work for you, are well-designed and follow platform standards.

Message dialogs with QMessageBox

The first built-in dialog type we'll look at is QMessageBox. This can be used to create information, warning, about or question dialogs — similar to the dialogs we've hand-built ourselves. The example below creates a simple QMessageBox and shows it.

Listing 52. basic/dialogs_3.py

```python
def button_clicked(self, s):
    dlg = QMessageBox(self)
    dlg.setWindowTitle("I have a question!")
    dlg.setText("This is a simple dialog")
    button = dlg.exec()

    # Look up the button enum entry for the result.
    button = QMessageBox.StandardButton(button)

    if button == QMessageBox.StandardButton.Ok:
        print("OK!")
```

🚀 **Run it!** You'll see a simple dialog with an *OK* button.

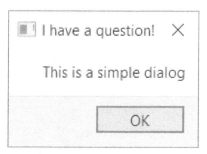

Figure 54. A QMessageBox dialog.

As with the dialog button box we looked at already, the buttons shown on a QMessageBox are also configured with a set of constants which can be combined with | to show multiple buttons. The full list of available button types is shown below.

Table 2. QMessageBox *available button types.*

Button types

QMessageBox.Ok	QMessageBox.Open
QMessageBox.Save	QMessageBox.SaveAll
QMessageBox.Cancel	QMessageBox.Close
QMessageBox.Discard	QMessageBox.Apply
QMessageBox.Reset	QMessageBox.RestoreDefaults
QMessageBox.Yes	QMessageBox.YesToAll
QMessageBox.No	QMessageBox.NoToAll
QMessageBox.Abort	QMessageBox.Retry
QMessageBox.Ignore	QMessageBox.Help
QMessageBox.NoButton	

You can also tweak the icon shown on the dialog by setting the icon with one of the following.

Table 3. QMessageBox *icon constants.*

Icon state	Description
QMessageBox.NoIcon	The message box does not have an icon.
QMessageBox.Question	The message is asking a question.
QMessageBox.Information	The message is informational only.
QMessageBox.Warning	The message is warning.
QMessageBox.Critical	The message indicates a critical problem.

For example, the following creates a question dialog with *Yes* and *No* buttons.

Listing 53. basic/dialogs_4.py

```python
from PyQt6.QtWidgets import (
    QApplication,
    QDialog,
    QMainWindow,
    QMessageBox,
    QPushButton,
)

class MainWindow(QMainWindow):

    # __init__ skipped for clarity
    def button_clicked(self, s):
        dlg = QMessageBox(self)
        dlg.setWindowTitle("I have a question!")
        dlg.setText("This is a question dialog")
        dlg.setStandardButtons(
            QMessageBox.StandardButton.Yes
            | QMessageBox.StandardButton.No
        )
        dlg.setIcon(QMessageBox.Icon.Question)
        button = dlg.exec()

        # Look up the button enum entry for the result.
        button = QMessageBox.StandardButton(button)

        if button == QMessageBox.StandardButton.Yes:
            print("Yes!")
        else:
            print("No!")
```

🚀 **Run it!** You'll see a question dialog with *Yes* and *No* buttons.

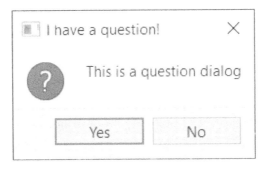

Figure 55. Question dialog created using QMessageBox.

Standard QMessageBox **dialogs**

To make things even simpler the QMessageBox also has a number of *static methods* which can be used to show these types of message dialog without first constructing a QMessageBox instance. These methods are shown below —

```
QMessageBox.about(parent, title, message)
QMessageBox.critical(parent, title, message)
QMessageBox.information(parent, title, message)
QMessageBox.question(parent, title, message)
QMessageBox.warning(parent, title, message)
```

The parent parameter is the window which the dialog will be a child of. If you're launching your dialog from your main window, you can use self to refer to the main window object. The following example creates a question dialog, as before, with *Yes* and *No* buttons.

Listing 54. basic/dialogs_5.py

```
def button_clicked(self, s):

    button = QMessageBox.question(
        self, "Question dialog", "The longer message"
    )

    if button == QMessageBox.StandardButton.Yes:
        print("Yes!")
    else:
        print("No!")
```

🚀 **Run it!** You'll see the same result, this time using the built in `.question()` method.

Figure 56. The built-in question dialog.

Notice that rather than call `exec()` we now simply call the dialog method and the dialog is created. The return value of each of the methods is the button which was pressed. We can detect what has been pressed by comparing the return value to the standard button constants.

The four `information`, `question`, `warning` and `critical` methods also accept optional `buttons` and `defaultButton` arguments which can be used to tweak the buttons shown on the dialog and select one by default. Generally though you don't want to change this from the default.

Listing 55. basic/dialogs_6.py

```python
def button_clicked(self, s):

    button = QMessageBox.critical(
        self,
        "Oh dear!",
        "Something went very wrong.",
        buttons=QMessageBox.StandardButton.Discard
        | QMessageBox.StandardButton.NoToAll
        | QMessageBox.StandardButton.Ignore,
        defaultButton=QMessageBox.StandardButton.Discard,
    )

    if button == QMessageBox.StandardButton.Discard:
        print("Discard!")
    elif button == QMessageBox.StandardButton.NoToAll:
        print("No to all!")
    else:
        print("Ignore!")
```

🚀 **Run it!** You'll see a critical dialog with customized buttons.

Figure 57. Critical error! This is a terrible dialog.

Asking for single values

Sometimes you need to get a single parameter from the user and want to be able to display a simple input dialog to get it. For this use-case PyQt6 provides the QInputDialog. This class can be used to get different types of data, as well as setting limits on the value returned by the user.

The *static methods* all accept a *parent* argument for the parent widget (usually self), a title argument for the dialog window title and a label to show next to the input, along with other type-specific controls. When called the methods show a dialog and once closed return a tuple of the *value* and *ok* which informs you whether the OK button was pressed. If *ok* is False then the dialog was closed.

Let's first look at the simplest example possible — a button launching a dialog to get a single integer value from the user. This uses the QDialog.get_int() *static method*, passing in the parent self, a window title and a prompt to show next to the input widget.

Listing 56. basic/dialogs_input 1.py

```python
import sys

from PyQt6.QtWidgets import (
    QApplication,
    QInputDialog,
    QMainWindow,
    QPushButton,
)


class MainWindow(QMainWindow):
    def __init__(self):
        super().__init__()

        self.setWindowTitle("My App")

        button1 = QPushButton("Integer")
        button1.clicked.connect(self.get_an_int)

        self.setCentralWidget(button1)

    def get_an_int(self):
        my_int_value, ok = QInputDialog.getInt(
            self, "Get an integer", "Enter a number"
        )
        print("Result:", ok, my_int_value)


app = QApplication(sys.argv)

window = MainWindow()
window.show()

app.exec()
```

🚀 **Run it!** You'll see a single button. Press it and you'll be prompted for a number.

So far so exciting. Let's extend this example to add a few more buttons, together with their handler methods. We'll hook the button's signals up to the method *slots* first and then step through implementing each input method.

Listing 57. basic/dialogs_input_2.py

```python
import sys

from PyQt6.QtWidgets import (
    QApplication,
    QInputDialog,
    QLineEdit,
    QMainWindow,
    QPushButton,
    QVBoxLayout,
    QWidget,
)


class MainWindow(QMainWindow):
    def __init__(self):
        super().__init__()

        self.setWindowTitle("My App")

        layout = QVBoxLayout()

        button1 = QPushButton("Integer")
        button1.clicked.connect(self.get_an_int)
        layout.addWidget(button1)

        button2 = QPushButton("Float")
        button2.clicked.connect(self.get_a_float)
        layout.addWidget(button2)

        button3 = QPushButton("Select")
        button3.clicked.connect(self.get_a_str_from_a_list)
        layout.addWidget(button3)

        button4 = QPushButton("String")
        button4.clicked.connect(self.get_a_str)
        layout.addWidget(button4)
```

```python
        button5 = QPushButton("Text")
        button5.clicked.connect(self.get_text)
        layout.addWidget(button5)

        container = QWidget()
        container.setLayout(layout)
        self.setCentralWidget(container)

    def get_an_int(self):
        my_int_value, ok = QInputDialog.getInt(
            self, "Get an integer", "Enter a number"
        )
        print("Result:", ok, my_int_value)

    def get_a_float(self):
        pass

    def get_a_str_from_a_list(self):
        pass

    def get_a_str(self):
        pass

    def get_text(self):
        pass


app = QApplication(sys.argv)

window = MainWindow()
window.show()

app.exec()
```

🚀 **Run it!** You'll see a list of push buttons which you can use to launch inputs, but only the *integer* input works for now.

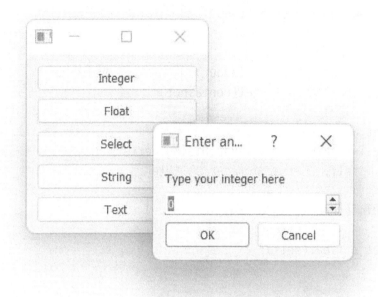

Figure 58. Dialog launcher demo. Click the buttons to launch dialogs to enter values.

Pressing on a button will call one of the input methods we've defined, let's implement them next. We'll step through each of the QInputDialog methods in turn, looking at the configuration options available and adding them to the example.

Integers

As we've already seen, to get a int value from the user, you can use the QInputDialog.getInt() method. This displays a standard Qt QDoubleSpinBox in a dialog. You can specify the initial value, as well as the *minimum* and *maximum* value range for the input, as well as the step size when using the arrow controls.

Listing 58. basic/dialogs_input_3.py

```python
def get_an_int(self):
    title = "Enter an integer"
    label = "Type your integer here"
    my_int_value, ok = QInputDialog.getInt(
        self, title, label, value=0, min=-5, max=5, step=1
    )
    print("Result:", ok, my_int_value)
```

Figure 59. Integer input dialog

 The value entered will be returned even if the user clicks "Cancel" to exit the dialog. You should *always* check the value of the ok return parameter before using the value.

Floats

For float types you can use the QInputDialog.getDouble() method — the *double* type is the C++ equivalent of *float* in Python. This is identical to the *getInt* input above, with the addition of a decimals argument to control the number of decimal places shown.

139

Listing 59. basic/dialogs_input_3.py

```python
def get_a_float(self):
    title = "Enter a float"
    label = "Type your float here"
    my_float_value, ok = QInputDialog.getDouble(
        self,
        title,
        label,
        value=0,
        min=-5.3,
        max=5.7,
        decimals=2,
    )
    print("Result:", ok, my_float_value)
```

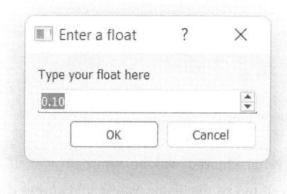

Figure 60. Float input dialog

Select from a list of strings

To select an item from a list of strings, you can use the QInputDialog.getItem()
method. The list of strings to select from is given using the items argument. You
can select which of the provided items is initially selected by setting the current
argument to the *index* of the selected item. By default the list is *editable*, meaning
that users can add new items to the list if they wish. You can disable this
behavior by passing editable=False.

Listing 60. basic/dialogs_input_3.py

```python
def get_a_str_from_a_list(self):
    title = "Select a string"
    label = "Select a fruit from the list"
    items = ["apple", "pear", "orange", "grape"]
    initial_selection = 2  # orange, indexed from 0
    my_selected_str, ok = QInputDialog.getItem(
        self,
        title,
        label,
        items,
        current=initial_selection,
        editable=False,
    )
    print("Result:", ok, my_selected_str)
```

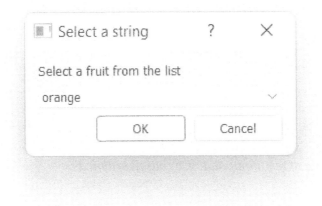

Figure 61. Input dialog for selection from a list of strings

Single line of text

To get a single line of text from the user you can use QInputDialog.getText. You can provide the initial contents of the input by passing it as the text argument. The mode argument lets you switch between *normal* and *password* modes where the entered text is shown as asterisks, by passing QLineEdit.EchoMode.Normal or

`QLineEdit.EchoMode.Password` respectively.

Listing 61. basic/dialogs_input_3.py

```
def get_a_str(self):
    title = "Enter a string"
    label = "Type your password"
    text = "my secret password"
    mode = QLineEdit.EchoMode.Password
    my_selected_str, ok = QInputDialog.getText(
        self, title, label, mode, text
    )
    print("Result:", ok, my_selected_str)
```

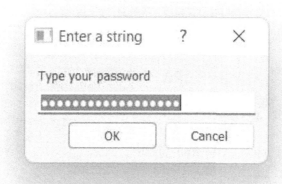

Figure 62. Single line of text input dialog, in password mode.

Multi-line text

Finally, to enter multi-line text you can use the `QLineEdit.getMultiLineText()`. This accepts only the initial state of the text.

Listing 62. basic/dialogs_input_3.py

```python
def get_text(self):
    title = "Enter text"
    label = "Type your novel here"
    text = "Once upon a time..."
    my_selected_str, ok = QInputDialog.getMultiLineText(
        self, title, label, text
    )
    print("Result:", ok, my_selected_str)
```

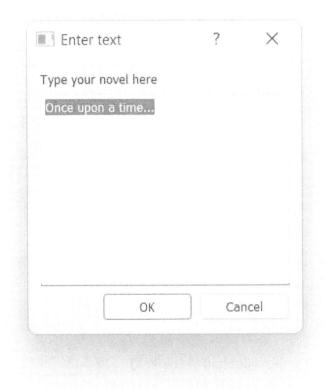

Figure 63. Multi-line text input dialog

🚀 **Run it!** With all the input methods implemented, you can now click on each button to see the different input dialogs appear.

Working with `QInputDialog` instances

The *static methods* described above are fine for most use-cases. However, if you want finer control over how the `QInputDialog` behaves you *can* create an instance of the `QInputDialog` and configure it before display—just like other dialog classes. Below is the same example, but using this approach instead.

Listing 63. basic/dialogs_input_instance.py

```python
import sys

from PyQt6.QtWidgets import (
    QApplication,
    QInputDialog,
    QLineEdit,
    QMainWindow,
    QPushButton,
    QVBoxLayout,
    QWidget,
)


class MainWindow(QMainWindow):
    def __init__(self):
        super().__init__()

        self.setWindowTitle("My App")

        layout = QVBoxLayout()

        button1 = QPushButton("Integer")
        button1.clicked.connect(self.get_an_int)
        layout.addWidget(button1)

        button2 = QPushButton("Float")
        button2.clicked.connect(self.get_a_float)
        layout.addWidget(button2)

        button3 = QPushButton("Select")
        button3.clicked.connect(self.get_a_str_from_a_list)
        layout.addWidget(button3)
```

```python
        button4 = QPushButton("String")
        button4.clicked.connect(self.get_a_str)
        layout.addWidget(button4)

        button5 = QPushButton("Text")
        button5.clicked.connect(self.get_text)
        layout.addWidget(button5)

        container = QWidget()
        container.setLayout(layout)
        self.setCentralWidget(container)

    def get_an_int(self):
        dialog = QInputDialog(self)
        dialog.setWindowTitle("Enter an integer")
        dialog.setLabelText("Type your integer here")
        dialog.setIntValue(0)
        dialog.setIntMinimum(-5)
        dialog.setIntMaximum(5)
        dialog.setIntStep(1)

        ok = dialog.exec()
        print("Result:", ok, dialog.intValue())

    def get_a_float(self):
        dialog = QInputDialog(self)
        dialog.setWindowTitle("Enter a float")
        dialog.setLabelText("Type your float here")
        dialog.setDoubleValue(0.1)
        dialog.setDoubleMinimum(-5.3)
        dialog.setDoubleMaximum(5.7)
        dialog.setDoubleStep(1.4)
        dialog.setDoubleDecimals(2)

        ok = dialog.exec()
        print("Result:", ok, dialog.doubleValue())

    def get_a_str_from_a_list(self):
        dialog = QInputDialog(self)
        dialog.setWindowTitle("Select a string")
        dialog.setLabelText("Select a fruit from the list")
        dialog.setComboBoxItems(["apple", "pear", "orange", "grape"])
        dialog.setComboBoxEditable(False)
```

```
            dialog.setTextValue("orange")

            ok = dialog.exec()
            print("Result:", ok, dialog.textValue())

    def get_a_str(self):
        dialog = QInputDialog(self)
        dialog.setWindowTitle("Enter a string")
        dialog.setLabelText("Type your password")
        dialog.setTextValue("my secret password")
        dialog.setTextEchoMode(QLineEdit.EchoMode.Password)

        ok = dialog.exec()
        print("Result:", ok, dialog.textValue())

    def get_text(self):
        dialog = QInputDialog(self)
        dialog.setWindowTitle("Enter text")
        dialog.setLabelText("Type your novel here")
        dialog.setTextValue("Once upon a time...")
        dialog.setOption(
            QInputDialog.InputDialogOption
.UsePlainTextEditForTextInput,
            True,
        )

        ok = dialog.exec()
        print("Result:", ok, dialog.textValue())


app = QApplication(sys.argv)

window = MainWindow()
window.show()

app.exec()
```

🚀 **Run it!** It should work as before — feel free to play around with the parameters to adjust how it behaves!

There are a few things to notice. Firstly, when you call `exec()` the return value is the equivalent to the `ok` value returned earlier (with 1 for `True` or 0 for `False`). To get the actual entered value, you need to use the type-specific methods, for example `.doubleValue()`, on the dialog object. Secondly, for the `QComboBox` selection from a list of strings, you use the same `.setTextValue()` (to set) and `.textValue()` (to get) methods as for the line or text inputs.

File dialogs

One of the most common use-cases for dialogs in applications is for working with files — whether documents that your application produces, or configuration settings that you want to persist between uses of your app. Helpfully, PyQt6 comes with built-in dialogs for opening files, selecting folders and saving files.

As we've mentioned, if you use Qt's built-in dialog tools then your app will follow platform standards. In the case of file dialogs, PyQt6 goes a step further and will use the platform's built-in dialogs for these operations, ensuring that your application is familiar to your users.

 Creating *good* file dialogs is hard, so I wouldn't recommend you try and roll your own.

In PyQt6 file dialogs are created using the `QFileDialog` class. For convenience it provides a number of *static methods* which you can call to display specific dialogs with minimal configuration. Below is a small demo using the `QFileDialog.getOpenFileName()` *static method* to get a filename to open.

Listing 64. basic/dialogs file 1.py

```python
import sys

from PyQt6.QtWidgets import (
    QApplication,
    QFileDialog,
    QMainWindow,
    QPushButton,
)


class MainWindow(QMainWindow):
    def __init__(self):
        super().__init__()

        self.setWindowTitle("My App")

        button1 = QPushButton("Open file")
        button1.clicked.connect(self.get_filename)

        self.setCentralWidget(button1)

    def get_filename(self):
        filename, selected_filter = QFileDialog.getOpenFileName(self)
        print("Result:", filename, selected_filter)


app = QApplication(sys.argv)

window = MainWindow()
window.show()

app.exec()
```

🚀 **Run it!** Click the button to launch the file open dialog. Select a file and
[**OK**] or [**Cancel**] the dialog to see what is returned.

As you can see the `QFileDialog.getOpenFilename()` returns *two* values. The first is the name of the file selected (or an empty string if the dialog is cancelled). The second is the *currently active file filter* — used for filtering visible files in the dialog. By default this will be `All Files (*)` and all files will be visible.

The file-based dialogs (open & save) all take a `filter` argument which is a `;;`-separated list of filter definition strings — this is a bit strange! There is also an `initialFilter` which is the string of the filter which is active when the dialog first opens. Let's take a look at how these filters are defined and how you can best work with them.

File filters

The Qt standard for *file filters* is a string consisting of the following format, where *User-friendly name* can be any text and the **ext* is the file-matching filter and extension. This should be included in brackets at the end of the filter string.

```
"User-friendly name (*.ext)"
```

If you want to provide multiple filters, you can separate them with `;;` double-semicolons. An example is shown below, including an * *All files* filter.

```
"Portable Network Graphics Image (*.png);;Comma Separated files
(*.csv);;All files (*)"
```

Below is our example updated to provide the above example filters to the `QFileDialog.getOpenFilename()` method.

Listing 65. basic/dialogs_file_2.py

```python
    def get_filename(self):
        filters = "Portable Network Graphics files (*.png);;Comma
Separated Values (*.csv);;All files (*)"
        print("Filters are:", filters)
        filename, selected_filter = QFileDialog.getOpenFileName(
            self,
            filter=filters,
        )
        print("Result:", filename, selected_filter)
```

> **!** You commonly see *.* used for the all-files filter, however in Qt
> this will **not** match files without an extension.

You can write your filters into a string like this, but it can get a bit unwieldly. If you want to select a given filter for the *initial* state, then you need to duplicate the text (or extract it) from this string. Instead, I recommend you store your file filter definitions as a list of strings, and then *join* the list using ;; before passing to the dialog method. This has the advantage that the initialFilter can be selected from this list by index.

```python
FILE_FILTERS = [
    "Portable Network Graphics files (*.png)",
    "Text files (*.txt)",
    "Comma Separated Values (*.csv)",
    "All files (*.*)",
]

initial_filter = FILE_FILTERS[2]  # *.csv
# construct the ;; separated filter string
filters = FILE_FILTERS.join(';;')
```

Our example is updated below to use this approach, with the FILE_FILTERS defined at the top of the file so they can be used by all the file methods.

Listing 66. basic/dialogs_file_2b.py

```python
import sys

from PyQt6.QtWidgets import (
    QApplication,
    QFileDialog,
    QMainWindow,
    QPushButton,
)

FILE_FILTERS = [
    "Portable Network Graphics files (*.png)",
    "Text files (*.txt)",
    "Comma Separated Values (*.csv)",
    "All files (*)",
]


class MainWindow(QMainWindow):
    def __init__(self):
        super().__init__()

        self.setWindowTitle("My App")

        button1 = QPushButton("Open file")
        button1.clicked.connect(self.get_filename)

        self.setCentralWidget(button1)

    def get_filename(self):
        initial_filter = FILE_FILTERS[3]  # Select one from the list.
        filters = ";;".join(FILE_FILTERS)
        print("Filters are:", filters)
        print("Initial filter:", initial_filter)

        filename, selected_filter = QFileDialog.getOpenFileName(
            self,
            filter=filters,
            initialFilter=initial_filter,
        )
        print("Result:", filename, selected_filter)


app = QApplication(sys.argv)
```

```
window = MainWindow()
window.show()

app.exec()
```

Configuring file dialogs

Now we understand the filters, let's extend our example to add handlers for more types of file operations. We'll then step through each of the QFileDialog methods to see the other configuration options available. Below we've added a series of buttons and hooked them up to file method slots to handle showing the different dialogs.

Listing 67. basic/dialogs_file_3.py

```python
import sys

from PyQt6.QtWidgets import (
    QApplication,
    QFileDialog,
    QMainWindow,
    QPushButton,
    QVBoxLayout,
    QWidget,
)

FILE_FILTERS = [
    "Portable Network Graphics files (*.png)",
    "Text files (*.txt)",
    "Comma Separated Values (*.csv)",
    "All files (*)",
]


class MainWindow(QMainWindow):
    def __init__(self):
        super().__init__()

        self.setWindowTitle("My App")
```

```python
        layout = QVBoxLayout()

        button1 = QPushButton("Open file")
        button1.clicked.connect(self.get_filename)
        layout.addWidget(button1)

        button2 = QPushButton("Open files")
        button2.clicked.connect(self.get_filenames)
        layout.addWidget(button2)

        button3 = QPushButton("Save file")
        button3.clicked.connect(self.get_save_filename)
        layout.addWidget(button3)

        button4 = QPushButton("Select folder")
        button4.clicked.connect(self.get_folder)
        layout.addWidget(button4)

        container = QWidget()
        container.setLayout(layout)
        self.setCentralWidget(container)

    def get_filename(self):
        initial_filter = FILE_FILTERS[3]  # Select one from the list.
        filters = ";;".join(FILE_FILTERS)
        print("Filters are:", filters)
        print("Initial filter:", initial_filter)

        filename, selected_filter = QFileDialog.getOpenFileName(
            self,
            filter=filters,
            initialFilter=initial_filter,
        )
        print("Result:", filename, selected_filter)

    def get_filenames(self):
        pass

    def get_save_filename(self):
        pass

    def get_folder(self):
```

```
        pass


app = QApplication(sys.argv)

window = MainWindow()
window.show()

app.exec()
```

🚀 **Run it!** You'll see a list of buttons which can be used to run the file methods — only the open file works for now.

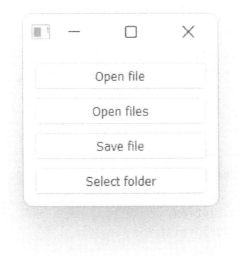

Figure 64. File dialog launcher demo.

Let's step through each of the file methods in turn and add them to our example.

Open a file

To select a single filename to open you can use the `QFileDialog.getOpenFileName()` method.

The *static methods* all accept a `parent` argument for the parent widget (usually `self`), and a `caption` argument for the dialog title. They also accept a `directory` argument which is the initial directory that the dialog will open in. Both `caption` and `directory` can be empty strings, in which case a default caption will be used and the dialog will open in the current folder.

In addition to the `caption` and `directory` this accepts `filter` and `initialFilter` arguments to configure the file filters. When it completes it returns the selected file as a string — containing the complete path — and the currently selected filter.

Listing 68. basic/dialogs_file_4.py

```python
def get_filename(self):
    caption = ""  # Empty uses default caption.
    initial_dir = ""  # Empty uses current folder.
    initial_filter = FILE_FILTERS[3]  # Select one from the list.
    filters = ";;".join(FILE_FILTERS)
    print("Filters are:", filters)
    print("Initial filter:", initial_filter)

    filename, selected_filter = QFileDialog.getOpenFileName(
        self,
        caption=caption,
        directory=initial_dir,
        filter=filters,
        initialFilter=initial_filter,
    )
    print("Result:", filename, selected_filter)
```

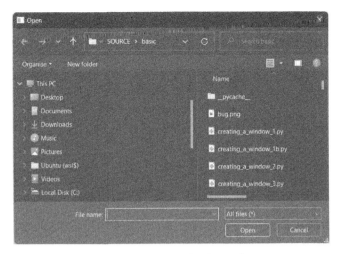

Figure 65. Standard Windows Open dialog, in dark mode.

Once you have the `filename` you can load it using standard Python. If the dialog was closed, the `filename` variable will be an empty string.

Listing 69. basic/dialogs_file_4b.py

```python
if filename:
    with open(filename, "r") as f:
        file_contents = f.read()
```

Open multiple files

Sometimes you want your users to be able to load multiple files at once — for example to load a collection of data files into your app. The `QFileDialog.getOpenFileNames()` method allows you to do this. It takes the same arguments as the single-file method above, the only difference being that it returns a *list of strings* for the selected file paths.

Listing 70. basic/dialogs_file_4.py

```python
def get_filenames(self):
    caption = ""  # Empty uses default caption.
    initial_dir = ""  # Empty uses current folder.
    initial_filter = FILE_FILTERS[1]  # Select one from the list.
    filters = ";;".join(FILE_FILTERS)
    print("Filters are:", filters)
    print("Initial filter:", initial_filter)

    filenames, selected_filter = QFileDialog.getOpenFileNames(
        self,
        caption=caption,
        directory=initial_dir,
        filter=filters,
        initialFilter=initial_filter,
    )
    print("Result:", filenames, selected_filter)
```

You can load the files from `filenames` by iterating and loading them just as in the previous example. Selecting a single file is still possible and will return a list with a single entry. If the dialog is closed without selecting a file `filenames` will be an empty list.

Listing 71. basic/dialogs_file_4b.py

```python
for filename in filenames:
    with open(filename, "r") as f:
        file_contents = f.read()
```

Save a file

To save a file you can use `QFileDialog.getSaveFileName()`

Listing 72. basic/dialogs file_4.py

```python
def get_save_filename(self):
    caption = ""  # Empty uses default caption.
    initial_dir = ""  # Empty uses current folder.
    initial_filter = FILE_FILTERS[2]  # Select one from the list.
    filters = ";;".join(FILE_FILTERS)
    print("Filters are:", filters)
    print("Initial filter:", initial_filter)

    filename, selected_filter = QFileDialog.getSaveFileName(
        self,
        caption=caption,
        directory=initial_dir,
        filter=filters,
        initialFilter=initial_filter,
    )
    print("Result:", filename, selected_filter)
```

Again, you can use the `filename` variable to save to the file using standard Python. If the dialog was closed without selecting a file, the `filename` variable will be an empty string. If the file exists it will be *overwritten* and the existing content lost.

You should *always* check to ensure that the user wants to overwrite a file. In the example below, we use `os.path.exists()` to check if the file exists and then show a `QMessageBox` to ask the user if they want to proceed to overwrite the existing file. If they answer *No*, the file will *not* be written. If the file doesn't exist, or the user answers *Yes* we write the file.

Listing 73. basic/dialogs_file_4b.py

```python
import os

        if filename:
            if os.path.exists(filename):
                # Existing file, ask the user for confirmation.
                write_confirmed = QMessageBox.question(
                    self,
                    "Overwrite file?",
                    f"The file {filename} exists. Are you sure you
want to overwrite it?",
                )
            else:
                # File does not exist, always-confirmed.
                write_confirmed = True

            if write_confirmed:
                with open(filename, "w") as f:
                    file_content = "YOUR FILE CONTENT"
                    f.write(file_content)
```

Always try to consider the mistakes your users may
make — such as clicking on the wrong file in the save
dialog — and give them the opportunity to save themselves.

Select a folder

To select an existing folder you can use `QFileDialog.getExistingDirectory()`

```python
folder_path = QFileDialog.getExistingDirectory(parent, caption="",
directory="", options=ShowDirsOnly)
```

By default the `QFileDialog.getExistingDirectory` will only show folders. You can
change this by passing in .

There are also *static methods* available for loading remote files, which return QUrl objects instead. These are QFileDialog.getSaveFileUrl(), QFileDialog.getOpenFileUrls(), QFileDialog.getOpenFileUrl() and for folders QFileDialog.getExistingDirectoryUrl(). See the Qt documentation for details.

If you want more control over how the file dialogs work you *can* create a QFileDialog instance and use the configuration methods instead. Below is the same file dialog demo but, rather than use the *static methods* above, we've created a QFileDialog instance and configured it before launching the dialog.

Listing 74. basic/dialogs_file_2.py

```python
import sys

from PyQt6.QtWidgets import (
    QApplication,
    QFileDialog,
    QLineEdit,
    QMainWindow,
    QPushButton,
    QVBoxLayout,
    QWidget,
)

FILE_FILTERS = [
    "Portable Network Graphics files (*.png)",
    "Text files (*.txt)",
    "Comma Separated Values (*.csv)",
    "All files (*)",
]


class MainWindow(QMainWindow):
    def __init__(self):
        super().__init__()

        self.setWindowTitle("My App")
```

```python
        layout = QVBoxLayout()

        button1 = QPushButton("Open file")
        button1.clicked.connect(self.get_filename)
        layout.addWidget(button1)

        button2 = QPushButton("Open files")
        button2.clicked.connect(self.get_filenames)
        layout.addWidget(button2)

        button3 = QPushButton("Save file")
        button3.clicked.connect(self.get_save_filename)
        layout.addWidget(button3)

        button4 = QPushButton("Select folder")
        button4.clicked.connect(self.get_folder)
        layout.addWidget(button4)

        container = QWidget()
        container.setLayout(layout)
        self.setCentralWidget(container)

    def get_filename(self):
        caption = "Open file"
        initial_dir = ""  # Empty uses current folder.
        initial_filter = FILE_FILTERS[3]  # Select one from the list.

        dialog = QFileDialog()
        dialog.setWindowTitle(caption)
        dialog.setDirectory(initial_dir)
        dialog.setNameFilters(FILE_FILTERS)
        dialog.selectNameFilter(initial_filter)
        dialog.setFileMode(QFileDialog.FileMode.ExistingFile)

        ok = dialog.exec()
        print(
            "Result:",
            ok,
            dialog.selectedFiles(),
            dialog.selectedNameFilter(),
        )
```

```python
    def get_filenames(self):
        caption = "Open files"
        initial_dir = ""  # Empty uses current folder.
        initial_filter = FILE_FILTERS[1]  # Select one from the list.

        dialog = QFileDialog()
        dialog.setWindowTitle(caption)
        dialog.setDirectory(initial_dir)
        dialog.setNameFilters(FILE_FILTERS)
        dialog.selectNameFilter(initial_filter)
        dialog.setFileMode(QFileDialog.FileMode.ExistingFiles)

        ok = dialog.exec()
        print(
            "Result:",
            ok,
            dialog.selectedFiles(),
            dialog.selectedNameFilter(),
        )

    def get_save_filename(self):
        caption = "Save As"
        initial_dir = ""  # Empty uses current folder.
        initial_filter = FILE_FILTERS[1]  # Select one from the list.

        dialog = QFileDialog()
        dialog.setWindowTitle(caption)
        dialog.setDirectory(initial_dir)
        dialog.setNameFilters(FILE_FILTERS)
        dialog.selectNameFilter(initial_filter)
        dialog.setFileMode(QFileDialog.FileMode.AnyFile)

        ok = dialog.exec()
        print(
            "Result:",
            ok,
            dialog.selectedFiles(),
            dialog.selectedNameFilter(),
        )

    def get_folder(self):
        caption = "Select folder"
        initial_dir = ""  # Empty uses current folder.
```

```
        dialog = QFileDialog()
        dialog.setWindowTitle(caption)
        dialog.setDirectory(initial_dir)
        dialog.setFileMode(QFileDialog.FileMode.Directory)

        ok = dialog.exec()
        print(
            "Result:",
            ok,
            dialog.selectedFiles(),
            dialog.selectedNameFilter(),
        )


app = QApplication(sys.argv)

window = MainWindow()
window.show()

app.exec()
```

🚀 **Run it!** You'll see the same dialog launcher with buttons as before.

You'll see that using this approach there is very little difference between the dialogs — you just need to set the appropriate *mode* and window title. In every case we retrieve the selected files using dialog.selectedFiles() which returns a list, even when only a single file is selected. Finally, note that using this approach you can pass the filters as a list of strings using dialog.setNameFilters() rather than joining them using ;; although that is still an option using dialog.setNameFilter() if you prefer.

You can use whichever approach you prefer. As before, the custom QFileDialog instances are much more configurable (we've only scratched the surface here) however the *static methods* have perfectly sensible defaults which will save you some time.

With all these methods at your disposal you should be able to create any dialogs that your application needs!

Qt also provides some less-commonly used dialogs for showing progress bars (QProgressDialog), one-off error messages (QErrorMessage), selecting colors (QColorDialog), selecting fonts (QFontDialog) and displaying *wizards* to guide users through tasks (QWizard). See the Qt documentation for details.

User-friendly Dialogs

It's particularly easy to create bad dialogs. From dialogs that trap users with confusing options to nested never-ending popups. There are plenty of ways to hurt your users.

Some examples of bad dialogs. (*)

Dialog buttons are defined by system standards. You may never have noticed that the OK & Cancel buttons are reversed on macOS & Linux vs. Windows, but your brain did!

Dialog button order is platform dependent.

If you do not follow standards, you'll confuse your users and cause them to make mistakes. With Qt you get this consistency for free when using the built-in controls. *Use them!*

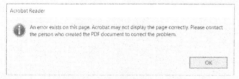

A real dialog from Adobe Acrobat Reader.

Error dialogs *always* annoy users. When you show an error dialog you are giving your users bad news. When you give someone bad news, you need to consider the impact it will have on them.

On the left is a real error dialog from Adobe Acrobat Reader. Notice how it explains that there is an error, what the consequences may be and potentially how to resolve it. But it still isn't *perfect*. The error is shown as an *information* dialog and the dialog is fired on every page. There is no way to suppress the repeated messages when moving around a document. The dialog text could also be improved to make it clear that the error is unrecoverable.

Good error messages should explain —
- What happened
- What was affected
- What are the consequences of it
- What can be done about it

An improved version of the Adobe Acrobat Reader DC dialog)

DO Take the time to make sure your dialogs are well designed.
DO Test error messages with *real users* & act on feedback.
DON'T Assume your users will understand programming terms or errors.

* Did you spot what's wrong with number 4? The default action is destructive!

9. Windows

In the previous chapter we looked at how to open *dialog* windows. These are special windows which (by default) grab the focus of the user, and run their own event loop, effectively blocking the execution of the rest of your app.

However, quite often you will want to open a second window in an application, without blocking the main window – for example, to show the output of some long-running process, or to display graphs or other visualizations. Alternatively, you may want to create an application that allows you to work on multiple documents at once, all in their own windows.

It's relatively straightforward to open new windows in PyQt6, but there are a few things to keep in mind to make sure they work well. In this tutorial we'll step through how to create a new window and how to show and hide external windows on demand.

Creating a new window

To create a new window in PyQt6 you just need to create a new instance of a widget object without a parent. This can be any widget (technically any subclass of QWidget) including another QMainWindow if you prefer.

 There is no restriction on the number of QMainWindow instances you can have, and if you need toolbars or menus on your second window you will need to use QMainWindow for that too.

As with your main window, *creating* a window is not sufficient, you must also show it.

Listing 75. basic/windows_1.py

```
import sys

from PyQt6.QtWidgets import (
```

```
        QApplication,
        QLabel,
        QMainWindow,
        QPushButton,
        QVBoxLayout,
        QWidget,
)


class AnotherWindow(QWidget):
    """
    This "window" is a QWidget. If it has no parent, it
    will appear as a free-floating window.
    """

    def __init__(self):
        super().__init__()
        layout = QVBoxLayout()
        self.label = QLabel("Another Window")
        layout.addWidget(self.label)
        self.setLayout(layout)


class MainWindow(QMainWindow):
    def __init__(self):
        super().__init__()
        self.button = QPushButton("Push for Window")
        self.button.clicked.connect(self.show_new_window)
        self.setCentralWidget(self.button)

    def show_new_window(self, checked):
        w = AnotherWindow()
        w.show()


app = QApplication(sys.argv)
w = MainWindow()
w.show()
app.exec()
```

If you run this, you'll see the main window. Clicking the button *may* show the second window, but if you see it it will only be visible for a fraction of a second.

What's happening?

```
def show_new_window(self, checked):
    w = AnotherWindow()
    w.show()
```

We are creating our second window inside this method, storing it in the variable w and showing it. However, once we leave this method the w variable will be cleaned up by Python, and the window destroyed. To fix this we need to keep a reference to the window *somewhere* — on the main window self object, for example.

Listing 76. basic/windows_1b.py

```
def show_new_window(self, checked):
    self.w = AnotherWindow()
    self.w.show()
```

Now, when you click the button to show the new window, it will persist.

Figure 66. The second window persisting.

However, what happens if you click the button again? The window will be re-created! This new window will replace the old in the self.w variable, and the previous window will be destroyed. You can see this more clearly if you change the AnotherWindow definition to show a random number in the label each time it is created.

169

Listing 77. basic/windows_2.py

```python
from random import randint

from PyQt6.QtWidgets import (
    QApplication,
    QLabel,
    QMainWindow,
    QPushButton,
    QVBoxLayout,
    QWidget,
)

class AnotherWindow(QWidget):
    """
    This "window" is a QWidget. If it has no parent, it
    will appear as a free-floating window.
    """

    def __init__(self):
        super().__init__()
        layout = QVBoxLayout()
        self.label = QLabel("Another Window % d" % randint(0, 100))
        layout.addWidget(self.label)
        self.setLayout(layout)
```

The __init__ block is only run when *creating* the window. If you keep clicking the button the number will change, showing that the window is being re-created.

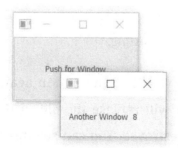

Figure 67. The number will change if the button is pressed again.

One solution is to simply check whether the window has already being created before creating it. The full example below shows this in action

Listing 78. basic/windows_3.py

```python
class MainWindow(QMainWindow):
    def __init__(self):
        super().__init__()
        self.w = None  # No external window yet.
        self.button = QPushButton("Push for Window")
        self.button.clicked.connect(self.show_new_window)
        self.setCentralWidget(self.button)


    def show_new_window(self, checked):
        if self.w is None:
            self.w = AnotherWindow()
        self.w.show()
```

This approach is fine for windows that you create temporarily, or need to change dependent on the current state of the program – for example if you want to show a particular plot, or log output. However, for many applications you have a number of standard windows that you want to be able to show/hide on demand.

In the next part we'll look at how to work with these types of windows.

Closing a window

As we previously saw, if no reference to a window is kept, it will be discarded (and closed). We can use this behavior to close a window, replacing the `show_new_window` method from the previous example with –

Listing 79. basic/windows_4.py

```python
def show_new_window(self, checked):
    if self.w is None:
        self.w = AnotherWindow()
    self.w.show()

    else:
        self.w = None  # Discard reference, close window.
```

By setting `self.w` to `None` (or any other value) the existing reference to the window will be lost, and the window will close. However, if we set it to any other value than `None` the first test will not pass anymore, and we will not be able to recreate a window.

This will only work if you have not kept a reference to this window somewhere else. To make sure the window closes regardless, you may want to explicitly call `.close()` on it.

Listing 80. basic/windows_4b.py

```python
def show_new_window(self, checked):
    if self.w is None:
        self.w = AnotherWindow()
        self.w.show()

    else:
        self.w.close()
        self.w = None  # Discard reference, close window.
```

Persistent windows

So far we've looked at how to create new windows on demand. However, sometimes you have a number of standard application windows. In this case it can often make more sense to create the additional windows first, then use `.show()` to display them when needed.

In the following example we create our external window in the __init__ block for the main window, and then our show_new_window method simply calls self.w.show() to display it.

Listing 81. basic/windows_5.py

```python
import sys
from random import randint

from PyQt6.QtWidgets import (
    QApplication,
    QLabel,
    QMainWindow,
    QPushButton,
    QVBoxLayout,
    QWidget,
)


class AnotherWindow(QWidget):
    """
    This "window" is a QWidget. If it has no parent, it
    will appear as a free-floating window.
    """

    def __init__(self):
        super().__init__()
        layout = QVBoxLayout()
        self.label = QLabel("Another Window % d" % randint(0, 100))
        layout.addWidget(self.label)
        self.setLayout(layout)


class MainWindow(QMainWindow):
    def __init__(self):
        super().__init__()
        self.w = AnotherWindow()
        self.button = QPushButton("Push for Window")
        self.button.clicked.connect(self.show_new_window)
        self.setCentralWidget(self.button)

    def show_new_window(self, checked):
```

```
        self.w.show()


app = QApplication(sys.argv)
w = MainWindow()
w.show()
app.exec()
```

If you run this, clicking on the button will show the window as before. Note that the window is only created once and calling `.show()` on an already visible window has no effect.

Showing & hiding windows

Once you have created a persistent window you can show and hide it without recreating it. Once hidden the window still exists, but will not be visible and accept mouse or other input. However you can continue to call methods on the window and update it's state – including changing it's appearance. Once re-shown any changes will be visible.

Below we update our main window to create a `toggle_window` method which checks, using `.isVisible()` to see if the window is currently visible. If it is not, it is shown using `.show()`, if it is already visible we hide it with `.hide()`.

```python
class MainWindow(QMainWindow):

    def __init__(self):
        super().__init__()
        self.w = AnotherWindow()
        self.button = QPushButton("Push for Window")
        self.button.clicked.connect(self.toggle_window)
        self.setCentralWidget(self.button)

    def toggle_window(self, checked):
        if self.w.isVisible():
            self.w.hide()

        else:
            self.w.show()
```

The complete working example of this persistent window and toggling the show/hide state is shown below.

Listing 82. basic/windows_6.py

```python
import sys
from random import randint

from PyQt6.QtWidgets import (
    QApplication,
    QLabel,
    QMainWindow,
    QPushButton,
    QVBoxLayout,
    QWidget,
)


class AnotherWindow(QWidget):
    """
    This "window" is a QWidget. If it has no parent, it
    will appear as a free-floating window.
    """

    def __init__(self):
```

```
            super().__init__()
            layout = QVBoxLayout()
            self.label = QLabel("Another Window % d" % randint(0, 100))
            layout.addWidget(self.label)
            self.setLayout(layout)


class MainWindow(QMainWindow):
    def __init__(self):
        super().__init__()
        self.w = AnotherWindow()
        self.button = QPushButton("Push for Window")
        self.button.clicked.connect(self.toggle_window)
        self.setCentralWidget(self.button)

    def toggle_window(self, checked):
        if self.w.isVisible():
            self.w.hide()

        else:
            self.w.show()


app = QApplication(sys.argv)
w = MainWindow()
w.show()
app.exec()
```

Again, the window is only created once – the window's __init__ block is not re-run (so the number in the label does not change) each time the window is re-shown.

Connecting signals between windows

In the signals chapter we saw how it was possible to connect widgets together directly using signals and slots. All we needed was for the destination widget to have been created and to have a reference to it via a variable. The same principle applies when connecting signals across windows — you can hook up signals in one window to slots in another, you just need to be able to access the slot.

In the example below, we connect a text input on our main window to a QLabel on a sub-window.

Listing 83. basic/windows_7.py

```python
import sys
from random import randint

from PyQt6.QtWidgets import (
    QApplication,
    QLabel,
    QMainWindow,
    QPushButton,
    QVBoxLayout,
    QWidget,
    QLineEdit,
)


class AnotherWindow(QWidget):
    """
    This "window" is a QWidget. If it has no parent, it
    will appear as a free-floating window.
    """

    def __init__(self):
        super().__init__()
        layout = QVBoxLayout()
        self.label = QLabel("Another Window")   ②
        layout.addWidget(self.label)
        self.setLayout(layout)


class MainWindow(QMainWindow):
    def __init__(self):
        super().__init__()
        self.w = AnotherWindow()
        self.button = QPushButton("Push for Window")
        self.button.clicked.connect(self.toggle_window)

        self.input = QLineEdit()
        self.input.textChanged.connect(self.w.label.setText)   ①
```

177

```
            layout = QVBoxLayout()
            layout.addWidget(self.button)
            layout.addWidget(self.input)
            container = QWidget()
            container.setLayout(layout)

            self.setCentralWidget(container)

        def toggle_window(self, checked):
            if self.w.isVisible():
                self.w.hide()

            else:
                self.w.show()


app = QApplication(sys.argv)
w = MainWindow()
w.show()
app.exec()
```

① The `AnotherWindow` window object is available via the variable `self.w`. The `QLabel` via `self.w.label` and the `.setText` slot by `self.w.label.setText`.

② When we create the `QLabel` we store a reference to it on `self` as `self.label`, so it is accessible externally on the object.

🚀 **Run it!** Type some text in the upper box, and you'll see it appear immediately on the label. The text will be updated even while the window is hidden — updating the state of widgets is not dependent on them being visible.

Of course, you're also free to connect signals on one window to methods on another. Anything goes, as long as it is accessible. Ensuring components are importable and accessible to one another is a good motivation for building a logical project structure. It often makes sense to hook up components centrally, in your main window/module to avoid cross-importing everything.

10. Events

Every interaction the user has with a Qt application is an *event.* There are many types of event, each representing a different type of interaction. Qt represents these events using *event objects* which package up information about what happened. These events are passed to specific *event handlers* on the widget where the interaction occurred.

By defining custom *event handlers* you can alter the way your widgets respond to these events. Event handlers are defined just like any other method, but the name is specific for the type of event they handle.

One of the main events which widgets receive is the `QMouseEvent`. QMouseEvent events are created for each and every mouse movement and button click on a widget. The following event handlers are available for handling mouse events —

Event handler	Event type moved
mouseMoveEvent	Mouse moved
mousePressEvent	Mouse button pressed
mouseReleaseEvent	Mouse button released
mouseDoubleClickEvent	Double click detected

For example, clicking on a widget will cause a `QMouseEvent` to be sent to the `.mousePressEvent` event handler on that widget. This handler can use the event object to find out information about what happened, such as what triggered the event and where specifically it occurred.

You can intercept events by sub-classing and overriding the handler method on the class. You can choose to filter, modify, or ignore events, passing them up to the normal handler for the event by calling the parent class function with `super()`. These could be added to your main window class as shown in the example below. In each case the argument e will receive the incoming event.

Listing 84. basic/events_1.py

```python
import sys

from PyQt6.QtCore import Qt
from PyQt6.QtWidgets import (
    QApplication,
    QLabel,
    QMainWindow,
    QTextEdit,
)


class MainWindow(QMainWindow):
    def __init__(self):
        super().__init__()
        self.label = QLabel("Click in this window")
        self.setCentralWidget(self.label)

    def mouseMoveEvent(self, e):
        self.label.setText("mouseMoveEvent")

    def mousePressEvent(self, e):
        self.label.setText("mousePressEvent")

    def mouseReleaseEvent(self, e):
        self.label.setText("mouseReleaseEvent")

    def mouseDoubleClickEvent(self, e):
        self.label.setText("mouseDoubleClickEvent")


app = QApplication(sys.argv)

window = MainWindow()
window.show()

app.exec()
```

🚀 **Run it!** Try moving and clicking (and double-clicking) in the window and watch the events appear.

You'll notice that mouse move events are only registered when you have the button pressed down. You can change this by calling `self.setMouseTracking(True)` on the window. You may also notice that the press (click) and double-click events both fire when the button is pressed down. Only the release event fires when the button is released. Typically to register a click from a user you should watch for both the mouse down *and* the release.

Inside the event handlers you have access to an event object. This object contains information about the event and can be used to respond differently depending on what exactly has occurred. We'll look at the mouse event objects next.

Mouse events

All mouse events in Qt are tracked with the `QMouseEvent` object, with information about the event being readable from the following event methods.

Method	Returns
`.button()`	Specific button that triggered this event
`.buttons()`	State of all mouse buttons (OR'ed flags)
`.position()`	Widget-relative position as a `QPoint` *integer*

You can use these methods within an event handler to respond to different events differently, or ignore them completely. The `.position()` method provides the widget-relative position information as a `QPoint` object, while buttons are reported using the mouse button types from the `Qt` namespace.

For example, the following allows us to respond differently to a left, right or middle click on the window.

Listing 85. basic/events_2.py

```python
    def mousePressEvent(self, e):
        if e.button() == Qt.MouseButton.LeftButton:
            # handle the left-button press in here
            self.label.setText("mousePressEvent LEFT")

        elif e.button() == Qt.MouseButton.MiddleButton:
            # handle the middle-button press in here.
            self.label.setText("mousePressEvent MIDDLE")

        elif e.button() == Qt.MouseButton.RightButton:
            # handle the right-button press in here.
            self.label.setText("mousePressEvent RIGHT")

    def mouseReleaseEvent(self, e):
        if e.button() == Qt.MouseButton.LeftButton:
            self.label.setText("mouseReleaseEvent LEFT")

        elif e.button() == Qt.MouseButton.MiddleButton:
            self.label.setText("mouseReleaseEvent MIDDLE")

        elif e.button() == Qt.MouseButton.RightButton:
            self.label.setText("mouseReleaseEvent RIGHT")

    def mouseDoubleClickEvent(self, e):
        if e.button() == Qt.MouseButton.LeftButton:
            self.label.setText("mouseDoubleClickEvent LEFT")

        elif e.button() == Qt.MouseButton.MiddleButton:
            self.label.setText("mouseDoubleClickEvent MIDDLE")

        elif e.button() == Qt.MouseButton.RightButton:
            self.label.setText("mouseDoubleClickEvent RIGHT")
```

The button identifiers are defined in the Qt namespace, as follows —

Identifier	Value (binary)	Represents
Qt.MouseButtons.NoButton	0 (000)	No button pressed, or the event is not related to button press.
Qt.MouseButtons.LeftButton	1 (001)	The left button is pressed
Qt.MouseButtons.RightButton	2 (010)	The right button is pressed.
Qt.MouseButtons.MiddleButton	4 (100)	The middle button is pressed.

 On right-handed mice the left and right button positions are reversed, i.e. pressing the right-most button will return Qt.MouseButtons.LeftButton. This means you don't need to account for the mouse orientation in your code.

 For a more in-depth look at how this all works check out Enums & the Qt Namespace later.

Context menus

Context menus are small context-sensitive menus which typically appear when right clicking on a window. Qt has support for generating these menus, and widgets have a specific event used to trigger them. In the following example we're going to intercept the .contextMenuEvent a QMainWindow. This event is fired whenever a context menu is *about to be* shown, and is passed a single value event of type QContextMenuEvent.

To intercept the event, we simply override the object method with our new method of the same name. So in this case we can create a method on our MainWindow subclass with the name contextMenuEvent and it will receive all events of this type.

Listing 86. basic/events_3.py

```python
import sys

from PyQt6.QtCore import Qt
from PyQt6.QtGui import QAction
from PyQt6.QtWidgets import (
    QApplication,
    QLabel,
    QMainWindow,
    QMenu,
)


class MainWindow(QMainWindow):
    def __init__(self):
        super().__init__()

    def contextMenuEvent(self, e):
        context = QMenu(self)
        context.addAction(QAction("test 1", self))
        context.addAction(QAction("test 2", self))
        context.addAction(QAction("test 3", self))
        context.exec(e.globalPos())


app = QApplication(sys.argv)

window = MainWindow()
window.show()

app.exec()
```

If you run the above code and right-click within the window, you'll see a context menu appear. You can set up `.triggered` slots on your menu actions as normal (and re-use actions defined for menus and toolbars).

When passing the initial position to the `exec()` method, this must be relative to the parent passed in while defining. In this case we pass `self` as the parent, so we can use the global position.

For completeness, there is also a signal-based approach to creating context menus.

Listing 87. basic/events_4.py

```python
class MainWindow(QMainWindow):
    def __init__(self):
        super().__init__()
        self.show()

        self.setContextMenuPolicy(
            Qt.ContextMenuPolicy.CustomContextMenu
        )
        self.customContextMenuRequested.connect(self.on_context_menu)

    def on_context_menu(self, pos):
        context = QMenu(self)
        context.addAction(QAction("test 1", self))
        context.addAction(QAction("test 2", self))
        context.addAction(QAction("test 3", self))
        context.exec(self.mapToGlobal(pos))
```

It's entirely up to you which you choose.

Event hierarchy

In pyqt6 every widget is part of two distinct hierarchies: the Python object hierarchy, and the Qt layout hierarchy. How you respond or ignore events can affect how your UI behaves.

Python inheritance forwarding

Often you may want to intercept an event, do something with it, yet still trigger the default event handling behavior. If your object is inherited from a standard widget, it will likely have sensible behavior implemented by default. You can trigger this by calling up to the parent implementation using super().

 This is the Python parent class, not the pyqt6 .parent().

```
def mousePressEvent(self, event):
    print("Mouse pressed!")
    super(self, MainWindow).contextMenuEvent(event)
```

The event will continue to behave as normal, yet you've added some non-interfering behavior.

Layout forwarding

When you add a widget to your application, it also gets another *parent* from the layout. The parent of a widget can be found by calling .parent(). Sometimes you specify these parents manually, such as for QMenu or QDialog, often it is automatic. When you add a widget to your main window for example, the main window will become the widget's parent.

When events are created for user interaction with the UI, these events are passed to the *uppermost* widget in the UI. If you click a button in a window, the button will receive the event before the window. If the first widget cannot handle the event, or chooses not to, the event will *bubble up* to the parent widget, which will be given a turn. This *bubbling* continues all the way up nested widgets, until the event is handled or it reaches the main window.

In your own event handlers you can choose to mark an event as *handled* by calling .accept() —

```
class CustomButton(Qbutton)
    def mousePressEvent(self, e):
        e.accept()
```

Alternatively, you can mark it as *unhandled* by calling .ignore() on the event object. In this case the event will continue to bubble up the hierarchy.

```
class CustomButton(Qbutton)
    def event(self, e):
        e.ignore()
```

If you want your widget to appear transparent to events, you can safely ignore events which you've actually responded to in some way. Similarly, you can choose to accept events you are not responding to in order to silence them.

 This is potentially confusing, since you might expect that calling .ignore() will ignore the event completely. This is not the case: your are ignoring the event for this widget only!

Qt Designer

So far we have been creating apps using Python code. This works great in many cases, but as your applications get larger, or interfaces more complicated, it can get a bit cumbersome to define all widgets programmatically. The good news is that Qt comes with a graphical editor — *Qt Designer* — which contains a drag-and-drop UI editor. Using *Qt Designer* you can define your UIs visually and then simply hook up the application logic later.

In this chapter we'll cover the basics of creating UIs with *Qt Designer*. The principles, layouts and widgets are identical, so you can apply everything you've already learnt. You'll also need your knowledge of the Python API to hook up your application logic later.

11. Installing Qt Designer

Qt Designer is available in the installation packages for Qt available from the Qt downloads page [https://www.qt.io/download-qt-installer]. Download and run the appropriate installer for your system and follow the platform-specific instructions below. Installing *Qt Designer* will not affect your PyQt6 installation.

> *Qt Creator vs. Qt Designer*
>
> You may also see mentions of *Qt Creator*. *Qt Creator* a fully-fledged IDE for Qt projects, while *Qt Designer* is the UI design component. *Qt Designer* is available within *Qt Creator* so you can install that instead if you wish, although it doesn't provide any added value for Python projects.

Windows

Qt Designer is not mentioned in the Windows Qt installer, but is automatically installed when you install any version of the Qt core libraries. For example, in the following screenshot we've opted to install the *MSVC 2017 64-bit* version of Qt — what you choose will have no effect on your *Designer* install.

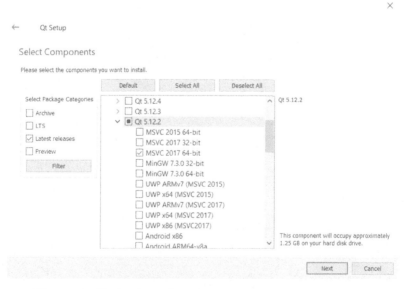

Figure 68. Installing Qt, will also install Qt Designer.

If you want to install *Qt Creator* it is listed under "Developer and Designer Tools". Rather confusingly, *Qt Designer* isn't in here.

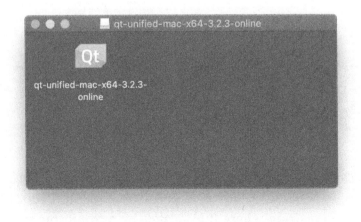

Figure 69. Installing the Qt Creator component.

macOS

Qt Designer is not mentioned in the macOS Qt installer, but is automatically installed when you install any version of the Qt core libraries. Download the installer from the Qt website — you can opt for the open source version.

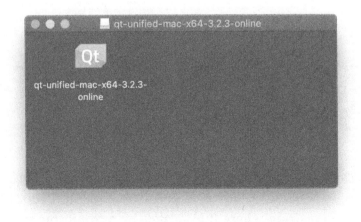

Figure 70. Inside the downloaded .dmg file you'll find the installer.

Open the installer to start the installation. Go through to where it asks you to choose which components to install. Select the *macOS* package under the latest version of Qt.

Figure 71. You only need the macOS package under the latest version.

Once the installation is complete, open the folder where you installed Qt. The launcher for *Designer* is under `<version>/clang_64/bin`. You'll notice that *Qt Creator* is also installed in the root of the Qt installation folder.

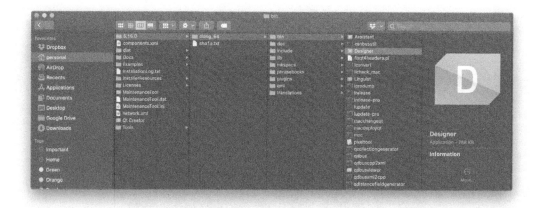

Figure 72. You can find the Designer launcher under the <version>/clang_64/bin folder.

You can run *Designer* from where it is located, or move it into your Applications folder so it is available to launch from the macOS Launchpad.

Linux (Ubuntu & Debian)

You can install *Qt Designer* using your package manager. Depending on your distribution and version you will have either *Qt5 Designer* or *Qt6 Designer* available. You can use either to develop UI designs for PyQt6.

Install *Qt5 Designer* with

```
sudo apt-get install qttools5-dev-tools
```

Or *Qt6 Designer* with

```
sudo apt-get install designer-qt6
```

Once installed, *Qt Designer* will be available in the launcher.

Figure 73. Qt Designer in Ubuntu launcher.

12. Getting started with Qt Designer

In this chapter we'll take a quick tour through using *Qt Designer* to design a UI and exporting that UI for use in your PyQt6 application. We'll only scratch the surface of what you can do with *Qt Designer* here. Once you've got the basics down, feel free to experiment more yourself.

Open up *Qt Designer* and you will be presented with the main window. The designer is available via the tab on the left hand side. However, to activate this you first need to start creating a .ui file.

Qt Designer

Qt Designer starts up with the *New Form* dialog. Here you can choose the type of interface you're building—this decides the base widget you will build your interface on. If you are starting an application then *Main Window* is usually the right choice. However, you can also create .ui files for dialog boxes and custom compound widgets.

 Form is the technical name given to a UI layout, since many UIs resemble a paper form with various input boxes.

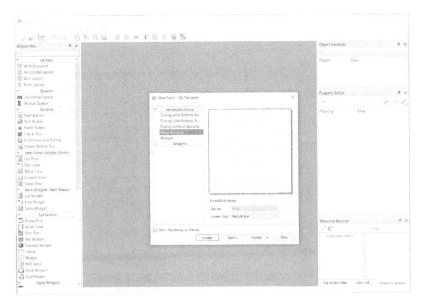

Figure 74. The Qt Designer interface

Click *Create* and a new UI will be created with a single empty widget in it. You're now ready to start designing your app.

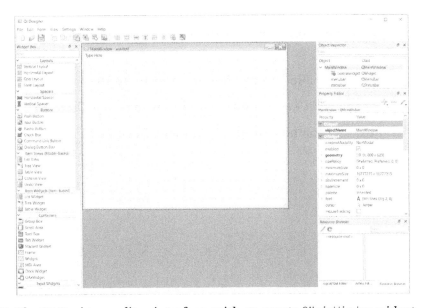

Figure 75. The Qt Designer editor interface, with an empty QMainWindow *widget.*

Qt Creator

If you've installed *Qt Creator*, the interface and process is slightly different. The left-hand side has a tab-like interface where you can select from the various components of the application. One of these is *Design*, which shows *Qt Designer* in the main panel.

Figure 76. The Qt Creator interface, with the Design section selected on the left. The Qt Designer interface is identical to the nested Designer.

 All the features of *Qt Designer* are available in *Qt Creator* but some aspects of the user interface are different.

To create a .ui file go to File → New File or Project... In the window that appears select *Qt* under *Files and Classes* on the left, then select *Qt Designer Form* on the right. You'll notice the icon has "ui" on it, showing the type of file you're creating.

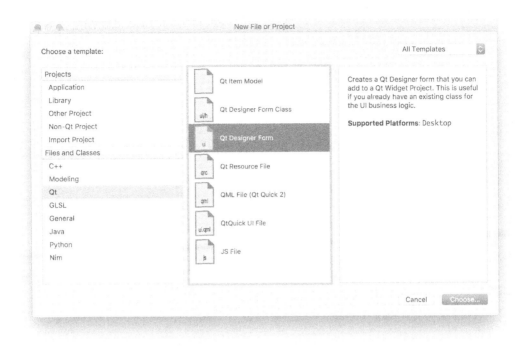

Figure 77. Create a new Qt .ui file.

In the next step you'll be asked what type of UI you want to create. For most applications *Main Window* is the right choice. However, you can also create .ui files for other dialog boxes or build custom widgets using QWidget (listed as "Widget").

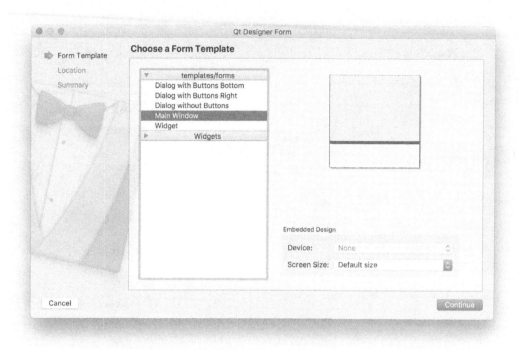

Figure 78. Select the type of widget to create, for most applications this will be Main Window.

Next choose a filename and save folder for your file. Save your `.ui` file with the same name as the class you'll be creating, just to make make subsequent commands simpler.

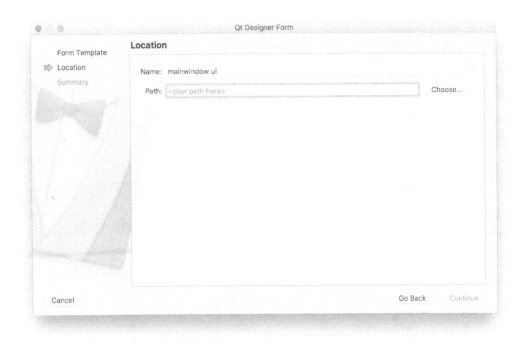

Figure 79. Choose save name and folder your your file.

Finally, you can choose to add the file to your version control system if you're using one. Feel free to skip this step — it doesn't affect your UI.

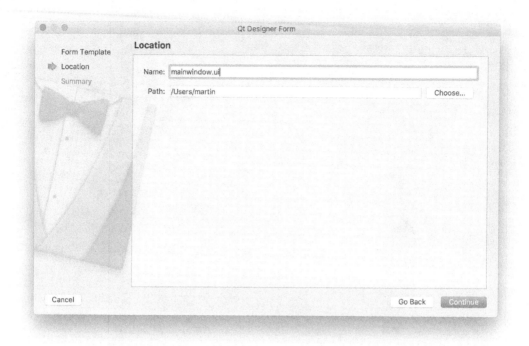

Figure 80. Optionally add the file to your version control, e.g. Git.

Laying out your Main Window

You'll be presented with your newly created main window in the UI designer. There isn't much to see to begin with, just a grey working area representing the window, together with the beginnings of a window menu bar.

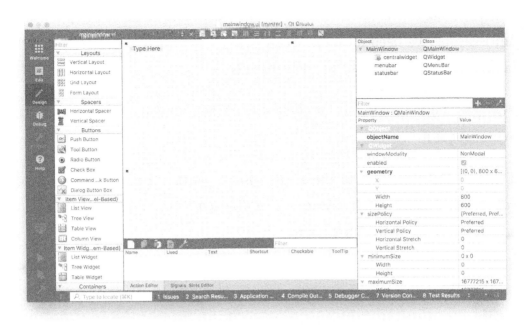

Figure 81. The initial view of the created main window.

You can resize the window by clicking the window and dragging the blue handles on each corner.

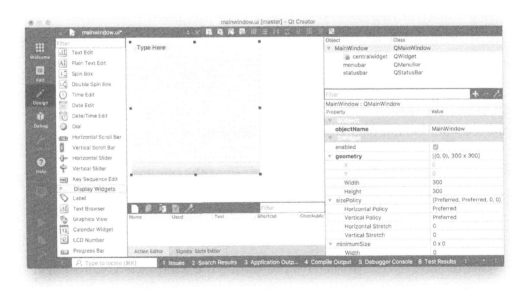

Figure 82. The main window resized to 300 x 300 pixels.

The first step in building an application is to add some widgets to your window. In our first applications we learnt that to set the central widget for a `QMainWindow` we need to use `.setCentralWidget()`. We also saw that to add multiple widgets with a layout, we need an intermediary `QWidget` to apply the layout to, rather than adding the layout to the window directly.

Qt Designer takes care of this for you automatically, although it's not particularly obvious about it.

To add multiple widgets to the main window with a layout, first drag your widgets onto the `QMainWindow`. Here we've dragged a `QLabel` and a `QPushButton`, it doesn't matter where you drop them.

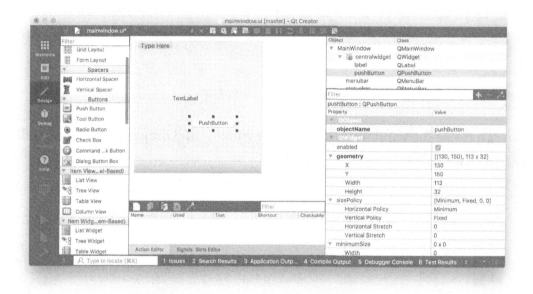

Figure 83. Main window with 1 labels and 1 button added.

We've created 2 widgets by dragging them onto the window, which made them children of that window. We can now apply a layout.

Find the `QMainWindow` in the right hand panel (it should be right at the top). Underneath you see *centralwidget* representing the window's central widget. The icon for the central widget shows the current layout applied. Initially it has a red circle-cross through it, showing that there is no layout active. Right click on the `QMainWindow` object, and find 'Layout' in the resulting dropdown.

Figure 84. Right click on the main window, and choose layout.

Next you'll see a list of layouts which you can apply to the window. Select *Lay Out Horizontally* and the layout will be applied to the widget.

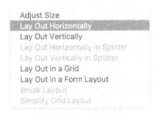

Figure 85. Select layout to apply to the main window.

The selected layout is applied to the *centralwidget* of the QMainWindow and the widgets are then added to the layout, being laid out according to the layout in place.

Note that you can drag and re-order the widgets within the layout, which will switch and move them around according to the layouts constraints. You can also select a different layout entirely, which is handy for prototyping and trying ideas out.

Don't try and add a layout without having widgets to go in it. The layout will collapse to zero size and will not be selectable!

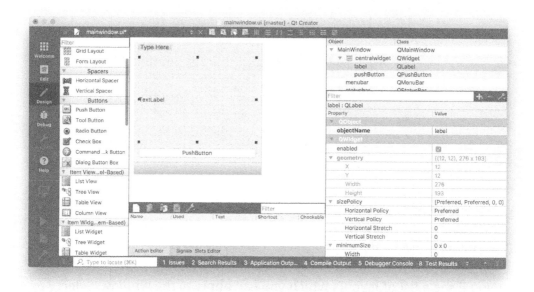

Figure 86. Vertical layout applied to widgets on the main window.

We've created a very simple UI in *Qt Designer*. The next step is to get this UI into our Python code and use it to construct a working application.

First save your .ui file — by default it will save at the location you chosen while creating it, although you can choose another location if you like. The .ui file is in XML format. To use our UI in Python, we can either load it directly from Python *or* first convert it to a Python .py file using the pyuic6 tool.

Loading your .ui file in Python

To load .ui files we can use the uic module included with PyQt6, specifically the uic.loadUI() method. This takes the filename of a UI file and loads it creating a fully-functional PyQt6 object.

Listing 88. designer/example_1.py

```python
import os
import sys

from PyQt6 import QtWidgets, uic

basedir = os.path.dirname(__file__)

app = QtWidgets.QApplication(sys.argv)

window = uic.loadUi(os.path.join(basedir, "mainwindow.ui"))
window.show()
app.exec()
```

To load a UI from the `__init__` block of an existing widget (e.g. a QMainWindow) you can use `uic.loadUI(filename, self)`.

Listing 89. designer/example_2.py

```python
import os
import sys

from PyQt6 import QtCore, QtGui, QtWidgets, uic

basedir = os.path.dirname(__file__)


class MainWindow(QtWidgets.QMainWindow):
    def __init__(self, *args, **kwargs):
        super().__init__(*args, **kwargs)
        uic.loadUi(os.path.join(basedir, "mainwindow.ui"), self)


app = QtWidgets.QApplication(sys.argv)
window = MainWindow()
window.show()
app.exec()
```

Converting your .ui file to Python

To generate a Python output file we can use the PyQt6 command line utility pyuic6. We run this, passing in the filename of the .ui file and the target file for output, with a -o parameter. The following will generate a Python file named MainWindow.py which contains our created UI. I use CamelCase on the filename to remind myself that it is a PyQt6 class file.

```
pyuic6 mainwindow.ui -o MainWindow.py
```

You can open the resulting MainWindow.py file in an editor to take a look, although you should *not* edit this file — if you do, any changes will be lost if you regenerate the UI from *Qt Designer*. The power of using *Qt Designer* is being able to edit and update your application as you go.

Building your application

Importing the resulting Python file works as for any other. You can import your class as follows. The pyuic6 tool appends Ui_ to the name of the object defined in *Qt Designer*, and it is this object you want to import.

```
from MainWindow import Ui_MainWindow
```

To create the main window in your application, create a class as normal but subclassing from both QMainWindow and your imported Ui_MainWindow class. Finally, call self.setupUi(self) from within the __init__ to trigger the setup of the interface.

```
class MainWindow(QMainWindow, Ui_MainWindow):
    def __init__(self, *args, obj=None, **kwargs):
        super(MainWindow, self).__init__(*args, **kwargs)
        self.setupUi(self)
```

That's it. Your window is now fully set up.

Adding application logic

You can interact with widgets created through *Qt Designer* just as you would those created with code. To make things simpler, `pyuic6` adds all widgets to the window object.

 The name used for objects can be found through *Qt Designer*. Simply click on it in the editor window, and then look for objectName in the properties panel.

In the following example we use the generated main window class to build a working application.

Listing 90. designer/compiled_example.py

```python
import random
import sys

from PyQt6.QtCore import Qt
from PyQt6.QtWidgets import QApplication, QMainWindow

from MainWindow import Ui_MainWindow


class MainWindow(QMainWindow, Ui_MainWindow):
    def __init__(self):
        super().__init__()
        self.setupUi(self)
        self.show()

        # You can still override values from your UI file within your
code,
        # but if possible, set them in Qt Creator. See the properties
panel.
        f = self.label.font()
        f.setPointSize(25)
        self.label.setAlignment(
            Qt.AlignmentFlag.AlignHCenter
            | Qt.AlignmentFlag.AlignVCenter
        )
        self.label.setFont(f)

        # Signals from UI widgets can be connected as normal.
        self.pushButton.pressed.connect(self.update_label)

    def update_label(self):
        n = random.randint(1, 6)
        self.label.setText("%d" % n)


app = QApplication(sys.argv)
w = MainWindow()
app.exec()
```

Notice that because we haven't set font size and alignment in the *Qt Designer* .ui definition, we must do so manually with code. You can change any widget parameters in this way, just as before. However, it is usually better to configure these things within *Qt Designer* itself.

You can set any widget properties through the properties panel on the bottom right of the window. Most widget properties are exposed here, for example, below we are updating the font size on the `QLabel` widget —

Figure 87. Setting the font size for the QLabel.

You can also configure alignment. For compound properties (where you can set multiple values, such as left + middle) they are nested.

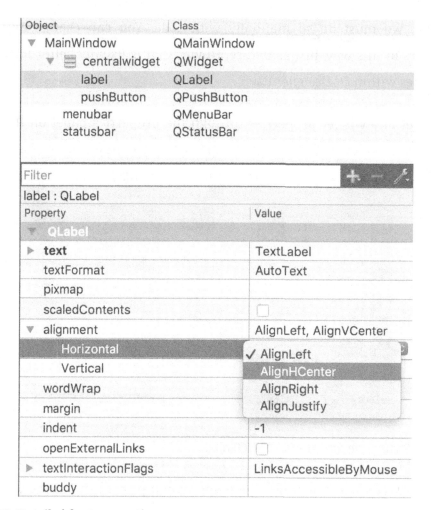

Object	Class
▼ MainWindow	QMainWindow
▼ ▤ centralwidget	QWidget
label	QLabel
pushButton	QPushButton
menubar	QMenuBar
statusbar	QStatusBar

Filter   **+ − 🔧**

label : QLabel

Property	Value
▼ QLabel	
▶ **text**	TextLabel
textFormat	AutoText
pixmap	
scaledContents	☐
▼ alignment	AlignLeft, AlignVCenter
Horizontal	✓ AlignLeft
Vertical	AlignHCenter
	AlignRight
	AlignJustify
wordWrap	
margin	
indent	-1
openExternalLinks	☐
▶ textInteractionFlags	LinksAccessibleByMouse
buddy	

Figure 88. Detailed font properties.

All object properties are able to be edited from both places — it's up to you whether you make a particular modification in code or in *Qt Designer*. As a general rule, it makes sense to keep *dynamic* changes in your code and the base or default state in your designed UI.

This introduction has only scratched the surface of what *Qt Designer* is capable of. I highly recommend you dig a little deeper and experiment — remember you can still add or adjust widgets from code afterwards.

Aesthetics

If you're not a designer, it can be difficult to create attractive and intuitive interfaces, or even know what they are. Thankfully there are simple rules you can follow to create interfaces that, if not necessarily beautiful, at least aren't *ugly*. The key concepts are — *alignment*, *groups* and *space*.

Alignment is about reducing visual noise. Think of the corners of widgets as alignment points and aim to minimize the number of unique alignment points in the UI. In practice, this means making sure the edges of elements in the interface line up with one another.

If you have differently sized inputs, align them against the edge you read from.

English is a left-to-right language, so if your application is in English, align the left.

The effect of alignment on interface clarity

Groups of related widgets gain context making them easier to understand. Structure your interface so related things are found together.

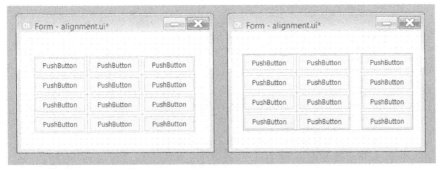

Group elements and add space between groups

Space is key to creating visually distinct regions in your interface — without space between groups, there are no groups! Keep spacing consistent and meaningful.

DO Use alignment to reduce visual noise in your interface.
DO Group related widgets together into logical sets.
DO Add consistent spacing between groups to clarify structure.

Theming

Out of the box Qt applications look *platform native*. That is, they take on the *look and feel* of the operating system they are running on. This means they look at home on any system and feel natural to users. But it can also mean they look a bit *boring*. Helpfully, Qt gives you complete control over the appearance of widgets in your application.

Whether you want your application to stand out, or you are designing custom widgets and want them to fit in, this chapter will explain how to do that in PyQt6.

13. Styles

Styles are Qt's way of making broad look and feel changes to applications, modifying how widgets are displayed and behave. Qt automatically applies platform-specific styles when running your application on a given platform — this is why your application looks like an macOS application when run on macOS and a Windows application on Windows. These platform-specific styles make use of native widgets on the host platform, meaning they are not available to use on other platforms.

However, the platform styles are not the only options you have for styling your applications. Qt also ships with a cross-platform style called *Fusion*, which provides a consistent cross-platform, modern, style for your applications.

Fusion

Qt's Fusion style gives you the benefit of UI consistency across all systems, at the expense of some consistency with the operating system standards. Which is more important will depend on how much control you need over the UI you are creating, how much you are customizing it and which widgets you are using.

> The Fusion style is a platform-agnostic style that offers a desktop-oriented look'n'feel. It implements the same design language as the Fusion style for Qt Widgets.

> — Qt Documentation

To enable the style, call .setStyle() on the QApplication instance, passing in the name of the style (in this case *Fusion*) as a string.

```
app - QApplication(sys.argv)
app.setStyle('Fusion')
#...
app.exec()
```

The widgets list example from earlier, but with the Fusion style applied, is shown below.

Figure 89. "Fusion" style widgets. They look identical on all platforms.

 There are more examples of widgets with Fusion style applied in the Qt documentation [https://doc.qt.io/archives/qt-5.8/gallery-fusion.html].

14. Palettes

The selection of colors used to draw the user interface in Qt are termed *palettes*. Both application level and widget-specific palettes are managed through `QPalette` objects. Palettes can be set at both the application and widget level, allowing you to set a global standard palette and override this on a per-widget basis. The global palette is normally defined by the Qt theme (itself normally dependent on the OS) but you can override this to change the look of your entire app.

The active global palette can be accessed from `QApplication.palette()` or by creating a new *empty* `QPalette` instance. For example —

```
from PyQt6.QtGui import QPalette
palette = QPalette()
```

You can modify the palette by calling `palette.setColor(role, color)` where *role* determines what the color is used for, `QColor` the color to use. The color used can either be a custom `QColor` object, or one of the built-in basic colors from the `Qt.GlobalColor` namespace.

```
palette.setColor(QPalette.ColorRole.Window, QColor(53,53,53))
palette.setColor(QPalette.ColorRole.WindowText, Qt.GlobalColor.white)
```

 There are some limitations when using palettes on Windows 10 and macOS platform-specific themes.

There are rather a lot of different *roles*. The main roles are shown in the table below —

Table 4. Main roles

Constant	Value	Description
`QPalette.ColorRole.Window`	10	Background color for windows.

Constant	Value	Description
`QPalette.ColorRole.WindowText`	0	Default text color for windows.
`QPalette.ColorRole.Base`	9	Background of text entry widgets, combobox drop down lists and toolbar handles. *Usually white or light*
`QPalette.ColorRole.AlternateBase`	16	Second `Base` color used in striped (alternating) rows — e.g. `QAbstractItemView.setAlternatingRowColors()`
`QPalette.ColorRole.ToolTipBase`	18	Background color for `QToolTip` and `QWhatsThis` hover indicators. Both tips use the `Inactive` group (see later) because they are not active windows.
`QPalette.ColorRole.ToolTipText`	19	Foreground color for `QToolTip` and `QWhatsThis`. Both tips use the `Inactive` group (see later) because they are not active windows.
`QPalette.ColorRole.PlaceholderText`	20	Color for placeholder text in widgets.
`QPalette.ColorRole.Text`	6	Text color for widgets colored with `Base` background. Must provide a good contrast with both Window and Base.
`QPalette.ColorRole.Button`	1	Default button background color. This can differ from `Window` but must provide good contrast with `ButtonText`.
`QPalette.ColorRole.ButtonText`	8	Text color used on buttons, must contrast with `Button` color.

Constant	Value	Description
QPalette.ColorRole.BrightText	7	Text color which is very different from WindowText, contrasts well with black. Used were other Text and WindowText colors would give poor contrast. Note: Not just used for text.

 You don't necessarily have to modify or set all of these in your custom palette, depending on widgets used in your application some can be omitted.

There are also smaller sets of roles used for 3D beveling on widgets and highlighting selected entries or links.

Table 5. 3D bevel roles

Constant	Value	Description
QPalette.ColorRole.Light	2	Lighter than Button color.
QPalette.ColorRole.Midlight	3	Between Button and Light.
QPalette.ColorRole.Dark	4	Darker than Button.
QPalette.ColorRole.Mid	5	Between Button and Dark.
QPalette.ColorRole.Shadow	11	A very dark color. By default, the shadow color is Qt.GlobalColor.black.

Table 6. Highlighting & links

Constant	Value	Description
QPalette.ColorRole.Highlight	12	A color to indicate a selected item or the current item. By default, the highlight color is Qt.GlobalColor.darkBlue.

Constant	Value	Description
QPalette.ColorRole.Highlighted Text	13	A text color that contrasts with Highlight. By default, the highlighted text Qt.GlobalColor.white.
QPalette.ColorRole.Link	14	A text color used for unvisited hyperlinks. By default, the link color is Qt.GlobalColor.blue.
QPalette.ColorRole.LinkVisited	15	A text color used for already visited hyperlinks. By default, the link-visited color is Qt.GlobalColor.magenta.

 There is also technically a QPalette.NoRole value for widget drawing states where no role is assigned, this can be ignored when creating palettes.

For parts of the UI which change when a widget is active, inactive or disabled you must set a color for each of these states. To do this, you can call palette.setColor(group, role, color) passing additional *group* parameter. The available groups are shown below —

Constant	Value
QPalette.ColorGroup.Disabled	1
QPalette.ColorGroup.Active	0
QPalette.ColorGroup.Inactive	2
QPalette.ColorGroup.Normal *synonym for Active*	0

For example, the following will set the WindowText color for a disabled window to *white* in the palette.

```
palette.setColor(QPalette.ColorGroup.Disabled, QPalette.ColorRole
.WindowText, Qt.GlobalColor.white)
```

Once the palette is defined, you can use .setPalette() to set it onto the
QApplication object to apply it to your application, or to a single widget. For
example, the following example will change the color of the window text and
background (here text is added using a QLabel).

Listing 91. themes/palette_test.py

```python
from PyQt6.QtWidgets import QApplication, QLabel
from PyQt6.QtGui import QPalette, QColor
from PyQt6.QtCore import Qt

import sys


app = QApplication(sys.argv)
palette = QPalette()
palette.setColor(QPalette.ColorRole.Window, QColor(0, 128, 255))
palette.setColor(QPalette.ColorRole.WindowText, Qt.GlobalColor.white)
app.setPalette(palette)

w = QLabel("Palette Test")
w.show()

app.exec()
```

When run, this gives the following output. The background of the window is
changed to a light blue, and the window text is white.

Figure 90. Changing the Window and WindowText colors.

To show palette use in practice and see some limitations of it, we'll now create an application using a custom dark palette.

 Using this palette all widgets will be drawn with a dark background, regardless of the dark mode state of your app. See later for using system dark modes.

While you should avoid overriding user settings in general, it can make sense in certain classes of applications such as photo viewers or video editors, where a bright UI will interfere with the users ability to judge color. The following app skeleton uses a custom palette by Jürgen Skrotzky [https://github.com/Jorgen-VikingGod/Qt-Frameless-Window-DarkStyle/blob/master/DarkStyle.cpp] to give the application a global dark theme.

```python
from PyQt6.QtWidgets import QApplication, QMainWindow
from PyQt6.QtGui import QPalette, QColor
from PyQt6.QtCore import Qt

import sys

darkPalette = QPalette()
darkPalette.setColor(QPalette.ColorRole.Window, QColor(53, 53, 53))
darkPalette.setColor(
    QPalette.ColorRole.WindowText, Qt.GlobalColor.white
)
darkPalette.setColor(
    QPalette.ColorGroup.Disabled,
    QPalette.ColorRole.WindowText,
    QColor(127, 127, 127),
)
darkPalette.setColor(QPalette.ColorRole.Base, QColor(42, 42, 42))
darkPalette.setColor(
    QPalette.ColorRole.AlternateBase, QColor(66, 66, 66)
)
darkPalette.setColor(
    QPalette.ColorRole.ToolTipBase, Qt.GlobalColor.white
)
darkPalette.setColor(
    QPalette.ColorRole.ToolTipText, Qt.GlobalColor.white
)
```

```python
darkPalette.setColor(QPalette.ColorRole.Text, Qt.GlobalColor.white)
darkPalette.setColor(
    QPalette.ColorGroup.Disabled,
    QPalette.ColorRole.Text,
    QColor(127, 127, 127),
)
darkPalette.setColor(QPalette.ColorRole.Dark, QColor(35, 35, 35))
darkPalette.setColor(QPalette.ColorRole.Shadow, QColor(20, 20, 20))
darkPalette.setColor(QPalette.ColorRole.Button, QColor(53, 53, 53))
darkPalette.setColor(
    QPalette.ColorRole.ButtonText, Qt.GlobalColor.white
)
darkPalette.setColor(
    QPalette.ColorGroup.Disabled,
    QPalette.ColorRole.ButtonText,
    QColor(127, 127, 127),
)
darkPalette.setColor(QPalette.ColorRole.BrightText, Qt.GlobalColor
.red)
darkPalette.setColor(QPalette.ColorRole.Link, QColor(42, 130, 218))
darkPalette.setColor(QPalette.ColorRole.Highlight, QColor(42, 130,
218))
darkPalette.setColor(
    QPalette.ColorGroup.Disabled,
    QPalette.ColorRole.Highlight,
    QColor(80, 80, 80),
)
darkPalette.setColor(
    QPalette.ColorRole.HighlightedText, Qt.GlobalColor.white
)
darkPalette.setColor(
    QPalette.ColorGroup.Disabled,
    QPalette.ColorRole.HighlightedText,
    QColor(127, 127, 127),
)

app = QApplication(sys.argv)
app.setPalette(darkPalette)

w = QMainWindow()  # Replace with your QMainWindow instance.
w.show()

app.exec()
```

As before, once the palette is constructed it must be applied to take effect. Here we apply it to the application as a whole by calling `app.setPalette()`. All widgets will adopt the theme once applied. You can use this skeleton to construct your own applications using this theme.

In the code examples with this book you can also find `themes/palette_dark_widgets.py` which reproduces the widgets demo, using this palette. The result on each platform is shown below.

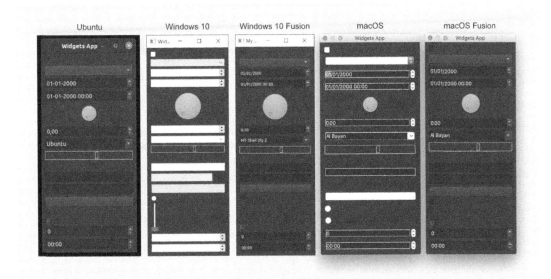

Figure 91. Custom dark palette on different platforms and themes

You'll notice that when using the default Windows and macOS themes some widgets do not have their colors applied correctly. This is because these themes make use of platform-native controls to give a true native feel. If you want to use a dark or heavily customized theme on Windows 10, it is recommended to use the *Fusion* style on these platforms.

Dark Mode

Darker themed OS and applications help to minimize eye strain and reduce sleep disturbance if working in the evening. Windows, macOS and Linux all provide support for dark mode themes, and the good news is that if you build your application with PyQt6 you get dark mode support for free.

Accessible Colors

As you start to building your own applications, you may be tempted to start fiddling with colors in the design — but wait! Your operating system has a standard theme which is respected by most software. Qt picks up this color scheme automatically and will apply it to your applications to help them fit in. Using these colors has some advantages —

1. Your app will look at home on your user's desktop
2. Your users are familiar with the meaning of contextual colors
3. Somebody else has spent time designing colors that work

Don't underestimate the value of #3! Designing good color schemes is hard, especially if you take accessibility issues into account — and you should!

If you want to replace the standard desktop color scheme, make sure that the benefits outweigh the costs & you've explored other options such as built-in dark modes on your target platforms.

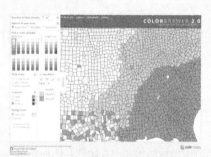

For **data visualization** applications I recommend using the *Color Brewer* color sets from Cynthia Brewer, which have both qualitative and quantitative schemes & are designed for maximum clarity.

For **contextual colors & highlights** or any other situation where you only need a few colors — e.g. status indicators — the coolors.co website lets you generate custom well-matched 4-color themes.

Colorbrewer2.org has quantitative and qualitative color schemes

Consistency makes the most of your palette. Use colors simply and effectively, restricting your palette as far as possible. If particular colors have meaning somewhere, use the same meaning everywhere. Avoid using multiple shades unless those shades have meaning.

Example color scheme from coolors.co

DO Consider using GUI-standard colors in your app.
DO When using custom colors, define a color scheme and stick to it.
DO Keep color-blind users in mind when choosing colors and contrasts.
DON'T Use standard colors for non-standard purposes, e.g. Red = OK.

15. Icons

Icons are small pictures which are used to aid navigation or understanding within a user interface. They are commonly found on buttons, either alongside or in place of text, or alongside actions in menus. By using easily recognizable indicators you can make your interface easier to use.

In PyQt6 you have a number of different options for how to source and integrate icons into your application. In this section we'll look at those options and the pros and cons of each.

Qt Standard Icons

The easiest way to add simple icons to your application is to use the built-in icons which ship with Qt itself. This small set of icons covers a number of standard use cases, from file operations, forward & backward arrows and message box indicators.

The full list of built-in icons follows.

Figure 92. Qt Builtin icons

You'll notice that this set of icons is a bit *restrictive*. If that's not a problem for the app you're building, or if you only need a few icons for your app it might still be a viable option for you.

The icons are accessible through the current application style using `QStyle.standardIcon(name)` or `QStyle.<constant>`. The full table of built-in icon names is shown below.

SP_ArrowBack	SP_DirIcon	SP_MediaSkipBackward
SP_ArrowDown	SP_DirLinkIcon	SP_MediaSkipForward
SP_ArrowForward	SP_DirOpenIcon	SP_MediaStop
SP_ArrowLeft	SP_DockWidgetCloseButton	SP_MediaVolume
SP_ArrowRight	SP_DriveCDIcon	SP_MediaVolumeMuted
SP_ArrowUp	SP_DriveDVDIcon	SP_MessageBoxCritical

SP_BrowserReload	SP_DriveFDIcon	SP_MessageBoxInformation
SP_BrowserStop	SP_DriveHDIcon	SP_MessageBoxQuestion
SP_CommandLink	SP_DriveNetIcon	SP_MessageBoxWarning
SP_ComputerIcon	SP_FileDialogBack	SP_TitleBarCloseButton
SP_CustomBase	SP_FileDialogContentsView	SP_TitleBarContextHelpButton
SP_DesktopIcon	SP_FileDialogDetailedView	SP_TitleBarMaxButton
SP_DialogApplyButton	SP_FileDialogEnd	SP_TitleBarMenuButton
SP_DialogCancelButton	SP_FileDialogInfoView	SP_TitleBarMinButton
SP_DialogCloseButton	SP_FileDialogListView	SP_TitleBarNormalButton
SP_DialogDiscardButton	SP_FileDialogNewFolder	SP_TitleBarShadeButton
SP_DialogHelpButton	SP_FileDialogStart	SP_TitleBarUnshadeButton
SP_DialogNoButton	SP_FileDialogToParent	SP_ToolBarHorizontalExtensionButton
SP_DialogOkButton	SP_FileIcon	SP_ToolBarVerticalExtensionButton
SP_DialogResetButton	SP_FileLinkIcon	SP_TrashIcon
SP_DialogSaveButton	SP_MediaPause	SP_VistaShield
SP_DialogYesButton	SP_MediaPlay	SP_DirClosedIcon
SP_MediaSeekBackward	SP_DirHomeIcon	SP_MediaSeekForward

You can access these icons directly via the QStyle namespace, as follows.

```
icon = QStyle.standardIcon(QStyle.SP_MessageBoxCritical)
button.setIcon(icon)
```

You can also use the style object from a specific widget. It doesn't matter which you use, since we're only accessing the built-ins anyway.

```
style = button.style()  # Get the QStyle object from the widget.
icon = style.standardIcon(style.SP_MessageBoxCritical)
button.setIcon(icon)
```

If you can't find an icon you need in this standard set, you will need to use one of the other approaches outlined below.

 While you *can* mix and match icons from different icon sets together, it's better to use a single style throughout to keep your app feeling coherent.

Icon files

If the standard icons aren't what you are looking for, or you need icons not available, you can use any custom icons you like. Icons can be any of the Qt supported image types on your platform, although for most use cases PNG or SVG images are preferable.

 To get list of supported image formats on your own platform you can call QtGui.QImageReader.supportedImageFormats().

Icon sets

If you're not a graphic designer you will save yourself a lot of time (and trouble) by using one of the many available icon sets. There are thousands of these available online, with varying licenses depending on their use in open source or commercial software.

In this book and example apps I've used the Fugue [http://p.yusukekamiyamane.com/] icon set, which is also free to use in your software with acknowledgement of the author. The Tango icon set is a large icon set developed for use on Linux, however there are no licensing requirements and it can be used on any platform.

Resource	Description	License
Fugue by p.yusukekamiyamane [http://p.yusukekamiyamane.com/]	3,570 16x16 icons in PNG format	CC BY 3.0
Diagona by p.yusukekamiyamane [http://p.yusukekamiyamane.com/]	400 16x16 and 10x10 icons in PNG format	CC BY 3.0
Tango Icons by The Tango Desktop Project [http://tango.freedesktop.org/Tango_Icon_Library]	Icons using the Tango project color theme.	Public domain

 While you do have control over the size of icons using in menus and toolbars, in most cases you should leave these as-is. A good standard icon size for menus is 20x20 pixels.

 Sizes smaller than this are fine too, the icon will be centered rather than scaled up.

Create your own

If you don't like any of the available icon sets, or want a unique look to your application, you can of course design your own icons. Icons can be created using any standard graphics software and saved as PNG images with transparent background. The icons should be square and of a resolution that they do not need to be scaled up or down when used in your application.

Using icon files

Once you have your icon files — whether from icon sets or self-drawn — they can

be used in your Qt applications by creating instances of QtGui.QIcon, passing in
the filename of the icon directly.

```
QtGui.QIcon("<filename>")
```

While you can use both absolute (complete) and relative (partial) to point to your
file, absolute paths are prone to break when distributing your applications.
Relative paths will work as long as the icon files are stored in the same location
relative to your script, although even this can be difficult to manage when
packaging.

 In order to create icon instances you must have already created
a QApplication instance. To ensure this is the case, you can
create your app instance at the top of your source file, or create
your QIcon instances in the __init__ for the widget or window
that uses them.

Free Desktop Specification Icons (Linux)

On Linux desktops there is a thing called the *Free Desktop Specification* which
defines standard names for icons for specific actions.

If your application uses these specific icon names (and loads the icon from a
"theme") then on Linux your application will use the current icon set which is
enabled on the desktop. The goal here is to ensure that all applications have the
same look & feel while remaining configurable.

To use these within Qt Designer you would select the drop-down and choose "Set
Icon From Theme..."

Figure 93. Selecting an icon theme

You then enter the **name** of the icon you want to use, e.g. document-new (see the full list of valid names [https://specifications.freedesktop.org/icon-naming-spec/latest/ar01s04.html]).

Figure 94. Selecting an icon theme

In code, you can get icons from the active Linux desktop theme using icon = QtGui.QIcon.fromTheme("document-new"). The following snippet produces a small window (button) with the "new document" icon showing, from the active theme.

Listing 92. icons/linux.py

```python
from PyQt6.QtWidgets import QApplication, QPushButton
from PyQt6.QtGui import QIcon

import sys

app = QApplication(sys.argv)
button = QPushButton("Hello")
icon = QIcon.fromTheme("document-new")
button.setIcon(icon)
button.show()

app.exec()
```

The resulting window will look like the following on Ubuntu, with the default icon theme.

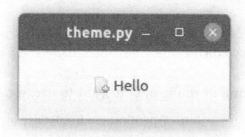

Figure 95. Linux Free Desktop Specification "document-new" icon

If you're developing a cross-platform application you can still make use of these standard icons on Linux. To do this, use your own icons for Windows and macOS and create a custom theme in Qt Designer, using the Free Desktop Specification names for the icons.

16. Qt Style Sheets (QSS)

So far we've looked at how you can apply custom colors to your PyQt6 apps using `QPalette`. However, there are many other customizations you can make to the appearance of widgets in Qt5. The system provided to allow this customization is called Qt Style Sheets (QSS).

QSS is conceptually very similar to Cascading Style Sheets (CSS) used to style the web, sharing a similar syntax and approach. In this section we'll look at some examples of QSS and how you can use it to modify widget appearance.

 Using QSS on widgets has a small performance impact, due to the need to look up the appropriate rules when redrawing widgets. However, unless you are doing very widget-heavy work this is unlikely to be of consequence.

Style editor

To make experimenting with QSS rules a little bit easier, we can create a simple demo app which allows rules to be input and applied to some example widgets. We'll use this to test out the various style properties and rules.

 The source code for the style viewer is shown below, but it's also available in the source code with this book.

Listing 93. themes/qss_tester.py

```python
import sys

from PyQt6.QtCore import Qt
from PyQt6.QtGui import QColor, QPalette
from PyQt6.QtWidgets import (
    QApplication,
    QCheckBox,
    QComboBox,
    QLabel,
```

```
        QLineEdit,
        QMainWindow,
        QPlainTextEdit,
        QPushButton,
        QSpinBox,
        QVBoxLayout,
        QWidget,
    )


    class MainWindow(QMainWindow):
        def __init__(self):
            super().__init__()

            self.setWindowTitle("QSS Tester")

            self.editor = QPlainTextEdit()
            self.editor.textChanged.connect(self.update_styles)

            layout = QVBoxLayout()
            layout.addWidget(self.editor)

            # Define a set of simple widgets.
            cb = QCheckBox("Checkbox")
            layout.addWidget(cb)

            combo = QComboBox()
            combo.setObjectName("thecombo")
            combo.addItems(["First", "Second", "Third", "Fourth"])
            layout.addWidget(combo)

            sb = QSpinBox()
            sb.setRange(0, 99999)
            layout.addWidget(sb)

            l = QLabel("This is a label")
            layout.addWidget(l)

            le = QLineEdit()
            le.setObjectName("mylineedit")
            layout.addWidget(le)

            pb = QPushButton("Push me!")
```

```
            layout.addWidget(pb)

        self.container = QWidget()
        self.container.setLayout(layout)

        self.setCentralWidget(self.container)

    def update_styles(self):
        qss = self.editor.toPlainText()
        self.setStyleSheet(qss)


app = QApplication(sys.argv)
app.setStyle("Fusion")

w = MainWindow()
w.show()

app.exec()
```

Running this app you'll see the following window, with a text editor at the top (where you can enter QSS rules) and a set of widgets to which these rules will be applied — we'll look at how applying rules and inheritance works in a bit.

Figure 96. QSS tester application, no rules applied.

Try entering the following style rules in the box at the top, and comparing the result with the screenshots to make sure it's working.

```
QLabel { background-color: yellow }
```

Figure 97. Applying background-color: yellow to QLabel

```
QLineEdit { background-color: rgb(255, 0, 0) }
```

Figure 98. Applying background-color: rgb(255, 0, 0) (red) to QLineEdit

```
QLineEdit {
    border-width: 7px;
    border-style: dashed;
    border-color: red;
}
```

Figure 99. Applying dashed red border to QLineEdit

Next we'll look in some detail at how these QSS rules are styling the widgets, gradually building up to some more complex rule sets.

 A full list of styleable widgets is available in the Qt documentation [https://doc.qt.io/qt-6/stylesheet-reference.html].

Styling properties

Next we'll go through the properties available to style widgets with QSS. These have been broken down into logical sections, containing properties that are related to one another to make it easier to digest. You can use the QSS rule tester app we just created to test these styles out on the various widgets.

The types used in the following tables are listed below. Some of these are compound types, made up of other entries.

 You can skip over this table for now, but will need it as a reference for interpreting the valid values for each property.

Property	Type	Description
Alignment	top | bottom | left | right | center	Horizontal and/or vertical alignment.
Attachment	scroll | fixed	Scroll or fixed attachment.
Background	Brush | Url | Repeat | Alignment	Compound type of Brush, Url,Repeat, andAlignment.
Boolean	0 | 1	True (1) or False (0).
Border	Border Style | Length | Brush	Shorthand border property.
Border Image	none | Url Number (stretch | repeat)	An image composed of nine parts (top left, top center, top right, center left, center, center right, bottom left, bottom center, and bottom right).

Property	Type	Description
Border Style	dashed | dot-dash | dot-dot-dash | dotted | double | groove | inset | outset | ridge | solid | none	The pattern used to draw a border.
Box Colors	Brush	Up to four values of Brush, specifying the top, right, bottom, and left edges of a box, respectively. If the left color is omitted will use right, if bottom is omitted will use top.
Box Lengths	Length	Up to four values of Length, specifying the top, right, bottom, and left edges of a box, respectively. If the left color is omitted will use right, if bottom is omitted will use top.
Brush	Color | Gradient | PaletteRole	A Color, Gradient or an entry in the Palette.
Color	rgb(r,g,b) | rgba(r,g,b,a) | hsv(h,s,v) | hsva(h,s,v,a) | hsl(h,s,l) | hsla(h,s,l,a) | #rrggbb | Color Name	Specifies a color as RGB (red, green, blue), RGBA (red, green, blue, alpha), HSV (hue, saturation, value), HSVA (hue, saturation, value, alpha), HSL (hue, saturation, lightness), HSLA (hue, saturation, lightness, alpha) or a named color. The rgb() or rgba() syntax can be used with integer values between 0 and 255, or with percentages.
Font	(Font Style | Font Weight) Font Size	Shorthand font property.

Property	Type	Description
Font Size	Length	The size of a font.
Font Style	normal | italic | oblique	The style of a font.
Font Weight	normal | bold | 100 | 200... | 900	The weight of a font.
Gradient	qlineargradient | qradialgradient | qconicalgradient	Lineargradients between start and end points. Radialgradients between a focal point and end points on a circle surrounding it. Conical gradients around a center point. See the QLinearGradient documentation [https://doc.qt.io/qt-6/stylesheet-reference.html#gradient] for syntax.
Icon	Url(disabled | active | normal | selected) (on | off)	A list of url,QIcon.ModeandQIcon.State. e.g. `file-icon:` `url(file.png),` `url(file_selected.png) selected;`
Length	Number(px | pt | em | ex)	A number followed by a measurement unit. If no unit is given, uses pixels in most contexts. One of px: pixels, pt: the size of one point (i.e., 1/72 of an inch), em: the em `width of the font (i.e., the width of 'M'), ex: the ex width of the font (i.e., the height of 'x')
Number	A decimal integer or a real number	e.g. 123, or 12.2312
Origin	margin | border | padding | content	See box model for more details.

Property	Type	Description
PaletteRole	alternate-base | base | bright-text | button | button-text | dark | highlight | highlighted-text | light | link | link-visited | mid | midlight | shadow | text | window | window-text	These values correspond the Color roles in the widget's QPalette, e.g. `color: palette(dark);`
Radius	Length	One or two occurrences of Length.
Repeat	repeat-x | repeat-y | repeat | no-repeat	repeat-x: Repeat horizontally. repeat-y: Repeat vertically. repeat: Repeat horizontally and vertically. no-repeat: Don't repeat.
Url	url(filename)	filename is the name of a file on disk or stored using the Qt Resource System.

The full details of these properties and types are also available in the QSS reference documentation [https://doc.qt.io/qt-6/stylesheet-reference.html#list-of-properties].

Text styles

We'll start with text properties which can be used to modify fonts, colors and styles (bold, italic, underline) of text. These can be applied to any widget or control.

Property	Type (Default)	Description
color	Brush (QPalette Foreground)	The color used to render text.

Property	Type (Default)	Description
font	Font	Shorthand notation for setting the text's font. Equivalent to specifying font-family, font-size, font-style, and/or font-weight
font-family	String	The font family.
font-size	Font Size	The font size. In this version of Qt, only pt and px metrics are supported.
font-style	normal | italic | oblique	The font style.
font-weight	Font Weight	The weight of the font.
selection-background-color	Brush (QPalette Highlight)	The background of selected text or items.
selection-color	Brush (Palette HighlightedText)	The foreground of selected text or items.
text-align	Alignment	The alignment of text and icon within the contents of the widget.
text-decoration	none | underline | overline | line-through	Additional text effects

The example snippet below, sets the color on the QLineEdit to *red*, the background color for selected text to *yellow* and the color of selected text to *blue*.

```
QLineEdit {
    color: red;
    selection-color: blue;
    selection-background-color: yellow;
}
```

Try this in the QSS tester to see the effect on the QLineEdit and it will give the following result. Notice that only the targeted widget (QLineEdit) is affected by the styles.

Figure 100. Applying text styles to a QLineEdit

We can apply this rule to two distinct types of widgets by giving them both as the target, separated by a comma.

```
QSpinBox, QLineEdit {
    color: red;
    selection-color: blue;
    selection-background-color: yellow;
}
```

Figure 101. Applying text styles to a QLineEdit & QSpinBox

In this final example, we apply the styles to the QSpinBox, QLineEdit and QPushButton, setting the font bold & italic and the text-align to **right**.

```
QSpinBox, QLineEdit, QPushButton {
    color: red;
    selection-color: blue;
    selection-background-color: yellow;
    font-style: italic;
    font-weight: bold;
    text-align: right;
}
```

This produces the result shown below. Notice that the text-align property has not affected the alignment of the QSpinBox or QLineEdit. For both these widgets alignment must be set using the .setAlignment() method, rather than styles.

Figure 102. Applying text styles to a QPushButton, QLineEdit & QSpinBox

Backgrounds

In addition to styling text you can also style the widget background, with both solid colors and images. For images there are a number of additional properties which define how the image is repeated and positioned within the widget area.

Property	Type (Default)	Description
background	Background	Shorthand notation for setting the background. Equivalent to specifying background-color, background-image, background-repeat, and/or background-position. See also background-origin, selection-background-color, background-clip, background-attachment and alternate-background-color.

Property	Type (Default)	Description
background-color	Brush	The background color used for the widget.
background-image	Url	The background image used for the widget. Semi-transparent parts of the image let the background-color shine through.
background-repeat	Repeat (both)	Whether and how the background image is repeated to fill the background-origin rectangle.
background-position	Alignment (top-left)	The alignment of the background image within the background-origin rectangle.
background-clip	Origin (border)	The widget's rectangle, in which the background is drawn.
background-origin	Origin (padding)	The widget's background rectangle, to use in conjunction with background-position and background-image.

The following example will apply the specified image over the background of our QPlainTextEdit which we are using to enter the rules.

```
QPlainTextEdit {
    color: white;
    background-image: url(../otje.jpg);
}
```

Images are referenced using the url() syntax, passing in the path to the file. Here we're using ../otje.jpg to point to a file in the parent directory.

Figure 103. A background image.

 While this syntax is identical to that used in CSS, remote files cannot be loaded with URLs.

To position the background in the widget you can use the background-position property. This defines the point of the image which will be aligned with the *same* point on the widget's *origin rectangle*. By default the *origin rectangle* is the padded area of the widget.

Figure 104. Examples of background position

A position of center, center therefore means the center of the image will be aligned with the center of the widget, along both axes.

```
QPlainTextEdit {
    color: white;
    background-image: url(../otje.jpg);
    background-position: center center;
}
```

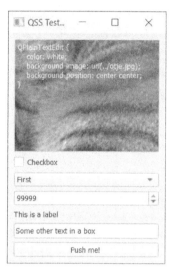

Figure 105. Centered background image.

To align the bottom-right of the image to the bottom-right of the *origin rectangle* of the widget, you would use.

```
QPlainTextEdit {
    color: white;
    background-image: url(../otje.jpg);
    background-position: bottom right;
}
```

The *origin rectangle* can be modified using the background-origin property. This accepts one of the values margin, border, padding or content which defines that specific box as the reference of background position alignment.

To understand what this means we'll need to take a look at the widget box model.

The widget Box Model

The term *box model* describes the relationships between the *boxes* (rectangles) which surround each widget and the effect these boxes have on the size or layout of widgets in relationship to one another. Each Qt widget is surrounded by four concentric boxes — from inside out, these are content, padding, border and margin.

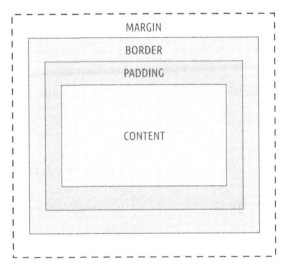

Figure 106. The box model.

Increasing the size of the inner boxes, increases the size of the outer boxes. This arrangement means, for example, that increasing the *padding* of a widget will add space between the content and the border, while increasing the dimensions of the border itself.

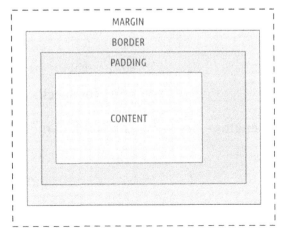

Figure 107. The effect on other boxes of adding padding to the right.

The properties available to modify the various boxes are given below.

Property	Type (Default)	Description
border	Border	Shorthand notation for setting the widget's border. Equivalent to specifying border-color, border-style, and/or border-width. Also border-top, border-right, border-bottom and border-left.
border-color	Box Colors (QPalette Foreground)	The color of all the border's edges. Also border-top-color, border-right-color, border-bottom-color, border-left-color for specific edges.
border-image	Border Image	The image used to fill the border. The image is cut into nine parts and stretched appropriately if necessary.
border-radius	Radius	The radius (curve) of the border's corners. Also border-top-left-radius, border-top-right-radius, border-bottom-right-radius and border-bottom-left-radius for specific corners.
border-style	Border Style (none)	The style of all the border's edges. Also border-top-style, border-right-style, border-bottom-style and border-left-style for specific edges.
border-width	Box Lengths	The width of the border. Also border-top-width, border-right-width, border-bottom-width and border-left-width.

Property	Type (Default)	Description
margin	Box Lengths	The widget's margins. Also margin-top, margin-right, margin-bottom and margin-left.
outline		The outline drawn around the object's border.
outline-color	Color	The color of the outline. See also border-color.
outline-offset	Length	The outline's offset from the border of the widget.
outline-style		Specifies the pattern used to draw the outline. See also border-style.
outline-radius		Adds rounded corners to the outline. Also outline-bottom-left-radius, outline-bottom-right-radius, outline-top-left-radius and outline-top-right-radius`". `padding,Box Lengths,"The widget's padding. Also padding-top, padding-right, padding-bottom and padding-left.

The following example modifies the margin, border and padding of the QPlainTextEdit widget.

```
QPlainTextEdit {
    margin: 10;
    padding: 10px;
    border: 5px solid red;
}
```

A note on units

In this example we're using px or *pixel* units for the *padding* and *border* The value for *margin* is also in pixels, as this is the default unit when none is specified. You can also use one of the following units —

- px pixels

- pt the size of one point (i.e. 1/72 of an inch)

- em the *em* width of the font (i.e. the width of 'M')

- ex the *ex* width of the font (i.e. the height of 'x')

Looking at the result in the QSS tester, you can see the padding *inside* the red border and the margin *outside* the red border.

Figure 108. The box model

You can also add a *radius* to the outline to add curved edges.

```
QPlainTextEdit {
    margin: 10;
    padding: 10px;
    border: 5px solid red;
    border-radius: 15px;
}
```

Figure 109. Borders with 15px radius (curve)

Sizing widgets

It is possible to control the size of widgets with QSS. However, while there are specific width and height properties (see later) these are only used to specify the sizes of sub-controls. To control widgets you must instead use the max- and min- properties.

Property	Type (Default)	Description
max-height	Length	The widget's or a subcontrol's maximum height.
max-width	Length	The widget's or a subcontrol's maximum width.
min-height	Length	The widget's or a subcontrol's minimum height.

Property	Type (Default)	Description
min-width	Length	The widget's or a subcontrol's minimum width.

If you provide a min-height property larger than the widget *usually* is, then the widget will be enlarged.

```
QLineEdit {
    min-height: 50;
}
```

Figure 110. Setting a min-height on a QLineEdit, to enlarge it.

However, when setting min-height the widget can of course be larger than this. To specify an exact size for a widget, you can specify both a min- and max- value for the dimension.

```
QLineEdit {
    min-height: 50;
    max-height: 50;
}
```

This will lock the widget to this height, preventing it from resizing in response to changes in content.

 Be careful about using this, as you can render widgets unreadable!

Widget specific styles

The styles we've looked at so far are generic and can be used with most widgets. However, there are also a number of widget-specific properties which can be set.

Property	Type (Default)	Description
alternate-background-color	Brush (QPalette AlternateBase)	The alternate background color used in QAbstractItemView subclasses.
background-attachment	Attachment (scroll)	Determines whether the background-image in a QAbstractScrollArea is scrolled or fixed with respect to the viewport.
button-layout	Number (SH_DialogButtonLayout)	The layout of buttons in a QDialogButtonBox or a QMessageBox. The possible values are 0 (Win), 1 (Mac), 2 (KDE), 3 (Gnome) and 5 (Android).

Property	Type (Default)	Description
dialogbuttonbox-buttons-have-icons	Boolean	Whether the buttons in a QDialogButtonBox show icons. If this property is set to 1, the buttons of a QDialogButtonBox show icons; if it is set to 0, the icons are not shown.
gridline-color	Color (SH_Table_GridLineColor)	The color of the grid line in a QTableView.
icon	Url+	The widget icon. The only widget currently supporting this property is QPushButton.
icon-size	Length	The width and height of the icon in a widget.
lineedit-password-character	Number (SH_LineEdit_PasswordCharacter)	The QLineEdit password character as a Unicode number.
lineedit-password-mask-delay	Number (SH_LineEdit_PasswordMaskDelay)	The QLineEdit password mask delay in milliseconds before lineedit-password-character is applied.
messagebox-text-interaction-flags	Number (SH_MessageBox_TextInteractionFlags)	The interaction behavior for text in a message box (from Qt.TextInteractionFlags).

Property	Type (Default)	Description
`opacity`	Number (`SH_ToolTipLabel_Opacity`)	The opacity for a widget (tooltips only) 0-255.
`paint-alternating-row-colors-for-empty-area`	bool	Whether a `QTreeView` paints alternating rows past the end of the data.
`show-decoration-selected`	Boolean (`SH_ItemView_ShowDecorationSelected`)	Controls whether selections in a `QListView` cover the entire row or just the extent of the text.
`titlebar-show-tooltips-on-buttons`	bool	Whether tool tips are shown on window title bar buttons.
`widget-animation-duration`	Number	How long an animation should last (milliseconds).

These only apply to the widgets specified in the description (or their subclasses).

Targeting

We've seen a range of different QSS properties and applied them to widgets based on their type. But how can you target individual widgets and how does Qt decide which rules to apply to which widgets and when? Next, we'll look at other options for targeting QSS rules and the effect of inheritance.

Type	Example	Description
Universal	`*`	Matches all widgets.
Type	`QPushButton`	Instances of QPushButton or its subclasses.

Type	Example	Description
Property	`QPushButton[flat="false"]`	Instances of `QPushButton` that are not flat. Can compare with *any* property that supports `.toString()`. Can also use `class="classname"`
Property contains	`QPushButton[property~="something"]`	Instances of `QPushButton` where property (a list of `QString`) does not contain the given value.
Class	`` `.QPushButton ``	Instances of QPushButton but not subclasses.
ID	`QPushButton#okButton`	A QPushButton instance whose object name is okButton.
Descendant	`QDialog QPushButton`	Instances of QPushButton that are descendants (children, grandchildren, etc.) of a QDialog.
Child	`QDialog > QPushButton`	Instances of QPushButton that are *immediate* children of a QDialog.

We'll look at each of these targeting rules in turn now, trying them out with our QSS tester.

Type

We've already seen *type targeting* in action in our QSS tester. Here we targeted rules against the type name of the individual widgets, for example `QComboBox` or `QLineEdit`.

Figure 111. Targeting a QComboBox does not affect other unrelated types.

However, targeting types in this way *also* targets any subclasses of that type. So for example, we can target QAbstractButton to target any types that derive from it.

```
QAbstractButton {
    background: orange;
}
```

Figure 112. Targeting a QAbstractButton affects all child classes

This behavior means that *all* widgets can be targeted using QWidget. For example, the following will set the background of all widgets to *red*.

```
QWidget {
    background: red;
}
```

Figure 113. QSS selection via parent classes.

Class .

Sometimes however you *want* to only target a specific class of widget, and not any subclasses. To do this you can use *class targeting* — by prepending a . to the name of the type.

The following targets instances of QWidget but *not* any classes derived from QWidget. In our QSS tester the only QWidget we have is the central widget used for holding the layout. So the following will change the background of *that* container widget orange.

```
.QWidget {
    background: orange;
}
```

Figure 114. Targeting a class specifically will not target subclasses

ID targeting

All Qt widgets have an *object name* which uniquely identifies them. When creating widgets in Qt Designer you use the object name to specify the name that the object is available under on the parent window. However, this relationship is just for convenience — you can set any *object name* you want for a widget in your own code. These names can then be used to target QSS rules directly to specific widgets.

In our QSS tester app we've set IDs on our QComboBox and QLineEdit for testing.

```
combo.setObjectName('thecombo')
le.setObjectName('mylineedit')
```

Property [property="<value>"]

You can target widgets by any widget property which is available as a string (or who's value has a .toString() method). This can be used to define some quite complex states on widgets.

The following is a simple example targeting a QPushButton by the text label.

261

```
QPushButton[text="Push me!"] {
    background: red;
}
```

Figure 115. Targeting a QPushButton by the label text

 Targeting widgets by their visible text is a *very bad idea* in general as it will introduce bugs as you try and translate your application or change labels.

Rules are applied to widgets when the stylesheet is first set and will not respond to changes in properties. If a property targeted by a QSS rule is modified, you must trigger a stylesheet recalculation for it to take effect — for example by re-setting the stylesheet again.

Descendant

To target descendants of a given type of widget, you can chain widgets together. The following example targets any QComboBox which is a child of a QMainWindow — whether it is an immediate child, or nested within other widgets or layouts.

```
QMainWindow QComboBox {
    background: yellow;
}
```

Figure 116. Targeting a QComboBox which is a child of a QMainWindow

To target *all* descendants you can use the global selector as the final element in the targeting. You can also chain many types together to target only those places in your app where that hierarchy exists.

```
QMainWindow QWidget * {
    background: yellow;
}
```

In our QSS tester application we have an outer QMainWindow, with a QWidget central widget holding the layout, and then our widgets in that layout. The rule above therefore matches only the individual widgets (which all have QMainWindow QWidget as parents, in that order).)

Figure 117. Targeting a QComboBox which is a child of a QMainWindow

Child >

You can also target a widget which is a *direct* child of another widget using the >
selector. This will only match where that exact hierarchy is in place.

For example, the following will *only* target the QWidget container which is a direct
child of the QMainWindow.

```
QMainWindow > QWidget {
    background: green;
}
```

But the following will not match anything, since in our QSS app the QComboBox
widget is *not* a direct child of the QMainWindow.

```
QMainWindow > QComboBox {    /* matches nothing */
    background: yellow;
}
```

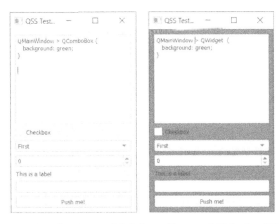

Figure 118. Targeting a QComboBox which is a direct child of a QWidget

Inheritance

Style sheets can be applied to QApplication and widgets and will apply to the styled widget and all of its children. A widget's effective style sheet is determined by combining the style sheets of all it's ancestors (parent, grandparent, ...all the way up to the window) plus style sheets on QApplication itself.

Rules are applied in order of *specificity*. That means, a rule which targets a specific widget by ID, will override a rule which targets *all* widgets of that type. For example, the following will set the background of the QLineEdit in our QSS tester app to blue — the specific ID overrides the generic widget rule.

```
QLineEdit#mylineedit {
    background: blue;
}

QLineEdit {
    background: red;
}
```

Figure 119. Specific ID targeting overrules generic widget targeting.

In cases where there are two conflicting rules the widgets' own style sheet will be preferred over inherited styles, and nearer ancestors will be preferred over more distance — parents will be preferred to grandparents for example.

No inherited properties

Widgets are only affected by rules which target them specifically. While rules can be *set* on a parent, they must still reference the target widget to affect it. Take the following rule —

```
QLineEdit {
    background: red;
}
```

If set on a QMainWindow all QLineEdit objects in that window will have a red background (assuming no other rules). However, if the following is set...

```
QMainWindow {
    background: red;
}
```

...only the QMainWindow itself will be set with a red background. The background color *itself* does not propogate to child widgets.

Figure 120. QSS properties do not propagate to children.

> If the child widgets have transparent backgrounds, the red *will* show through however.

Unless targeted by a matching rule, a widget will use its default system style values for each property. Widgets do not inherit style properties from parent widgets, even inside compound widgets, and widgets must be targeted by rules directly to be affected by them.

> This is in contrast with CSS, where elements can inherit values from their parents.

Pseudo-selectors

So far we've looked at static styling, using properties to change the default appearance of a widget. However, QSS also allows you to style in response to dynamic widget states. An example of this is the highlight you see when buttons are hovered with the mouse — the highlight helps to indicate that the widget has focus and will respond if you click it.

There are many other uses for active styling, from usability (highlighting lines of data, or specific tabs) to visualizing data hierarchies. These can all be achieved using *pseudo-selectors* in QSS. Pseudo-selectors make QSS rules apply only in particular circumstances.

There are a lot of different pseudo selectors which you can apply to widgets. Some such as `:hover` are generic and can be used with all widgets, others are widget-specific. The full list is given below —

Pseudo-State	Description
`:active`	Widget is part of an active window.
`:adjoins-item`	The `::branch` of a `QTreeView` is adjacent to an item.
`:alternate`	Set for every alternate row when painting the row of a `QabstractItemView` (`QabstractItemView.alternatingRowColors()` is `True`)
`:bottom`	Positioned at the bottom, e.g. a `QTabBar` that has its tabs at the bottom.
`:checked`	Item is checked, e.g. the checked state of QAbstractButton.
`:closable`	Items can be closed, e.g. a `QDockWidget` has `QDockWidget.DockWidgetClosable` enabled.
`:closed`	Item is in the closed state, e.g. an non-expanded item in a `QtreeView`.
`:default`	Item is the default action, e.g. a default `QPushButton` or a default action in a `QMenu`.
`:disabled`	Item is disabled.
`:editable`	`QcomboBox` is editable.
`:enabled`	Item is enabled.
`:exclusive`	Item is part of an exclusive item group, e.g. a menu item in a exclusive `QActionGroup`.

Pseudo-State	Description
:first	Item is the first in a list, e.g. the first tab in a `QtabBar`.
:flat	Item is flat, e.g. a flat `QpushButton`.
:floatable	Items can be floated, e.g. the `QDockWidget` has `QDockWidget.DockWidgetFloatable` enabled.
:focus	Item has input focus.
:has-children	Item has children, e.g. an item in a `QTreeView` with child items.
:has-siblings	Item has siblings, e.g. an item in a `QTreeView` with siblings.
:horizontal	Item has horizontal orientation
:hover	Mouse is hovering over the item.
:indeterminate	Item has indeterminate state, e.g. a `QCheckBox` or `QRadioButton` is partially checked.
:last	Item is the last (in a list), e.g. the last tab in a `QTabBar`.
:left	Item is positioned at the left, e.g. a `QTabBar` that has its tabs positioned at the left.
:maximized	Item is maximized, e.g. a maximized `QMdiSubWindow`.
:middle	Item is in the middle (in a list), e.g. a tab that is not in the beginning or the end in a `QTabBar`.
:minimized	Item is minimized, e.g. a minimized `QMdiSubWindow`.
:movable	Item can be moved around, e.g. the QDockWidget has `QDockWidget.DockWidgetMovable` enabled.
:no-frame	Item has no frame, e.g. a frameless `QSpinBox` or `QLineEdit`.

Pseudo-State	Description
:non-exclusive	Item is part of a non-exclusive item group, e.g. a menu item in a non-exclusive QActionGroup.
:off	Items that can be toggled, this applies to items in the "off" state.
:on	Items that can be toggled, this applies to widgets in the "on" state.
:only-one	Item is the only one (in a list), e.g. a lone tab in a QTabBar.
:open	Item is in the open state, e.g. an expanded item in a QTreeView, or a QComboBox or` QPushButton ` with an open menu.
:next-selected	Next item is selected, e.g. the selected tab of a QTabBar is next to this item.
:pressed	Item is being pressed using the mouse.
:previous-selected	Previous item is selected, e.g. a tab in a QTabBar that is next to the selected tab.
:read-only	Item is marked read only or non-editable, e.g. a read only QLineEdit or a non-editable QComboBox.
:right	Item is positioned at the right, e.g. a QTabBar that has its tabs positioned at the right.
:selected	Item is selected, e.g. the selected tab in a QTabBar or the selected item in a QMenu.
:top	Item is positioned at the top, e.g. a QTabBar that has its tabs positioned at the top.
:unchecked	Item is unchecked.
:vertical	Item has vertical orientation.

Pseudo-State	Description
`:window`	Widget is a window (i.e a top level widget).

We can use the QSS tester to see pseudo-selectors in action. For example, the following will change the background of the `QPushButton` *red* when the mouse hovers over the widget.

```
QPushButton:hover {
    background: red;
}
```

The following will change the background of all widgets when they are hovered.

```
*:hover {
    background: red;
}
```

Hovering a widget means all it's parents are also hovered (the mouse is within their bounding box) as the image below shows.

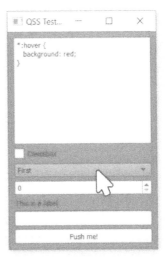

Figure 121. Left, QPushButton highlighted when hovered. Right, when a widget is hovered all parent widgets are also hovered.

You can also *negate* pseudo-selectors using !. This means that the rule will become active when that selector is inactive. For example the following...

```
QPushButton:!hover {
    background: yellow;
}
```

...will make the QPushButton yellow when it is *not hovered*.

You can also chain multiple pseudo-selectors together. For example, the following will set the background of a QCheckBox green when it is *checked* and *not hovered*, and yellow when it is *checked* and *hovered*.

```
QCheckBox:checked:!hover {
    background: green;
}

QCheckBox:checked:hover {
    background: yellow;
}
```

Figure 122. Chained pseudo selectors for hover state.

As for all other rules, you can also chain them using "," separators to make the defined rule apply to both (or many) cases. For example, the following will set a checkbox background green when it is *checked* OR *hovered*.

```
QCheckBox:checked, QCheckBox:hover {
    background: yellow;
}
```

Styling Widget Sub controls

Many widgets are constructed from a combination of other sub-widgets or *controls*. QSS provides syntax for addressing these sub-controls directly, so you can make style changes to sub-controls individually. These sub-controls can be addressed by using the :: (double-colon) selector, followed by an identifier for the given sub control.

A good example of such a widget is the QComboBox. The following style snip applies a custom style directly to the down-arrow on the right hand of the combo box.

```
QComboBox::drop-down {
    background: yellow;
    image: url('puzzle.png')
}
```

Figure 123. Setting background and icon for a QComboBox dropdown with QSS.

There are quite a few sub-control selectors available in QSS, which are listed below. You'll notice that many of them apply only to specific widgets (or types of widgets).

Sub-Control	Description
::add-line	Button to move to next line on a QScrollBar.
::add-page	Space between the handle and the add-line of a QScrollBar.
::branch	Branch indicator of a QTreeView.
::chunk	Progress chunk of a QProgressBar.
::close-button	Close button of a QDockWidget or tabs of QTabBar.
::corner	Corner between two scrollbars in a QAbstractScrollArea.
::down-arrow	Down arrow of a QComboBox, QHeaderView, QScrollBar or QSpinBox.
::down-button	Down button of a QScrollBar or a QSpinBox.
::drop-down	Drop-down button of a QComboBox.

Sub-Control	Description
::float-button	Float button of a QDockWidget.
::groove	Groove of a QSlider.
::indicator	Indicator of a QAbstractItemView, a QCheckBox, a QRadioButton, a checkable QMenu item or a checkable QGroupBox.
::handle	Handle of a QScrollBar, a QSplitter, or a QSlider.
::icon	Icon of a QAbstractItemView or a QMenu.
::item	Item of a QAbstractItemView, a QMenuBar, a QMenu, or a QStatusBar.
::left-arrow	Left arrow of a QScrollBar.
::left-corner	Left corner of a QTabWidget, e.g. control the left corner widget in a QTabWidget.
::menu-arrow	Arrow of a QToolButton with a menu.
::menu-button	Menu button of a QToolButton.
::menu-indicator	Menu indicator of a QPushButton.
::right-arrow	Right arrow of a QMenu or a QScrollBar.
::pane	The pane (frame) of a QTabWidget.
::right-corner	The right corner of a QTabWidget. For example, this control can be used to control the position the right corner widget in a QTabWidget.
::scroller	The scroller of a QMenu or QTabBar.
::section	The section of a QHeaderView.
::separator	The separator of a QMenu or in a QMainWindow.
::sub-line	The button to subtract a line of a QScrollBar.

Sub-Control	Description
::sub-page	The region between the handle (slider) and the sub-line of a QScrollBar.
::tab	The tab of a QTabBar or QToolBox.
::tab-bar	The tab bar of a QTabWidget. This subcontrol exists only to control the position of the QTabBar inside the QTabWidget. To style the tabs use the ::tab subcontrol.
::tear	The tear indicator of a QTabBar.
::tearoff	The tear-off indicator of a QMenu.
::text	The text of a QAbstractItemView.
::title	The title of a QGroupBox or a QDockWidget.
::up-arrow	The up arrow of a QHeaderView (sort indicator), QScrollBar or a QSpinBox.
::up-button	The up button of a QSpinBox.

The following targets the up and down buttons of a QSpinBox turning the background red and green respectively.

```
QSpinBox::up-button {
    background: green;
}

QSpinBox::down-button {
    background: red;
}
```

Figure 124. Setting background to the QSpinBox up and down buttons.

The arrows *inside* the up or down buttons are also separately targetable. Below we're setting them with custom plus and minus icons — note we also need to resize the buttons to fit.

```
QSpinBox {
    min-height: 50;
}

QSpinBox::up-button {
    width: 50;
}

QSpinBox::up-arrow {
    image: url('plus.png');
}

QSpinBox::down-button {
    width: 50;
}

QSpinBox::down-arrow {
    image: url('minus.png')
}
```

Figure 125. Setting background to the QSpinBox up and down buttons.

Subcontrol pseudostates

You can use pseudostates to target subcontrols, just as for other widgets. To do this, simply chain the pseudostate after the control. For example —

```
QSpinBox::up-button:hover {
    background: green;
}

QSpinBox::down-button:hover {
    background: red;
}
```

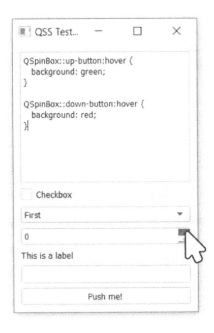

Figure 126. Combining subcontrol selectors with pseudo-selectors.

Positioning Sub-controls

Using QSS you also get precise control over the position of subcontrols inside widgets. These allow adjustment in position either *relative* to their normal position, or in *absolute* reference to their parent widget. We'll look at these positioning methods below.

Property	Type (Default)	Description
position	relative | absolute (relative)	Whether offsets specified using left, right, top, and bottom are relative or absolute coordinates.

Property	Type (Default)	Description
bottom	Length	If position is relative (the default), moves a subcontrol by a certain offset up; specifying bottom: y is then equivalent to specifying top: -y. If position is absolute, the bottom property specifies the subcontrol's bottom edge in relation to the parent's bottom edge (see also subcontrol-origin).
left	Length	If position=relative move a subcontrol right by the given offset (i.e. specifies additional space on the left). If position is absolute, specifies the distance from the left edge of the parent.
right	Length	If position=relative move a subcontrol left by the given offset (i.e. specifies additional space on the right). If position is absolute, specifies the distance from the right edge of the parent.

Property	Type (Default)	Description
top	Length	If position=relative move a subcontrol down the given offset (i.e. specifies additional space on the top). If position is absolute, specifies the distance from the top edge of the parent.

By default, positioning is *relative*. In this mode, the *left*, *right*, *top* and *bottom* properties define additional spacing to be added on the respective side. This means, somewhat confusingly, that *left* moves widgets *right*.

 To help you remember, think of these as "add space to the *left*" and so on.

```
QSpinBox {
    min-height: 100;
}

QSpinBox::up-button {
    width: 50;
}

QSpinBox::down-button {
    width: 50;
    left: 5;
}
```

Figure 127. Adjusting the position of subcontrols with left.

When position is set to *absolute*, the *left, right, top* and *bottom* properties define the spacing between the widget and and it's parent's identical edges. So, for example, top: 5, left: 5 will position a widget so it's top and left edges are 5 pixels from it's parent's top and left edge.

```
QSpinBox {
    min-height: 100;
}

QSpinBox::up-button {
    width: 50;
}

QSpinBox::down-button {
    position: absolute;
    width: 50;
    right: 25;
}
```

Below you can see the effect of positioning the down button using *absolute*, placing it 25 pixels from the right.

Figure 128. Adjusting the position of subcontrols absolute.

This is not the most practical example, but it demonstrates one constraint on positioning sub-controls in this way — you cannot position a subcontrol outside it's parent's bounding box.

Subcontrol styles

Finally, there are number of QSS properties which specifically target sub-controls for styling. These are shown below — see the description for the specific affected widgets and controls.

Property	Type (Default)	Description
image	Url+	The image that is drawn in the contents rectangle of a subcontrol. Setting the image property on subcontrols implicitly sets the width and height of the sub-control (unless the image is a SVG).

Property	Type (Default)	Description
image-position	alignment	The alignment of the image. Image's position can be specified using relative or absolute position. See relative and absolute for explanation.
height	Length	The height of a subcontrol. If you want a widget with a fixed height, set the min-height and max-height to the same value.
spacing	Length	Internal spacing in the widget.
subcontrol-origin	Origin (padding)	The origin rectangle of the subcontrol within the parent element.
subcontrol-position	Alignment	The alignment of the subcontrol within the origin rectangle specified by subcontrol-origin.
width	Length	The width of a subcontrol. If you want a widget with a fixed width, set the min-width and max-width to the same value.

Editing Stylesheets in Qt Designer

So far the examples we've seen have applied QSS to widgets using code. However, you can also set stylesheets on widgets from within Qt Designer.

To set a QSS stylesheet on a widget in Qt Designer, right-click on the widget and select "Change stylesheet..." from the context menu.

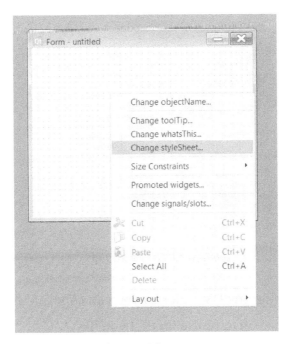

Figure 129. Accessing the QSS editor for a widget.

This will open up the following window, where you can enter QSS rules as text, which will be applied to this widget (and any children which match the rules).

Figure 130. The QSS editor in Qt Designer.

As well as entering rules as text, the QSS editor in Qt Designer gives you access to a resource lookup tool, color selection widget and a gradient designer. This tool (shown below) provides a number of built-in gradients you can add to your rules, but you can also define your own custom gradients if you prefer.

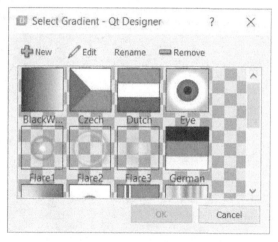

Figure 131. The QSS gradient designer in Qt Designer.

Gradients are defined using QSS rules so you can copy and paste them elsewhere (including into your code) to re-use them if you like.

Listing 94. The Dutch flag using a QSS qlineargradient rule.

```
QWidget {
background: qlineargradient(spread:pad, x1:0, y1:0, x2:0, y2:1, stop
:0 rgba(255, 0, 0, 255), stop:0.339795 rgba(255, 0, 0, 255), stop
:0.339799 rgba(255, 255, 255, 255), stop:0.662444 rgba(255, 255, 255,
255), stop:0.662469 rgba(0, 0, 255, 255), stop:1 rgba(0, 0, 255,
255))
}
```

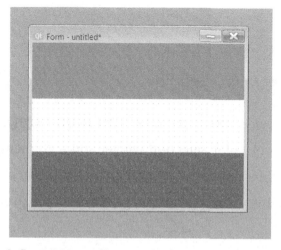

Figure 132. The "Dutch flag" QSS gradient applied to a QWidget in Qt Designer

Model View Architecture

...with proper design, the features come cheaply.

— Dennis Ritchie

As you start to build more complex applications with PyQt6 you'll likely come across issues keeping widgets in sync with your data.

Data stored in widgets (e.g. a simple `QListWidget`) is not easy to manipulate from Python — changes require you to get an item, get the data, and then set it back. The default solution to this is to keep an external data representation in Python, and then either duplicate updates to the both the data and the widget, or simply rewrite the whole widget from the data. As you start to work with larger data this approach can start to have performance impacts on your application.

Thankfully Qt has a solution for this — ModelViews. ModelViews are a powerful alternative to the standard display widgets, which use a standardized model interface to interact with data sources — from simple data structures to external databases. This isolates your data, meaning you can keep it in any structure you like, while the view takes care of presentation and updates.

This chapter introduces the key aspects of Qt's ModelView architecture and uses it to build a simple desktop Todo application in PyQt6.

17. The Model View Architecture — Model View Controller

Model–View–Controller (MVC) is an architectural pattern used for developing user interfaces. It divides an application into three interconnected parts, separating the internal representation of data from how it is presented to and accepted from the user.

The MVC pattern splits the interface into the following components —

- **Model** holds the data structure which the app is working with.

- **View** is any representation of information as shown to the user, whether graphical or tables. Multiple views of the same data are allowed.

- **Controller** accepts input from the user, transforms it into commands and applies these to the model or view.

In Qt land the distinction between the View & Controller gets a little murky. Qt accepts input events from the user via the OS and delegates these to the widgets (Controller) to handle. However, widgets also handle presentation of their own state to the user, putting them squarely in the View. Rather than agonize over where to draw the line, in Qt-speak the View and Controller are instead merged together creating a Model/ViewController architecture — called "Model View" for simplicity.

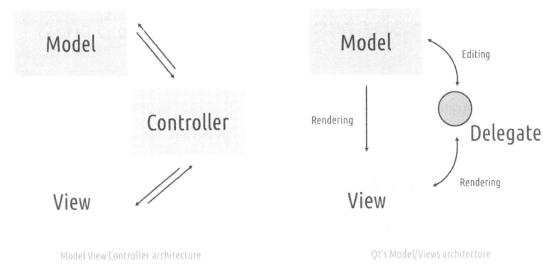

Figure 133. Comparing the MVC model and the Qt Model/View architecture.

Importantly, the distinction between the *data* and *how it is presented* is preserved.

The Model View

The Model acts as the interface between the data store and the ViewController. The Model holds the data (or a reference to it) and presents this data through a standardized API which Views then consume and present to the user. Multiple Views can share the same data, presenting it in completely different ways.

You can use any "data store" for your model, including for example a standard Python list or dictionary, or a database (via Qt itself, or SQLAlchemy) — it's entirely up to you.

The two parts are essentially responsible for —

1. The **model** stores the data, or a reference to it and returns individual or ranges of records, and associated metadata or *display* instructions.

2. The **view** requests data from the model and displays what is returned on the widget.

18. A simple Model View — a Todo List

To demonstrate how to use the ModelViews in practice, we'll put together a very simple implementation of a desktop Todo List. This will consist of a `QListView` for the list of items, a `QLineEdit` to enter new items, and a set of buttons to add, delete, or mark items as done.

 The files for this example are in the source code.

The UI

The simple UI was laid out using Qt Creator and saved as `mainwindow.ui`. The `.ui` file is included in the downloads for this book.

Figure 134. Designing the UI in Qt Creator

The `.ui` file was converted to a Python file as described previously using the command-line tool.

This generates a `MainWindow.py` file which contains our custom window class as designed in Qt Designer. This can be imported in our application code as normal — a basic skeleton app to display our UI is shown below.

Listing 95. model-views/todo_skeleton.py

```python
import sys

from PyQt6 import QtCore, QtGui, QtWidgets
from PyQt6.QtCore import Qt

from MainWindow import Ui_MainWindow


class MainWindow(QtWidgets.QMainWindow, Ui_MainWindow):
    def __init__(self):
        super().__init__()
        self.setupUi(self)


app = QtWidgets.QApplication(sys.argv)
window = MainWindow()
window.show()
app.exec()
```

🚀 **Run it!** You'll see the window appear, although nothing is functional yet.

Figure 135. The MainWindow

The widgets in the interface were given the IDs shown in the table below.

objectName	Type	Description
todoView	QListView	The list of current todos
todoEdit	QLineEdit	The text input for creating a new todo item
addButton	QPushButton	Create the new todo, adding it to the todos list
deleteButton	QPushButton	Delete the current selected todo, removing it from the todos list
completeButton	QPushButton	Mark the current selected todo as done

We'll use these identifiers to hook up the application logic later.

The Model

We define our custom model by subclassing from a base implementation, allowing us to focus on the parts unique to our model. Qt provides a number of different model bases, including lists, trees and tables (ideal for spreadsheets).

For this example we are displaying the result to a QListView. The matching base model for this is QAbstractListModel. The outline definition for our model is shown below.

Listing 96. model-views/todo_1.py

```python
class TodoModel(QAbstractListModel):
    def __init__(self, todos=None):
        super().__init__()
        self.todos = todos or []

    def data(self, index, role):
        if role == Qt.ItemDataRole.DisplayRole:
            status, text = self.todos[index.row()]
            return text

    def rowCount(self, index):
        return len(self.todos)
```

The `.todos` variable is our data store. The two methods rowcount() and data() are standard Model methods we must implement for a list model. We'll go through these in turn below.

.todos list

The data store for our model is .todos, a simple Python list in which we'll store a tuple of values in the format [(bool, str), (bool, str), (bool, str)] where bool is the *done* state of a given entry, and str is the text of the todo.

We initialize self.todo to an empty list on startup, unless a list is passed in via the todos keyword argument.

self.todos = todos or [] will set self.todos to the provided todos value if it is *truthy* (i.e. anything other than an empty list, the bool ` False` or None the default value), otherwise it will be set to the empty list [].

To create an instance of this model we can simply do —

```
model = TodoModel()   # create an empty todo list
```

Or to pass in an existing list —

```
todos = [(False, 'an item'), (False, 'another item')]
model = TodoModel(todos)
```

.rowcount()

The .rowcount() method is called by the view to get the number of rows in the current data. This is required for the view to know the maximum index it can request from the data store (rowcount - 1). Since we're using a Python list as our data store, the return value for this is simply the len() of the list.

.data()

This is the core of your model, which handles requests for data from the view and returns the appropriate result. It receives two parameters index and role.

index is the position/coordinates of the data which the view is requesting, accessible by two methods .row() and .column() which give the position in each dimension. For a list view, column can be ignored.

For our QListView, the column is always 0 and can be ignored. But you would need to use this for 2D data, for example in a spreadsheet view.

`role` is a flag indicating the *type* of data the view is requesting. This is because the `.data()` method actually has more responsibility than just the core data. It also handles requests for style information, tooltips, status bars, etc. — basically anything that could be informed by the data itself.

The naming of `Qt.ItemDataRole.DisplayRole` is a bit weird, but this indicates that the *view* is asking us "please give me data for display". There are other *roles* which the `data` can receive for styling requests or requesting data in "edit-ready" format.

Role	Value	Description
`Qt.ItemDataRole.DisplayRole`	0	The key data to be rendered in the form of text. QString [https://doc.qt.io/qt-6/qstring.html]
`Qt.ItemDataRole.DecorationRole`	1	The data to be rendered as a decoration in the form of an icon. QColor [https://doc.qt.io/qt-6/qcolor.html], QIcon [https://doc.qt.io/qt-6/qicon.html] or QPixmap [https://doc.qt.io/qt-6/qpixmap.html]
`Qt.ItemDataRole.EditRole`	2	The data in a form suitable for editing in an editor. QString [https://doc.qt.io/qt-6/qstring.html]
`Qt.ItemDataRole.ToolTipRole`	3	The data displayed in the item's tooltip. QString [https://doc.qt.io/qt-6/qstring.html]
`Qt.ItemDataRole.StatusTipRole`	4	The data displayed in the status bar. QString [https://doc.qt.io/qt-6/qstring.html]

Role	Value	Description
Qt.ItemDataRole.WhatsThisRole	5	The data displayed for the item in "What's This?" mode. QString [https://doc.qt.io/qt-6/qstring.html]
Qt.ItemDataRole.SizeHintRole	13	The size hint for the item that will be supplied to views. QSize [https://doc.qt.io/qt-6/qsize.html]

For a full list of available *roles* that you can receive see the Qt ItemDataRole documentation [https://doc.qt.io/qt-6/qt.html#ItemDataRole-enum]. Our todo list will only be using Qt.ItemDataRole.DisplayRole and Qt.ItemDataRole.DecorationRole.

Basic implementation

The code below shows the basic model we've created in the application skeleton, which has the code necessary to take the model and display it — although it is empty! We'll add our model code and application logic to this base.

Listing 97. model-views/todo_1b.py

```python
import sys

from PyQt6.QtCore import QAbstractListModel, Qt
from PyQt6.QtWidgets import QApplication, QMainWindow

from MainWindow import Ui_MainWindow


class TodoModel(QAbstractListModel):
    def __init__(self, todos=None):
        super().__init__()
        self.todos = todos or []

    def data(self, index, role):
        if role == Qt.ItemDataRole.DisplayRole:
            status, text = self.todos[index.row()]
            return text

    def rowCount(self, index):
        return len(self.todos)


class MainWindow(QMainWindow, Ui_MainWindow):
    def __init__(self):
        super().__init__()
        self.setupUi(self)
        self.model = TodoModel()
        self.todoView.setModel(self.model)


app = QApplication(sys.argv)
window = MainWindow()
window.show()
app.exec()
```

We define our TodoModel as before and initialize the MainWindow object. In the __init__ for the MainWindow we create an instance of our todo model and set this model on the todo_view. Save this file as todo.py and run it with —

```
python3 todo.py
```

While there isn't much to see yet, the `QListView` and our model are actually working — if you add some default data to the `TodoModel` in the `MainWindow` class you'll see it appear in the list.

```
self.model = TodoModel(todos=[(False, 'my first todo')])
```

Figure 136. QListView showing hard-coded todo item

You can keep adding items manually like this and they will show up in order in the `QListView`. Next we'll make it possible to add items from within the application.

First create a new method on the `MainWindow` named `add`. This is our callback which will take care of adding the current text from the input as a new todo. Connect this method to the addButton.pressed signal at the end of the __init__ block.

Listing 98. model-views/todo_2.py

```python
class MainWindow(QMainWindow, Ui_MainWindow):
    def __init__(self):
        super().__init__()
        self.setupUi(self)
        self.model = TodoModel()
        self.todoView.setModel(self.model)
        # Connect the button.
        self.addButton.pressed.connect(self.add)

    def add(self):
        """
        Add an item to our todo list, getting the text from the
QLineEdit .todoEdit
        and then clearing it.
        """
        text = self.todoEdit.text()
        # Remove whitespace from the ends of the string.
        text = text.strip()
        if text:  # Don't add empty strings.
            # Access the list via the model.
            self.model.todos.append((False, text))
            # Trigger refresh.
            self.model.layoutChanged.emit()   ①
            # Empty the input
            self.todoEdit.setText("")
```

① Here we're emitting a model signal .layoutChanged to let the view know that the *shape* of the data has been altered. This triggers a refresh of the entirety of the view. If you omit this line, the todo will still be added but the QListView won't update.

If just the data is altered, but the number of rows/columns are unaffected you can use the .dataChanged() signal instead. This also defines an altered region in the data using a top-left and bottom-right location to avoid redrawing the entire view.

Hooking up the other actions

We can now connect the rest of the button's signals and add helper functions for performing the *delete* and *complete* operations. We add the button signals to the __init__ block as before.

```
self.addButton.pressed.connect(self.add)
self.deleteButton.pressed.connect(self.delete)
self.completeButton.pressed.connect(self.complete)
```

Then define a new delete method as follows —

Listing 99. model-views/todo_3.py

```
class MainWindow(QMainWindow, Ui_MainWindow):

    def delete(self):
        indexes = self.todoView.selectedIndexes()
        if indexes:
            # Indexes is a single-item list in single-select mode.
            index = indexes[0]
            # Remove the item and refresh.
            del self.model.todos[index.row()]
            self.model.layoutChanged.emit()
            # Clear the selection (as it is no longer valid).
            self.todoView.clearSelection()
```

We use self.todoView.selectedIndexes to get the indexes (actually a list of a single item, as we're in single-selection mode) and then use the .row() as an index into our list of todos on our model. We delete the indexed item using Python's del operator, and then trigger a layoutChanged signal because the shape of the data has been modified.

Finally, we clear the active selection since the item you selected is now gone and the position itself could be out of bounds (if you had selected the last item).

You could make this smarter and select the adjacent item in the list instead.

The `complete` method looks like this —

Listing 100. model-views/todo_4.py

```python
class MainWindow(QMainWindow, Ui_MainWindow):

    def complete(self):
        indexes = self.todoView.selectedIndexes()
        if indexes:
            index = indexes[0]
            row = index.row()
            status, text = self.model.todos[row]
            self.model.todos[row] = (True, text)
            # .dataChanged takes top-left and bottom right, which are
equal
            # for a single selection.
            self.model.dataChanged.emit(index, index)
            # Clear the selection (as it is no longer valid).
            self.todoView.clearSelection()
```

This uses the same indexing as for delete, but this time we fetch the item from the model `.todos` list and then replace the status with `True`.

 We have to do this fetch-and-replace, as our data is stored as Python tuples which cannot be modified.

The key difference here vs. standard Qt widgets is that we make changes directly to our data, and simply need to notify Qt that some change has occurred — updating the widget state is handled automatically.

Using DecorationRole

If you run the application you should now find that adding and deleting both work, but while completing items is working, there is no indication of it in the view. We need to update our model to provide the view with an indicator to display when an item is complete. The updated model is shown below.

Listing 101. model-views/todo_5.py

```python
import os


basedir = os.path.dirname(__file__)


tick = QImage(os.path.join(basedir, "tick.png"))


class TodoModel(QAbstractListModel):
    def __init__(self, *args, todos=None, **kwargs):
        super(TodoModel, self).__init__(*args, **kwargs)
        self.todos = todos or []

    def data(self, index, role):
        if role == Qt.ItemDataRole.DisplayRole:
            status, text = self.todos[index.row()]
            return text

        if role == Qt.ItemDataRole.DecorationRole:
            status, text = self.todos[index.row()]
            if status:
                return tick

    def rowCount(self, index):
        return len(self.todos)
```

 We load the icons using the basedir technique introduced earlier, to ensure the paths are correct however the script is run. The icon I'm using is taken from the Fugue set by p.yusukekamiyamane [http://p.yusukekamiyamane.com/]

We're using a tick icon tick.png to indicate completed items, which we load into a `QImage` object named `tick`. In the model we've implemented a handler for the `Qt.ItemDataRole.DecorationRole` which returns the tick icon for rows whose `status` is `True` (for complete).

 Instead of an icon you can also return a color, e.g. `QtGui.QColor('green')` which will be drawn as solid square.

Running the app you should now be able to mark items as complete.

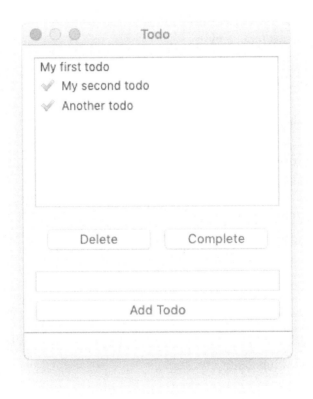

Figure 137. Todos complete

A persistent data store

Our todo app works nicely, but it has one fatal flaw — it forgets your todos as soon as you close the application. While thinking you have nothing to do when you do may help to contribute to short-term feelings of Zen, long term it's probably a bad idea.

The solution is to implement some sort of persistent data store. The simplest approach is a simple file store, where we load items from a JSON or Pickle file at startup and write back any changes.

To do this we define two new methods on our MainWindow class — load and save. These load data from a JSON file name data.json (if it exists, ignoring the error if it doesn't) to self.model.todos and write the current self.model.todos out to the same file, respectively.

Listing 102. model-views/todo_6.py

```
def load(self):
    try:
        with open("data.json", "r") as f:
            self.model.todos = json.load(f)
    except Exception:
        pass

def save(self):
    with open("data.json", "w") as f:
        data = json.dump(self.model.todos, f)
```

To persist the changes to the data we need to add the .save() handler to the end of any method that modifies the data, and the .load() handler to the __init__ block after the model has been created.

The final code looks like this —

Listing 103. mode-views/todo_complete.py

```
import json
import os
import sys

from PyQt6.QtCore import QAbstractListModel, Qt
from PyQt6.QtGui import QImage
from PyQt6.QtWidgets import QApplication, QMainWindow
```

```python
from MainWindow import Ui_MainWindow

basedir = os.path.dirname(__file__)

tick = QImage(os.path.join(basedir, "tick.png"))


class TodoModel(QAbstractListModel):
    def __init__(self, todos=None):
        super().__init__()
        self.todos = todos or []

    def data(self, index, role):
        if role == Qt.ItemDataRole.DisplayRole:
            status, text = self.todos[index.row()]
            return text

        if role == Qt.ItemDataRole.DecorationRole:
            status, text = self.todos[index.row()]
            if status:
                return tick

    def rowCount(self, index):
        return len(self.todos)


class MainWindow(QMainWindow, Ui_MainWindow):
    def __init__(self):
        super().__init__()
        self.setupUi(self)
        self.model = TodoModel()
        self.load()
        self.todoView.setModel(self.model)
        self.addButton.pressed.connect(self.add)
        self.deleteButton.pressed.connect(self.delete)
        self.completeButton.pressed.connect(self.complete)

    def add(self):
        """
        Add an item to our todo list, getting the text from the
QLineEdit .todoEdit
        and then clearing it.
```

```python
            """
            text = self.todoEdit.text()
            # Remove whitespace from the ends of the string.
            text = text.strip()
            if text:  # Don't add empty strings.
                # Access the list via the model.
                self.model.todos.append((False, text))
                # Trigger refresh.
                self.model.layoutChanged.emit()
                # Empty the input
                self.todoEdit.setText("")
                self.save()

        def delete(self):
            indexes = self.todoView.selectedIndexes()
            if indexes:
                # Indexes is a single-item list in single-select mode.
                index = indexes[0]
                # Remove the item and refresh.
                del self.model.todos[index.row()]
                self.model.layoutChanged.emit()
                # Clear the selection (as it is no longer valid).
                self.todoView.clearSelection()
                self.save()

        def complete(self):
            indexes = self.todoView.selectedIndexes()
            if indexes:
                index = indexes[0]
                row = index.row()
                status, text = self.model.todos[row]
                self.model.todos[row] = (True, text)
                # .dataChanged takes top-left and bottom right, which are
    equal
                # for a single selection.
                self.model.dataChanged.emit(index, index)
                # Clear the selection (as it is no longer valid).
                self.todoView.clearSelection()
                self.save()

        def load(self):
            try:
                with open("data.json", "r") as f:
```

```
                self.model.todos = json.load(f)
        except Exception:
            pass

    def save(self):
        with open("data.json", "w") as f:
            data = json.dump(self.model.todos, f)


app = QApplication(sys.argv)
window = MainWindow()
window.show()
app.exec()
```

If the data in your application has the potential to get large or more complex, you may prefer to use an actual database to store it. Qt provides models for interacting with SQL databases which we'll cover shortly.

 For another interesting example of a QListView see my example media player application [https://www.pythonguis.com/apps/failamp-multimedia-player/]. This uses the Qt built-in QMediaPlaylist as the datastore, with the contents displayed to a QListView.

19. Tabular data in ModelViews, with numpy & pandas

In the previous section we covered an introduction to the Model View architecture. However, we only touched on one of the model views — `QListView`. There are two other Model Views available in PyQt6 — `QTableView` and `QTreeView` which provide tabular (Excel-like) and tree (file directory browser-like) views using the same `QStandardItemModel`.

In this part we'll look at how to use `QTableView` from PyQt6, including how to model your data, format values for display and add conditional formatting.

You can use model views with *any* data source, as long as your model returns that data in a format that Qt can understand. Working with tabular data in Python opens up a number of possibilities for how we load and work with that data. Here we'll start with a simple nested list of lists and then move onto integrating your Qt application with the popular *numpy* and *pandas* libraries. This will provide you with a great foundation for building data-focused applications.

Introduction to `QTableView`

`QTableView` is a Qt view widget which presents data in a spreadsheet-like table view. Like all widgets in the *Model View Architecture* this uses a separate *model* to provide data and presentation information to the view. Data in the model can be updated as required, and the view notified of these changes to redraw/display the changes. By customizing the model it is possible to have a huge amount of control over how the data is presented.

To use the model we'll need a basic application structure and some dummy data. A simple working example is shown below, which defines a custom model with a simple nested-list as a data store.

Listing 104. tableview_demo.py

```python
import sys
from PyQt6 import QtCore, QtGui, QtWidgets
from PyQt6.QtCore import Qt


class TableModel(QtCore.QAbstractTableModel):
    def __init__(self, data):
        super().__init__()
        self._data = data

    def data(self, index, role):
        if role == Qt.ItemDataRole.DisplayRole:
            # See below for the nested-list data structure.
            # .row() indexes into the outer list,
            # .column() indexes into the sub-list
            return self._data[index.row()][index.column()]

    def rowCount(self, index):
        # The length of the outer list.
        return len(self._data)

    def columnCount(self, index):
        # The following takes the first sub-list, and returns
        # the length (only works if all rows are an equal length)
        return len(self._data[0])


class MainWindow(QtWidgets.QMainWindow):
    def __init__(self):
        super().__init__()

        self.table = QtWidgets.QTableView()

        data = [
            [4, 1, 3, 3, 7],
            [9, 1, 5, 3, 8],
            [2, 1, 5, 3, 9],
        ]

        self.model = TableModel(data)
        self.table.setModel(self.model)
```

```
        self.setCentralWidget(self.table)


app = QtWidgets.QApplication(sys.argv)
window = MainWindow()
window.show()
app.exec()
```

As in our earlier model view examples, we create the `QTableView` widget, then create an instance of our custom model (which we've written to accept the data source as a parameter) and then we set the model on the view. That's all we need to do — the view widget now uses the model to get the data, and determine how to draw it.

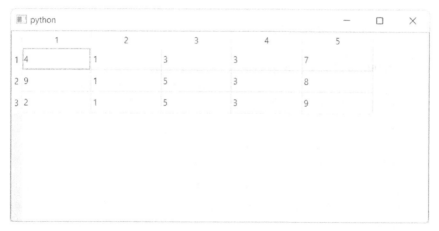

Figure 138. Basic table example

Nested `list` as a 2-dimensional data store

For a table you need a 2D data structure, with columns and rows. As shown in the example above you can model a simple 2D data structure using a nested Python `list`. We'll take a minute to look at this data structure, and it's limitations, below —

```
table = [
    [4, 1, 3, 3, 7],
    [9, 1, 5, 3, 8],
    [2, 1, 5, 3, 9],
]
```

The nested list is a "list of lists of values" — an outer list containing a number of sub-lists which themselves contain the values. With this structure, to index into individual values (or "cells") you must index twice, first to return one of the inner list objects and then again to index into that list.

The typical arrangement is for the outer list to hold the *rows* and each nested list to contain the values for the *columns*. With this arrangement when you index, you index first by *row*, then by *column* — making the example above a 3 row, 5 column table. Helpfully, this matches the visual layout in the source code.

The first index into the table will return a nested sub-list —

```
row = 2
col = 4

>>> table[row]
[2, 1, 5, 3, 9]
```

Which you then index again to return the value —

```
>>> table[row][col]
9
```

Note that using this type of structure you can't easily return an entire *column*, you would instead need to iterate all the rows. However, you are of course free to flip things on their head and use the first index as *column* depending on whether accessing by column or row is more useful to you.

```
table = [
  [4, 9, 2],
  [1, 1, 1],
  [3, 5, 5],
  [3, 3, 2],
  [7, 8, 9],
]

row = 4  # reversed
col = 2  # reversed

>>> table[col]
[3, 5, 5]

>>> table[col][row]
9
```

 Nothing about this data structure enforces equal row or column lengths — one row can be 5 elements long, another 200. However, inconsistencies will lead to errors on the table view. See the alternative data stores later if you're working with large or complex data tables.

Next we'll look in a bit more detail at our custom TableModel and see how it works with this simple data structure to display the values.

Writing a custom QAbstractTableModel

In the *Model View Architecture* the model is responsible for providing both the data and presentation metadata for display by the view. In order to interface between our data object and the view we need to write our own custom model, which understands the structure of our data.

To write our custom model we can create a subclass of QAbstractTableModel. The only *required* methods for a custom table model are data, rowCount and columnCount. The first returns data (or presentation information) for given locations in the table, while the latter two must return a single integer value for the dimensions of the data source.

```python
class TableModel(QtCore.QAbstractTableModel):

    def __init__(self, data):
        super(TableModel, self).__init__()
        self._data = data

    def data(self, index, role):
        if role == Qt.ItemDataRole.DisplayRole:
            # See below for the nested-list data structure.
            # .row() indexes into the outer list,
            # .column() indexes into the sub-list
            return self._data[index.row()][index.column()]

    def rowCount(self, index):
        # The length of the outer list.
        return len(self._data)

    def columnCount(self, index):
        # The following takes the first sub-list, and returns
        # the length (only works if all rows are an equal length)
        return len(self._data[0])
```

 QtCore.QAbstractTableModel is an *abstract base class* meaning it does not have implementations for the methods. If you try and use it directly, it will not work. You must sub-class it.

In the __init__ constructor we accept a single parameter data which we store as the instance attribute self._data so we can access it from our methods. The passed in data structure is stored by reference, so any external changes will be reflected here.

To notify the model of changes you need to trigger the model's layoutChanged signal, using self.model.layoutChanged.emit().

The `data` method is called with two values `index` and `role`. The `index` parameter gives the location in the table for which information is currently being requested, and has two methods `.row()` and `.column()` which give the row and column number *in the view* respectively. In our example, the data is stored as a nested list, and the row and column indices are used to index as follows `data[row][column]`.

The view has no knowledge of the structure of the source data, and it is the responsibility of the model to translate between the view's *row* and *column* and the relevant positions in your own data store.

The `role` parameter describes what *kind* of information the method should return on this call. To get the data to display, the view calls this model's `data` method with the `role` of `Qt.ItemDataRole.DisplayRole`. However, `role` can have many other values including `Qt.ItemDataRole.BackgroundRole`, `Qt.ItemDataRole.CheckStateRole`, `Qt.ItemDataRole.DecorationRole`, `Qt.ItemDataRole.FontRole`, `Qt.ItemDataRole.TextAlignmentRole` and `Qt.ItemDataRole.ForegroundRole`, which each expect particular values in response (see later).

> `Qt.ItemDataRole.DisplayRole` actually expects a string to be returned, although other basic Python types including `float`, `int` and `bool` will also be displayed using their default string representations. However, formatting these types to your strings is usually preferable.

We'll cover how to use these other role types later, for now it is only necessary to know that you **must** check the role type is `Qt.ItemDataRole.DisplayRole` before returning your data for display.

The two custom methods `columnCount` and `rowCount` return the number of columns and rows in our data structure. In the case of a nested list of lists in the arrangement we're using here, the number of rows is simply the number of elements in the outer list, and the number of columns is the number of elements in **one of** the inner lists — assuming they are all equal.

 If these methods return values that are too high you will see out of bounds errors, if they return values that are too low, you'll see the table cut off.

Formatting numbers and dates

The data returned by the model for display is expected to be a string. While `int` and `float` values will also be displayed, using their default string representation, complex Python types will not. To display these, or to override the default formatting of `float` , `int` or `bool` values, you must format these to strings yourself.

You might be tempted to do this by converting your data to a table of strings in advance. However, by doing this you make it very difficult to continue working with the data in your table, whether for calculations or for updates.

Instead, you should use the model's `data` method to perform the string conversion on demand. By doing this you can continue to work with the original data, yet have complete control over how it is presented to the user — including changing this on the fly through configuration.

Below is a simple custom formatter which looks up the values in our data table, and displays them in a number of different ways depending on the Python `type` of the data.

Listing 105. tableview_format_1.py

```python
import sys
from datetime import datetime    ①

from PyQt6 import QtCore, QtGui, QtWidgets
from PyQt6.QtCore import Qt


class TableModel(QtCore.QAbstractTableModel):
    def __init__(self, data):
        super().__init__()
        self._data = data

    def data(self, index, role):
        if role == Qt.ItemDataRole.DisplayRole:
            # Get the raw value
            value = self._data[index.row()][index.column()]

            # Perform per-type checks and render accordingly.
            if isinstance(value, datetime):
                # Render time to YYY-MM-DD.
                return value.strftime("%Y-%m-%d")

            if isinstance(value, float):
                # Render float to 2 dp
                return "%.2f" % value

            if isinstance(value, str):
                # Render strings with quotes
                return '"%s"' % value

            # Default (anything not captured above: e.g. int)
            return value

    def rowCount(self, index):
        return len(self._data)

    def columnCount(self, index):
        return len(self._data[0])
```

① Note the additional import for `from datetime import datetime` at the top of the file.

Use this together with the modified sample data below to see it in action.

```
data = [
    [4, 9, 2],
    [1, -1, 'hello'],
    [3.023, 5, -5],
    [3, 3, datetime(2017,10,1)],
    [7.555, 8, 9],
]
```

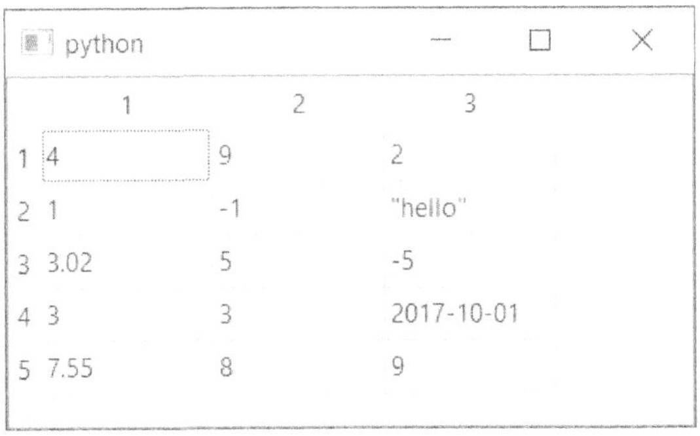

Figure 139. Custom data formatting

So far we've only looked at how we can customize how the data itself is formatted. However, the model interface gives you far more control over the display of table cells including colors and icons. In the next part we'll look at how to use the model to customize QTableView appearance.

Styles & Colors with Roles

Using colors and icons to highlight cells in data tables can help make data easier to find and understand, or help users to select or mark data of interest. Qt allows for complete control of all of these from the model, by responding to the relevant *role* on the data method.

The types expected to be returned in response to the various role types are shown below.

Role	Type
Qt.ItemDataRole.BackgroundRole	QBrush (also QColor)
Qt.ItemDataRole.CheckStateRole	Qt.CheckState
Qt.ItemDataRole.DecorationRole	QIcon, QPixmap, QColor
Qt.ItemDataRole.DisplayRole	QString (also int, float, bool)
Qt.ItemDataRole.FontRole	QFont
Qt.ItemDataRole.SizeHintRole	QSize
Qt.ItemDataRole.TextAlignmentRole	Qt.Alignment
Qt.ItemDataRole.ForegroundRole	QBrush (also QColor)

By responding to a particular combination of role and index we can modify the appearance of particular cells, columns or rows in the table — for example, setting a blue background for all cells in the 3rd column.

Listing 106. tableview_format_2.py

```python
def data(self, index, role):
    if (
        role == Qt.ItemDataRole.BackgroundRole
        and index.column() == 2
    ):
        # See below for the data structure.
        return QtGui.QColor(Qt.GlobalColor.blue)

    # existing `if role == Qt.ItemDataRole.DisplayRole:` block
hidden
    # hidden for clarity.
```

By using the index to lookup values from our own data, we can also customize appearance based on values in our data. We'll go through some of the more common use-cases below.

Text alignment

In our previous formatting examples we had used text formatting to display `float` down to 2 decimal places. However, it's also common when displaying numbers to right-align them, to make it easier to compare across lists of numbers. This can be accomplished by returning `Qt.Alignment.AlignRight` in response to `Qt.ItemDataRole.TextAlignmentRole` for any numeric values.

The modified `data` method is shown below. We check for `role == Qt.ItemDataRole.TextAlignmentRole` and look up the value by index as before, then determine if the value is numeric. If it is we can return `Qt.Alignment.AlignVCenter` + `Qt.Alignment.AlignRight` to align in the middle vertically, and on the right horizontally.

Listing 107. tableview_format_3.py

```python
def data(self, index, role):
    if role == Qt.ItemDataRole.TextAlignmentRole:
        value = self._data[index.row()][index.column()]

        if isinstance(value, int) or isinstance(value, float):
            # Align right, vertical middle.
            return (
                Qt.AlignmentFlag.AlignVCenter
                | Qt.AlignmentFlag.AlignRight
            )

    # existing `if role == Qt.ItemDataRole.DisplayRole:` block
hidden
    # hidden for clarity.
```

 Other alignments are possible, including `Qt.Alignment.AlignHCenter` to align center horizontally. You can combine them together by OR-ing them together e.g. `Qt.Alignment.AlignBottom | Qt.Alignment.AlignRight`.

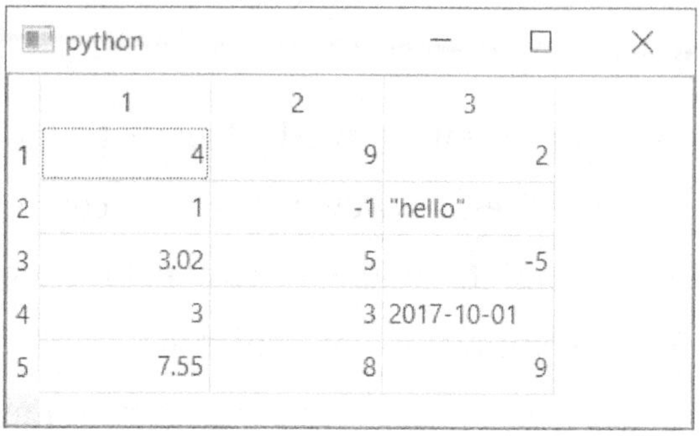

Figure 140. QTableView cell alignment

Text colors

If you've used spreadsheets like Excel you might be familiar with the concept of *conditional formatting*. These are rules you can apply to cells (or rows, or columns) which change text and background colors of cells depending on their value.

This can be useful to help visualize data, for example using red for negative numbers or highlighting ranges of numbers (e.g. low … high) with a gradient of blue to red.

First, the below example implements a handler which checks if the value in the indexed cell is numeric, and below zero. If it is, then the handler returns the text (foreground) color red.

Listing 108. tableview_format_4.py

```python
def data(self, index, role):
    if role == Qt.ItemDataRole.ForegroundRole:
        value = self._data[index.row()][index.column()]

        if (
            isinstance(value, int) or isinstance(value, float)
        ) and value < 0:
            return QtGui.QColor("red")

    # existing `if role == Qt.ItemDataRole.DisplayRole:` block hidden
    # hidden for clarity.
```

If you add this to your model's data handler, all negative numbers will now appear red.

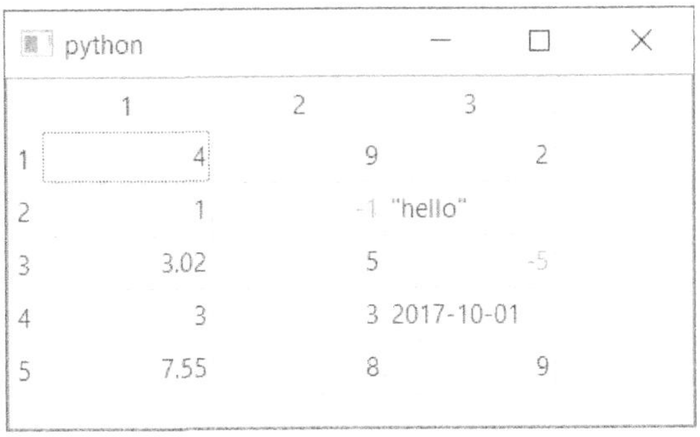

Figure 141. QTableView text formatting, with red negative numbers

Number range gradients

The same principle can be used to apply gradients to numeric values in a table to, for example, highlight low and high values. First we define our color scale, which is taken from colorbrewer2.org [http://colorbrewer2.org/#type=diverging& scheme=RdBu&n=11].

```python
COLORS = ['#053061', '#2166ac', '#4393c3', '#92c5de', '#d1e5f0',
          '#f7f7f7', '#fddbc7', '#f4a582', '#d6604d', '#b2182b', '#67001f']
```

Next we define our custom handler, this time for `Qt.ItemDataRole.BackgroundRole`. This takes the value at the given index, checks that this is numeric then performs a series of operations to constrain it to the range 0...10 required to index into our list.

Listing 109. tableview_format_5.py

```python
def data(self, index, role):
    if role == Qt.ItemDataRole.BackgroundRole:
        value = self._data[index.row()][index.column()]
        if isinstance(value, int) or isinstance(value, float):
            value = int(value)  # Convert to integer for
indexing.

            # Limit to range -5 ... +5, then convert to 0..10
            value = max(-5, value)  # values < -5 become -5
            value = min(5, value)  # valaues > +5 become +5
            value = value + 5  # -5 becomes 0, +5 becomes + 10

            return QtGui.QColor(COLORS[value])

        # existing `if role == Qt.ItemDataRole.DisplayRole:` block
hidden
        # hidden for clarity.
```

The logic used here for converting the value to the gradient is very basic, cutting off high/low values, and not adjusting to the range of the data. However, you can adapt this as needed, as long as the end result of your handler is to return a `QColor` or `QBrush`

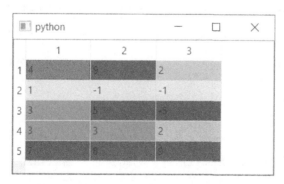

Figure 142. QTableView with number-range color gradients

322

Icon & Image decoration

Each table cell contains a small *decoration* area which can be used to display icons, images or a solid block of color, on the left hand side next to the data. This can be used to indicate data type, e.g. calendars for dates, ticks and crosses for bool values, or for a more subtle conditional-formatting for number ranges.

Below are some simple implementations of these ideas.

Indicating bool/date data types with icons

For dates we'll use Python's built-in datetime type. First, add the following import to the top of your file to import this type.

```
from datetime import datetime
```

Then, update the data (set in the MainWindow.__init__) to add datetime and bool (True or False values), for example.

```
data = [
    [True, 9, 2],
    [1, 0, -1],
    [3, 5, False],
    [3, 3, 2],
    [datetime(2019, 5, 4), 8, 9],
]
```

With these in place, you can update your model data method to show icons and formatted dates for date types, with the following code.

Listing 110. tableview_format_6.py

```python
import os


basedir = os.path.dirname(__file__)


class TableModel(QtCore.QAbstractTableModel):
    def __init__(self, data):
        super().__init__()
        self._data = data

    def data(self, index, role):
        if role == Qt.ItemDataRole.DisplayRole:
            value = self._data[index.row()][index.column()]
            if isinstance(value, datetime):
                return value.strftime("%Y-%m-%d")

            return value

        if role == Qt.ItemDataRole.DecorationRole:
            value = self._data[index.row()][index.column()]
            if isinstance(value, datetime):
                return QtGui.QIcon(
                    os.path.join(basedir, "calendar.png")
                )

    def rowCount(self, index):
        return len(self._data)

    def columnCount(self, index):
        return len(self._data[0])
```

 We load the icons using the basedir technique introduced earlier, to ensure the paths are correct however the script is run.

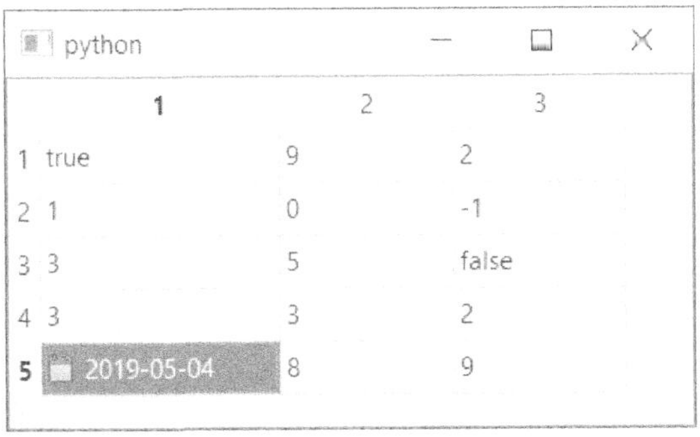

Figure 143. QTableView formatted dates with indicator icon

The following shows how to use ticks and cross for boolean `True` and `False` values respectively.

Listing 111. tableview_format_7.py

```python
def data(self, index, role):
    if role == Qt.ItemDataRole.DecorationRole:
        value = self._data[index.row()][index.column()]
        if isinstance(value, bool):
            if value:
                return QtGui.QIcon("tick.png")

        return QtGui.QIcon("cross.png")
```

You can of course combine the above together, or any other mix of `Qt.ItemDataRole.DecorationRole` and `Qt.ItemDataRole.DisplayRole` handlers. It's usually simpler to keep each type grouped under the same *if* branch, or as your model becomes more complex, to create sub-methods to handle each role.

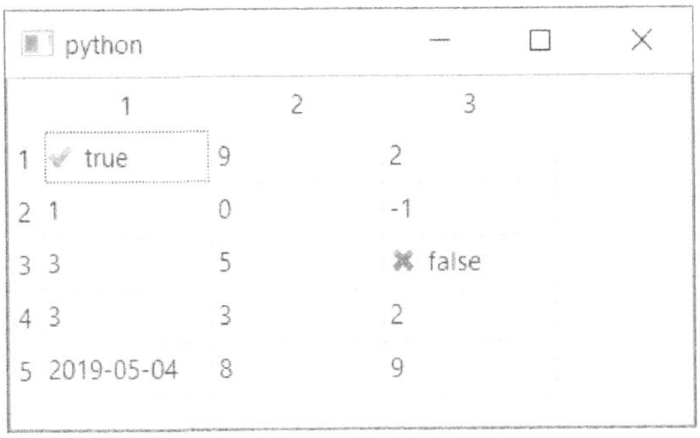

Figure 144. QTableView boolean indicators

Color blocks

If you return a QColor for Qt.ItemDataRole.DecorationRole a small square of color will be displayed on the left hand side of the cell, in the icon location. This is identical to the earlier Qt.ItemDataRole.BackgroundRole conditional formatting example, except now handling and responding to Qt.ItemDataRole.DecorationRole.

Listing 112. tableview_format_8.py

```python
def data(self, index, role):
    if role == Qt.ItemDataRole.DecorationRole:
        value = self._data[index.row()][index.column()]

        if isinstance(value, datetime):
            return QtGui.QIcon(
                os.path.join(basedir, "calendar.png")
            )

        if isinstance(value, bool):
            if value:
                return QtGui.QIcon(
                    os.path.join(basedir, "tick.png")
                )

            return QtGui.QIcon(os.path.join(basedir,
"cross.png"))

        if isinstance(value, int) or isinstance(value, float):
            value = int(value)

            # Limit to range -5 ... +5, then convert to 0..10
            value = max(-5, value)  # values < -5 become -5
            value = min(5, value)   # valaues > +5 become +5
            value = value + 5  # -5 becomes 0, +5 becomes + 10

            return QtGui.QColor(COLORS[value])
```

Figure 145. QTableView color block decorations

Alternative Python data structures

So far in our examples we've used simple nested Python lists to hold our data for display. This is fine for simple tables of data, however if you're working with large data tables there are some other better options in Python, which come with additional benefits. In the next parts we'll look at two Python data table libraries — *numpy* and *pandas* — and how to integrate these with Qt.

Numpy

Numpy is a library which provides support for large multi-dimensional arrays or matrix data structures in Python. The efficient and high-performance handling of large arrays makes *numpy* ideal for scientific and mathematical applications. This also makes *numpy* arrays a good data store for large, single-typed, data tables in PyQt6.

Using numpy as a data source

To support *numpy* arrays we need to make a number of changes to the model, first modifying the indexing in the `data` method and then changing the row and column count calculations for `rowCount` and `columnCount`.

The standard *numpy* API provides element-level access to 2D arrays, by passing the row and column in the same slicing operation, e.g. `_data[index.row(), index.column()]`. This is more efficient than indexing in two steps, as for the `list` of `list` examples.

In *numpy* the dimensions of an array are available through .shape which returns a tuple of dimensions along each axis in turn. We get the length of each axis by selecting the correct item from this tuple, e.g. _data.shape[0] gets the size of the first axis.

The following complete example shows how to display a *numpy* array using Qt's QTableView via a custom model.

Listing 113. model-views/tableview_numpy.py

```python
import sys

import numpy as np
from PyQt6 import QtCore, QtGui, QtWidgets
from PyQt6.QtCore import Qt


class TableModel(QtCore.QAbstractTableModel):
    def __init__(self, data):
        super().__init__()
        self._data = data

    def data(self, index, role):
        if role == Qt.ItemDataRole.DisplayRole:
            # Note: self._data[index.row()][index.column()] will also
work
            value = self._data[index.row(), index.column()]
            return str(value)

    def rowCount(self, index):
        return self._data.shape[0]

    def columnCount(self, index):
        return self._data.shape[1]


class MainWindow(QtWidgets.QMainWindow):
    def __init__(self):
        super().__init__()

        self.table = QtWidgets.QTableView()
```

```
        data = np.array(
            [
                [1, 9, 2],
                [1, 0, -1],
                [3, 5, 2],
                [3, 3, 2],
                [5, 8, 9],
            ]
        )

        self.model = TableModel(data)
        self.table.setModel(self.model)

        self.setCentralWidget(self.table)
        self.setGeometry(600, 100, 400, 200)


app = QtWidgets.QApplication(sys.argv)
window = MainWindow()
window.show()
app.exec()
```

While simple Python types such as `int` and `float` are displayed without converting to strings, *numpy* uses it's own types (e.g. `numpy.int32`) for array values. In order for these to be displayed we **must** first convert them to strings.

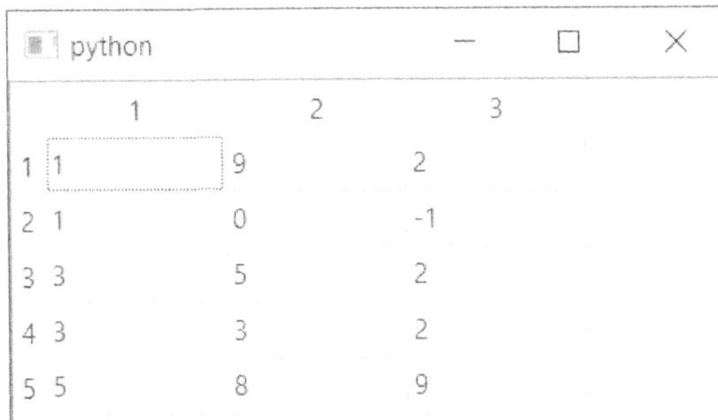

Figure 146. QTableView with numpy array

With QTableView only 2D arrays can be displayed, however if you have a higher dimensional data structure you can combine the QTableView with a tabbed or scrollbar UI, to allow access to and display of these higher dimensions.

Pandas

Pandas is a Python library commonly used for data manipulation and analysis. It provides a nice API for loading 2D tabular data from various data sources and performing data analysis on it. By using the *numpy* DataTable as your QTableView model you can use these APIs to load and analyse your data from right within your application.

Using Pandas as a data source

The modifications of the model to work with *numpy* are fairly minor, requiring changes to the indexing in the data method and modifications to rowCount and columnCount. The changes for rowCount and columnCount are identical to *numpy* with *pandas* using a _data.shape tuple to represent the dimensions of the data.

For indexing we use the *pandas* .iloc method, for indexed locations — i.e. lookup by column and/or row index. This is done by passing the row and then column to the slice _data.iloc[index.row(), index.column()].

The following complete example shows how to display a *pandas* data frame using Qt QTableView via a custom model.

Listing 114. model-views/tableview_pandas.py

```
import sys

import pandas as pd
from PyQt6 import QtCore, QtGui, QtWidgets
from PyQt6.QtCore import Qt


class TableModel(QtCore.QAbstractTableModel):
```

```python
    def __init__(self, data):
        super().__init__()
        self._data = data

    def data(self, index, role):
        if role == Qt.ItemDataRole.DisplayRole:
            value = self._data.iloc[index.row(), index.column()]
            return str(value)

    def rowCount(self, index):
        return self._data.shape[0]

    def columnCount(self, index):
        return self._data.shape[1]

    def headerData(self, section, orientation, role):
        if role == Qt.ItemDataRole.DisplayRole:
            if orientation == Qt.Orientation.Horizontal:
                return str(self._data.columns[section])

            if orientation == Qt.Orientation.Vertical:
                return str(self._data.index[section])


class MainWindow(QtWidgets.QMainWindow):
    def __init__(self):
        super().__init__()

        self.table = QtWidgets.QTableView()

        data = pd.DataFrame(
            [
                [1, 9, 2],
                [1, 0, -1],
                [3, 5, 2],
                [3, 3, 2],
                [5, 8, 9],
            ],
            columns=["A", "B", "C"],
            index=["Row 1", "Row 2", "Row 3", "Row 4", "Row 5"],
        )

        self.model = TableModel(data)
```

```
        self.table.setModel(self.model)

        self.setCentralWidget(self.table)
        self.setGeometry(600, 100, 400, 200)


app = QtWidgets.QApplication(sys.argv)
window = MainWindow()
window.show()
app.exec()
```

An interesting extension here is to use the table header of the QTableView to display row and *pandas* column header values, which can be taken from DataFrame.index and DataFrame.columns respectively.

	A	B	C
Row 1	1	9	2
Row 2	1	0	-1
Row 3	3	5	2
Row 4	3	3	2
Row 5	5	8	9

Figure 147. QTableView pandas DataTable, with column and row headers

For this we need to implement a Qt.ItemDataRole.DisplayRole handler in a custom headerData method. This receives section, the index of the row/column (0...n), orientation which can be either Qt.Orientations.Horizontal for the column headers, or Qt.Orientations.Vertical for the row headers, and role which works the same as for the data method.

 The headerData method also receives other roles, which can be used to customize the appearance of the headers further.

Conclusion

In this chapter we've covered the basics of using QTableView and a custom model to display tabular data in your applications. This was extended to demonstrate how to format data and decorate cells with icons and colors. Finally, we demonstrated using QTableView with tabular data from *numpy* and *pandas* structures including displaying custom column and row headers.

 If you want to run calculations on your table data, take a look at Using the thread pool.

20. Querying SQL databases with Qt models

So far we've used table models to access data loaded or stored in the application itself — from simple lists of lists to *numpy* and *pandas* tables. However, all of these approaches have in common that the data that you are viewing must be loaded entirely into memory.

To simplify interaction with SQL databases Qt provides a number of SQL models which can be connected to views to display the output of SQL queries, or database tables. In this chapter we'll look at two alternatives — displaying database data in a QTableView and with QDataWidgetMapper which allows you to map database fields to Qt widgets.

Which model you use depends on whether you want read-only access to a database, read-write access or read-only access with relationships (querying more than one table). In the next sections we'll look at each of those options in turn.

The following examples start from this simple skeleton, showing a table view in a window, but with no model set.

Listing 115. databases/tableview.py

```python
import os
import sys

from PyQt6.QtCore import Qt
from PyQt6.QtWidgets import QApplication, QMainWindow, QTableView


class MainWindow(QMainWindow):
    def __init__(self):
        super().__init__()

        self.table = QTableView()

        # self.model = ?
        # self.table.setModel(self.model)

        self.setCentralWidget(self.table)


app = QApplication(sys.argv)
window = MainWindow()
window.show()
app.exec()
```

Before we connect a model, running this will just show an empty window.

For these examples we're using a SQLite file database `demo.sqlite` which is included in the downloads for this book.

You can use your own database if you prefer, including both SQLite databases or database servers (PostgreSQL, MySQL, etc.). See Authenticating with QSqlDatabase for instructions on how to connect to remote servers.

Connecting to a database

To be able to display data from a database in your app, you must first connect with it. Both server (IP, e.g. PostgreSQL or MySQL) and file-based (SQLite) databases are supported by Qt, the only difference being in how you set them up.

For all these examples we're using the Chinook sample database [https://github.com/ lerocha/chinook-database] — a sample database designed for testing and demos. The database represents a digital media store, including tables for artists, albums, media tracks, invoices and customers.

 A copy of the SQLite version of this database is included in the code with this book, named `chinook.sqlite`. You can also download the latest version from here [https://github.com/lerocha/ chinook-database/raw/master/ChinookDatabase/DataSources/ Chinook_Sqlite.sqlite].

```python
import os

from PyQt6.QtSql import QSqlDatabase

basedir = os.path.dirname(__file__)

db = QSqlDatabase("QSQLITE")
db.setDatabaseName(os.path.join(basedir, "chinook.sqlite"))
db.open()
```

 Where you place this code will depend on your application. Often you want to create a single database connection and use it throughout your app — in this case it's best to create a separate module, e.g. db.py to hold this (and other related functionality).

The process is the same for all databases — create the database object, set the name and then *open* the database to initialize the connection. However, if you want to connect to a remote database there are a few extra parameters. See

Displaying a table with `QSqlTableModel`

The simplest thing you can do once you've connected your app to a database store, is to display a single table in your application. To do this we can use `QSqlTableModel`. This model displays data directly from the table, allowing editing.

First we need to create the instance of the table model, passing in the database *object* we've created above. Then we need to set the source table to query data from — this is the name of the table in the database, here <table name>. Finally we need to call `.select()` on the model.

```
model = QSqlTableModel(db=db)
model.setTable('<table name>')
model.select()
```

By calling `.select()` we tell the model to query the database and keep the result, ready for display. To display this data in a `QTableView` we simply need to pass it to the views `.setModel()` method.

```
table = QTableView()
table.setModel(self.model)
```

The data will be displayed in the table model and can be browsed using the scrollbar. See below for the full code, which loads the database and displays the *track* table in the view.

Listing 116. tableview_tablemodel.py

```python
import os
import sys

from PyQt6.QtCore import QSize, Qt
from PyQt6.QtSql import QSqlDatabase, QSqlTableModel
from PyQt6.QtWidgets import QApplication, QMainWindow, QTableView

basedir = os.path.dirname(__file__)

db = QSqlDatabase("QSQLITE")
db.setDatabaseName(os.path.join(basedir, "chinook.sqlite"))
db.open()


class MainWindow(QMainWindow):
    def __init__(self):
        super().__init__()

        self.table = QTableView()

        self.model = QSqlTableModel(db=db)

        self.table.setModel(self.model)

        self.model.setTable("Track")
        self.model.select()

        self.setMinimumSize(QSize(1024, 600))
        self.setCentralWidget(self.table)


app = QApplication(sys.argv)
window = MainWindow()
window.show()
app.exec()
```

This will give you the following window when run.

	TrackId	Name	AlbumId	MediaTypeId	GenreId	Composer	Milliseconds	Bytes
1	1	...To Rock (We ...	1	1	1	Angus Young, Malcolm Young...	343719	11170334
2	2	Balls to the Wall	2	2	1		342562	5510424
3	3	Fast As a Shark	3	2	1	Kaufman, U. Dirkschneider & ...	230619	3990994
4	4	Restless and Wild	3	2	1	Kaufman, U. ...	252051	4331779
5	5	Princess of the Dawn	3	2	1	Deaffy & R.A. Smith-Diesel	375418	6290521
6	6	Put The Finger On You	1	1	1	Angus Young, Malcolm Young....	205662	6713451
7	7	Let's Get It Up	1	1	1	Angus Young, Malcolm Young....	233926	7636561
8	8	Inject The Venom	1	1	1	Angus Young, Malcolm Young....	210834	6852860
9	9	Snowballed	1	1	1	Angus Young, Malcolm Young...	203102	6599424
10	10	Evil Walks	1	1	1	Angus Young, Malcolm Young....	263497	8611245
11	11	C.O.D.	1	1	1	Angus Young, Malcolm Young....	199836	6566314
12	12	Breaking The Rules	1	1	1	Angus Young, Malcolm Young....	263288	8596840
13	13	Night Of The Long Knives	1	1	1	Angus Young, Malcolm Young....	205688	6706347
14	14	Spellbound	1	1	1	Angus Young, Malcolm Young....	270863	8817038
15	15	Go Down	4	1	1	AC/DC	331180	10847611

Figure 148. The tracks table displayed in a `QTableView`*.*

You can resize the columns by dragging the right hand edge. Resize to fit the contents by double-clicking on the right hand edge.

Editing the data

Database data displayed in a `QTableView` is editable by default — just double-click on any cell and you will be able to modify the contents. The changes are persisted back to the database immediately after you finish editing.

Qt provides some control over this editing behavior, which you may want to change depending on the type of app you are building. Qt terms these behaviors *editing strategy* and they can be one of the following -

Strategy	Description
`QSqlTableModel.EditStrategy.OnFieldChange`	Changes are applied automatically, when the user deselects the edited cell.
`QSqlTableModel.EditStrategy.OnRowChange`	Changes are applied automatically, when the user selects a different row.

Strategy	Description
QSqlTableModel.EditStrategy.OnManualSubmit	Changes are cached in the model, and written to the database only when .submitAll() is called, or discarded when revertAll() is called.

You can set the current edit strategy for the model by calling .setEditStrategy on it. For example —

```
self.model.setEditStrategy(QSqlTableModel.EditStrategy.OnRowChange)
```

Sorting columns

To sort the table by a given column, we can call .setSort() on the model, passing in the column index and Qt.SortOrder.AscendingOrder or Qt.SortOrder.DescendingOrder.

Listing 117. databases/tableview_tablemodel_sort.py

```
self.model.setTable("Track")
self.model.setSort(2, Qt.SortOrder.DescendingOrder)
self.model.select()
```

This must be done *before* the call to .select(). If you want to sort after you've got the data, you can perform another .select() call to refresh.

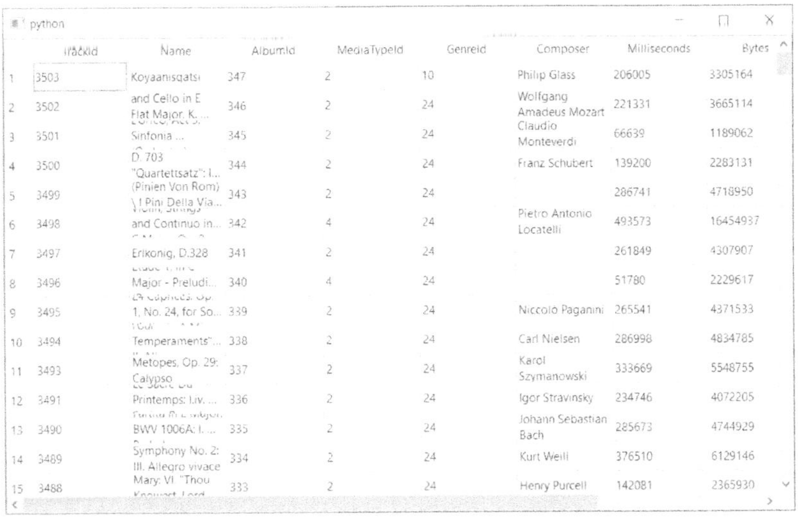

	TrackId	Name	AlbumId	MediaTypeId	GenreId	Composer	Milliseconds	Bytes
1	3503	Koyaanisqatsi	347	2	10	Philip Glass	206005	3305164
2	3502	and Cello in E Flat Major, K. ...	346	2	24	Wolfgang Amadeus Mozart	221331	3665114
3	3501	Sinfonia ...	345	2	24	Claudio Monteverdi	66639	1189062
4	3500	D. 703 "Quartettsatz": I...	344	2	24	Franz Schubert	139200	2283131
5	3499	(Pinien Von Rom) \ I Pini Della Via...	343	2	24		286741	4718950
6	3498	and Continuo in...	342	4	24	Pietro Antonio Locatelli	493573	16454937
7	3497	Erlkonig, D.328	341	2	24		261849	4307907
8	3496	Major - Preludi...	340	4	24		51780	2229617
9	3495	1, No. 24, for So...	339	2	24	Niccolo Paganini	265541	4371533
10	3494	Temperaments"...	338	2	24	Carl Nielsen	286998	4834785
11	3493	Metopes, Op. 29: Calypso	337	2	24	Karol Szymanowski	333669	5548755
12	3491	Printemps: I.iv. ...	336	2	24	Igor Stravinsky	234746	4072205
13	3490	BWV 1006A: I. ...	335	2	24	Johann Sebastian Bach	285673	4744929
14	3489	Symphony No. 2: III. Allegro vivace	334	2	24	Kurt Weill	376510	6129146
15	3488	Mary: VI. "Thou	333	2	24	Henry Purcell	142081	2365930

Figure 149. The tracks table sorted on column index 2, the `album_id`.

You may prefer to sort the table using the *column name* rather than the column index. To do this, you can look up the column index with the name.

Listing 118. databases/tableview_tablemodel_sortname.py

```
        self.model.setTable("Track")
        idx = self.model.fieldIndex("Milliseconds")
        self.model.setSort(idx, Qt.SortOrder.DescendingOrder)
        self.model.select()
```

The table is now sorted on the `milliseconds` column.

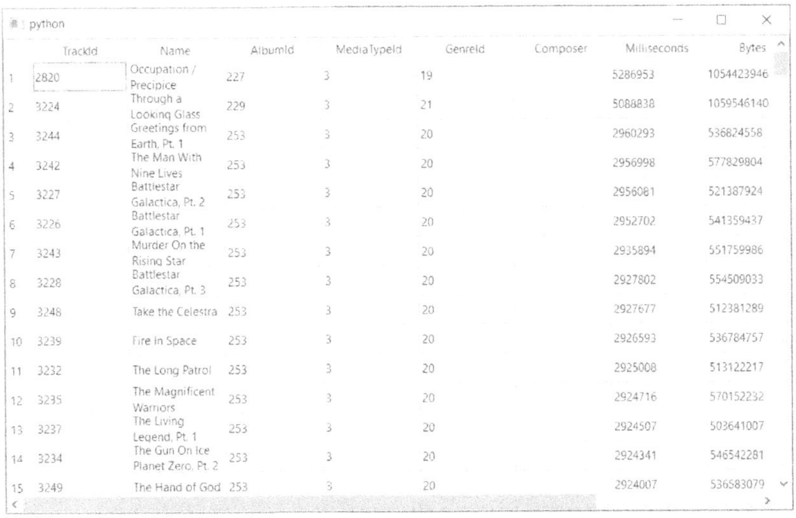

	TrackId	Name	AlbumId	MediaTypeId	GenreId	Composer	Milliseconds	Bytes
1	2820	Occupation / Precipice	227	3	19		5286953	1054423946
2	3224	Through a Looking Glass	229	3	21		5088838	1059546140
3	3244	Greetings from Earth, Pt. 1	253	3	20		2960293	536824558
4	3242	The Man With Nine Lives	253	3	20		2956998	577829804
5	3227	Battlestar Galactica, Pt. 2	253	3	20		2956081	521387924
6	3226	Battlestar Galactica, Pt. 1	253	3	20		2952702	541359437
7	3243	Murder On the Rising Star	253	3	20		2935894	551759986
8	3228	Battlestar Galactica, Pt. 3	253	3	20		2927802	554509033
9	3248	Take the Celestra	253	3	20		2927677	512381289
10	3239	Fire in Space	253	3	20		2926593	536784757
11	3232	The Long Patrol	253	3	20		2925008	513122217
12	3235	The Magnificent Warriors	253	3	20		2924716	570152232
13	3237	The Living Legend, Pt. 1	253	3	20		2924507	503641007
14	3234	The Gun On Ice Planet Zero, Pt. 2	253	3	20		2924341	546542281
15	3249	The Hand of God	253	3	20		2924007	536583079

Figure 150. The tracks table sorted on the `milliseconds` *column.*

Column titles

By default the column header titles on the table come from the column names in the database. Often this isn't very user-friendly, so you can replace them with proper titles using `.setHeaderData`, passing in the column index, the direction — horizontal (top) or vertical (left) header — and the label.

Listing 119. database/tableview_tablemodel_titles.py

```
        self.model.setTable("Track")
        self.model.setHeaderData(1, Qt.Orientation.Horizontal,
"Name")
        self.model.setHeaderData(
            2, Qt.Orientation.Horizontal, "Album (ID)"
        )
        self.model.setHeaderData(
            3, Qt.Orientation.Horizontal, "Media Type (ID)"
        )
        self.model.setHeaderData(
            4, Qt.Orientation.Horizontal, "Genre (ID)"
        )
        self.model.setHeaderData(
            5, Qt.Orientation.Horizontal, "Composer"
        )
        self.model.select()
```

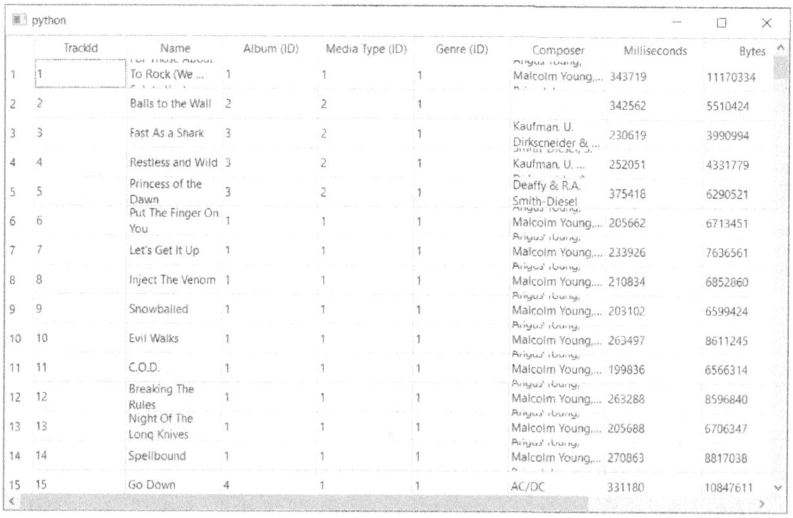

python

	TrackId	Name	Album (ID)	Media Type (ID)	Genre (ID)	Composer	Milliseconds	Bytes
1	1	To Rock (We ...	1	1	1	Malcolm Young,...	343719	11170334
2	2	Balls to the Wall	2	2	1		342562	5510424
3	3	Fast As a Shark	3	2	1	Kaufman, U. Dirkscneider & ...	230619	3990994
4	4	Restless and Wild	3	2	1	Kaufman, U. ...	252051	4331779
5	5	Princess of the Dawn	3	2	1	Deaffy & R.A. Smith-Diesel	375418	6290521
6	6	Put The Finger On You	1	1	1	Malcolm Young,...	205662	6713451
7	7	Let's Get It Up	1	1	1	Malcolm Young,...	233926	7636561
8	8	Inject The Venom	1	1	1	Malcolm Young,...	210834	6852860
9	9	Snowballed	1	1	1	Malcolm Young,...	203102	6599424
10	10	Evil Walks	1	1	1	Malcolm Young,...	263497	8611245
11	11	C.O.D.	1	1	1	Malcolm Young,...	199836	6566314
12	12	Breaking The Rules	1	1	1	Malcolm Young,...	263288	8596840
13	13	Night Of The Long Knives	1	1	1	Malcolm Young,...	205688	6706347
14	14	Spellbound	1	1	1	Malcolm Young,...	270863	8817038
15	15	Go Down	4	1	1	AC/DC	331180	10847611

Figure 151. The tracks table with nicer column titles.

As when sorting, it is not always convenient to use the column indexes for this — if the column order changes in the database, the names set in your application will be out of sync.

As before, we can use .fieldIndex() to lookup the index for a given name. You can go a step further and define a Python dict of column name and title to apply in one go, when setting up the model.

Listing 120. database/tableview_tablemodel_titlesname.py

```
        self.model.setTable("Track")
        column_titles = {
            "Name": "Name",
            "AlbumId": "Album (ID)",
            "MediaTypeId": "Media Type (ID)",
            "GenreId": "Genre (ID)",
            "Composer": "Composer",
        }
        for n, t in column_titles.items():
            idx = self.model.fieldIndex(n)
            self.model.setHeaderData(idx, Qt.Orientation.Horizontal,
  t)

        self.model.select()
```

Selecting columns

Often you will not want to display all the columns from a table. You can select which columns to display by removing columns from the model. To do this call .removeColumns() passing in the index of the first column to remove and the number of subsequent columns.

```
self.model.removeColumns(2, 5)
```

Once removed the columns will no longer be shown on the table. You can use the same name-lookup approach used for column labelling to remove columns by name.

```
columns_to_remove = ['name', 'something']

for cn in columns_to_remove:
    idx = self.model.fieldIndex(cn)
    self.model.removeColumns(idx, 1)
```

 Removing columns in this way just removes them from the view. If you want to filter the columns out with SQL see the query models below.

Filtering a table

We can filter the table by calling .setFilter() on the model, passing in a parameter which describes the filter. The filter parameter can be any valid SQL WHERE clause without the WHERE prepended. For example name="Martin" to match exactly, or name LIKE "Ma%" to match fields beginning with "Ma".

In case you're not familiar with SQL, below are a few example search patterns you can use to perform different types of searches.

Pattern	Description
field="{}"	Field matches the string exactly.
field LIKE "{}%"	Field begins with the given string.
field LIKE "%{}"	Field ends with the given string.
field LIKE "%{}%"	Field contains the given string.

In each example {} is the search string, which you must interpolate using python "{}".format(search_str). Unlike the sort, the filter will be applied automatically to the data, without the need to call .select() again.

 If .select() hasn't been called yet, the filter will be applied the first time it is.

In the following example we add a QLineEdit field and hook this up to search the table on the track name field. We connect the line edit changed signal to construct and apply the filter to the model.

Listing 121. databases/tableview_tablemodel_filter.py

```python
import os
import sys

from PyQt6.QtCore import QSize, Qt
from PyQt6.QtSql import QSqlDatabase, QSqlTableModel
from PyQt6.QtWidgets import (
    QApplication,
    QLineEdit,
    QMainWindow,
    QTableView,
    QVBoxLayout,
    QWidget,
)

basedir = os.path.dirname(__file__)

db = QSqlDatabase("QSQLITE")
db.setDatabaseName(os.path.join(basedir, "chinook.sqlite"))
db.open()


class MainWindow(QMainWindow):
    def __init__(self):
        super().__init__()

        container = QWidget()
        layout = QVBoxLayout()

        self.search = QLineEdit()
        self.search.textChanged.connect(self.update_filter)
        self.table = QTableView()

        layout.addWidget(self.search)
        layout.addWidget(self.table)
        container.setLayout(layout)
```

```python
        self.model = QSqlTableModel(db=db)

        self.table.setModel(self.model)

        self.model.setTable("Track")
        self.model.select()

        self.setMinimumSize(QSize(1024, 600))
        self.setCentralWidget(container)

    def update_filter(self, s):
        filter_str = 'Name LIKE "%{}%"'.format(s)
        self.model.setFilter(filter_str)


app = QApplication(sys.argv)
window = MainWindow()
window.show()
app.exec()
```

	TrackId	Name	AlbumId	MediaTypeId	GenreId	Composer	Milliseconds	Bytes
1	4	Restless and Wild	3	2	1	Kaufman, U. ...	252051	4331779
2	32	Deuces Are Wild	5	1	1	Steven Tyler, Jim Vallance	215875	7074167
3	775	Call Of The Wild	61	1	1	Ian Gillian, Rog...	293851	9575295
4	1245	Wildest Dreams	98	1	13	Adrian Smith/ Steve Harris	232777	9312384
5	1869	Where The Wild Things Are	153	1	3	Hetfield, Ulrich, Newsted	414380	13571280
6	1973	Wild Side	162	1	3	Nikki Sixx/Tommy Lee/Vince Neil	276767	9116997
7	2312	Near Wild Heaven	187	1	4	Stipe/Mike Mill...	199862	6610009
8	2627	Wild Hearted Son	213	1	1		266893	8670550
9	2633	Wild Flower	213	1	1		215536	7084321
10	2697	I Go Wild	218	1	1	Jagger/Richards	264019	8630833
11	2930	Ride Your Wild ...	232	1	1	U2	316551	10304369
12	2944	Wild Honey	233	1	1	Bono, Larry ...	226768	7466069

Figure 152. Filtering the tracks table on the name.

 This is prone to SQL injection attacks.

While this works, this is *really* bad way to enable searching on a table, since the user can construct invalid or malicious SQL statements. For example, try entering the single character " in the search box — the filtering will stop working, and won't work again until you restart the app.

This is because you've created an invalid SQL statement e.g.

```
'name LIKE "%"%"'
```

The ideal way to work around this problem is to use parameterized queries — leaving escaping of the input to the database, to ensure that nothing dangerous or malformed is passed. However, this isn't possible with the Qt filter interface, we can only pass a string.

For simple plain-text searching we can instead simply strip out any non-alphanumeric or space characters from the string. It will depend on your use case whether this is appropriate.

```python
import re

s = re.sub('[\W_]+', '', s)
query = 'field="%s"' % s
```

Putting that into our filter method from our example, we get the following code.

Listing 122. databases/tableview_tablemodel_filter_clean.py

```python
def update_filter(self, s):
    s = re.sub("[\W_]+", "", s)
    filter_str = 'Name LIKE "%{}%"'.format(s)
    self.model.setFilter(filter_str)
```

Try running the example again, and entering " — and any other garbage you can think of. You should find that the search continues to work.

Displaying related data with
QSqlRelationalTableModel

In the previous examples we've used QSqlTableModel to display data from a single table. However, in relational databases tables can have *relationships* with other tables and it is often useful to be able to view that related data inline.

Relationships in relational databases are handled through *foreign keys*. These are a (usually) numeric value, stored in a column of one table, which references the *primary key* for a row in another table.

An example of a *foreign key* in our example *tracks* table would be album_id or genre_id. Both are numeric values which point to records in the *album* and *genre* table respectively. Displaying these values to the user (1, 2, 3.. etc.) is not helpful because they have no meaning themselves.

What would be nicer, would be to pull through the name of the album, or the genre and display it in our table view. For that, we can use QSqlRelationalTableModel.

The setup for this model is identical for the previous. To define the relationships we call .setRelation() passing the column index, and a QSqlRelation object.

```
from PyQt6.QtSql import QSqlRelation, QSqlRelationalTableModel

self.model = QSqlRelationalTableModel(db=db)

relation = QSqlRelation('<related_table>',
'<related_table_foreign_key_column', '<column_to_display>')
self.model.setRelation(<column>, relation)
```

The QSqlRelation object accepts three arguments, first the related *table* we will be pulling data from, the *foreign key column* on that table, and finally the *column* to pull data from.

For our test database *tracks* table, the following will pull data from the related tables for album ID, media_type ID and genre ID (columns 3, 4, 5 respectively).

Listing 123. databases/tableview_relationalmodel.py

```
        self.model.setTable("Track")
        self.model.setRelation(
            2, QSqlRelation("Album", "AlbumId", "Title")
        )
        self.model.setRelation(
            3, QSqlRelation("MediaType", "MediaTypeId", "Name")
        )
        self.model.setRelation(
            4, QSqlRelation("Genre", "GenreId", "Name")
        )
        self.model.select()
```

When run you will see the three _id columns have been replaced by the data pulled through from the related tables. The columns take the names of the related fields, if they don't clash, or have a name constructed for them.

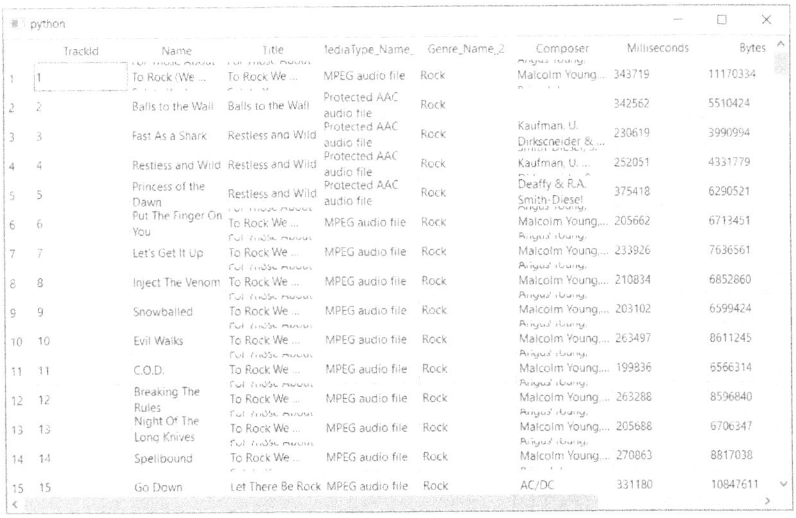

python

	TrackId	Name	Title	ediaType_Name_	Genre_Name_2	Composer	Milliseconds	Bytes
1	1	To Rock (We ...	To Rock We ...	MPEG audio file	Rock	Malcolm Young,...	343719	11170334
2	2	Balls to the Wall	Balls to the Wall	Protected AAC audio file	Rock		342562	5510424
3	3	Fast As a Shark	Restless and Wild	Protected AAC audio file	Rock	Kaufman, U. Dirkscneider & ...	230619	3990994
4	4	Restless and Wild	Restless and Wild	Protected AAC audio file	Rock	Kaufman, U. ...	252051	4331779
5	5	Princess of the Dawn	Restless and Wild	Protected AAC audio file	Rock	Deaffy & R.A. Smith-Diesel	375418	6290521
6	6	Put The Finger On You	To Rock We ...	MPEG audio file	Rock	Malcolm Young,...	205662	6713451
7	7	Let's Get It Up	To Rock We ...	MPEG audio file	Rock	Malcolm Young,...	233926	7636561
8	8	Inject The Venom	To Rock We ...	MPEG audio file	Rock	Malcolm Young,...	210834	6852860
9	9	Snowballed	To Rock We ...	MPEG audio file	Rock	Malcolm Young,...	203102	6599424
10	10	Evil Walks	To Rock We ...	MPEG audio file	Rock	Malcolm Young,...	263497	8611245
11	11	C.O.D.	To Rock We ...	MPEG audio file	Rock	Malcolm Young,...	199836	6566314
12	12	Breaking The Rules	To Rock We ...	MPEG audio file	Rock	Malcolm Young,...	263288	8596840
13	13	Night Of The Long Knives	To Rock We ...	MPEG audio file	Rock	Malcolm Young,...	205688	6706347
14	14	Spellbound	To Rock We ...	MPEG audio file	Rock	Malcolm Young,...	270863	8817038
15	15	Go Down	Let There Be Rock	MPEG audio file	Rock	AC/DC	331180	10847611

Figure 153. Displaying data from related fields.

Using QSqlRelationalDelegate **to edit related fields.**

If you try and edit fields in a QSqlRelationalTableModel you'll notice a problem — while you can edit the fields on the base table (here *Tracks*) any edits you make to the related fields (e.g. *Album Title*) are not saved. These fields are currently only views to the data.

Valid values for related fields are limited by the values in the related table — to have more choices, we need to add another row to the related table. Since the options are restricted, it often makes sense to display the choices in a QComboBox. Qt comes with a model item delegate which can do this lookup and display for us — QSqlRelationalDelegate.

Listing 124. databases/tableview_relationalmodel_delegate.py

```python
self.model.setTable("Track")
self.model.setRelation(
    2, QSqlRelation("Album", "AlbumId", "Title")
)
self.model.setRelation(
    3, QSqlRelation("MediaType", "MediaTypeId", "Name")
)
self.model.setRelation(
    4, QSqlRelation("Genre", "GenreId", "Name")
)

delegate = QSqlRelationalDelegate(self.table)
self.table.setItemDelegate(delegate)

self.model.select()
```

This delegate automatically handles the mapping for *any* relational fields. We simply create the delegate passing in the QTableView instance, and then set the resulting delegate on the model, everything is taken care of automatically.

Running this you will see drop-downs when you edit the related fields.

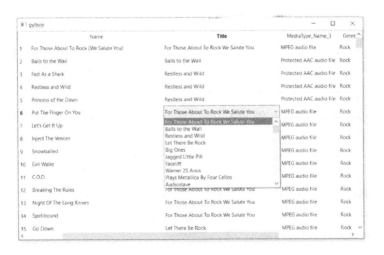

Figure 154. Making relatable fields editable through a drop-down with QSqlRelationalDelegate

Generic queries with `QSqlQueryModel`

So far we've been displaying an entire database table on our `QTableView` with some optional column filtering and sorting. However, Qt also allows for displaying more complex queries using `QSqlQueryModel`. In this part we'll look at how we can use `QSqlQueryModel` to display an SQL query, starting first with a simple single-table query and then relational and parameterized queries.

The process for querying with this model is slightly different. Rather than passing the database to the model constructor, here we instead create a `QSqlQuery` object which takes the database connection, and then pass *that* to the model.

```
query = QSqlQuery("SELECT name, composer FROM track ", db=db)
```

This means that you can use a single `QSqlQueryModel` and perform queries on different databases if you like. The complete working example of this query is shown below.

Listing 125. databases/tableview_querymodel.py

```python
import os
import sys

from PyQt6.QtCore import QSize, Qt
from PyQt6.QtSql import QSqlDatabase, QSqlQuery, QSqlQueryModel
from PyQt6.QtWidgets import QApplication, QMainWindow, QTableView

basedir = os.path.dirname(__file__)

db = QSqlDatabase("QSQLITE")
db.setDatabaseName(os.path.join(basedir, "chinook.sqlite"))
db.open()


class MainWindow(QMainWindow):
    def __init__(self):
        super().__init__()

        self.table = QTableView()

        self.model = QSqlQueryModel()
        self.table.setModel(self.model)

        query = QSqlQuery("SELECT Name, Composer FROM track ", db=db)

        self.model.setQuery(query)

        self.setMinimumSize(QSize(1024, 600))
        self.setCentralWidget(self.table)


app = QApplication(sys.argv)
window = MainWindow()
window.show()
app.exec()
```

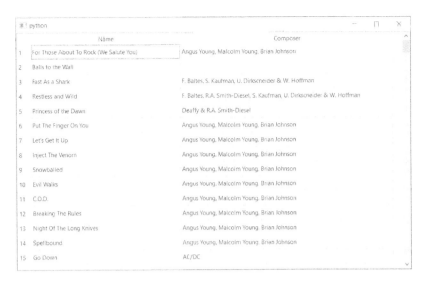

Figure 155. Performing a simple query.

In this first example we've performed a very simple query against our *track* table, only returning two fields from that table. However, the `QSqlQuery` object can be used for more complex queries, including cross-table joins and parameterized queries — where we can pass values in to modify the query.

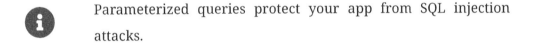

Parameterized queries protect your app from SQL injection attacks.

In the following example we extend the simple query to add a related look up on the *album* table. In addition we bind a `album_title` parameter which is used for a *contains* search against the album table.

Listing 126. databases/tableview_querymodel_parameter.py

```python
import os
import sys

from PyQt6.QtCore import QSize, Qt
from PyQt6.QtSql import QSqlDatabase, QSqlQuery, QSqlQueryModel
from PyQt6.QtWidgets import QApplication, QMainWindow, QTableView

basedir = os.path.dirname(__file__)

db = QSqlDatabase("QSQLITE")
db.setDatabaseName(os.path.join(basedir, "chinook.sqlite"))
db.open()


class MainWindow(QMainWindow):
    def __init__(self):
        super().__init__()

        self.table = QTableView()

        self.model = QSqlQueryModel()
        self.table.setModel(self.model)

        query = QSqlQuery(db=db)
        query.prepare(
            "SELECT Name, Composer, Album.Title FROM Track "
            "INNER JOIN Album ON Track.AlbumId = Album.AlbumId "
            "WHERE Album.Title LIKE '%' || :album_title || '%' "
        )
        query.bindValue(":album_title", "Sinatra")
        query.exec()

        self.model.setQuery(query)
        self.setMinimumSize(QSize(1024, 600))
        self.setCentralWidget(self.table)


app = QApplication(sys.argv)
window = MainWindow()
window.show()
app.exec()
```

Now that we want to add parameters to the query, we cannot pass it to `QSqlQuery` as it is created. Doing this would execute it immediately, without the parameter-replacement. Instead we now need to pass the query into `.prepare()`, telling the driver to identify parameters in the query and wait for the values.

Next, we bind each of our parameters using `.bindValue()` and finally call `query.exec()` to actually perform the query on the database.

This parameterized query is the equivalent of the following SQL —

```
SELECT Name, Composer, Album.Title FROM Track
INNER JOIN Album ON Track.AlbumId = Album.AlbumId
WHERE Album.Title LIKE '%Sinatra%'
```

This gives the following result —

Figure 156. The result of the parameterised query.

In this last example we add three search fields — one for the track title, one for the artist and one for the album title. We connect the `.textChanged` signals from each of these to a custom method that updates the parameters for the query.

Listing 127. databases/tableview_querymodel_search.py

```
import os
```

355

```python
import sys

from PyQt6.QtCore import QSize, Qt
from PyQt6.QtSql import QSqlDatabase, QSqlQuery, QSqlQueryModel
from PyQt6.QtWidgets import (
    QApplication,
    QHBoxLayout,
    QLineEdit,
    QMainWindow,
    QTableView,
    QVBoxLayout,
    QWidget,
)

basedir = os.path.dirname(__file__)

db = QSqlDatabase("QSQLITE")
db.setDatabaseName(os.path.join(basedir, "chinook.sqlite"))
db.open()


class MainWindow(QMainWindow):
    def __init__(self):
        super().__init__()

        container = QWidget()
        layout_search = QHBoxLayout()

        self.track = QLineEdit()
        self.track.setPlaceholderText("Track name...")
        self.track.textChanged.connect(self.update_query)

        self.composer = QLineEdit()
        self.composer.setPlaceholderText("Artist name...")
        self.composer.textChanged.connect(self.update_query)

        self.album = QLineEdit()
        self.album.setPlaceholderText("Album name...")
        self.album.textChanged.connect(self.update_query)

        layout_search.addWidget(self.track)
        layout_search.addWidget(self.composer)
        layout_search.addWidget(self.album)
```

```python
        layout_view = QVBoxLayout()
        layout_view.addLayout(layout_search)

        self.table = QTableView()

        layout_view.addWidget(self.table)

        container.setLayout(layout_view)

        self.model = QSqlQueryModel()
        self.table.setModel(self.model)

        self.query = QSqlQuery(db=db)

        self.query.prepare(
            "SELECT Name, Composer, Album.Title FROM Track "
            "INNER JOIN Album ON Track.AlbumId=Album.AlbumId WHERE "
            "Track.Name LIKE '%' || :track_name || '%' AND "
            "Track.Composer LIKE '%' || :track_composer || '%' AND "
            "Album.Title LIKE '%' || :album_title || '%'"
        )

        self.update_query()

        self.setMinimumSize(QSize(1024, 600))
        self.setCentralWidget(container)

    def update_query(self, s=None):

        # Get the text values from the widgets.
        track_name = self.track.text()
        track_composer = self.composer.text()
        album_title = self.album.text()

        self.query.bindValue(":track_name", track_name)
        self.query.bindValue(":track_composer", track_composer)
        self.query.bindValue(":album_title", album_title)

        self.query.exec()
        self.model.setQuery(self.query)
```

```
app = QApplication(sys.argv)
window = MainWindow()
window.show()
app.exec()
```

If you run this you can search the database using each of the fields independently, with the results updating automatically each time the search query changes.

Figure 157. The result of the multi-parameter search query.

QDataWidgetMapper

In all the examples so far we've displayed the output data from the database in a table, using `QTableView`. While this often makes sense for *viewing* data, for data input or editing it is usually preferable to display the inputs as a form which can be typed into and tabbed between.

 These are called create, read, update and delete (CRUD) operations and interfaces.

The full working example is shown below.

Listing 128. databases/widget_mapper.py

```python
import os
import sys

from PyQt6.QtCore import QSize, Qt
from PyQt6.QtSql import QSqlDatabase, QSqlTableModel
from PyQt6.QtWidgets import (
    QApplication,
    QComboBox,
    QDataWidgetMapper,
    QDoubleSpinBox,
    QFormLayout,
    QLabel,
    QLineEdit,
    QMainWindow,
    QSpinBox,
    QWidget,
)


basedir = os.path.dirname(__file__)


db = QSqlDatabase("QSQLITE")
db.setDatabaseName(os.path.join(basedir, "chinook.sqlite"))
db.open()


class MainWindow(QMainWindow):
    def __init__(self):
        super().__init__()

        form = QFormLayout()

        self.track_id = QSpinBox()
        self.track_id.setRange(0, 2147483647)
        self.track_id.setDisabled(True)
        self.name = QLineEdit()
        self.album = QComboBox()
        self.media_type = QComboBox()
        self.genre = QComboBox()
        self.composer = QLineEdit()

        self.milliseconds = QSpinBox()
        self.milliseconds.setRange(0, 2147483647)  ①
        self.milliseconds.setSingleStep(1)
```

```
            self.bytes = QSpinBox()
            self.bytes.setRange(0, 2147483647)
            self.bytes.setSingleStep(1)

            self.unit_price = QDoubleSpinBox()
            self.unit_price.setRange(0, 999)
            self.unit_price.setSingleStep(0.01)
            self.unit_price.setPrefix("$")

            form.addRow(QLabel("Track ID"), self.track_id)
            form.addRow(QLabel("Track name"), self.name)
            form.addRow(QLabel("Composer"), self.composer)
            form.addRow(QLabel("Milliseconds"), self.milliseconds)
            form.addRow(QLabel("Bytes"), self.bytes)
            form.addRow(QLabel("Unit Price"), self.unit_price)

            self.model = QSqlTableModel(db=db)

            self.mapper = QDataWidgetMapper()   ②
            self.mapper.setModel(self.model)

            self.mapper.addMapping(self.track_id, 0)   ③
            self.mapper.addMapping(self.name, 1)
            self.mapper.addMapping(self.composer, 5)
            self.mapper.addMapping(self.milliseconds, 6)
            self.mapper.addMapping(self.bytes, 7)
            self.mapper.addMapping(self.unit_price, 8)

            self.model.setTable("Track")
            self.model.select()   ④

            self.mapper.toFirst()   ⑤

            self.setMinimumSize(QSize(400, 400))

            widget = QWidget()
            widget.setLayout(form)
            self.setCentralWidget(widget)

app = QApplication(sys.argv)
window = MainWindow()
```

```
window.show()
app.exec()
```

① Widgets must be configured to accept all valid values from the table.

② One QDataWidgetMapper for all widgets.

③ Widgets are mapped to _columns.

④ Perform the select to populate the model.

⑤ Step the mapper forward to the first record.

If you run this example, you'll see the following window. The self.mapper.toFirst() call selects the first record in the table and this is then displayed in the mapped widgets.

Figure 158. Viewing a record via mapped widgets.

We currently can't change which record we are viewing or save any changes we make to records. To make this possible we can add 3 buttons — one each for browse *previous* and *next* through the records, and *save* to commit changes to the database. To do this we can hook up some QPushButton widgets to the *mapper* slots .toPrevious, .toNext and .submit.

Update the end of the __init__ method to add the following, adding the widgets into the existing layout.

Listing 129. databases/widget_mapper_controls.py

```python
        self.setMinimumSize(QSize(400, 400))

        controls = QHBoxLayout()

        prev_rec = QPushButton("Previous")
        prev_rec.clicked.connect(self.mapper.toPrevious)

        next_rec = QPushButton("Next")
        next_rec.clicked.connect(self.mapper.toNext)

        save_rec = QPushButton("Save Changes")
        save_rec.clicked.connect(self.mapper.submit)

        controls.addWidget(prev_rec)
        controls.addWidget(next_rec)
        controls.addWidget(save_rec)

        layout.addLayout(form)
        layout.addLayout(controls)

        widget = QWidget()
        widget.setLayout(layout)
        self.setCentralWidget(widget)
```

You will also need to update the imports at the top of the file to import
QPushButton and QHBoxLayout.

Listing 130. databases/widget_mapper_controls.py

```python
from PyQt6.QtWidgets import (
    QApplication,
    QComboBox,
    QDataWidgetMapper,
    QDoubleSpinBox,
    QFormLayout,
    QHBoxLayout,
    QLabel,
    QLineEdit,
    QMainWindow,
    QPushButton,
    QSpinBox,
    QVBoxLayout,
    QWidget,
)
```

Now you can browse between records in the *Tracks* table, make changes to the track data and submit these changes to the database. The full source code for this example is available at `databases/widget_mapper_controls.py` in the book source code.

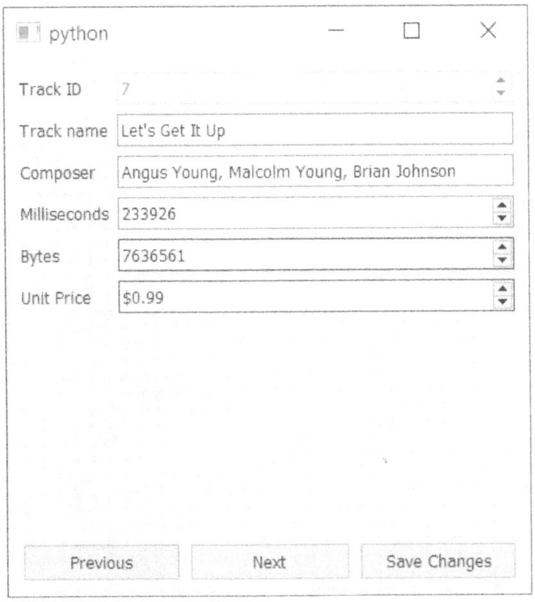

Figure 159. Viewing records, with previous/next controls and save to submit.

Authenticating with QSqlDatabase

In the examples so far we've used SQLite database files. But often you'll want to connect to a remote SQL server instead. That requires a few additional parameters, including the hostname (where the database is located) and a username and password if appropriate.

```python
# Create database connection.
db = QSqlDatabase('<driver>')
db.setHostName('<localhost>')
db.setDatabaseName('<databasename>')
db.setUserName('<username>')
db.setPassword('<password>')
db.open()
```

NOTE: The value of `<driver>` can be any one of the following `['QSQLITE', 'QMYSQL', 'QMYSQL3', 'QODBC', 'QODBC3', 'QPSQL', 'QPSQL7']`. To get this list on your system run `QSqlDatabase.drivers()`.

That's it! Once the connection is established, the models will behave exactly as before.

Custom Widgets

As we've seen, Qt comes with a wide range of widgets built-in, which you can use to build your applications. Even so, sometimes these simple widgets are not enough — maybe you need an input for some custom types, or want to visualize data in a unique way. In Qt you are free to create your own widgets, either from scratch or by combining existing widgets.

In this chapter we'll see how to use bitmap graphics and custom signals to create your very own widgets.

Figure 160. A custom color-gradient input, one of the widgets in our library.

 You may also want to check out our custom widget library [https://www.pythonguis.com/widgets/].

21. Bitmap Graphics in Qt

The first step towards creating custom widgets in PyQt6 is understanding bitmap (pixel-based) graphic operations. All standard widgets draw themselves as bitmaps on a rectangular "canvas" that forms the shape of the widget. Once you understand how this works you can draw any custom widget you like!

INFO: Bitmaps are rectangular grids of *pixels*, where each pixel (and its color) is represented by a number of "bits". They are distinct from vector graphics, where the image is stored as a series of line (or *vector*) drawing shapes which are used to form the image. If you're viewing vector graphics on your screen they are being *rasterised* — converted into a bitmap image — to be displayed as pixels on the screen.

In this tutorial we'll take a look at QPainter, Qt's API for performing bitmap graphic operations and the basis for drawing your own widgets. We'll go through some basic drawing operations and finally put it all together to create our own little Paint app.

QPainter

Bitmap drawing operations in Qt are handled through the QPainter class. This is a generic interface which can be used to draw on various *surfaces* including, for example, QPixmap. In this chapter we'll look at the QPainter drawing methods, first using primitive operations on a QPixmap surface, and then building a simple Paint application using what we've learnt.

To make this easy to demonstrate we'll be using the following stub application which handles creating our container (a QLabel) creating a pixmap canvas, setting that into the container and adding the container to the main window.

Listing 131. bitmap/stub.py

```python
import sys

from PyQt6.QtCore import Qt
from PyQt6.QtGui import QPixmap
from PyQt6.QtWidgets import QApplication, QLabel, QMainWindow


class MainWindow(QMainWindow):
    def __init__(self):
        super().__init__()

        self.label = QLabel()
        self.canvas = QPixmap(400, 300)     ①
        self.canvas.fill(Qt.GlobalColor.white)     ②

        self.setCentralWidget(self.label)
        self.draw_something()

    def draw_something(self):
        pass


app = QApplication(sys.argv)
window = MainWindow()
window.show()
app.exec()
```

① Create the `QPixmap` object we'll draw onto.

② Fill the entire canvas with white (so we can see our line).

 Why do we use `QLabel` to draw on? The `QLabel` widget can also be used to show images, and it's the simplest widget available for displaying a `QPixmap`.

We need to fill our canvas with white to begin with as depending on the platform and current dark mode, the background can be anything from light gray to black. We can start by drawing something really simple.

Listing 132. /bitmap/line.py

```python
import sys

from PyQt6.QtCore import Qt
from PyQt6.QtGui import QPainter, QPixmap
from PyQt6.QtWidgets import QApplication, QLabel, QMainWindow


class MainWindow(QMainWindow):
    def __init__(self):
        super().__init__()

        self.label = QLabel()
        self.canvas = QPixmap(400, 300)      ①
        self.canvas.fill(Qt.GlobalColor.white)      ②
        self.label.setPixmap(self.canvas)
        self.setCentralWidget(self.label)
        self.draw_something()

    def draw_something(self):
        painter = QPainter(self.canvas)
        painter.drawLine(10, 10, 300, 200)      ③
        painter.end()
        self.label.setPixmap(self.canvas)


app = QApplication(sys.argv)
window = MainWindow()
window.show()
app.exec()
```

① Create the `QPixmap` object we'll draw onto.

② Fill the entire canvas with white (so we can see our line).

③ Draw a line from (10, 10) to (300, 200). The coordinates are x, y with 0, 0 in the top left.

Save this to a file and run it and you should see the following — a single black line inside the window frame —

Figure 161. A single black line on the canvas.

All the drawing occurs within the draw_something method — we create a QPainter instance, passing in the canvas (self.label.pixmap()) and then issue a command to draw a line. Finally we call .end() to close the painter and apply the changes.

 You would usually also need to call .update() to trigger a refresh of the widget, but as we're drawing before the application window is shown a refresh is already going to occur automatically.

The coordinate system of QPainter puts 0, 0 in the top-left of the canvas, with x increasing towards the right and y increasing *down* the image. This may be surprising if you're used to graphing where 0, 0 is in the bottom-left.

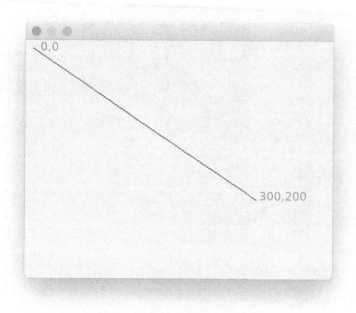

Figure 162. Black line annotated with the coordinates.

Drawing primitives

QPainter provides a huge number of methods for drawing shapes and lines on a bitmap surface (in 5.12 there are 192 QPainter specific non-event methods). The good news is that most of these are overloaded methods which are simply different ways of calling the same base methods.

For example, there are 5 different drawLine methods, all of which draw the same line, but differ in how the coordinates of what to draw are defined.

Method	Description
drawLine(line)	Draw a QLine instance
drawLine(line)	Draw a QLineF instance
drawLine(x1, y1, x2, y2)	Draw a line between x1, y2 and x2, y2 (both int).

Method	Description
drawLine(p1, p2)	Draw a line between point p1 and p2 (both QPoint)
drawLine(p1, p2)	Draw a line between point p1 and p2 (both QPointF)

If you're wondering what the difference is between a QLine and a QLineF , the latter has its coordinates specified as float. This is convenient if you have float positions as the result of other calculations, but otherwise not so much.

Ignoring the F-variants, we have 3 unique ways to draw a line — with a line object, with two sets of coordinates (x1, y1), (x2, y2) or with two QPoint objects. When you discover that a QLine itself is defined as `QLine(const QPoint & p1, const QPoint & p2)` or `QLine(int x1, int y1, int x2, int y2)` you see that they are all in fact, exactly the same thing. The different call signatures are simply there for convenience.

 Given the x1, y1, x2, y2 coordinates, the two QPoint objects would be defined as QPoint(x1, y1) and QPoint(x2, y2).

So, leaving out the duplicates we have the following draw operations —drawArc , drawChord, drawConvexPolygon, drawEllipse,drawLine, drawPath, drawPie, drawPoint, drawPolygon, drawPolyline, drawRect, drawRects and drawRoundedRect. To avoid get overwhelmed we'll focus first on the primitive shapes and lines first and return to the more complicated operations once we have the basics down.

 For each example, replace the draw_something method in your stub application and re-run it to see the output.

drawPoint

This draws a point, or *pixel* at a given point on the canvas. Each call to drawPoint draws one pixel. Replace your draw_something code with the following.

Listing 133. bitmap/point.py

```python
def draw_something(self):
    painter = QPainter(self.canvas)
    painter.drawPoint(200, 150)
    painter.end()
    self.label.setPixmap(self.canvas)
```

If you re-run the file you will see a window, but this time there is a single dot, in black in the middle of it. You may need to move the window around to spot it.

Figure 163. Drawing a single point (pixel) with QPainter.

That really isn't much to look at. To make things more interesting we can change the color and size of the point we're drawing. In PyQt6 the color and thickness of lines is defined using the active *pen* on the QPainter. You can set this by creating a QPen instance and applying it.

Listing 134. bitmap/point_with_pen.py

```python
def draw_something(self):
    painter = QPainter(self.canvas)
    pen = QPen()
    pen.setWidth(40)
    pen.setColor(QColor("red"))
    painter.setPen(pen)
    painter.drawPoint(200, 150)
    painter.end()
    self.label.setPixmap(self.canvas)
```

This will give the following mildly more interesting result..

Figure 164. A big red dot.

You are free to perform multiple draw operations with your QPainter until the painter is *ended*. Drawing onto the canvas is very quick — here we're drawing 10k dots at random.

Listing 135. bitmap/points.py

```
from random import choice, randint  ①

    def draw_something(self):
        painter = QPainter(self.canvas)
        pen = QPen()
        pen.setWidth(3)
        painter.setPen(pen)

        for n in range(10000):
            painter.drawPoint(
                200 + randint(-100, 100),
                150 + randint(-100, 100),  # x  # y
            )
        painter.end()
        self.label.setPixmap(self.canvas)
```

① Add this import at the top of the file.

The dots are 3 pixel-width and black (the default pen).

Figure 165. 10k 3-pixel dots on a canvas.

You will often want to update the current pen while drawing — e.g. to draw multiple points in different colors while keeping other characteristics (width) the same. To do this without recreating a new QPen instance each time you can get the current active pen from the QPainter using pen = painter.pen(). You can also re-apply an existing pen multiple times, changing it each time.

Listing 136. bitmap/points_color.py

```python
def draw_something(self):
    colors = [
        "#FFD141",
        "#376F9F",
        "#0D1F2D",
        "#E9EBEF",
        "#EB5160",
    ]

    painter = QPainter(self.canvas)
    pen = QPen()
    pen.setWidth(3)
    painter.setPen(pen)

    for n in range(10000):
        # pen = painter.pen() you could get the active pen here
        pen.setColor(QColor(choice(colors)))
        painter.setPen(pen)
        painter.drawPoint(
            200 + randint(-100, 100),
            150 + randint(-100, 100),  # x  # y
        )
    painter.end()
    self.label.setPixmap(self.canvas)
```

Will produce the following output —

Figure 166. Random pattern of 3 width dots.

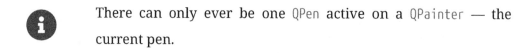

There can only ever be one `QPen` active on a `QPainter` — the current pen.

That's about as much excitement as you can have drawing dots onto a screen, so we'll move on to look at some other drawing operations.

drawLine

We already drew a line on the canvas at the beginning to test things are working. But what we didn't try was setting the pen to control the line appearance.

Listing 137. bitmap/line_with_pen.py

```python
def draw_something(self):
    painter = QPainter(self.canvas)
    pen = QPen()
    pen.setWidth(15)
    pen.setColor(QColor("blue"))
    painter.setPen(pen)
    painter.drawLine(QPoint(100, 100), QPoint(300, 200))
    painter.end()
    self.label.setPixmap(self.canvas)
```

In this example we're also using `QPoint` to define the two points to connect with a line, rather than passing individual `x1`, `y1`, `x2`, `y2` parameters — remember that both methods are functionally identical.

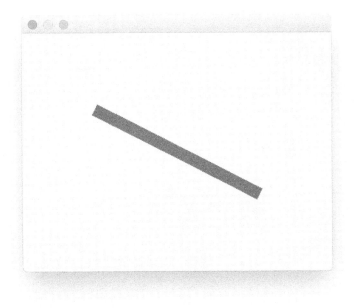

Figure 167. A thick blue line.

drawRect, drawRects **and** drawRoundedRect

These functions all draw rectangles, defined by a series of points, or by `QRect` or `QRectF` instances.

Listing 138. bitmap/rect.py

```python
def draw_something(self):
    painter = QPainter(self.canvas)
    pen = QPen()
    pen.setWidth(3)
    pen.setColor(QColor("#EB5160"))
    painter.setPen(pen)
    painter.drawRect(50, 50, 100, 100)
    painter.drawRect(60, 60, 150, 100)
    painter.drawRect(70, 70, 100, 150)
    painter.drawRect(80, 80, 150, 100)
    painter.drawRect(90, 90, 100, 150)
    painter.end()
    self.label.setPixmap(self.canvas)
```

 A square is just a rectangle with the same width and height

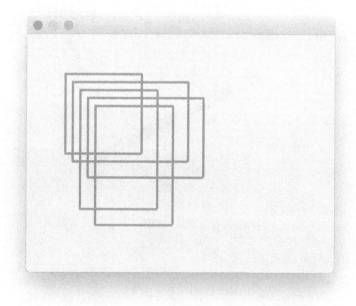

Figure 168. Drawing rectangles.

You can also replace the multiple calls to drawRect with a single call to drawRects passing in multiple QRect objects. This will product exactly the same result.

```
painter.drawRects(
    QtCore.QRect(50, 50, 100, 100),
    QtCore.QRect(60, 60, 150, 100),
    QtCore.QRect(70, 70, 100, 150),
    QtCore.QRect(80, 80, 150, 100),
    QtCore.QRect(90, 90, 100, 150),
)
```

Drawn shapes can be filled in PyQt6 by setting the current active painter *brush*, passing in a QBrush instance to painter.setBrush(). The following example fills all rectangles with a patterned yellow color.

Listing 139. bitmap/rect_with_brush.py

```
def draw_something(self):
    painter = QPainter(self.canvas)
    pen = QPen()
    pen.setWidth(3)
    pen.setColor(QColor("#376F9F"))
    painter.setPen(pen)

    brush = QBrush()
    brush.setColor(QColor("#FFD141"))
    brush.setStyle(Qt.BrushStyle.Dense1Pattern)
    painter.setBrush(brush)

    painter.drawRects(
        QRect(50, 50, 100, 100),
        QRect(60, 60, 150, 100),
        QRect(70, 70, 100, 150),
        QRect(80, 80, 150, 100),
        QRect(90, 90, 100, 150),
    )
    painter.end()
    self.label.setPixmap(self.canvas)
```

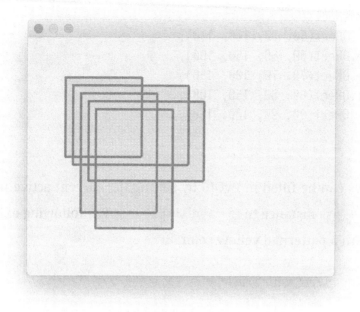

Figure 169. Filled rectangles.

As for the pen, there is only ever one brush active on a given painter, but you can switch between them or change them while drawing. There are a number of brush style patterns available [https://doc.qt.io/qt-6/qt.html#BrushStyle-enum]. You'll probably use `Qt.BrushStyle.SolidPattern` more than any others though.

 You **must** set a style to see any fill at all as the default is `Qt.BrushStyle.NoBrush`.

The `drawRoundedRect` methods draw a rectangle, but with rounded edges, and so take two extra parameters for the x & y *radius* of the corners.

Listing 140. bitmap/roundrect.py

```python
def draw_something(self):
    painter = QPainter(self.canvas)
    pen = QPen()
    pen.setWidth(3)
    pen.setColor(QColor("#376F9F"))
    painter.setPen(pen)
    painter.drawRoundedRect(40, 40, 100, 100, 10, 10)
    painter.drawRoundedRect(80, 80, 100, 100, 10, 50)
    painter.drawRoundedRect(120, 120, 100, 100, 50, 10)
    painter.drawRoundedRect(160, 160, 100, 100, 50, 50)
    painter.end()
    self.label.setPixmap(self.canvas)
```

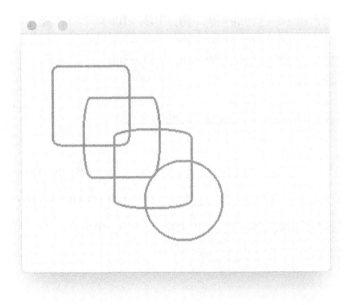

Figure 170. Rounded rectangles.

There is an optional final parameter to toggle between the x & y ellipse radii of the corners being defined in absolute pixel terms `Qt.SizeMode.RelativeSize` (the default) or relative to the size of the rectangle (passed as a value 0...100). Pass `Qt.SizeMode.RelativeSize` to enable this.

drawEllipse

The final primitive draw method we'll look at now is drawEllipse which can be used to draw an *ellipse* or a *circle*.

 A circle is just an ellipse with an equal width and height.

Listing 141. bitmap/ellipse.py

```
def draw_something(self):
    painter = QPainter(self.canvas)
    pen = QPen()
    pen.setWidth(3)
    pen.setColor(QColor(204, 0, 0))  # r, g, b
    painter.setPen(pen)

    painter.drawEllipse(10, 10, 100, 100)
    painter.drawEllipse(10, 10, 150, 200)
    painter.drawEllipse(10, 10, 200, 300)
    painter.end()

    self.label.setPixmap(self.canvas)
```

In this example drawEllipse is taking 4 parameters, with the first two being the x & y position of the *top left of the rectangle* in which the ellipse will be drawn, while the last two parameters are the width and height of that rectangle respectively.

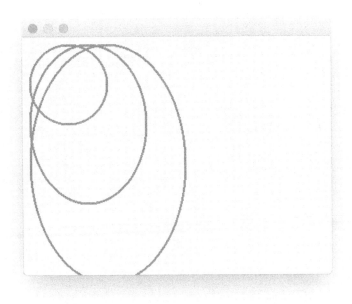

Figure 171. Drawing an ellipse with x, y, width, height or QRect.

 You can achieve the same by passing in a QRect

There is another call signature which takes the *center of the ellipse* as the first parameter, provided as QPoint or QPointF object, and then a x and y *radius*. The example below shows it in action.

```
painter.drawEllipse(QtCore.QPoint(100, 100), 10, 10)
painter.drawEllipse(QtCore.QPoint(100, 100), 15, 20)
painter.drawEllipse(QtCore.QPoint(100, 100), 20, 30)
painter.drawEllipse(QtCore.QPoint(100, 100), 25, 40)
painter.drawEllipse(QtCore.QPoint(100, 100), 30, 50)
painter.drawEllipse(QtCore.QPoint(100, 100), 35, 60)
```

Figure 172. Drawing an ellipse using Point & radius.

You can fill ellipses using the same QBrush approach described for rectangles.

Text

Finally, we'll take a brief tour through the QPainter text drawing methods. To control the current font on a QPainter you use setFont passing in a QFont instance. With this you can control the family, weight and size (among other things) of the text you write. The color of the text is still defined using the current pen, however the width of the pen has no effect.

Listing 142. bitmap/text.py

```python
def draw_something(self):
    painter = QPainter(self.canvas)

    pen = QPen()
    pen.setWidth(1)
    pen.setColor(QColor("green"))
    painter.setPen(pen)

    font = QFont()
    font.setFamily("Times")
    font.setBold(True)
    font.setPointSize(40)
    painter.setFont(font)

    painter.drawText(100, 100, "Hello, world!")
    painter.end()
    self.label.setPixmap(self.canvas)
```

You can also specify location with `QPoint` or `QPointF`.

Figure 173. Bitmap text hello world example.

There are also methods for drawing text within a specified area. Here the parameters define the x & y position and the width & height of the bounding box. Text outside this box is clipped (hidden). The 5th parameter *flags* can be used to control alignment of the text within the box among other things.

```
painter.drawText(100, 100, 100, 100, Qt.AlignmentFlag.AlignHCenter,
'Hello, world!')
```

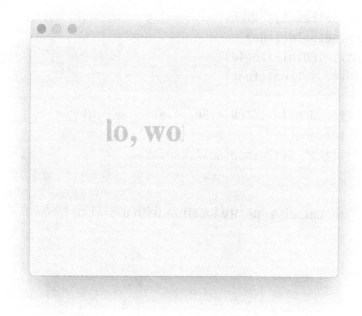

Figure 174. Bounding box clipped on drawText.

You have complete control over the display of text by setting the active font on the painter via a QFont object. Check out the QFont documentation [https://doc.qt.io/qt-6/qfont.html] for more information.

A bit of fun with QPainter

That got a bit heavy, so let's take a breather and make something fun. So far we've been programmatically defining the draw operations to perform on the QPixmap surface. But we can just as easily draw in response to user input — for example allowing a user to scribble all over the canvas. Let's take what we've learned so far and use it to build a rudimentary Paint app.

We can start with the same simple application outline, adding a `mouseMoveEvent` handler to the `MainWindow` class in place of our draw method. Here we take the current position of the user's mouse and draw it to the canvas.

Listing 143. bitmap/paint_start.py

```python
import sys

from PyQt6.QtCore import Qt
from PyQt6.QtGui import QPainter, QPixmap
from PyQt6.QtWidgets import QApplication, QLabel, QMainWindow


class MainWindow(QMainWindow):
    def __init__(self):
        super().__init__()

        self.label = QLabel()
        self.canvas = QPixmap(400, 300)
        self.canvas.fill(Qt.GlobalColor.white)
        self.label.setPixmap(self.canvas)
        self.setCentralWidget(self.label)

    def mouseMoveEvent(self, e):
        pos = e.position()
        painter = QPainter(self.canvas)
        painter.drawPoint(pos.x(), pos.y())
        painter.end()
        self.label.setPixmap(self.canvas)


app = QApplication(sys.argv)
window = MainWindow()
window.show()
app.exec()
```

Widgets by default only receive mouse move events when a mouse button is pressed, unless *mouse tracking* is enabled. This can be configured using the `.setMouseTracking` method — setting this to `True` (it is `False` by default) will track the mouse continuously.

If you save this and run it you should be able to move your mouse over the screen and click to draw individual points. It should look something like this —

Figure 175. Drawing individual mouseMoveEvent points.

The issue here is that when you move the mouse around quickly it actually jumps between locations on the screen, rather than moving smoothly from one place to the next. The `mouseMoveEvent` is fired for each location the mouse is in, but that's not enough to draw a continuous line, unless you move *very slowly*.

The solution to this is to draw *lines* instead of *points*. On each event we simply draw a line from where we were (previous .x() and .y()) to where we are now (current .x() and .y()). We can do this by tracking last_x and last_y ourselves.

We also need to *forget* the last position when releasing the mouse, or we'll start drawing from that location again after moving the mouse across the page — i.e. we won't be able to break the line.

Listing 144. bitmap/paint_line.py

```python
import sys

from PyQt6.QtCore import Qt
from PyQt6.QtGui import QPainter, QPixmap
from PyQt6.QtWidgets import QApplication, QLabel, QMainWindow


class MainWindow(QMainWindow):
    def __init__(self):
        super().__init__()

        self.label = QLabel()
        self.canvas = QPixmap(400, 300)
        self.canvas.fill(Qt.GlobalColor.white)
        self.label.setPixmap(self.canvas)
        self.setCentralWidget(self.label)

        self.last_x, self.last_y = None, None

    def mouseMoveEvent(self, e):
        pos = e.position()
        if self.last_x is None:  # First event.
            self.last_x = pos.x()
            self.last_y = pos.y()
            return  # Ignore the first time.

        painter = QPainter(self.canvas)
        painter.drawLine(self.last_x, self.last_y, pos.x(), pos.y())
        painter.end()

        self.label.setPixmap(self.canvas)
```

```
        # Update the origin for next time.
        self.last_x = pos.x()
        self.last_y = pos.y()

    def mouseReleaseEvent(self, e):
        self.last_x = None
        self.last_y = None


app = QApplication(sys.argv)
window = MainWindow()
window.show()
app.exec()
```

If you run this you should be able to scribble on the screen as you would expect.

Figure 176. Drawing with the mouse, using a continuous line.

It's still a bit dull, so let's add a simple palette to allow us to change the pen color.

This requires a bit of re-architecting to ensure the mouse position is detected accurately. So far we've using the `mouseMoveEvent` on the `QMainWindow` . When we only have a single widget in the window this is fine — as long as you don't resize the window, the coordinates of the container and the single nested widget line up. However, if we add other widgets to the layout this won't hold — the coordinates of the `QLabel` will be offset from the window, and we'll be drawing in the wrong location.

This is easily fixed by moving the mouse handling onto the `QLabel` itself— it's event coordinates are always relative to itself. This we wrap up as an individual `Canvas` object, which handles the creation of the pixmap surface, sets up the x & y locations and the holds the current pen color (set to black by default).

 This self-contained `Canvas` is a drop-in drawable surface you could use in your own apps.

Listing 145. bitmap/paint.py

```python
import sys

from PyQt6.QtCore import QPoint, QSize, Qt
from PyQt6.QtGui import QColor, QPainter, QPen, QPixmap
from PyQt6.QtWidgets import (
    QApplication,
    QHBoxLayout,
    QLabel,
    QMainWindow,
    QPushButton,
    QVBoxLayout,
    QWidget,
)

class Canvas(QLabel):
    def __init__(self):
        super().__init__()
        self._pixmap = QPixmap(600, 300)
```

```python
        self._pixmap.fill(Qt.GlobalColor.white)
        self.setPixmap(self._pixmap)

        self.last_x, self.last_y = None, None
        self.pen_color = QColor("#000000")

    def set_pen_color(self, c):
        self.pen_color = QColor(c)

    def mouseMoveEvent(self, e):
        pos = e.position()
        if self.last_x is None:  # First event.
            self.last_x = pos.x()
            self.last_y = pos.y()
            return  # Ignore the first time.

        painter = QPainter(self._pixmap)
        p = painter.pen()
        p.setWidth(4)
        p.setColor(self.pen_color)
        painter.setPen(p)
        painter.drawLine(self.last_x, self.last_y, pos.x(), pos.y())
        painter.end()
        self.setPixmap(self._pixmap)

        # Update the origin for next time.
        self.last_x = pos.x()
        self.last_y = pos.y()

    def mouseReleaseEvent(self, e):
        self.last_x = None
        self.last_y = None
```

For the color selection we're going to build a custom widget, based off QPushButton. This widget accepts a `color` parameter which can be a QColor instance, or a color name ('red', 'black') or hex value. This color is set on the background of the widget to make it identifiable. We can use the standard QPushButton.pressed signal to hook it up to any actions.

Listing 146. bitmap/paint.py

```python
COLORS = [
    # 17 undertones https://lospec.com/palette-list/17undertones
    "#000000",
    "#141923",
    "#414168",
    "#3a7fa7",
    "#35e3e3",
    "#8fd970",
    "#5ebb49",
    "#458352",
    "#dcd37b",
    "#fffee5",
    "#ffd035",
    "#cc9245",
    "#a15c3e",
    "#a42f3b",
    "#f45b7a",
    "#c24998",
    "#81588d",
    "#bcb0c2",
    "#ffffff",
]
class QPaletteButton(QPushButton):
    def __init__(self, color):
        super().__init__()
        self.setFixedSize(QSize(24, 24))
        self.color = color
        self.setStyleSheet("background-color: %s;" % color)
```

With those two new parts defined, we simply need to iterate over our list of colors, create a QPaletteButton for each, passing in the color. Then connect its pressed signal to the set_pen_color handler on the canvas (indirectly through a lambda to pass the additional color data) and add it to the palette layout.

Listing 147. bitmap/paint.py

```python
class MainWindow(QMainWindow):
    def __init__(self):
        super().__init__()

        self.canvas = Canvas()

        w = QWidget()
        l = QVBoxLayout()
        w.setLayout(l)
        l.addWidget(self.canvas)

        palette = QHBoxLayout()
        self.add_palette_buttons(palette)
        l.addLayout(palette)

        self.setCentralWidget(w)

    def add_palette_buttons(self, layout):
        for c in COLORS:
            b = QPaletteButton(c)
            b.pressed.connect(lambda c=c: self.canvas.set_pen_color(
c))
            layout.addWidget(b)


app = QApplication(sys.argv)
window = MainWindow()
window.show()
app.exec()
```

This should give you a fully-functioning multicolor paint application, where you can draw lines on the canvas and select colors from the palette.

Figure 177. Unfortunately, it doesn't make you good.

Unfortunately, it doesn't make you a good artist.

Spray

For a final bit of fun you can switch out the `mouseMoveEvent` with the following to draw with a "spray can" effect instead of a line. This is simulated using `random.gauss` to generate a series of *normally distributed* dots around the current mouse position which we plot with `drawPoint`.

Listing 148. bitmap/spraypaint.py

```python
import random
import sys

from PyQt6.QtCore import QSize, Qt
from PyQt6.QtGui import QColor, QPainter, QPen, QPixmap
from PyQt6.QtWidgets import (
    QApplication,
    QHBoxLayout,
    QLabel,
    QMainWindow,
    QPushButton,
    QVBoxLayout,
    QWidget,
)
```

```
SPRAY_PARTICLES = 100
SPRAY_DIAMETER = 10

class Canvas(QLabel):
    def __init__(self):
        super().__init__()
        self._pixmap = QPixmap(600, 300)
        self._pixmap.fill(Qt.GlobalColor.white)
        self.setPixmap(self._pixmap)

        self.pen_color = QColor("#000000")

    def set_pen_color(self, c):
        self.pen_color = QColor(c)

    def mouseMoveEvent(self, e):
        pos = e.position()
        painter = QPainter(self._pixmap)
        p = painter.pen()
        p.setWidth(1)
        p.setColor(self.pen_color)
        painter.setPen(p)

        for n in range(SPRAY_PARTICLES):
            xo = random.gauss(0, SPRAY_DIAMETER)
            yo = random.gauss(0, SPRAY_DIAMETER)
            painter.drawPoint(pos.x() + xo, pos.y() + yo)

        self.setPixmap(self._pixmap)
```

 For the spray can we don't need to track the previous position, as we always spray around the current point.

Define the SPRAY_PARTICLES and SPRAY_DIAMETER variables at the top of your file and import the random standard library module. The image below shows the spray behavior when using the following settings:

```
import random

SPRAY_PARTICLES = 100
SPRAY_DIAMETER = 10
```

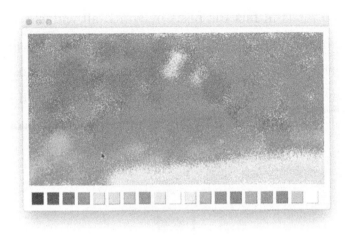

Figure 178. Just call me Picasso.

If you want a challenge, you could try adding an additional button to toggle between draw and spray mode, or an input widget to define the brush/spray diameter.

 For a fully-functional drawing app written with Python & Qt check out Piecasso [https://github.com/learnpyqt/15-minute-apps/tree/master/paint] in our "Minute apps" repository on Github.

This introduction should have given you a good idea of what you can do with QPainter. As described, this system is the basis of all widget drawing. If you want to look further, check out the widget .paint() method, which receives a QPainter instance, to allow the widget to draw on itself. The same methods you've learnt here can be used in .paint() to draw some basic custom widgets.

22. Creating Custom Widgets

In the previous chapter we introduced QPainter and looked at some basic bitmap drawing operations which you can used to draw dots, lines, rectangles and circles on a QPainter *surface* such as a QPixmap. This process of *drawing on a surface* with QPainter is in fact the basis by which all widgets in Qt are drawn. Now you know how to use QPainter you know how to draw your own custom widgets! In this chapter we'll take what we've learnt so far and use it to construct a completely new *custom* widget. For a working example we'll be building the following widget — a customizable PowerBar meter with a dial control.

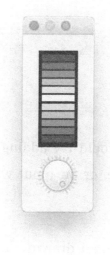

Figure 179. PowerBar meter.

This widget is actually a mix of a *compound widget* and *custom widget* in that we are using the built-in Qt QDial component for the dial, while drawing the power bar ourselves. We then assemble these two parts together into a parent widget which can be dropped into place seamlessly in any application, without needing to know how it's put together. The resulting widget provides the common QAbstractSlider interface with some additions for configuring the bar display.

After following this example you will be able to build your very own custom widgets — whether they are compounds of built-ins or completely novel self-drawn wonders.

Getting started

As we've previously seen compound widgets are simply widgets with a layout applied, which itself contains >1 other widget. The resulting "widget" can then be used as any other, with the internals hidden/exposed as you like.

The outline for our **PowerBar** widget is given below — we'll build our custom widget up gradually from this outline stub.

Listing 149. custom-widgets/stub.py

```python
import sys

from PyQt6 import QtCore, QtGui, QtWidgets
from PyQt6.QtCore import Qt


class _Bar(QtWidgets.QWidget):
    pass


class PowerBar(QtWidgets.QWidget):
    """
    Custom Qt Widget to show a power bar and dial.
    Demonstrating compound and custom-drawn widget.
    """

    def __init__(self, parent=None, steps=5):
        super().__init__(parent)

        layout = QtWidgets.QVBoxLayout()
        self._bar = _Bar()
        layout.addWidget(self._bar)

        self._dial = QtWidgets.QDial()
        layout.addWidget(self._dial)

        self.setLayout(layout)


app = QtWidgets.QApplication(sys.argv)
volume = PowerBar()
volume.show()
app.exec()
```

This simply defines our custom power bar is defined in the _Bar object — here just unaltered subclass of QWidget. The PowerBar widget (which is the complete widget) combines this, using a QVBoxLayout with the built in QDial to display them together.

We don't need to create a `QMainWindow` since any widget without a parent is a window in it's own right. Our custom `PowerBar` widget will appear as any normal window.

You can run this file at any time to see your widget in action. Run it now and you should see something like this:

Figure 180. PowerBar dial.

If you stretch the window down you'll see the dial has more space above it than below — this is being taken up by our (currently invisible) `_Bar` widget.

paintEvent

The `paintEvent` handler is the core of all widget drawing in PyQt6. Every complete and partial re-draw of a widget is triggered through a `paintEvent` which the widget handles to draw itself. A `paintEvent` can be triggered by —

- repaint() [https://doc.qt.io/qt-6/qwidget.html#repaint] or update() [https://doc.qt.io/qt-6/qwidget.html#update] was called

- the widget was obscured and has now been uncovered

- the widget has been resized

— but it can also occur for many other reasons. What is important is that when a `paintEvent` is triggered your widget is able to redraw it.

If a widget is simple enough (like ours is) you can often get away with simply redrawing the entire thing any time *anything* happens. But for more complicated widgets this can get very inefficient. For these cases the `paintEvent` includes the specific region that needs to be updated. We'll make use of this in later, more complicated examples.

For now we'll do something very simple, and just fill the entire widget with a single color. This will allow us to see the area we're working with to start drawing the bar. Add the following code to the `_Bar` class.

Listing 150. custom-widgets/powerbar_1.py

```python
def paintEvent(self, e):
    painter = QtGui.QPainter(self)
    brush = QtGui.QBrush()
    brush.setColor(QtGui.QColor("black"))
    brush.setStyle(Qt.BrushStyle.SolidPattern)
    rect = QtCore.QRect(
        0,
        0,
        painter.device().width(),
        painter.device().height(),
    )
    painter.fillRect(rect, brush)
```

Positioning

Now we can see the `_Bar` widget we can tweak its positioning and size. If you drag around the shape of the window you'll see the two widgets changing shape to fit the space available. This is what we want, but the `QDial` is also expanding vertically more than it should, and leaving empty space we could use for the bar.

Figure 181. PowerBar stretched leaves empty space.

We can use setSizePolicy on our _Bar widget to make sure it expands as far as possible. By using the QSizePolicy.MinimumExpanding the provided sizeHint will be used as a minimum, and the widget will expand as much as possible.

Listing 151. custom-widgets/powerbar_2.py

```python
class _Bar(QtWidgets.QWidget):
    def __init__(self):
        super().__init__()

        self.setSizePolicy(
            QtWidgets.QSizePolicy.Policy.MinimumExpanding,
            QtWidgets.QSizePolicy.Policy.MinimumExpanding,
        )

    def sizeHint(self):
        return QtCore.QSize(40, 120)

    def paintEvent(self, e):
        painter = QtGui.QPainter(self)
        brush = QtGui.QBrush()
        brush.setColor(QtGui.QColor("black"))
        brush.setStyle(Qt.BrushStyle.SolidPattern)
        rect = QtCore.QRect(
            0,
            0,
            painter.device().width(),
            painter.device().height(),
        )
        painter.fillRect(rect, brush)
```

It's still not *perfect* as the QDial widget resizes itself a bit awkwardly, but our bar is now expanding to fill all the available space.

Figure 182. PowerBar with policy set to QSizePolicy.MinimumExpanding.

With the positioning sorted we can now move on to define our paint methods to draw our PowerBar meter in the top part (currently black) of the widget.

Updating the display

We now have our canvas completely filled in black, next we'll use QPainter draw commands to actually draw something on the widget.

Before we start on the bar, we've got a bit of testing to do to make sure we can update the display with the values of our dial. Update the _Bar.paintEvent with the following code.

Listing 152. custom-widgets/powerbar_3.py

```python
def paintEvent(self, e):
    painter = QtGui.QPainter(self)

    brush = QtGui.QBrush()
    brush.setColor(QtGui.QColor("black"))
    brush.setStyle(Qt.BrushStyle.SolidPattern)
    rect = QtCore.QRect(
        0,
        0,
        painter.device().width(),
        painter.device().height(),
    )
    painter.fillRect(rect, brush)

    # Get current state.
    dial = self.parent()._dial
    vmin, vmax = dial.minimum(), dial.maximum()
    value = dial.value()

    pen = painter.pen()
    pen.setColor(QtGui.QColor("red"))
    painter.setPen(pen)

    font = painter.font()
    font.setFamily("Times")
    font.setPointSize(18)
    painter.setFont(font)

    painter.drawText(
        25, 25, "{}-->{}<--{}".format(vmin, value, vmax)
    )
    painter.end()
```

This draws the black background as before, then uses .parent() to access our
parent PowerBar widget and through that the QDial via _dial. From there we get
the current value, as well as the allowed range minimum and maximum values.
Finally we draw those using the painter, just like we did in the previous part.

We're leaving handling of the current value, min and max values to the QDial here, but we could also store that value ourselves and use signals to/from the dial to keep things in sync.

Run this, wiggle the dial around and .....nothing happens. Although we've defined the paintEvent handler we're not triggering a repaint when the dial changes.

You can force a refresh by resizing the window, as soon as you do this you should see the text appear. Neat, but terrible UX — "just resize your app to see your settings!"

To fix this we need to hook up our _Bar widget to repaint itself in response to changing values on the dial. We can do this using the QDial.valueChanged`signal, hooking it up to a custom slot method which calls `.refresh() — triggering a full-repaint.

Add the following method to the _Bar widget.

Listing 153. custom-widgets/powerbar_4.py

```
def _trigger_refresh(self):
    self.update()
```

...and add the following to the __init__ block for the parent PowerBar widget.

Listing 154. custom-widgets/powerbar_4.py

```
self._dial = QtWidgets.QDial()
self._dial.valueChanged.connect(self._bar._trigger_refresh)
layout.addWidget(self._dial)
```

If you re-run the code now, you will see the display updating automatically as you turn the dial (click and drag with your mouse). The current value is displayed as text.

Figure 183. PowerBar displaying current value as text.

Drawing the bar

Now we have the display updating and displaying the current value of the dial, we can move onto drawing the actual bar display. This is a little complicated, with a bit of maths to calculate bar positions, but we'll step through it to make it clear what's going on.

The sketch below shows what we are aiming for — a series of **N** boxes, inset from the edges of the widget, with spaces between them.

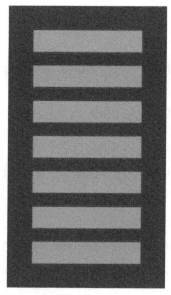

Figure 184. The bar segments and layout we're aiming for.

Calculating what to draw

The number of boxes to draw is determined by the current value — and how far along it is between the minimum and maximum value configured for the QDial. We already have that information in the example above.

```
dial = self.parent()._dial
vmin, vmax = dial.minimum(), dial.maximum()
value = dial.value()
```

If value is half way between vmin and vmax then we want to draw half of the boxes (if we have 4 boxes total, draw 2). If value is at vmax we want to draw them all.

To do this we first convert our value into a number between 0 and 1, where 0 = vmin and 1 = vmax. We first subtract vmin from value to adjust the range of possible values to start from zero — i.e. from vmin···vmax to 0···(vmax-vmin). Dividing this value by vmax-vmin (the new maximum) then gives us a number between 0 and 1.

The trick then is to multiply this value (called pc below) by the number of steps and that gives us a number between 0 and 5 — the number of boxes to draw.

```
pc = (value - vmin) / (vmax - vmin)
n_steps_to_draw = int(pc * 5)
```

We're wrapping the result in int to convert it to a whole number (rounding down) to remove any partial boxes.

Update the drawText method in your paint event to write out this number instead.

Listing 155. custom-widgets/powerbar_5.py

```python
def paintEvent(self, e):
    painter = QtGui.QPainter(self)

    brush = QtGui.QBrush()
    brush.setColor(QtGui.QColor("black"))
    brush.setStyle(Qt.BrushStyle.SolidPattern)
    rect = QtCore.QRect(
        0,
        0,
        painter.device().width(),
        painter.device().height(),
    )
    painter.fillRect(rect, brush)

    # Get current state.
    dial = self.parent()._dial
    vmin, vmax = dial.minimum(), dial.maximum()
    value = dial.value()

    pen = painter.pen()
    pen.setColor(QtGui.QColor("red"))
    painter.setPen(pen)

    font = painter.font()
    font.setFamily("Times")
    font.setPointSize(18)
    painter.setFont(font)

    pc = (value - vmin) / (vmax - vmin)
    n_steps_to_draw = int(pc * 5)
    painter.drawText(25, 25, "{}".format(n_steps_to_draw))
    painter.end()
```

As you turn the dial you will now see a number between 0 and 5.

Drawing boxes

Next we want to convert this number 0...5 to a number of bars drawn on the canvas. Start by removing the drawText and font and pen settings, as we no longer need those.

To draw accurately we need to know the size of our canvas — i.e the size of the widget. We will also add a bit of padding around the edges to give space around the edges of the blocks against the black background.

 All measurements in the QPainter are in pixels.

Listing 156. custom-widgets/powerbar_6.py

```
padding = 5

# Define our canvas.
d_height = painter.device().height() - (padding * 2)
d_width = painter.device().width() - (padding * 2)
```

We take the height and width and subtract `2 * padding` from each — it's 2x because we're padding both the left and right (and top and bottom) edges. This gives us our resulting *active canvas* area in d_height and d_width.

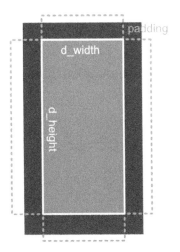

Figure 185. The padding on the outside of the layout.

We need to break up our d_height into 5 equal parts, one for each block — we can calculate that height simply by d_height / 5. Additionally, since we want spaces between the blocks we need to calculate how much of this step size is taken up by space (top and bottom, so halved) and how much is actual block.

Listing 157. custom-widgets/powerbar_6.py

```
        step_size = d_height / 5
        bar_height = step_size * 0.6
```

These values are all we need to draw our blocks on our canvas. To do this we count up to the number of steps-1 starting from 0 using range and then draw a fillRect over a region for each block.

Listing 158. custom-widgets/powerbar_6.py

```
        brush.setColor(QtGui.QColor("red"))

        for n in range(n_steps_to_draw):
            ypos = (1 + n) * step_size
            rect = QtCore.QRect(
                padding,
                padding + d_height - int(ypos),
                d_width,
                int(bar_height),
            )
            painter.fillRect(rect, brush)
```

There is a lot going on in the placement calculations for the blocks, so let's step through those first.

The box to draw with fillRect is defined as a QRect object to which we pass, in turn, the left x, top y, width and height.

The *width* is the full canvas width minus the padding, which we previously calculated and stored in d_width. The *left x* is similarly just the padding value (5px) from the left hand side of the widget.

The *height* of the bar bar_height`we calculated as 0.6 times the `step_size.

This leaves parameter 2 d_height - ((1 + n) * step_size) which gives the *top y* position of the rectangle to draw. This is the only calculation that changes as we draw the blocks.

Remember that y coordinates in QPainter start at the top and increase down the canvas. This means that plotting at d_height will be plotting at the very bottom of the canvas.

To draw a block at the very bottom we must start drawing at d_height-step_size i.e. one block up to leave space to draw downwards.

In our bar meter we're drawing blocks, in turn, starting at the bottom and working upwards. So our very first block must be placed at d_height-step_size and the second at d_height-(step_size*2). Our loop iterates from 0 upwards, so we can achieve this with the following formula —

```
ypos = (1 + n) * step_size
y = d_height - ypos
```

This produces the following layout.

In the picture below the current value of n has been printed over the box, and a blue box has been drawn around the complete step_size so you can see the padding and spacers in effect.

Figure 186. Showing the whole area (in blue) taken up by each segment.

Putting this all together gives the following code, which when run will produce a working power-bar widget with blocks in red. You can drag the wheel back and forth and the bars will move up and down in response.

Listing 159. custom-widgets/powerbar_6b.py

```python
import sys

from PyQt6 import QtCore, QtGui, QtWidgets
from PyQt6.QtCore import Qt


class _Bar(QtWidgets.QWidget):
    def __init__(self):
        super().__init__()

        self.setSizePolicy(
            QtWidgets.QSizePolicy.Policy.MinimumExpanding,
            QtWidgets.QSizePolicy.Policy.MinimumExpanding,
        )

    def sizeHint(self):
        return QtCore.QSize(40, 120)

    def paintEvent(self, e):
        painter = QtGui.QPainter(self)

        brush = QtGui.QBrush()
        brush.setColor(QtGui.QColor("black"))
```

```python
        brush.setStyle(Qt.BrushStyle.SolidPattern)
        rect = QtCore.QRect(
            0,
            0,
            painter.device().width(),
            painter.device().height(),
        )
        painter.fillRect(rect, brush)

        # Get current state.
        dial = self.parent()._dial
        vmin, vmax = dial.minimum(), dial.maximum()
        value = dial.value()

        pc = (value - vmin) / (vmax - vmin)
        n_steps_to_draw = int(pc * 5)

        padding = 5

        # Define our canvas.
        d_height = painter.device().height() - (padding * 2)
        d_width = painter.device().width() - (padding * 2)

        step_size = d_height / 5
        bar_height = step_size * 0.6

        brush.setColor(QtGui.QColor("red"))

        for n in range(n_steps_to_draw):
            ypos = (1 + n) * step_size
            rect = QtCore.QRect(
                padding,
                padding + d_height - int(ypos),
                d_width,
                int(bar_height),
            )
            painter.fillRect(rect, brush)
        painter.end()

    def _trigger_refresh(self):
        self.update()
```

```python
class PowerBar(QtWidgets.QWidget):
    """
    Custom Qt Widget to show a power bar and dial.
    Demonstrating compound and custom-drawn widget.
    """

    def __init__(self, parent=None, steps=5):
        super().__init__(parent)

        layout = QtWidgets.QVBoxLayout()
        self._bar = _Bar()
        layout.addWidget(self._bar)

        self._dial = QtWidgets.QDial()
        self._dial.valueChanged.connect(self._bar._trigger_refresh)
        layout.addWidget(self._dial)

        self.setLayout(layout)


app = QtWidgets.QApplication(sys.argv)
volume = PowerBar()
volume.show()
app.exec()
```

Figure 187. The basic complete PowerBar.

That already does the job, but we can go further to provide more customization, add some UX improvements and improve the API for working with our widget.

416

Customizing the Bar

We now have a working power bar, controllable with a dial. But it's nice when creating widgets to provide options to configure the behavior of your widget to make it more flexible. In this part we'll add methods to set customizable numbers of segments, colors, padding and spacing.

The elements we're going to provide customization for are —

Option	Description
number of bars	How many bars are displayed on the widget
colors	Individual colors for each of the bars
background color	The color of the draw canvas (default black)
padding	Space around the widget edge, between bars and edge of canvas
bar height / bar percent	Proportion (0...1) of the bar which is solid (the rest will be spacing between adjacent bars)

We can store each of these as attributes on the `_bar` object, and use them from the `paintEvent` method to change its behavior.

The `_Bar.__init__` is updated to accept an initial argument for either the number of bars (as an integer) or the colors of the bars (as a list of `QColor`, hex values or names). If a number is provided, all bars will be colored red. If the a list of colors is provided the number of bars will be determined from the length of the color list. Default values for `self._bar_solid_percent`, `self._background_color`, `self._padding` are also set.

Listing 160. custom-widgets/powerbar_7.py

```python
class _Bar(QtWidgets.QWidget):
    def __init__(self, steps):
        super().__init__()

        self.setSizePolicy(
            QtWidgets.QSizePolicy.Policy.MinimumExpanding,
            QtWidgets.QSizePolicy.Policy.MinimumExpanding,
        )

        if isinstance(steps, list):
            # list of colors.
            self.n_steps = len(steps)
            self.steps = steps

        elif isinstance(steps, int):
            # int number of bars, defaults to red.
            self.n_steps = steps
            self.steps = ["red"] * steps

        else:
            raise TypeError("steps must be a list or int")

        self._bar_solid_percent = 0.8
        self._background_color = QtGui.QColor("black")
        self._padding = 4  # n-pixel gap around edge.
```

Likewise we update the `PowerBar.__init__` to accept the steps parameter, and pass it through.

Listing 161. custom-widgets/powerbar_7.py

```python
class PowerBar(QtWidgets.QWidget):
    """
    Custom Qt Widget to show a power bar and dial.
    Demonstrating compound and custom-drawn widget.
    """

    def __init__(self, parent=None, steps=5):
        super().__init__(parent)

        layout = QtWidgets.QVBoxLayout()
        self._bar = _Bar(steps)

        layout.addWidget(self._bar)

        self._dial = QtWidgets.QDial()
        self._dial.valueChanged.connect(self._bar._trigger_refresh)
        layout.addWidget(self._dial)

        self.setLayout(layout)
```

We now have the parameters in place to update the `paintEvent` method. The modified code is shown below.

Listing 162. custom-widgets/powerbar_7.py

```python
    def paintEvent(self, e):
        painter = QtGui.QPainter(self)

        brush = QtGui.QBrush()
        brush.setColor(self._background_color)
        brush.setStyle(Qt.BrushStyle.SolidPattern)
        rect = QtCore.QRect(
            0,
            0,
            painter.device().width(),
            painter.device().height(),
        )
        painter.fillRect(rect, brush)
```

```python
        # Get current state.
        dial = self.parent()._dial
        vmin, vmax = dial.minimum(), dial.maximum()
        value = dial.value()

        # Define our canvas.
        d_height = painter.device().height() - (self._padding * 2)
        d_width = painter.device().width() - (self._padding * 2)

        # Draw the bars.
        step_size = d_height / self.n_steps
        bar_height = step_size * self._bar_solid_percent

        # Calculate the y-stop position, from the value in range.
        pc = (value - vmin) / (vmax - vmin)
        n_steps_to_draw = int(pc * self.n_steps)

        for n in range(n_steps_to_draw):
            brush.setColor(QtGui.QColor(self.steps[n]))
            ypos = (1 + n) * step_size
            rect = QtCore.QRect(
                self._padding,
                self._padding + d_height - int(ypos),
                d_width,
                int(bar_height),
            )
            painter.fillRect(rect, brush)

    painter.end()
```

You can now experiment with passing in different values for the __init__ to
PowerBar, e.g. increasing the number of bars, or providing a color list. Some
examples are shown below.

 A good source of hex color palettes is the Bokeh source
[https://github.com/bokeh/bokeh/blob/master/bokeh/palettes.py].

```
PowerBar(10)
PowerBar(3)
PowerBar(["#5e4fa2", "#3288bd", "#66c2a5", "#abdda4", "#e6f598",
"#ffffbf", "#fee08b", "#fdae61", "#f46d43", "#d53e4f", "#9e0142"])
PowerBar(["#a63603", "#e6550d", "#fd8d3c", "#fdae6b", "#fdd0a2",
"#feedde"])
```

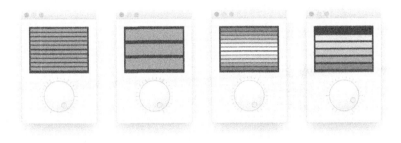

Figure 188. Some PowerBar examples.

You could fiddle with the padding settings through the variables e.g. self._bar_solid_percent but it'd be nicer to provide proper methods to set these.

 We're following the Qt standard of camelCase method names for these external methods for consistency with the others inherited from QDial.

Listing 163. custom-widgets/powerbar_8.py

```python
    def setColor(self, color):
        self._bar.steps = [color] * self._bar.n_steps
        self._bar.update()

    def setColors(self, colors):
        self._bar.n_steps = len(colors)
        self._bar.steps = colors
        self._bar.update()

    def setBarPadding(self, i):
        self._bar._padding = int(i)
        self._bar.update()

    def setBarSolidPercent(self, f):
        self._bar._bar_solid_percent = float(f)
        self._bar.update()

    def setBackgroundColor(self, color):
        self._bar._background_color = QtGui.QColor(color)
        self._bar.update()
```

In each case we set the private variable on the `_bar` object and then call
`_bar.update()` to trigger a redraw of the widget. The method support changing
the color to a single color, or updating a list of them — setting a list of colors can
also be used to change the number of bars.

 There is no method to set the bar count, since expanding a list of
colors would be tricky. But feel free to try adding this yourself!

Here's an example using 25px padding, a fully solid bar and a grey background.

```python
bar = PowerBar(["#49006a", "#7a0177", "#ae017e", "#dd3497",
"#f768a1", "#fa9fb5", "#fcc5c0", "#fde0dd", "#fff7f3"])
bar.setBarPadding(2)
bar.setBarSolidPercent(0.9)
bar.setBackgroundColor('gray')
```

With these settings you get the following result.

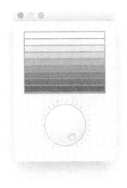

Figure 189. Configuring the PowerBar.

Adding the QAbstractSlider Interface

We've added methods to configure the behavior of the power bar. But we currently provide no way to configure the standard QDial methods — for example, setting the min, max or step size — from our widget. We could work through and add wrapper methods for all of these, but it would get very tedious very quickly.

```
# Example of a single wrapper, we'd need 30+ of these.
def setNotchesVisible(self, b):
    return self._dial.setNotchesVisible(b)
```

Instead we can add a little handler onto our outer widget to automatically look for methods (or attributes) on the QDial instance, if they don't exist on our class directly. This way we can implement our own methods, yet still get all the QAbstractSlider goodness for free.

The wrapper is shown below, implemented as a custom __getattr__ method.

Listing 164. custom-widgets/powerbar_8.py

```python
def __getattr__(self, name):
    if name in self.__dict__:
        return self[name]

    try:
        return getattr(self._dial, name)
    except AttributeError:
        raise AttributeError(
            "'{}' object has no attribute '{}'".format(
                self.__class__.__name__, name
            )
        )
```

When accessing a property (or method) — e.g. when we call PowerBar.setNotchesVisible(true) Python internally uses __getattr__ to get the property from the current object. This handler does this through the object dictionary self.__dict__. We've overridden this method to provide our custom handling logic.

Now, when we call PowerBar.setNotchesVisible(true), this handler first looks on our current object (a PowerBar instance) to see if .setNotchesVisible exists and if it does uses it. If **not** it then calls getattr() on self._dial instead returning what it finds there. This gives us access to all the methods of QDial from our custom `PowerBar` widget.

If QDial doesn't have the attribute either, and raises an AttributeError we catch it and raise it again from our custom widget, where it belongs.

This works for any properties or methods, including signals. So the standard QDial signals such as .valueChanged are available too.

Thanks to these changes we can also simplify the code in our paintEvent to get the current state from .parent() directly, rather than .parent()._dial. This doesn't alter behavior at all, but makes things more readable.

Listing 165. custom-widgets/powerbar_8.py

```python
def paintEvent(self, e):
    painter = QtGui.QPainter(self)

    brush = QtGui.QBrush()
    brush.setColor(self._background_color)
    brush.setStyle(Qt.BrushStyle.SolidPattern)
    rect = QtCore.QRect(
        0,
        0,
        painter.device().width(),
        painter.device().height(),
    )
    painter.fillRect(rect, brush)

    # Get current state.
    parent = self.parent()
    vmin, vmax = parent.minimum(), parent.maximum()
    value = parent.value()

    # Define our canvas.
    d_height = painter.device().height() - (self._padding * 2)
    d_width = painter.device().width() - (self._padding * 2)

    # Draw the bars.
    step_size = d_height / self.n_steps
    bar_height = step_size * self._bar_solid_percent

    # Calculate the y-stop position, from the value in range.
    pc = (value - vmin) / (vmax - vmin)
    n_steps_to_draw = int(pc * self.n_steps)

    for n in range(n_steps_to_draw):
        brush.setColor(QtGui.QColor(self.steps[n]))
        ypos = (1 + n) * step_size
        rect = QtCore.QRect(
            self._padding,
            self._padding + d_height - int(ypos),
            d_width,
            int(bar_height),
```

```
            )
            painter.fillRect(rect, brush)

        painter.end()
```

Updating from the Meter display

Currently you can update the current value of the PowerBar meter by twiddling with the dial. But it would be nice if you could also update the value by clicking a position on the power bar, or by dragging you mouse up and down. To do this we can update our _Bar widget to handle mouse events.

Listing 166. custom-widgets/powerbar_9.py

```python
class _Bar(QtWidgets.QWidget):

    clickedValue = QtCore.pyqtSignal(int)
    def _calculate_clicked_value(self, e):
        parent = self.parent()
        vmin, vmax = parent.minimum(), parent.maximum()
        d_height = self.size().height() + (self._padding * 2)
        step_size = d_height / self.n_steps
        click_y = e.y() - self._padding - step_size / 2

        pc = (d_height - click_y) / d_height
        value = int(vmin + pc * (vmax - vmin))
        self.clickedValue.emit(value)

    def mouseMoveEvent(self, e):
        self._calculate_clicked_value(e)

    def mousePressEvent(self, e):
        self._calculate_clicked_value(e)
```

In the __init__ block for the PowerBar widget we can connect to the _Bar.clickedValue signal and send the values to self._dial.setValue to set the current value on the dial.

```
# Take feedback from click events on the meter.
self._bar.clickedValue.connect(self._dial.setValue)
```

If you run the widget now, you'll be able to click around in the bar area and the value will update, and the dial rotate in sync.

The final code

Below is the complete final code for our PowerBar meter widget, called PowerBar.

Listing 167. custom-widgets/powerbar.py

```python
from PyQt6 import QtCore, QtGui, QtWidgets
from PyQt6.QtCore import Qt


class _Bar(QtWidgets.QWidget):

    clickedValue = QtCore.pyqtSignal(int)

    def __init__(self, steps):
        super().__init__()

        self.setSizePolicy(
            QtWidgets.QSizePolicy.Policy.MinimumExpanding,
            QtWidgets.QSizePolicy.Policy.MinimumExpanding,
        )

        if isinstance(steps, list):
            # list of colors.
            self.n_steps = len(steps)
            self.steps = steps

        elif isinstance(steps, int):
            # int number of bars, defaults to red.
            self.n_steps = steps
            self.steps = ["red"] * steps

        else:
            raise TypeError("steps must be a list or int")
```

```python
        self._bar_solid_percent = 0.8
        self._background_color = QtGui.QColor("black")
        self._padding = 4  # n-pixel gap around edge.

    def paintEvent(self, e):
        painter = QtGui.QPainter(self)

        brush = QtGui.QBrush()
        brush.setColor(self._background_color)
        brush.setStyle(Qt.BrushStyle.SolidPattern)
        rect = QtCore.QRect(
            0,
            0,
            painter.device().width(),
            painter.device().height(),
        )
        painter.fillRect(rect, brush)

        # Get current state.
        parent = self.parent()
        vmin, vmax = parent.minimum(), parent.maximum()
        value = parent.value()

        # Define our canvas.
        d_height = painter.device().height() - (self._padding * 2)
        d_width = painter.device().width() - (self._padding * 2)

        # Draw the bars.
        step_size = d_height / self.n_steps
        bar_height = step_size * self._bar_solid_percent

        # Calculate the y-stop position, from the value in range.
        pc = (value - vmin) / (vmax - vmin)
        n_steps_to_draw = int(pc * self.n_steps)

        for n in range(n_steps_to_draw):
            brush.setColor(QtGui.QColor(self.steps[n]))
            ypos = (1 + n) * step_size
            rect = QtCore.QRect(
                self._padding,
                self._padding + d_height - int(ypos),
                d_width,
```

```python
                    int(bar_height),
                )
                painter.fillRect(rect, brush)

        painter.end()

    def sizeHint(self):
        return QtCore.QSize(40, 120)

    def _trigger_refresh(self):
        self.update()

    def _calculate_clicked_value(self, e):
        parent = self.parent()
        vmin, vmax = parent.minimum(), parent.maximum()
        d_height = self.size().height() + (self._padding * 2)
        step_size = d_height / self.n_steps
        click_y = e.y() - self._padding - step_size / 2

        pc = (d_height - click_y) / d_height
        value = int(vmin + pc * (vmax - vmin))
        self.clickedValue.emit(value)

    def mouseMoveEvent(self, e):
        self._calculate_clicked_value(e)

    def mousePressEvent(self, e):
        self._calculate_clicked_value(e)


class PowerBar(QtWidgets.QWidget):
    """
    Custom Qt Widget to show a power bar and dial.
    Demonstrating compound and custom-drawn widget.
    """

    def __init__(self, parent=None, steps=5):
        super().__init__(parent)

        layout = QtWidgets.QVBoxLayout()
        self._bar = _Bar(steps)
        layout.addWidget(self._bar)
```

```python
        # Create the QDial widget and set up defaults.
        # - we provide accessors on this class to override.
        self._dial = QtWidgets.QDial()
        self._dial.setNotchesVisible(True)
        self._dial.setWrapping(False)
        self._dial.valueChanged.connect(self._bar._trigger_refresh)

        # Take feedback from click events on the meter.
        self._bar.clickedValue.connect(self._dial.setValue)

        layout.addWidget(self._dial)
        self.setLayout(layout)

    def __getattr__(self, name):
        if name in self.__dict__:
            return self[name]

        try:
            return getattr(self._dial, name)
        except AttributeError:
            raise AttributeError(
                "'{}' object has no attribute '{}'".format(
                    self.__class__.__name__, name
                )
            )

    def setColor(self, color):
        self._bar.steps = [color] * self._bar.n_steps
        self._bar.update()

    def setColors(self, colors):
        self._bar.n_steps = len(colors)
        self._bar.steps = colors
        self._bar.update()

    def setBarPadding(self, i):
        self._bar._padding = int(i)
        self._bar.update()

    def setBarSolidPercent(self, f):
        self._bar._bar_solid_percent = float(f)
        self._bar.update()
```

```
def setBackgroundColor(self, color):
    self._bar._background_color = QtGui.QColor(color)
    self._bar.update()
```

You'll notice that this version of the file does not create an instance of
QApplication or PowerBar itself — it is intended to be used as a library. You can add
this file into your own projects and then import with from powerbar import
PowerBar to use this widget in your own apps. The example below adds the
PowerBar` to a standard main window layout.

Listing 168. custom-widgets/powerbar_demo.py

```python
import sys
from PyQt6.QtWidgets import (
    QApplication,
    QMainWindow,
    QVBoxLayout,
    QWidget,
)

from powerbar import PowerBar


class MainWindow(QMainWindow):
    def __init__(self):
        super().__init__()

        layout = QVBoxLayout()

        powerbar = PowerBar(steps=10)
        layout.addWidget(powerbar)

        container = QWidget()
        container.setLayout(layout)
        self.setCentralWidget(container)


app = QApplication(sys.argv)
w = MainWindow()
w.show()
app.exec()
```

You should be able to use many of these ideas in creating your own custom widgets. For some more examples, take a look at the Learn PyQt widget library [https://www.pythonguis.com/widgets/] — these widgets are all open source and free to use in your own projects.

23. Using Custom Widgets in Qt Designer

In the previous chapter we built a custom *PowerBar* widget. The resulting widget can be used as-is in your own applications by importing and adding to layouts, just as for any built-in widget. But what if you're building your application UI using *Qt Designer*? Can you add custom widgets there too?

The answer is — yes!

In this short chapter we'll step through the process for adding custom widgets to your own *Qt Designer* applications. The process can be a little confusing, but if you follow the steps below you'll be able to use any of your custom widgets in UIs you create in *Designer*.

 You can use the same approach for adding custom widgets from other libraries, such as *PyQtGraph* or *matplotlib*.

Background

The first thing to understand is that you *can't* load and display your custom widgets in Qt Designer. The widgets available in *Designer* are built-in and it has no way to interpret your Python code to discover what you've created.

Instead, to insert your widgets into the UI you add *placeholder* widgets and then tell *Designer* that you want to replace the placeholder with your custom widget in the application when it is run.

Inside *Qt Designer* you will see the placeholder. You can change the same parameters as you would on any widget of the same type and these *will* be passed to your custom widget. When you load the UI in your Python application PyQt6 will substitute your custom widget where it belongs.

In Qt this process of replacing placeholder widgets is known as *promoting*. The built-in widget is *promoted* into your custom widget.

Writing *Promotable* **Custom Widgets**

Promoting widgets allows you to switch a placeholder widget used in Qt Designer with your own custom widget. When implementing your custom widget, you *must* subclass from another existing PyQt6 widget — even if that is the base QWidget. You must also ensure the your custom widget implements the default *constructor* of the widget you subclass. In most cases, that just means accepting parent as a first argument to your __init__ method.

 If your custom widget throws an error, check the parameters that PyQt6 is trying to pass it in the compiled UI file.

To promote to a custom widget, the custom widget must be in *a separate file* from where the compiled UI will be imported. However, you *can* define multiple custom widgets in the same file if you wish.

 This restriction is to avoid circular imports — if your application file imports the compiled UI file and this in turn imports your application file, this will not work.

Once you have your custom widget defined in a file, take a note of the *file name* and the *class name*. You will need these to *promote* the widget in Qt Designer.

Creating & Promoting Widgets in Designer

Choose where you want your custom widget to appear in your UI and add the *placeholder widget*. There is no rule here, but generally if your custom widget inherits from another Qt widget, use that widget as the placeholder. For example, if you've created a custom widget based on QLabel use Label as your placeholder. This allows you to access the label's standard properties within *Designer* to customize your custom widget.

Figure 190. Simple UI layout, with a placeholder Widget on the left hand side.

You *won't* be able alter any custom widget properties in *Designer*—*Qt Designer* doesn't know anything about your custom widget or how it works. Do this in your code!

Once you've added the widgets you can *promote* them. Select the widgets you want to promote, right click and chose **Promote to ...**

Figure 191. Promoting widgets via the right click menu.

At the bottom of the dialog you can add a *New Promoted Class*. Enter the class name—the name of your custom widget's Python class, e.g. PowerBar—and the Python file containing the class as the *header file*, omitting the .py suffix.

Qt will auto-suggest the filename based on the class name, but will append a .h (the C++ standard suffix for *header files*). You *must* remove the .h even if the filename is correct.

If your custom widget is defined in a class in a sub-folder, provided the *full Python dot-notation* to the file, the same way you would for other imports. For example, perhaps you placed the file under ui/widgets/powerbar.py then enter ui.widgets.powerbar as the *header file.*

Figure 192. Adding the class name and header file.

Click "Add" to define the promotion. You can then select the promotion in the list at the top and click *Promote* to actually promote your widgets.

Figure 193. Selecting the promotion and applying it to your widgets.

The widgets will be promoted, and show their new class name (here PowerBar).

Figure 194. Promoted widgets showing in the UI hierarchy.

Save the UI file and compile it using the `pyuic` tool as before.

```
pyuic6 mainwindow.ui -o MainWindow.py
```

If you open the generated file, you'll see custom `PowerBar` class is now used to construct a widget in the `setupUi` method and a new import has been added at the bottom of the file.

```
class Ui_MainWindow(object):
    def setupUi(self, MainWindow):
        # etc...
        self.widget = PowerBar(self.centralwidget)


    # etc...


    def retranslateUi(self, MainWindow):
        _translate = QtCore.QCoreApplication.translate
        MainWindow.setWindowTitle(_translate("MainWindow",
"MainWindow"))
        self.label.setText(_translate("MainWindow", "Some custom
widgets here next to the PowerBar (left)."))
        self.pushButton.setText(_translate("MainWindow", "A button"))
from powerbar import PowerBar
```

You can use the compiled UI file as normal. You *don't* need to import your custom widget into your application since this is handled in the compiled UI file.

Listing 169. custom-widgets/promote_test.py

```python
import random
import sys

from PyQt6.QtCore import Qt
from PyQt6.QtWidgets import QApplication, QMainWindow

from MainWindow import Ui_MainWindow


class MainWindow(QMainWindow, Ui_MainWindow):
    def __init__(self):
        super().__init__()
        self.setupUi(self)
        self.show()


app = QApplication(sys.argv)
w = MainWindow()
app.exec()
```

When you run the app your custom widgets will be loaded and automatically appear in the right place.

Figure 195. PowerBar custom widget showing in the app.

Most errors you see will be due to imports. The first step should always be to check the import at the bottom of the compiled UI file, to see if it makes sense. Is the target file reachable?

Third-party widgets

You can use this same technique to add other third-party widgets to your applications too. The process is exactly the same, you just need to refer to the widget by the fully-qualified Python import path and use the appropriate class names. Below, are some example configurations for common third-party widgets.

 We'll be covering how to use these libraries in a later chapter!

PyQtGraph

Use `PlotWidget` as the *promoted class name* and `pyqtgraph` as the *header file* in *Qt Designer*. Use `QWidget` as the *placeholder* widget. The PyQtGraph plot widget will work as-is in the generated UI file.

See the `custom-widgets/pyqtgraph_demo.py` file in the source code downloads for this book for a working demo.

Figure 196. PyQtGraph plot widget added via widget promotion.

Matplotlib

The `matplotlib` custom widget `FigureCanvasQTAgg` cannot be used directly in *Qt Designer* because the constructor doesn't accept `parent` as the first parameter, expecting a `Figure` object instead.

We can work around this by adding a simple wrapper class, defined below.

Listing 170. custom-widgets/mpl.py

```
from matplotlib.backends.backend_qtagg import FigureCanvasQTAgg
from matplotlib.figure import Figure


class MplCanvas(FigureCanvasQTAgg):
    def __init__(self, parent=None, width=5, height=4, dpi=100):
        fig = Figure(figsize=(width, height), dpi=dpi)
        self.axes = fig.add_subplot(111)
        super().__init__(fig)
```

Add this file to your project named `mpl.py` and then use `MplCanvas` as the *promoted class name* and `mpl` as the *header file* in *Qt Designer*. Use `QWidget` as the *placeholder* widget.

See the `custom-widgets/matplotlib_demo.py` file in the source code downloads for this book for a working demo.

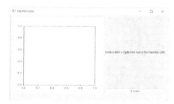

Figure 197. matplotlib plot widget added via widget promotion.

Using these techniques you should be able to use any custom widgets you come across in your PyQt6 applications.

Familiarity & Skeuomorphism

One of the most powerful tools you can exploit when building user interfaces is *familiarity*. That is, giving your users the sense that your interface is something they have used before. Familiar interfaces are often described as being *intuitive.* There is nothing naturally intuitive about moving a mouse pointer around a screen and clicking on square-ish bumps. But, after spending years doing exactly that, there is something very familiar about it.

Search for *familiarity in* user interfaces led to *skeuomorphism.* Skeuomorphism is the application of non-functional design cues from objects, where those design elements are functional. That can mean using common interface elements, or making interfaces which look like real objects. While in recent years GUI trends have moved back to abstract "flat" designs, all modern user-interfaces retain skeuomorphic touches.

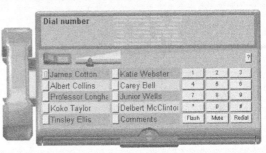

RealPhone — One of IBM's RealThings™

The modern desktop calculator is a good example. When we perform calculations we put the result at the *bottom*. So why is the screen on the top of a calculator? Because otherwise it would be obscured by your hand. The screen position is *functional.*

Calculator & upside down calculator (Windows 10)

For calculators on computers, this position is retained even though it is non-functional — the mouse pointer will not obscure the screen and input is often via the keyboard. But if you opened up a calculator and it had the screen at the bottom you would be confused. It looks *upside down.* It's *weird* or *unintuitive* despite being perfectly usable. This is the essence of skeuomorphism — making user interfaces feel more intuitive by exploiting the familiarity of users with existing objects.

Where your own software sits on this scale is up to you. The important thing is to be aware of existing interfaces and to exploit them where possible to improve usability of your own apps. Your users will thank you for it!

DO Take inspiration from existing interfaces when designing your own.
DO Include skeuomorphic elements where they *help* your users.

Concurrent Execution

> A computer shall not waste your time or require you to do more work than is strictly necessary.

— Jef Raskin, Second Law of User Interface Design

The event loop started by calling `.exec()` on your `QApplication` object runs within the same thread as your Python code. The thread which runs this event loop — commonly referred to as the *GUI thread* — also handles all window communication with the host operating system.

By default, any execution triggered by the event loop will also run synchronously within this thread. In practice this means that any time your PyQt6 application spends *doing something* in your code, window communication and GUI interaction are frozen.

If what you're doing is simple, and returns control to the GUI loop quickly, this freeze will be imperceptible to the user. However, if you need to perform longer-running tasks, for example opening/writing a large file, downloading some data, or rendering some complex image, there are going to be problems. To your user the application will appear to be unresponsive. Because your app is no longer communicating with the OS the OS will think it has crashed — on macOS you see the spinning wheel of death, on Windows the window will dim. That's not a good look.

The solution is simple — get your work out of the *GUI thread*. PyQt6 provides straightforward interfaces to accomplish exactly that.

24. Introduction to Threads & Processes

Below is a minimal stub application for PyQt6 which will allow us to demonstrate the problem and later to fix it. You can copy and paste this into a new file, and save it with an appropriate filename like `concurrent.py`.

Listing 171. bad_example_1.py

```python
import sys
import time

from PyQt6.QtCore import QTimer
from PyQt6.QtWidgets import (
    QApplication,
    QLabel,
    QMainWindow,
    QPushButton,
    QVBoxLayout,
    QWidget,
)


class MainWindow(QMainWindow):
    def __init__(self):
        super().__init__()

        self.counter = 0

        layout = QVBoxLayout()

        self.l = QLabel("Start")
        b = QPushButton("DANGER!")
        b.pressed.connect(self.oh_no)

        layout.addWidget(self.l)
        layout.addWidget(b)

        w = QWidget()
        w.setLayout(layout)
```

```
        self.setCentralWidget(w)

        self.show()

        self.timer = QTimer()
        self.timer.setInterval(1000)
        self.timer.timeout.connect(self.recurring_timer)
        self.timer.start()

    def oh_no(self):
        time.sleep(5)

    def recurring_timer(self):
        self.counter += 1
        self.l.setText("Counter: %d" % self.counter)


app = QApplication(sys.argv)
window = MainWindow()
app.exec()
```

🚀 **Run it!** A window will appear, containing a button and a number counting upwards.

Figure 198. The number will increase by 1 every second, as long as the event loop is running.

This is generated by a simple recurring timer, firing once per second. Think of this as our *event loop indicator* — a simple way to let us known that out application is ticking over normally. There is also a button with the word **"DANGER!"**. Push it.

Figure 199. Push the button.

You'll notice that each time you push the button the counter stops ticking and your application freezes entirely. On Windows you may see the window turn pale, indicating it is not responding, while on macOS you may see the spinning wheel of death.

What appears as a *frozen interface* is in fact caused by the Qt event loop being blocked from processing (and responding to) window events. Your clicks on the window as still registered by the host OS and sent to your application, but because it's sat in your big ol' lump of code (time.sleep), it can't accept or react to them. Your app does not respond and the OS and it interprets this as a freeze or hang.

The wrong approach

The simplest way get around this is to accept events from within your code. This allows Qt to continue to respond to the host OS and your application will stay responsive. You can do this easily by using the static .processEvents() function on the QApplication class. Simply add a line like the following, somewhere in your long-running code block:

```
QApplication.processEvents()
```

If we take our long-running `time.sleep` code and break it down into multiple steps, we can insert `.processEvents` in between. The code for this would be:

```
def oh_no(self):
    for n in range(5):
        QApplication.processEvents()
        time.sleep(1)
```

Now when you push the button your code is entered as before. However, now `QApplication.processEvents()` intermittently passes control back to Qt, and allows it to respond to OS events as normal. Qt will now accept events *and handle them* before returning to run the remainder of your code.

This works, but it's horrible for a couple of reasons.

Firstly, when you pass control back to Qt, your code is no longer running. This means that whatever long-running thing you're trying to do will take *longer*. That is probably not what you want.

Secondly, processing events outside the main event loop causes your application to branch off into handling code (e.g. for triggered slots, or events) while in your loop. If your code depends on/responds to external state this can cause undefined behavior. The code below demonstrates this in action:

Listing 172. bad_example_2.py

```
import sys
import time

from PyQt6.QtCore import QTimer
from PyQt6.QtWidgets import (
    QApplication,
    QLabel,
    QMainWindow,
    QPushButton,
    QVBoxLayout,
    QWidget,
)
```

```python
class MainWindow(QMainWindow):
    def __init__(self):
        super().__init__()

        self.counter = 0

        layout = QVBoxLayout()

        self.l = QLabel("Start")
        b = QPushButton("DANGER!")
        b.pressed.connect(self.oh_no)

        c = QPushButton("?")
        c.pressed.connect(self.change_message)

        layout.addWidget(self.l)
        layout.addWidget(b)

        layout.addWidget(c)

        w = QWidget()
        w.setLayout(layout)

        self.setCentralWidget(w)

        self.show()

    def change_message(self):
        self.message = "OH NO"

    def oh_no(self):
        self.message = "Pressed"

        for _ in range(100):
            time.sleep(0.1)
            self.l.setText(self.message)
            QApplication.processEvents()


app = QApplication(sys.argv)
window = MainWindow()
```

```
app.exec()
```

If you run this code you'll see the counter as before. Pressing "DANGER!" will change the displayed text to "Pressed", as defined at the entry point to the oh_no function. However, if you press the "?" button while oh_no is still running you'll see that the message changes. State is being changed from outside your loop.

This is a toy example. However, if you have multiple long-running processes within your application, with each calling QApplication.processEvents() to keep things ticking, your application behavior can quickly become unpredictable.

Threads and Processes

If you take a step back and think about what you want to happen in your application, it can probably be summed up with "stuff to happen at the same time as other stuff happens". There are two main approaches to running independent tasks on a computer: *threads* and *processes*.

Threads share the same memory space, so are quick to start up and consume minimal resources. The shared memory makes it trivial to pass data between threads, however reading/writing memory from different threads can lead to race conditions or segfaults. In Python there is the added issue that multiple threads are bound by the same Global Interpreter Lock GIL — meaning non-GIL-releasing Python code can only execute in one thread at a time. However, this is not a major issue with PyQt6 where most of the time is spent outside of Python.

Processes use separate memory space (and an entirely separate Python interpreter). This side-steps any potential problems with the GIL, but at the cost of slower start-up times, larger memory overhead and complexity in sending/receiving data.

For simplicity's sake it usually makes sense to use threads. Processes in Qt are better suited to running and communicating with external programs. In this chapter we'll look at the options available to you from within Qt to move work onto separate threads and processes.

25. Using the thread pool

Qt provides a very simple interface for running jobs in other threads, which is exposed nicely in PyQt6. This is built around two classes — QRunnable and QThreadPool. The former is the container for the work you want to perform, while the latter is the manager for your working threads.

The neat thing about using QThreadPool is that it handles queuing and execution of workers for you. Other than queuing up jobs and retrieving the results there is not very much to do at all.

Using QRunnable

To define a custom QRunnable you can subclass the base QRunnable class, then place the code you wish you execute within the run() method. The following is an implementation of our long running time.sleep job as a QRunnable. Add the following code above the MainWindow class definition.

Listing 173. concurrent/qrunnable_1.py

```python
class Worker(QRunnable):
    """
    Worker thread
    """

    @pyqtSlot()
    def run(self):
        """
        Your code goes in this method
        """
        print("Thread start")
        time.sleep(5)
        print("Thread complete")
```

Executing our function in another thread is simply a matter of creating an instance of the Worker and then passing it to our QThreadPool instance.

We create an instance of a thread pool in the __init__ block.

Listing 174. concurrent/qrunnable_1.py

```python
class MainWindow(QMainWindow):
    def __init__(self):
        super().__init__()

        self.threadpool = QThreadPool()
        print(
            "Multithreading with maximum %d threads"
            % self.threadpool.maxThreadCount()
        )
```

Finally, replace the oh_no method with the following to create and submit the worker to the pool.

Listing 175. concurrent/qrunnable_1.py

```python
    def oh_no(self):
        worker = Worker()
        self.threadpool.start(worker)
```

Now, clicking on the button will create a worker to handle the (long-running) process and spin that off into another thread via the QThreadPool pool. If there are not enough threads available to process incoming workers, they'll be queued and executed in order at a later time.

🚀 **Run it!** You'll see that your application now handles you frantically bashing the button with no problems.

Figure 200. The simple `QRunnable` *example app. The counter will increase by one every second — as long as the GUI thread is running.*

Look at the output in the console to see workers starting and finishing.

```
Multithreading with maximum 12 threads
Thread start
Thread start
Thread start
Thread complete
Thread complete
Thread complete
```

Check what happens if you hit the button multiple times. You should see your threads executed immediately *up to* the number reported by `.maxThreadCount`. If you hit the button again after there are already this number of active workers, the subsequent workers will be queued until a thread becomes available.

In this example we've let `QThreadPool` decide the *ideal* number of active threads to use. This number differs on different computers and is designed to get the optimum performance. However, sometimes you have a need for a *specific* number of threads — in that case, you can use `.setMaxThreadCount` to set this value explicitly. This value is *per thread pool*.

Using `QThreadPool.start()`

In the previous example we created a `QRunnable` object ourselves and passed it to the `QThreadPool` to have them executed. However, for simple use-cases, Qt provides a convenience method through `QThreadPool.start()` which can handle the execution of arbitrary Python functions and methods. Qt creates the necessary QRunnable objects for you and queues them on the pool.

In the example below we've put our work in a do_some_work method and modified our oh_no method to pass this to the thread pool's .start() method.

Listing 176. concurrent/qthreadpool_start_1.py

```python
def oh_no(self):
    self.threadpool.start(self.do_some_work)

@pyqtSlot()
def do_some_work(self):
    print("Thread start")
    time.sleep(5)
    print("Thread complete")

def recurring_timer(self):
    self.counter += 1
    self.l.setText("Counter: %d" % self.counter)
```

Pressing the button will execute our do_some_work method on the QThreadPool.

 You can start more than one thread this way. Try pressing the button until you reach the *maximum number of concurrent threads*. No new threads will start until there is space in the pool.

This approach works fine for many simple tasks. Within your executed function you *do* have access to signals and can use them to emit data. You cannot *receive* signals — there is nowhere to connect them — but you can interact with variables through the self object.

Update your code to add the following custom_signal and modify the work method to emit this signal and update the self.counter variable.

Listing 177. concurrent/qthreadpool_start_2.py

```python
class MainWindow(QMainWindow):

    custom_signal = pyqtSignal()

    def __init__(self):
        super().__init__()

        # Connect our custom signal to a handler.
        self.custom_signal.connect(self.signal_handler)
        # etc.

    def oh_no(self):
        self.threadpool.start(self.do_some_work)

    @pyqtSlot()
    def do_some_work(self):
        print("Thread start")
        # Emit our custom signal.
        self.custom_signal.emit()
        for n in range(5):
            time.sleep(1)
        self.counter = self.counter - 10
        print("Thread complete")

    def signal_handler(self):
        print("Signal received!")

    def recurring_timer(self):
        self.counter += 1
        self.l.setText("Counter: %d" % self.counter)
```

If you run this example you'll notice that while the work method is running in another thread (the sleep does not interrupt the counter) we are still able to emit signals and modify the self.counter variable.

 You *cannot* modify the GUI directly from another thread — attempting to do so will crash your application.

You *can* modify the GUI using signals. For example, try connecting a str signal to the label's .setText method.

While this is a handy little interface, often you'll find yourself wanting more control over, or more structured communication with, your running threads. Next we'll look at some more complicated examples using QRunnable to show what's possible.

Extending QRunnable

If you want to pass custom data into the execution function you can set up your runner to take *arguments* or *keywords* and then store that data on the QRunnable self object. The data will then be accessible from within the run method.

Listing 178. concurrent/qrunnable_2.py

```python
class Worker(QRunnable):
    """
    Worker thread

    :param args: Arguments to make available to the run code
    :param kwargs: Keywords arguments to make available to the run
    :code
    :
    """

    def __init__(self, *args, **kwargs):
        super().__init__()
        self.args = args
        self.kwargs = kwargs

    @pyqtSlot()
    def run(self):
        """
            Initialize the runner function with passed self.args,
        self.kwargs.
        """

        print(self.args, self.kwargs)


    def oh_no(self):
        worker = Worker("some", "arguments", keywords=2)
        self.threadpool.start(worker)
```

 As functions are also objects in Python, you can also pass a function to execute in to your runner. See The Generic for an example.

Thread IO

Sometimes it's helpful to be able to pass back *state* and *data* from running workers. This could include the outcome of calculations, raised exceptions or ongoing progress (think progress bars). Qt provides the *signals and slots* framework which allows you to do just that and is thread-safe, allowing safe communication directly from running threads to your GUI frontend. *Signals* allow you to .emit values, which are then picked up elsewhere in your code by *slot* functions which have been linked with .connect.

Below is a simple WorkerSignals class defined to contain a number of example signals.

 Custom signals can only be defined on objects derived from QObject. Since QRunnable is not derived from QObject we can't define the signals there directly. A custom QObject to hold the signals is the simplest solution.

Listing 179. concurrent/qrunnable_3.py

```python
class WorkerSignals(QObject):
    """
    Defines the signals available from a running worker thread.

    Supported signals are:

    finished
        No data

    error
        `str` Exception string

    result
        `dict` data returned from processing

    """

    finished = pyqtSignal()
    error = pyqtSignal(str)
    result = pyqtSignal(dict)
```

In this example we've defined 3 custom signals:

1. *finished* signal, with no data to indicate when the task is complete.

2. *error* signal which receives a `tuple` of `Exception` type, `Exception` value and formatted traceback.

3. *result* signal receiving any `object` type from the executed function.

You may not find a need for all of these signals, but they are included to give an indication of what is possible. In the following code we use these signals to notify about completion and errors in a simple calculation worker.

Listing 180. concurrent/qrunnable_3.py

```python
import random
import sys
import time

from PyQt6.QtCore import (
    QObject,
    QRunnable,
    QThreadPool,
    QTimer,
    pyqtSignal,
    pyqtSlot,
)
from PyQt6.QtWidgets import (
    QApplication,
    QLabel,
    QMainWindow,
    QPushButton,
    QVBoxLayout,
    QWidget,
)


class WorkerSignals(QObject):
    """
    Defines the signals available from a running worker thread.

    Supported signals are:

    finished
        No data
```

```
    error
        `str` Exception string

    result
        `dict` data returned from processing

    """


    finished = pyqtSignal()
    error = pyqtSignal(str)
    result = pyqtSignal(dict)


class Worker(QRunnable):
    """
    Worker thread

    :param args: Arguments to make available to the run code
    :param kwargs: Keywords arguments to make available to the run
    :code
    :
    """


    def __init__(self, iterations=5):
        super().__init__()
        self.signals = (
            WorkerSignals()
        )  # Create an instance of our signals class.
        self.iterations = iterations

    @pyqtSlot()
    def run(self):
        """
                Initialize the runner function with passed self.args,
        self.kwargs.
        """
        try:
            for n in range(self.iterations):
                time.sleep(0.01)
                v = 5 / (40 - n)

        except Exception as e:
```

```python
                self.signals.error.emit(str(e))

        else:
            self.signals.finished.emit()
            self.signals.result.emit({"n": n, "value": v})



class MainWindow(QMainWindow):
    def __init__(self):
        super().__init__()

        self.threadpool = QThreadPool()
        print(
            "Multithreading with maximum %d threads"
            % self.threadpool.maxThreadCount()
        )

        self.counter = 0

        layout = QVBoxLayout()

        self.l = QLabel("Start")
        b = QPushButton("DANGER!")
        b.pressed.connect(self.oh_no)

        layout.addWidget(self.l)
        layout.addWidget(b)

        w = QWidget()
        w.setLayout(layout)

        self.setCentralWidget(w)

        self.show()

        self.timer = QTimer()
        self.timer.setInterval(1000)
        self.timer.timeout.connect(self.recurring_timer)
        self.timer.start()

    def oh_no(self):
        worker = Worker(iterations=random.randint(10, 50))
        worker.signals.result.connect(self.worker_output)
```

461

```
            worker.signals.finished.connect(self.worker_complete)
            worker.signals.error.connect(self.worker_error)
            self.threadpool.start(worker)

    def worker_output(self, s):
        print("RESULT", s)

    def worker_complete(self):
        print("THREAD COMPLETE!")

    def worker_error(self, t):
        print("ERROR: %s" % t)

    def recurring_timer(self):
        self.counter += 1
        self.l.setText("Counter: %d" % self.counter)


app = QApplication(sys.argv)
window = MainWindow()
app.exec()
```

You can connect your own handler functions to these signals to receive notification of completion (or the result) of threads. The example is designed to occasionally throw a *division by zero* exception, which you'll see in the output.

```
Multithreading with maximum 12 threads
THREAD COMPLETE!
RESULT {'n': 16, 'value': 0.20833333333333334}
ERROR: division by zero
THREAD COMPLETE!
RESULT {'n': 11, 'value': 0.1724137931034483}
THREAD COMPLETE!
RESULT {'n': 22, 'value': 0.2777777777777778}
ERROR: division by zero
```

In the next section we'll look at a number of different variations on this approach which allow you to do some interesting things using QThreadPool in your own applications.

26. QRunnable examples

QThreadPool and QRunnable are an incredibly flexible way to run things in other threads. By tweaking the signals and parameters you can perform any tasks you can imagine. In this chapter we'll look some examples for how to construct runners for particular scenarios.

All the examples follow the same general pattern — a custom QRunnable class with custom WorkerSignals. The difference is in what we pass to the runner, what it does with those parameters, and how we hook up the signals.

Listing 181. concurrent/qrunnable_base.py

```python
import sys
import time
import traceback

from PyQt6.QtCore import (
    QObject,
    QRunnable,
    QThreadPool,
    pyqtSignal,
    pyqtSlot,
)
from PyQt6.QtWidgets import QApplication, QMainWindow


class WorkerSignals(QObject):
    pass


class Worker(QRunnable):
    def __init__(self, *args, **kwargs):
        super().__init__()
        # Store constructor arguments (re-used for processing)
        self.args = args
        self.kwargs = kwargs
        self.signals = WorkerSignals()

    @pyqtSlot()
    def run(self):
        pass


class MainWindow(QMainWindow):
    def __init__(self):
        super().__init__()
        self.show()


app = QApplication(sys.argv)
window = MainWindow()
app.exec()
```

The progress watcher

If you're using threads to perform long-running actions you should keep your users informed about how the task is progressing. A common way to do this is by showing the user a *progress bar* which indicates, with a bar filling left to right, how much of the task is complete. In order to show a progress bar for your tasks, you need to emit the current progress state from your worker.

To do this we can define another signal called progress on the WorkerSignals object. This signal emits on each loop a number from 0..100 as the "task" progresses. The output of this progress signal is connected to a standard QProgressBar shown on the statusbar of our main window.

Listing 182. concurrent/qrunnable_progress.py

```python
import sys
import time

from PyQt6.QtCore import (
    QObject,
    QRunnable,
    QThreadPool,
    QTimer,
    pyqtSignal,
    pyqtSlot,
)
from PyQt6.QtWidgets import (
    QApplication,
    QLabel,
    QMainWindow,
    QProgressBar,
    QPushButton,
    QVBoxLayout,
    QWidget,
)


class WorkerSignals(QObject):
    """
    Defines the signals available from a running worker thread.
```

```python
        progress
            int progress complete,from 0-100
        """

    progress = pyqtSignal(int)


class Worker(QRunnable):
    """
    Worker thread

    Inherits from QRunnable to handle worker thread setup, signals
    and wrap-up.
    """

    def __init__(self):
        super().__init__()

        self.signals = WorkerSignals()

    @pyqtSlot()
    def run(self):
        total_n = 1000
        for n in range(total_n):
            progress_pc = int(
                100 * float(n + 1) / total_n
            )  # Progress 0-100% as int
            self.signals.progress.emit(progress_pc)
            time.sleep(0.01)


class MainWindow(QMainWindow):
    def __init__(self, *args, **kwargs):
        super().__init__(*args, **kwargs)

        layout = QVBoxLayout()

        self.progress = QProgressBar()

        button = QPushButton("START IT UP")
        button.pressed.connect(self.execute)
```

```python
            layout.addWidget(self.progress)
            layout.addWidget(button)

            w = QWidget()
            w.setLayout(layout)

            self.setCentralWidget(w)

            self.show()

            self.threadpool = QThreadPool()
            print(
                "Multithreading with maximum %d threads"
                % self.threadpool.maxThreadCount()
            )

    def execute(self):
        worker = Worker()
        worker.signals.progress.connect(self.update_progress)

        # Execute
        self.threadpool.start(worker)

    def update_progress(self, progress):
        self.progress.setValue(progress)


app = QApplication(sys.argv)
window = MainWindow()
app.exec()
```

Figure 201. Progress bar showing current progress for a long-running worker.

If you press the button while another runner is already working, you'll notice a problem — the two runners emit their progress to the same progress bar, so the values will jump back and forward.

Tracking multiple workers with a single progress bar is possible — we just need two things: somewhere to *store* the progress values for each worker, and a unique identifier for each worker. On each progress update, we can then calculate the *average* progress across all workers, and display that.

Listing 183. concurrent/qrunnable_progress_many.py

```python
import random
import sys
import time
import uuid

from PyQt6.QtCore import (
    QObject,
    QRunnable,
    QThreadPool,
    QTimer,
    pyqtSignal,
    pyqtSlot,
)
from PyQt6.QtWidgets import (
    QApplication,
    QLabel,
    QMainWindow,
    QProgressBar,
    QPushButton,
    QVBoxLayout,
    QWidget,
)


class WorkerSignals(QObject):
    """
    Defines the signals available from a running worker thread.

    progress
        int progress complete,from 0-100
    """
```

```python
    progress = pyqtSignal(str, int)
    finished = pyqtSignal(str)


class Worker(QRunnable):
    """
    Worker thread

    Inherits from QRunnable to handle worker thread setup, signals
    and wrap-up.
    """

    def __init__(self):
        super().__init__()
        self.job_id = uuid.uuid4().hex   ①
        self.signals = WorkerSignals()

    @pyqtSlot()
    def run(self):
        total_n = 1000
        delay = random.random() / 100  # Random delay value.
        for n in range(total_n):
            progress_pc = int(100 * float(n + 1) / total_n)   ②
            self.signals.progress.emit(self.job_id, progress_pc)
            time.sleep(delay)

        self.signals.finished.emit(self.job_id)


class MainWindow(QMainWindow):
    def __init__(self):
        super().__init__()

        layout = QVBoxLayout()

        self.progress = QProgressBar()

        button = QPushButton("START IT UP")
        button.pressed.connect(self.execute)

        self.status = QLabel("0 workers")

        layout.addWidget(self.progress)
```

```python
        layout.addWidget(button)
        layout.addWidget(self.status)

        w = QWidget()
        w.setLayout(layout)

        # Dictionary holds the progress of current workers.
        self.worker_progress = {}

        self.setCentralWidget(w)

        self.show()

        self.threadpool = QThreadPool()
        print(
            "Multithreading with maximum %d threads"
            % self.threadpool.maxThreadCount()
        )

        self.timer = QTimer()
        self.timer.setInterval(100)
        self.timer.timeout.connect(self.refresh_progress)
        self.timer.start()

    def execute(self):
        worker = Worker()
        worker.signals.progress.connect(self.update_progress)
        worker.signals.finished.connect(self.cleanup)    ③

        # Execute
        self.threadpool.start(worker)

    def cleanup(self, job_id):
        if job_id in self.worker_progress:
            del self.worker_progress[job_id]    ④

            # Update the progress bar if we've removed a value.
            self.refresh_progress()

    def update_progress(self, job_id, progress):
        self.worker_progress[job_id] = progress

    def calculate_progress(self):
```

```
        if not self.worker_progress:
            return 0

        return sum(v for v in self.worker_progress.values()) / len(
            self.worker_progress
        )

    def refresh_progress(self):
        # Calculate total progress.
        progress = self.calculate_progress()
        print(self.worker_progress)
        self.progress.setValue(progress)
        self.status.setText("%d workers" % len(self.worker_progress))


app = QApplication(sys.argv)
window = MainWindow()
app.exec()
```

① Use a unique UUID4 identifier for this runner.

② Progress 0-100% as an integer.

③ When the job finishes, we need to cleanup (delete) the workers progress.

④ Delete the progress for the finished worker.

If you run this, you'll see the global progress bar along with an indicator to show how many active workers there are running.

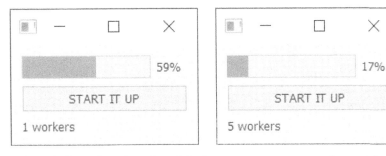

Figure 202. The window showing the global progress state, together with the number of active workers.

Checking the console output for the script you can see the actual status for each of the individual workers.

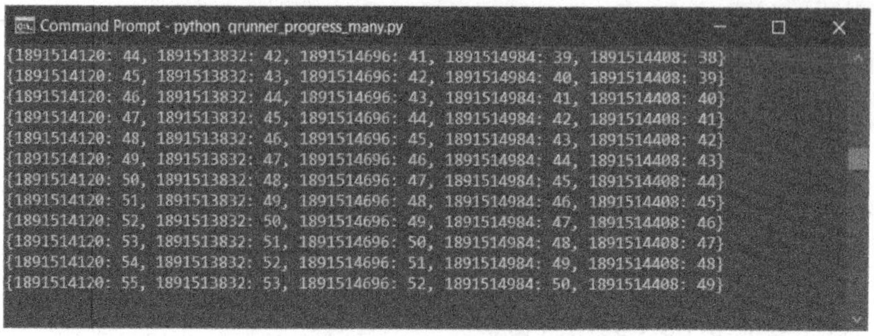

Figure 203. Check the shell output to see the individual worker progress.

Removing the worker immediately means that the progress will jump *backwards* when a job finishes — removing 100 from the average calculation will cause the average to fall. You can postpone the cleanup if you like, for example the following will only remove the entries when *all* progress bars reach 100.

Listing 184. concurrent/qrunnable_progress_many_2.py

```python
import random
import sys
import time
import uuid

from PyQt6.QtCore import (
    QObject,
    QRunnable,
    QThreadPool,
    QTimer,
    pyqtSignal,
    pyqtSlot,
)
from PyQt6.QtWidgets import (
    QApplication,
    QLabel,
    QMainWindow,
    QProgressBar,
    QPushButton,
    QVBoxLayout,
    QWidget,
)


class WorkerSignals(QObject):
```

```python
    """
    Defines the signals available from a running worker thread.

    progress
        int progress complete,from 0-100
    """

    progress = pyqtSignal(str, int)
    finished = pyqtSignal(str)


class Worker(QRunnable):
    """
    Worker thread

    Inherits from QRunnable to handle worker thread setup, signals
    and wrap-up.
    """

    def __init__(self):
        super().__init__()
        self.job_id = uuid.uuid4().hex   ①
        self.signals = WorkerSignals()

    @pyqtSlot()
    def run(self):
        total_n = 1000
        delay = random.random() / 100   # Random delay value.
        for n in range(total_n):
            progress_pc = int(100 * float(n + 1) / total_n)   ②
            self.signals.progress.emit(self.job_id, progress_pc)
            time.sleep(delay)

        self.signals.finished.emit(self.job_id)


class MainWindow(QMainWindow):
    def __init__(self):
        super().__init__()

        layout = QVBoxLayout()

        self.progress = QProgressBar()
```

```python
        button = QPushButton("START IT UP")
        button.pressed.connect(self.execute)

        self.status = QLabel("0 workers")

        layout.addWidget(self.progress)
        layout.addWidget(button)
        layout.addWidget(self.status)

        w = QWidget()
        w.setLayout(layout)

        # Dictionary holds the progress of current workers.
        self.worker_progress = {}

        self.setCentralWidget(w)

        self.show()

        self.threadpool = QThreadPool()
        print(
            "Multithreading with maximum %d threads"
            % self.threadpool.maxThreadCount()
        )

        self.timer = QTimer()
        self.timer.setInterval(100)
        self.timer.timeout.connect(self.refresh_progress)
        self.timer.start()

    def execute(self):
        worker = Worker()
        worker.signals.progress.connect(self.update_progress)
        worker.signals.finished.connect(self.cleanup)   ③

        # Execute
        self.threadpool.start(worker)

    def cleanup(self, job_id):
        if all(v == 100 for v in self.worker_progress.values()):
            self.worker_progress.clear()  # Empty the dict.
```

```python
            # Update the progress bar if we've removed a value.
            self.refresh_progress()

    def update_progress(self, job_id, progress):
        self.worker_progress[job_id] = progress

    def calculate_progress(self):
        if not self.worker_progress:
            return 0

        return sum(v for v in self.worker_progress.values()) / len(
            self.worker_progress
        )

    def refresh_progress(self):
        # Calculate total progress.
        progress = self.calculate_progress()
        print(self.worker_progress)
        self.progress.setValue(progress)
        self.status.setText("%d workers" % len(self.worker_progress))


app = QApplication(sys.argv)
window = MainWindow()
app.exec()
```

While this works, and is fine for simple use-cases, it would be nicer if this worker state (and control) could be wrapped up into it's own *manager* component rather than being handled through the main window. Take a look at the later The Manager section to see how we can do that.

The calculator

Threading is a good option when you need to perform complex calculations. If you're using the Python *numpy*, *scipy* or *pandas* libraries then these calculations may also release the Python Global Interpreter Lock (GIL) meaning both your GUI and calculation thread can run at full speed.

In this example we'll create a number of workers which are all performing some simple calculations. The results of these calculations will be returned to the GUI thread and displayed in a plot.

 We cover PyQtGraph in detail in Plotting with PyQtGraph, for now just focus on the QRunnable.

Listing 185. concurrent/qrunnable_calculator.py

```python
import random
import sys
import time
import uuid

from PyQt6.QtCore import (
    QObject,
    QRunnable,
    QThreadPool,
    QTimer,
    pyqtSignal,
    pyqtSlot,
)
from PyQt6.QtWidgets import (
    QApplication,
    QMainWindow,
    QPushButton,
    QVBoxLayout,
    QWidget,
)
import pyqtgraph as pg
```

```python
class WorkerSignals(QObject):
    """
    Defines the signals available from a running worker thread.

    data
        tuple data point (worker_id, x, y)
    """

    data = pyqtSignal(tuple)  ①


class Worker(QRunnable):
    """
    Worker thread

    Inherits from QRunnable to handle worker thread setup, signals
    and wrap-up.
    """

    def __init__(self):
        super().__init__()
        self.worker_id = uuid.uuid4().hex  # Unique ID for this
worker.
        self.signals = WorkerSignals()

    @pyqtSlot()
    def run(self):

        total_n = 1000
        y2 = random.randint(0, 10)
        delay = random.random() / 100  # Random delay value.
        value = 0

        for n in range(total_n):
            # Dummy calculation, each worker will produce different
values,
            # because of the random y & y2 values.
            y = random.randint(0, 10)
            value += n * y2 - n * y

            self.signals.data.emit((self.worker_id, n, value))  ②
            time.sleep(delay)
```

```
class MainWindow(QMainWindow):
    def __init__(self):
        super().__init__()

        self.threadpool = QThreadPool()

        self.x = {}  # Keep timepoints.
        self.y = {}  # Keep data.
        self.lines = {}  # Keep references to plotted lines, to
update.

        layout = QVBoxLayout()
        self.graphWidget = pg.PlotWidget()
        self.graphWidget.setBackground("w")
        layout.addWidget(self.graphWidget)

        button = QPushButton("Create New Worker")
        button.pressed.connect(self.execute)

        # layout.addWidget(self.progress)
        layout.addWidget(button)

        w = QWidget()
        w.setLayout(layout)

        self.setCentralWidget(w)

        self.show()

    def execute(self):
        worker = Worker()
        worker.signals.data.connect(self.receive_data)

        # Execute
        self.threadpool.start(worker)

    def receive_data(self, data):
        worker_id, x, y = data  ③

        if worker_id not in self.lines:
            self.x[worker_id] = [x]
            self.y[worker_id] = [y]
```

```
            # Generate a random color.
            pen = pg.mkPen(
                width=2,
                color=(
                    random.randint(100, 255),
                    random.randint(100, 255),
                    random.randint(100, 255),
                ),
            )
            self.lines[worker_id] = self.graphWidget.plot(
                self.x[worker_id], self.y[worker_id], pen=pen
            )
            return

        # Update existing plot/data
        self.x[worker_id].append(x)
        self.y[worker_id].append(y)

        self.lines[worker_id].setData(
            self.x[worker_id], self.y[worker_id]
        )


app = QApplication(sys.argv)
window = MainWindow()
app.exec()
```

① Setup a custom signal to pass out the data. Using `tuple` allows you to send out any number of values wrapped in a `tuple`.

② Here we're emitting a *worker_id*, *x* and *y* value.

③ Receiver slot unpacks the data.

Once you've received the data from a worker, you can do what you like with it — perhaps add it to a table or model view. Here we're storing the *x* and *y* values in `dict` objects keyed by the *worker_id*. That keeps the data for each worker separate and allows us to plot them individually.

If you run this example press the button you'll see a line appear on the plot and gradually extend. If you press the button again, another worker will start, returning more data and adding another line to the plot. Each worker generates data at a different rate, each generating 100 values.

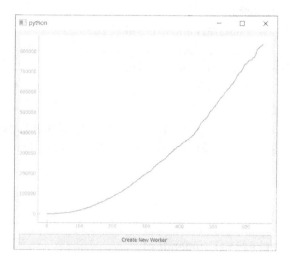

Figure 204. Plot output from a single runner after a few iterations.

You can start new workers up to the *max threads* available on your machine. After generating 100 values workers will shut-down and the next queued worker will start up — adding it's values as a new line.

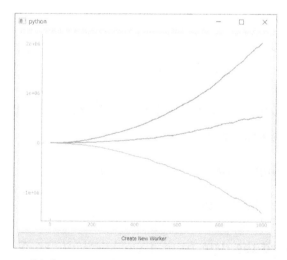

Figure 205. Plot from multiple runners.

The `tuple` is of course optional, you could send back bare strings if you have only one runner, or don't need to associated outputs with a source. It is also possible to send a `bytestring`, or any other type of data, by setting up the signals appropriately.

Stopping a running QRunnable

Once you've started a QRunnable there is, by default, no way to stop it. This isn't very nice from a usability point of view — if a user starts task by mistake, they then have to sit and wait for it to finish. Unfortunately, there is no way to *kill* a runner, however we can ask it nicely to stop. In this example we'll look at how we can use *flags* to indicate to the runner that it needs to stop.

In computing *flags* are variables that are used to signal a current or change in state. Think of how ships use flags to communicate with one another.

Figure 206. Lima, "You should stop your vessel instantly."

The code below implements a simple runner with a progress bar which increases every 0.01 seconds from left to right, and a **[Stop]** button. If you click **[Stop]** the worker will exit, stopping the progress bar permanently.

Listing 186. concurrent/qrunnable_stop.py

```python
import sys
import time

from PyQt6.QtCore import (
    QObject,
    QRunnable,
    Qt,
    QThreadPool,
    pyqtSignal,
    pyqtSlot,
)
from PyQt6.QtWidgets import (
    QApplication,
    QHBoxLayout,
    QMainWindow,
    QProgressBar,
```

```python
        QPushButton,
        QWidget,
    )


class WorkerKilledException(Exception):
    pass


class WorkerSignals(QObject):
    progress = pyqtSignal(int)


class JobRunner(QRunnable):

    signals = WorkerSignals()

    def __init__(self):
        super().__init__()

        self.is_killed = False    ①

    @pyqtSlot()
    def run(self):
        try:
            for n in range(100):
                self.signals.progress.emit(n + 1)
                time.sleep(0.1)

                if self.is_killed:    ②
                    raise WorkerKilledException

        except WorkerKilledException:
            pass    ③

    def kill(self):    ④
        self.is_killed = True


class MainWindow(QMainWindow):
    def __init__(self):
        super().__init__()
```

```
        # Some buttons
        w = QWidget()
        l = QHBoxLayout()
        w.setLayout(l)

        btn_stop = QPushButton("Stop")

        l.addWidget(btn_stop)

        self.setCentralWidget(w)

        # Create a statusbar.
        self.status = self.statusBar()
        self.progress = QProgressBar()
        self.status.addPermanentWidget(self.progress)

        # Thread runner
        self.threadpool = QThreadPool()

        # Create a runner
        self.runner = JobRunner()
        self.runner.signals.progress.connect(self.update_progress)
        self.threadpool.start(self.runner)

        btn_stop.pressed.connect(self.runner.kill)

        self.show()

    def update_progress(self, n):
        self.progress.setValue(n)


app = QApplication(sys.argv)
w = MainWindow()
app.exec()
```

① The flag to indicate whether the runner should be killed is called `.is_killed`.

② On each loop we test to see whether `.is_killed` is `True` in which case we throw an exception.

③ Catch the exception, we could emit a *finished* or *error* signal here.

④ .kill() convenience function so we can call worker.kill() to kill it.

If you want to stop the worker without throwing an error, you can simply return from the run method, e.g.

```
def run(self):
    for n in range(100):
        self.signals.progress.emit(n + 1)
        time.sleep(0)

        if self.is_killed:
            return
```

In the above example we only have a single worker. However, in many applications you will have more. How do you handle stopping workers when you have multiple runners running?

If you want the stop to stop *all* workers, then nothing is changed. You can simply hook all the workers up to the same "Stop" signal, and when that signal is fired — e.g. by pressing a button — all the workers will stop simultaneously.

If you want to be able to stop individual workers you would either need to create a separate button somewhere in your UI for each runner, or implement a *manager* to keep track of workers and provide a nicer interface to kill them. Take a look at The Manager for a working example.

Pausing a runner

Pausing a runner is a rarer requirement — normally you want things to go *as fast as possible.* But sometimes you may want to put a worker to "sleep" so it temporarily stops reading from a data source. You can do this with a small modification to the approach used to stop the runner. The code to do this is shown below.

The paused runner still takes up a slot in the thread pool, limiting the number of concurrent tasks that can be run. Use carefully!

Listing 187. concurrent/qrunnable_pause.py

```python
import sys
import time

from PyQt6.QtCore import (
    QObject,
    QRunnable,
    Qt,
    QThreadPool,
    pyqtSignal,
    pyqtSlot,
)
from PyQt6.QtWidgets import (
    QApplication,
    QHBoxLayout,
    QMainWindow,
    QProgressBar,
    QPushButton,
    QWidget,
)


class WorkerKilledException(Exception):
    pass


class WorkerSignals(QObject):
    progress = pyqtSignal(int)


class JobRunner(QRunnable):

    signals = WorkerSignals()

    def __init__(self):
        super().__init__()
```

```python
        self.is_paused = False
        self.is_killed = False

    @pyqtSlot()
    def run(self):
        for n in range(100):
            self.signals.progress.emit(n + 1)
            time.sleep(0.1)

            while self.is_paused:
                time.sleep(0)   ①

            if self.is_killed:
                raise WorkerKilledException

    def pause(self):
        self.is_paused = True

    def resume(self):
        self.is_paused = False

    def kill(self):
        self.is_killed = True


class MainWindow(QMainWindow):
    def __init__(self):
        super().__init__()

        # Some buttons
        w = QWidget()
        l = QHBoxLayout()
        w.setLayout(l)

        btn_stop = QPushButton("Stop")
        btn_pause = QPushButton("Pause")
        btn_resume = QPushButton("Resume")

        l.addWidget(btn_stop)
        l.addWidget(btn_pause)
        l.addWidget(btn_resume)
```

```
        self.setCentralWidget(w)

        # Create a statusbar.
        self.status = self.statusBar()
        self.progress = QProgressBar()
        self.status.addPermanentWidget(self.progress)

        # Thread runner
        self.threadpool = QThreadPool()

        # Create a runner
        self.runner = JobRunner()
        self.runner.signals.progress.connect(self.update_progress)
        self.threadpool.start(self.runner)

        btn_stop.pressed.connect(self.runner.kill)
        btn_pause.pressed.connect(self.runner.pause)
        btn_resume.pressed.connect(self.runner.resume)

        self.show()

    def update_progress(self, n):
        self.progress.setValue(n)


app = QApplication(sys.argv)
w = MainWindow()
app.exec()
```

① You can put a higher value that 0 in the sleep call if you don't want to check if it's time to wake up very often.

If you run this example you'll see a progress bar moving from left to right. If you click **[Pause]** the worker will pause. If you then click **[Resume]** the worker will continue from where it started. If you click **[Stop]** the worker will stop, permanently, as before.

Rather than throw an exception when receiving the is_paused signal, we enter a pause loop. This stops execution of the worker, but does not exit the run method or terminate the worker.

By using `while self.is_paused:` for this loop, we will exit the loop as soon as the worker is unpaused, and resume what we were doing before.

 You *must* include the `time.sleep()` call. This zero-second pause allows for Python to release the GIL, so this loop will not block other execution. Without that sleep you have a *busy loop* which will waste resources while doing nothing. Increase the sleep value if you want to check less often.

The Communicator

When running a thread you frequently want to be able get output from what is happening, while it's happening.

In this example we'll create a runner which performs requests to remote servers in a separate thread, and dumps the output to a logger. We'll also look at how we can pass a custom *parser* into the runner to extra data we're interested in from the requests.

 If you want to log data from external processes, rather than threads, take a look at Running External processes and Running external commands & processes.

Dumping data

In this first example we'll just dump the raw data (HTML) from each request to the output, using a custom signal.

Listing 188. concurrent/qrunnable_io.py

```python
import sys

import requests
from PyQt6.QtCore import (
    QObject,
    QRunnable,
    QThreadPool,
    QTimer,
    pyqtSignal,
    pyqtSlot,
)
from PyQt6.QtWidgets import (
    QApplication,
    QLabel,
    QMainWindow,
    QPlainTextEdit,
    QPushButton,
    QVBoxLayout,
```

```python
    QWidget,
)


class WorkerSignals(QObject):
    """
    Defines the signals available from a running worker thread.

    data
        tuple of (identifier, data)
    """

    data = pyqtSignal(tuple)


class Worker(QRunnable):
    """
    Worker thread

    Inherits from QRunnable to handle worker thread setup, signals
    and wrap-up.

    :param id: The id for this worker
    :param url: The url to retrieve
    """

    def __init__(self, id, url):
        super().__init__()
        self.id = id
        self.url = url

        self.signals = WorkerSignals()

    @pyqtSlot()
    def run(self):
        r = requests.get(self.url)

        for line in r.text.splitlines():
            self.signals.data.emit((self.id, line))


class MainWindow(QMainWindow):
    def __init__(self):
```

```python
        super().__init__()

        self.urls = [
            "https://www.pythonguis.com/",
            "https://www.mfitzp.com/",
            "https://www.google.com",
            "https://academy.pythonguis.com/",
        ]

        layout = QVBoxLayout()

        self.text = QPlainTextEdit()
        self.text.setReadOnly(True)

        button = QPushButton("GO GET EM!")
        button.pressed.connect(self.execute)

        layout.addWidget(self.text)
        layout.addWidget(button)

        w = QWidget()
        w.setLayout(layout)

        self.setCentralWidget(w)

        self.show()

        self.threadpool = QThreadPool()
        print(
            "Multithreading with maximum %d threads"
            % self.threadpool.maxThreadCount()
        )

    def execute(self):
        for n, url in enumerate(self.urls):
            worker = Worker(n, url)
            worker.signals.data.connect(self.display_output)

            # Execute
            self.threadpool.start(worker)

    def display_output(self, data):
        id, s = data
```

```
        self.text.appendPlainText("WORKER %d: %s" % (id, s))


app = QApplication(sys.argv)
window = MainWindow()
app.exec()
```

If you run this example and press the button you'll see the HTML output from a number of websites, prepended by the worker ID that retrieve them. Note that output from different workers is interleaved.

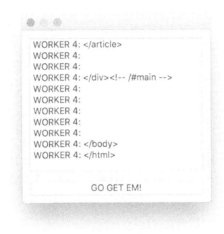

Figure 207. Logging output from multiple workers to the main window.

The tuple is of course optional, you could send back bare strings if you have only one runner, or don't need to associated outputs with a source. It is also possible to send a bytestring, or any other type of data, by setting up the signals appropriately.

Parsing data

Often you are not interested in the raw data from the thread (whether from a server or other external device) and instead want to process the data in some way first. In this example we create custom parsers, which can extract *specific* data from pages requested. We can create multiple workers, each receiving a different list of sites and parsers.

493

Listing 189. concurrent/qrunnable_io_parser.py

```python
        self.parsers = {   ①
            # Regular expression parsers, to extract data from the
HTML.
            "title": re.compile(
                r"<title.*?>(.*?)<\/title>", re.M | re.S
            ),
            "h1": re.compile(r"<h1.*?>(.*?)<\/h1>", re.M | re.S),
            "h2": re.compile(r"<h2.*?>(.*?)<\/h2>", re.M | re.S),
        }
```

① The parsers are defined as a series of compiled regular expressions. But you can define parsers however you like.

Listing 190. concurrent/qrunnable_io_parser.py

```python
    def execute(self):
        for n, url in enumerate(self.urls):
            worker = Worker(n, url, self.parsers)   ①
            worker.signals.data.connect(self.display_output)

            # Execute
            self.threadpool.start(worker)
```

① Pass the list of parsers to each worker.

Listing 191. concurrent/qrunnable_io_parser.py

```
class Worker(QRunnable):
    """

    Worker thread

    Inherits from QRunnable to handle worker thread setup, signals
    and wrap-up.

    :param id: The id for this worker
    :param url: The url to retrieve
    """

    def __init__(self, id, url, parsers):
        super().__init__()
        self.id = id
        self.url = url
        self.parsers = parsers

        self.signals = WorkerSignals()

    @pyqtSlot()
    def run(self):
        r = requests.get(self.url)

        data = {}
        for name, parser in self.parsers.items():    ①
            m = parser.search(r.text)
            if m:    ②
                data[name] = m.group(1).strip()

        self.signals.data.emit((self.id, data))
```

① Iterate the parser list we passed to the worker. Run each parser on the data
   for this page.

② If the regular expression matched, add the data to our data dictionary.

Running this, you'll see the output from each worker, with the H1, H2 and TITLE
tags extracted.

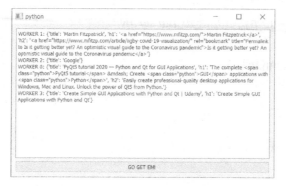

Figure 208. Displaying parsed output from multiple workers.

If you are building tools to extract data from websites, take a look at BeautifulSoup 4 [https://www.crummy.com/software/BeautifulSoup/bs4/doc/] which is far more robust than using regular expressions.

The Generic

You won't always know ahead of time what you want to use workers for. Or you may have a number of similar functions to perform and want a regular API for running them. In that case you can take advantage of the fact that in Python functions are objects to build a *generic* runner which accepts not just arguments, but also the function to run.

In the following example we create a single Worker class and then use it to run a number of different functions. With this setup you can pass in any Python function and have it executed in a separate thread.

The complete working example is given below, showcasing the custom QRunnable worker together with the worker & progress signals. You should be able to adapt this code to any application you develop.

Listing 192. concurrent/qrunnable_generic.py

```python
import sys
import time
import traceback

from PyQt6.QtCore import (
    QObject,
    QRunnable,
    QThreadPool,
    QTimer,
    pyqtSignal,
    pyqtSlot,
)
from PyQt6.QtWidgets import (
    QApplication,
    QLabel,
    QMainWindow,
    QPushButton,
    QVBoxLayout,
    QWidget,
)
```

```python
def execute_this_fn():
    for _ in range(0, 5):
        time.sleep(1)

    return "Done."


class WorkerSignals(QObject):
    """
    Defines the signals available from a running worker thread.

    Supported signals are:

    finished
        No data

    error
        `tuple` (exctype, value, traceback.format_exc() )

    result
        `object` data returned from processing, anything

    """

    finished = pyqtSignal()
    error = pyqtSignal(tuple)
    result = pyqtSignal(object)


class Worker(QRunnable):
    """
    Worker thread

    Inherits from QRunnable to handle worker thread setup, signals
and wrap-up.

    :param callback: The function callback to run on this worker
    :thread. Supplied args and
                        kwargs will be passed through to the runner.
    :type callback: function
    :param args: Arguments to pass to the callback function
    :param kwargs: Keywords to pass to the callback function
```

```python
        :
    """

    def __init__(self, fn, *args, **kwargs):
        super().__init__()
        # Store constructor arguments (re-used for processing)
        self.fn = fn
        self.args = args
        self.kwargs = kwargs
        self.signals = WorkerSignals()

    @pyqtSlot()
    def run(self):
        """
        Initialize the runner function with passed args, kwargs.
        """

        # Retrieve args/kwargs here; and fire processing using them
        try:
            result = self.fn(*self.args, **self.kwargs)
        except:
            traceback.print_exc()
            exctype, value = sys.exc_info()[:2]
            self.signals.error.emit(
                (exctype, value, traceback.format_exc())
            )
        else:
            self.signals.result.emit(
                result
            )  # Return the result of the processing
        finally:
            self.signals.finished.emit()  # Done


class MainWindow(QMainWindow):
    def __init__(self):
        super().__init__()

        self.counter = 0

        layout = QVBoxLayout()

        self.l = QLabel("Start")
```

499

```python
        b = QPushButton("DANGER!")
        b.pressed.connect(self.oh_no)

        layout.addWidget(self.l)
        layout.addWidget(b)

        w = QWidget()
        w.setLayout(layout)

        self.setCentralWidget(w)

        self.show()

        self.threadpool = QThreadPool()
        print(
            "Multithreading with maximum %d threads"
            % self.threadpool.maxThreadCount()
        )

        self.timer = QTimer()
        self.timer.setInterval(1000)
        self.timer.timeout.connect(self.recurring_timer)
        self.timer.start()

    def print_output(self, s):
        print(s)

    def thread_complete(self):
        print("THREAD COMPLETE!")

    def oh_no(self):
        # Pass the function to execute
        worker = Worker(
            execute_this_fn
        )  # Any other args, kwargs are passed to the run function
        worker.signals.result.connect(self.print_output)
        worker.signals.finished.connect(self.thread_complete)

        # Execute
        self.threadpool.start(worker)

    def recurring_timer(self):
        self.counter += 1
```

```
        self.l.setText("Counter: %d" % self.counter)


app = QApplication(sys.argv)
window = MainWindow()
app.exec()
```

The generic function approach adds a limitation that may not be immediately obvious — the run function does not have access to the `self` object of your runner, and therefore cannot access the signals to emit the data itself. We can only emit the return value of the function, once it has ended. While you can return a compound type, such as a `tuple`, to return multiple values, you can't get progress signals or in-progress data.

However, there is a way around this. Since you can pass anything you want **into** the custom function, you can also pass `self` or the `self.signals` object to make them available to you.

Listing 193. concurrent/qrunnable_generic_callback.py

```
import sys
import time
import traceback

from PyQt6.QtCore import (
    QObject,
    QRunnable,
    QThreadPool,
    QTimer,
    pyqtSignal,
    pyqtSlot,
)
from PyQt6.QtWidgets import (
    QApplication,
    QLabel,
    QMainWindow,
    QPushButton,
    QVBoxLayout,
    QWidget,
```

```python
    )

def execute_this_fn(signals):
    for n in range(0, 5):
        time.sleep(1)
        signals.progress.emit(n * 100 / 4)

    return "Done."


class WorkerSignals(QObject):
    """
    Defines the signals available from a running worker thread.

    Supported signals are:

    finished
        No data

    error
        `tuple` (exctype, value, traceback.format_exc() )

    result
        `object` data returned from processing, anything

    progress
        `int` indicating % progress

    """

    finished = pyqtSignal()
    error = pyqtSignal(tuple)
    result = pyqtSignal(object)
    progress = pyqtSignal(int)


class Worker(QRunnable):
    """
    Worker thread

    Inherits from QRunnable to handle worker thread setup, signals
and wrap-up.
```

```python
        :param callback: The function callback to run on this worker
        :thread. Supplied args and
                        kwargs will be passed through to the runner.
        :type callback: function
        :param args: Arguments to pass to the callback function
        :param kwargs: Keywords to pass to the callback function
        :
        """

    def __init__(self, fn, *args, **kwargs):
        super().__init__()
        # Store constructor arguments (re-used for processing)
        self.fn = fn
        self.args = args
        self.kwargs = kwargs
        self.signals = WorkerSignals()

        # Add the callback to our kwargs
        kwargs["signals"] = self.signals

    @pyqtSlot()
    def run(self):
        """
        Initialize the runner function with passed args, kwargs.
        """

        # Retrieve args/kwargs here; and fire processing using them
        try:
            result = self.fn(*self.args, **self.kwargs)
        except Exception:
            traceback.print_exc()
            exctype, value = sys.exc_info()[:2]
            self.signals.error.emit(
                (exctype, value, traceback.format_exc())
            )
        else:
            self.signals.result.emit(
                result
            )  # Return the result of the processing
        finally:
            self.signals.finished.emit()  # Done
```

```python
class MainWindow(QMainWindow):
    def __init__(self):
        super().__init__()

        self.counter = 0

        layout = QVBoxLayout()

        self.l = QLabel("Start")
        b = QPushButton("DANGER!")
        b.pressed.connect(self.oh_no)

        layout.addWidget(self.l)
        layout.addWidget(b)

        w = QWidget()
        w.setLayout(layout)

        self.setCentralWidget(w)

        self.show()

        self.threadpool = QThreadPool()
        print(
            "Multithreading with maximum %d threads"
            % self.threadpool.maxThreadCount()
        )

        self.timer = QTimer()
        self.timer.setInterval(1000)
        self.timer.timeout.connect(self.recurring_timer)
        self.timer.start()

    def progress_fn(self, n):
        print("%d%% done" % n)

    def print_output(self, s):
        print(s)

    def thread_complete(self):
        print("THREAD COMPLETE!")
```

```
    def oh_no(self):
        # Pass the function to execute
        worker = Worker(
            execute_this_fn
        )  # Any other args, kwargs are passed to the run function
        worker.signals.result.connect(self.print_output)
        worker.signals.finished.connect(self.thread_complete)
        worker.signals.progress.connect(self.progress_fn)

        # Execute
        self.threadpool.start(worker)

    def recurring_timer(self):
        self.counter += 1
        self.l.setText("Counter: %d" % self.counter)


app = QApplication(sys.argv)
window = MainWindow()
app.exec()
```

Note that for this to work, your custom function must be able to accept the additional argument. You can do this by defining the functions with **kwargs to silently swallow the extra arguments if they aren't used.

```
def execute_this_fn(**kwargs):    ①
    for _ in range(0, 5):
        time.sleep(1)

    return "Done."
```

① The signals keyword argument is swallowed up by **kwargs.

Running External processes

So far we've looked how we can run Python code in another *thread*. Sometimes however you need to run external programs — such as command line programs — in another *process*.

You actually have two options when starting external processes with PyQt6. You can either use Python's built-in subprocess module to start the processes, or you can use Qt's QProcess.

 For more information on running external processes using QProcess take a look at the Running external commands & processes chapter.

Starting a new process always comes with a small execution cost and will block your GUI momentarily. This is usually not perceptible but it can add up depending on your use case and may have performance impacts. You can get around this by starting your processes in another thread.

If you want to communicate with the process in real-time you will need a separate thread to avoid blocking the GUI. QProcess handles this separate thread for you internally, but with Python subprocess you will need to do this yourself.

In this QRunnable example we use instances of workers to handle starting external processes through Python subprocess. This keeps the startup cost of the process out of the GUI thread and also allows us to interact with the processes directly through Python.

Listing 194. concurrent/qrunnable_process.py

```python
import subprocess
import sys

from PyQt6.QtCore import (
    QObject,
    QRunnable,
```

```python
    QThreadPool,
    pyqtSignal,
    pyqtSlot,
)
from PyQt6.QtWidgets import (
    QApplication,
    QMainWindow,
    QPlainTextEdit,
    QPushButton,
    QVBoxLayout,
    QWidget,
)


class WorkerSignals(QObject):
    """
    Defines the signals available from a running worker thread.

    Supported signals are:

    finished: No data
    result: str
    """

    result = pyqtSignal(
        str
    )  # Send back the output from the process as a string.
    finished = pyqtSignal()


class SubProcessWorker(QRunnable):
    """
    ProcessWorker worker thread

    Inherits from QRunnable to handle worker thread setup, signals
and wrap-up.

    :param command: command to execute with `subprocess`.

    """

    def __init__(self, command):
        super().__init__()
```

```python
        # Store constructor arguments (re-used for processing).
        self.signals = WorkerSignals()

        # The command to be executed.
        self.command = command

    @pyqtSlot()
    def run(self):
        """
        Execute the command, returning the result.
        """
        output = subprocess.getoutput(self.command)
        self.signals.result.emit(output)
        self.signals.finished.emit()


class MainWindow(QMainWindow):
    def __init__(self):
        super().__init__()

        # Some buttons
        layout = QVBoxLayout()

        self.text = QPlainTextEdit()
        layout.addWidget(self.text)

        btn_run = QPushButton("Execute")
        btn_run.clicked.connect(self.start)

        layout.addWidget(btn_run)

        w = QWidget()
        w.setLayout(layout)
        self.setCentralWidget(w)

        # Thread runner
        self.threadpool = QThreadPool()

        self.show()

    def start(self):
        # Create a runner
```

```
        self.runner = SubProcessWorker("python dummy_script.py")
        self.runner.signals.result.connect(self.result)
        self.threadpool.start(self.runner)

    def result(self, s):
        self.text.appendPlainText(s)


app = QApplication(sys.argv)
w = MainWindow()
app.exec()
```

 The "external program" in this example is a simple Python script
python dummy_script.py. However can replace this with any
other program you like.

Running processes have two streams of output — *standard out* and *standard
error*. The standard output returns the actual result of the execution (if any)
while standard error returns any error *or* logging information.

In this example we're running the external script using subprocess.getoutput.
This runs the external program, waiting for it to complete before returning. Once
it has completed, getoutput returns both the *standard output* and *standard error*
together as a single string.

Parsing the result

You don't have to pass the output as-is. If you have post-processing to do on the
output from the command, it can make sense to handle this in your worker
thread as well, to keep it self-contained. The worker can then return the data to
your GUI thread in a structured format, ready to be used.

In the following example, we pass in a function to post-process the result of the
demo script to extract the values of interest into a dictionary. This data is used to
update widgets on the GUI side.

Listing 195. concurrent/qrunnable_process_result.py

```python
import subprocess
import sys
from collections import namedtuple

from PyQt6.QtCore import (
    QObject,
    QRunnable,
    QThreadPool,
    pyqtSignal,
    pyqtSlot,
)
from PyQt6.QtWidgets import (
    QApplication,
    QLineEdit,
    QMainWindow,
    QPushButton,
    QSpinBox,
    QVBoxLayout,
    QWidget,
)


def extract_vars(l):
    """
    Extracts variables from lines, looking for lines
    containing an equals, and splitting into key=value.
    """
    data = {}
    for s in l.splitlines():
        if "=" in s:
            name, value = s.split("=")
            data[name] = value

    data["number_of_lines"] = len(l)
    return data


class WorkerSignals(QObject):
    """
    Defines the signals available from a running worker thread.

    Supported signals are:
```

```python
    finished: No data
    result: dict
    """

    result = pyqtSignal(dict)  # Send back the output as dictionary.
    finished = pyqtSignal()


class SubProcessWorker(QRunnable):
    """
    ProcessWorker worker thread

    Inherits from QRunnable to handle worker thread setup, signals
and wrap-up.

    :param command: command to execute with `subprocess`.

    """

    def __init__(self, command, process_result=None):
        super().__init__()

        # Store constructor arguments (re-used for processing).
        self.signals = WorkerSignals()

        # The command to be executed.
        self.command = command

        # The post-processing fn.
        self.process_result = process_result

    @pyqtSlot()
    def run(self):
        """
        Execute the command, returning the result.
        """

        output = subprocess.getoutput(self.command)

        if self.process_result:
            output = self.process_result(output)

        self.signals.result.emit(output)
```

```python
        self.signals.finished.emit()


class MainWindow(QMainWindow):
    def __init__(self):
        super().__init__()

        # Some buttons
        layout = QVBoxLayout()

        self.name = QLineEdit()
        layout.addWidget(self.name)

        self.country = QLineEdit()
        layout.addWidget(self.country)

        self.website = QLineEdit()
        layout.addWidget(self.website)

        self.number_of_lines = QSpinBox()
        layout.addWidget(self.number_of_lines)

        btn_run = QPushButton("Execute")
        btn_run.clicked.connect(self.start)

        layout.addWidget(btn_run)

        w = QWidget()
        w.setLayout(layout)
        self.setCentralWidget(w)

        # Thread runner
        self.threadpool = QThreadPool()

        self.show()

    def start(self):
        # Create a runner
        self.runner = SubProcessWorker(
            "python dummy_script.py", process_result=extract_vars
        )
        self.runner.signals.result.connect(self.result)
        self.threadpool.start(self.runner)
```

```
    def result(self, data):
        print(data)
        self.name.setText(data["name"])
        self.country.setText(data["country"])
        self.website.setText(data["website"])
        self.number_of_lines.setValue(data["number_of_lines"])


app = QApplication(sys.argv)
w = MainWindow()
app.exec()
```

The simple parser in this case looks for any lines with a = in them, splits on this to produce a name and a value, which are then stored in a dict. However, you can use any tools you like to extract data from the string output.

Because getoutput *blocks* until the program is complete, we cannot see how the program is running — for example, to get progress information. In the next example we'll show how to get live output from a running process.

Tracking progress

Often external programs will output progress information to the console. You might want to capture this and either show it to your users, or use it to generate a progress bar.

For the result of the execution you usually want to capture standard out, for the progress to capture *standard error.* In this following example we capture both. As well as the command, we pass a custom parser function to the worker, to capture the current worker progress and emit it as a number 0-99.

This example is quite complex. The full source code is available in the source code with the book, but here we'll cover the key differences to the simpler one.

Listing 196. concurrent/qrunnable_process_parser.py

```python
@pyqtSlot()
def run(self):
    """
    Initialize the runner function with passed args, kwargs.
    """

    result = []

    with subprocess.Popen(    ①
        self.command,
        bufsize=1,
        stdout=subprocess.PIPE,
        stderr=subprocess.STDOUT,    ②
        universal_newlines=True,
    ) as proc:
        while proc.poll() is None:
            data = proc.stdout.readline()    ③
            result.append(data)
            if self.parser:    ④
                value = self.parser(data)
                if value:
                    self.signals.progress.emit(value)

    output = "".join(result)

    self.signals.result.emit(output)
```

① Run using Popen to give us access to output streams.

② We pipe *standard error* out together with *standard output*.

③ Read a line from the process (or wait for one).

④ Pass all collected data so far to the parser.

Parsing is handled by this simple parser function, which takes in a string and matches the regular expression `Total complete: (\d+)%`.

Listing 197. concurrent/qrunnable_process_parser.py

```python
progress_re = re.compile("Total complete: (\d+)%")


def simple_percent_parser(output):
    """
    Matches lines using the progress_re regex,
    returning a single integer for the % progress.
    """
    m = progress_re.search(output)
    if m:
        pc_complete = m.group(1)
        return int(pc_complete)
```

The parser is passed into the runner along with the command — this means we can use a generic runner for all subprocesses and handle the output differently for different commands.

Listing 198. concurrent/qrunnable_process_parser.py

```python
    def start(self):
        # Create a runner
        self.runner = SubProcessWorker(
            command="python dummy_script.py",
            parser=simple_percent_parser,
        )
        self.runner.signals.result.connect(self.result)
        self.runner.signals.progress.connect(self.progress.setValue)
        self.threadpool.start(self.runner)
```

In this simple example we only pass the *latest* line from the process, since our custom script outputs lines like `Total complete: 25%`. That means that we only need the *latest* line to be able to calculate the current progress.

Sometimes however, scripts can be a bit less helpful. For example `ffmpeg` the video encoder outputs the duration of the video file to be processed once at the beginning, then outputs the *duration* that has currently been processed. To calculate the % of progress you need *both* values.

To do that, you can pass the collected output to the parser instead. There is an example of this in the source code with the book, named `concurrent/qrunnable_process_parser_elapsed.py`.

The Manager

In the previous examples we've created a number of different `QRunnable` implementations that can be used for different purposes in your application. In all cases you can run as many of these runners as you like, on the same or multiple `QThreadPool` pools. However, sometimes you will want to keep track of the runners which you have running in order to do something with their output, or provide users with control over the runners directly.

`QThreadPool` itself does not give you access to the currently running runners, so we need to create our own *manager* ourselves, through which we start and control our workers.

The example below brings together some of the other worker features already introduced — progress, pause and stop control — together with the model views to present individual progress bars. This manager will likely work as a drop-in for most use-cases you have for running threads.

 This is quite a complex example, the full source code is available in the resources for the book. Here we'll go through the key parts of the `QRunnable` manager in turn.

The worker manager

The worker manager class holds the threadpool, our workers and their progress and state information. It is derived from `QAbstractListModel` meaning it also provides a Qt model-like interface, allowing for it to be used as the model for a `QListView` — providing a per-worker progress bar and status indicator. The status tracking is handled through a number of internal signals, which attach automatically to every added worker.

Listing 199. concurrent/qrunnable_manager.py

```
class WorkerManager(QAbstractListModel):
    """
```

```
        Manager to handle our worker queues and state.
        Also functions as a Qt data model for a view
        displaying progress for each worker.

        """

        _workers = {}
        _state = {}

        status = pyqtSignal(str)

        def __init__(self):
            super().__init__()

            # Create a threadpool for our workers.
            self.threadpool = QThreadPool()
            # self.threadpool.setMaxThreadCount(1)
            self.max_threads = self.threadpool.maxThreadCount()
            print(
                "Multithreading with maximum %d threads" % self
.max_threads
            )

            self.status_timer = QTimer()
            self.status_timer.setInterval(100)
            self.status_timer.timeout.connect(self.notify_status)
            self.status_timer.start()

        def notify_status(self):
            n_workers = len(self._workers)
            running = min(n_workers, self.max_threads)
            waiting = max(0, n_workers - self.max_threads)
            self.status.emit(
                "{} running, {} waiting, {} threads".format(
                    running, waiting, self.max_threads
                )
            )

        def enqueue(self, worker):
            """

            Enqueue a worker to run (at some point) by passing it to the
QThreadPool.
            """
```

```python
        worker.signals.error.connect(self.receive_error)
        worker.signals.status.connect(self.receive_status)
        worker.signals.progress.connect(self.receive_progress)
        worker.signals.finished.connect(self.done)

        self.threadpool.start(worker)
        self._workers[worker.job_id] = worker

        # Set default status to waiting, 0 progress.
        self._state[worker.job_id] = DEFAULT_STATE.copy()

        self.layoutChanged.emit()

    def receive_status(self, job_id, status):
        self._state[job_id]["status"] = status
        self.layoutChanged.emit()

    def receive_progress(self, job_id, progress):
        self._state[job_id]["progress"] = progress
        self.layoutChanged.emit()

    def receive_error(self, job_id, message):
        print(job_id, message)

    def done(self, job_id):
        """
        Task/worker complete. Remove it from the active workers
        dictionary. We leave it in worker_state, as this is used to
        to display past/complete workers too.
        """
        del self._workers[job_id]
        self.layoutChanged.emit()

    def cleanup(self):
        """
        Remove any complete/failed workers from worker_state.
        """
        for job_id, s in list(self._state.items()):
            if s["status"] in (STATUS_COMPLETE, STATUS_ERROR):
                del self._state[job_id]
        self.layoutChanged.emit()

    # Model interface
```

```
    def data(self, index, role):
        if role == Qt.ItemDataRole.DisplayRole:
            # See below for the data structure.
            job_ids = list(self._state.keys())
            job_id = job_ids[index.row()]
            return job_id, self._state[job_id]

    def rowCount(self, index):
        return len(self._state)
```

Workers are constructed outside the manager and passed in via .enqueue(). This connects all signals and adds the worker to the thread pool`. It will be executed, as normal once a thread is available.

The worker's are kept in an internal dictionary _workers keyed by the job id. There is a separate dictionary _state which stores the status and progress information about the workers. We keep them separate so we can delete jobs once complete, keeping an accurate count, yet continue to show information about completed jobs until cleared.

Signals from each submitted workers are connected to slots on the manager, which update the _state dictionary, print error messages or delete the completed job. Once any state is updated, we must call .layoutChanged() to trigger a refresh of the model view. The _clear_ method iterates through the _state list and removes any that are complete or have failed.

Lastly, we set up a timer to regularly trigger a method to emit the current thread counts as a status message. The number of active threads is the *minimum* of the number of _workers and the max_threads. The waiting threads is the number of _workers _minus_ the max_threads (as long as it is more than zero). The message is shown on the main window status bar.

The worker

The worker itself follows the same pattern as all our previous examples. The only *requirement* for our manager is the addition of a .job_id property which is set

520

when the worker is created.

The signals from the workers must include this *job id* so the manager knows which worker sent the signal — updating the correct status, progress and finished states.

The worker itself is a simply dummy worker, which iterates 100 times (1 for each % progress) and performs a simple calculation. This worker calculation generates a series of numbers, but is constructed to occasionally throw *division by zero* errors.

Listing 200. concurrent/qrunnable_manager.py

```python
class WorkerSignals(QObject):
    """
    Defines the signals available from a running worker thread.

    Supported signals are:

    finished
        No data

    error
        `tuple` (exctype, value, traceback.format_exc() )

    result
        `object` data returned from processing, anything

    progress
        `int` indicating % progress

    """

    error = pyqtSignal(str, str)
    result = pyqtSignal(str, object)   # We can send anything back.

    finished = pyqtSignal(str)
    progress = pyqtSignal(str, int)
    status = pyqtSignal(str, str)
```

```python
class Worker(QRunnable):
    """
    Worker thread

    Inherits from QRunnable to handle worker thread setup, signals
and wrap-up.

    :param args: Arguments to pass for the worker
    :param kwargs: Keywords to pass for the worker

    """

    def __init__(self, *args, **kwargs):
        super().__init__()

        # Store constructor arguments (re-used for processing).
        self.signals = WorkerSignals()

        # Give this job a unique ID.
        self.job_id = str(uuid.uuid4())

        # The arguments for the worker
        self.args = args
        self.kwargs = kwargs

        self.signals.status.emit(self.job_id, STATUS_WAITING)

    @pyqtSlot()
    def run(self):
        """
        Initialize the runner function with passed args, kwargs.
        """

        self.signals.status.emit(self.job_id, STATUS_RUNNING)

        x, y = self.args

        try:

            value = random.randint(0, 100) * x
            delay = random.random() / 10
            result = []
```

```
            for n in range(100):
                # Generate some numbers.
                value = value / y
                y -= 1

                # The following will sometimes throw a division by
zero error.

                result.append(value)

                # Pass out the current progress.
                self.signals.progress.emit(self.job_id, n + 1)
                time.sleep(delay)

        except Exception as e:
            print(e)
            # We swallow the error and continue.
            self.signals.error.emit(self.job_id, str(e))
            self.signals.status.emit(self.job_id, STATUS_ERROR)

        else:
            self.signals.result.emit(self.job_id, result)
            self.signals.status.emit(self.job_id, STATUS_COMPLETE)

        self.signals.finished.emit(self.job_id)
```

In addition to the progress signals we've seen before, we also have a *status* signal which emits one of the following statuses. Exceptions are caught and both the exception text and the error state are emitted using *error* and *status*.

Listing 201. concurrent/qrunnable_manager.py

```python
STATUS_WAITING = "waiting"
STATUS_RUNNING = "running"
STATUS_ERROR = "error"
STATUS_COMPLETE = "complete"


STATUS_COLORS = {
    STATUS_RUNNING: "#33a02c",
    STATUS_ERROR: "#e31a1c",
    STATUS_COMPLETE: "#b2df8a",
}

DEFAULT_STATE = {"progress": 0, "status": STATUS_WAITING}
```

Each of the active statuses have assigned colors which will be used in drawing on the progress bar.

Custom row display

We're using a QListView for the progress bar display. Normally a list view displays a simple text value for each row. To modify this we use a QItemDelegate which allows us to paint a custom widget for each row.

Listing 202. concurrent/qrunnable_manager.py

```python
class ProgressBarDelegate(QStyledItemDelegate):
    def paint(self, painter, option, index):
        # data is our status dict, containing progress, id, status
        job_id, data = index.model().data(
            index, Qt.ItemDataRole.DisplayRole
        )
        if data["progress"] > 0:
            color = QColor(STATUS_COLORS[data["status"]])

            brush = QBrush()
            brush.setColor(color)
            brush.setStyle(Qt.BrushStyle.SolidPattern)

            width = option.rect.width() * data["progress"] / 100

            rect = QRect(
                option.rect
            )  # Copy of the rect, so we can modify.
            rect.setWidth(width)

            painter.fillRect(rect, brush)

        pen = QPen()
        pen.setColor(Qt.GlobalColor.black)
        painter.drawText(
            option.rect, Qt.AlignmentFlag.AlignLeft, job_id
        )
```

We get the data for the current row from the model using
`index.model().data(index, Qt.ItemDataRole.DisplayRole)`. This is calling the
`.data()` method on our custom model (manager) passing in the `index` and `role`. In
our `.data()` method we are returning two bits of data — `job_id` and the `state`
dictionary, containing *progress* and *status* keys.

For active jobs (`progress > 0`) *status* is used to select a color for the bar. This is
drawn as a rectangle of the item row size `option.rect()`, with the width adjusted
by the % completion. Finally, we write the `job_id` text over the top of this.

Starting a job

With everything in place, we can now enqueue jobs by calling `.self.worker.enqueue()` passing in arguments to the worker.

Listing 203. concurrent/qrunnable_manager.py

```python
def start_worker(self):
    x = random.randint(0, 1000)
    y = random.randint(0, 1000)

    w = Worker(x, y)
    w.signals.result.connect(self.display_result)
    w.signals.error.connect(self.display_result)

    self.workers.enqueue(w)
```

The `.enqueue()` method accepts a constructed worker and attaches the internal signals to it to track progress. However, we can still attach any other external signals that we want.

Figure 209. The manager interface, where you can start new jobs and see progress.

Also, while this example has only a single worker class, you can use this same manager with any other QRunnable-derived classes, as long as they have the same signals available. This means you can use a single worker manager to manage all the workers in your app.

 Take a look at the full code in the source files with this book and experiment modifying the manager to your needs — for example, try adding kill & pause functionality, generic function runners.

Stopping jobs

We can start jobs, and some of them die due to errors. But what if we want to stop jobs that are taking too long? The QListView allows us to select rows and through the selected row we can kill a specific worker. The method below is linked to a button, and looks up the worker from the current selected item in the list.

Listing 204. concurrent/qrunnable_manager_stop.py

```
def stop_worker(self):
    selected = self.progress.selectedIndexes()
    for idx in selected:
        job_id, _ = self.workers.data(
            idx, Qt.ItemDataRole.DisplayRole
        )
        self.workers.kill(job_id)
```

In addition to this we need to modify the delegate to draw the currently selected item and update the worker and manager to pass through the *kill* signal. Take a look at the full source for this example to see how it all fits together.

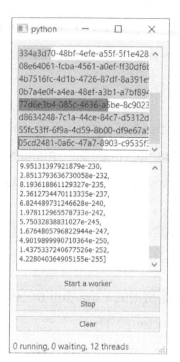

Figure 210. The manager, selecting a job allows you to stop it.

27. Long-running threads

In the examples we've looked at so far we've been using QRunnable objects to execute *tasks* using the QThreadPool. The tasks we submitted were handled in order by the thread pool, with the maximum concurrency constrained by the pool.

But what if you want something to execute *right now* regardless of what else is happening? Or, perhaps you want to keep a thread running in the background the *entire time* your application is running — to interact with some remote service or hardware, or to stream data through for processing. In that case the thread pool architecture may not be appropriate.

In this chapter we'll look at PyQt6's persistent thread interface QThread. It provides a very similar interface to the QRunnable objects you've already seen, but gives you complete control over when and how the thread is run.

Using QThread

Just like in the QRunnable examples, the QThread class acts as a wrapper around the code you want to execute in another thread. It handles the start up and shifting of the work to a separate thread, as well as managing and shutting down the thread once it completes. You just need to provide the code to execute. This is done by subclassing QThread and implementing a run() method.

A simple thread

Let's start with a simple example. Below, we've implemented a worker thread which can perform arithmetic for us. We have added a single signal to the thread which we can use to send data out of the thread.

Listing 205. concurrent/qthread_1.py

```
import sys
import time
```

```python
from PyQt6.QtCore import QThread, pyqtSignal, pyqtSlot
from PyQt6.QtWidgets import QApplication, QLabel, QMainWindow


class Thread(QThread):
    """
    Worker thread
    """

    result = pyqtSignal(str)   ①

    @pyqtSlot()
    def run(self):
        """
        Your code goes in this method
        """
        print("Thread start")
        counter = 0
        while True:
            time.sleep(0.1)
            # Output the number as a formatted string.
            self.result.emit(f"The number is {counter}")
            counter += 1
        print("Thread complete")


class MainWindow(QMainWindow):
    def __init__(self):
        super().__init__()

        # Create thread and start it.
        self.thread = Thread()
        self.thread.start()   ②

        label = QLabel("Output will appear here")

        # Connect signal, so output appears on label.
        self.thread.result.connect(label.setText)

        self.setCentralWidget(label)
        self.show()
```

```
app = QApplication(sys.argv)
window = MainWindow()
app.exec()
```

① Unlike QRunnable the QThread class *does* inherit from QObject so we can define the signals on the thread object itself.

② Call .start() to start the thread, *not* .run()!

If you run this example you'll see a number in a window counting upwards. Not very exciting! But this counting is happening on a *separate thread* from your GUI and the result is being emitted using signals. This means the GUI isn't blocked by the work taking place (although normal Python GIL rules apply).

Figure 211. QThread counter with the result displayed via a signal.

Try increasing the duration of the sleep() call and you'll see that, even with the thread blocked the main GUI continues to run as normal.

 If you usually work with numpy or other libraries, experiment with using them to perform more complex calculations in the thread.

 You will *usually* want to add signals of some kind to your thread for communication.

Thread control

Now we can start our thread, but we have no way to stop it. Unlike QRunnable the QThread class *has* a built-in method .terminate() which can be used to *immediately* kill a running thread. This is not a clean shutdown — the thread will simply stop wherever it was, and no Python exception will be thrown.

Listing 206. concurrent/qthread_2.py

```python
class MainWindow(QMainWindow):
    def __init__(self):
        super().__init__()

        # Create thread and start it.
        self.thread = Thread()
        self.thread.start()

        label = QLabel("Output will appear here")
        button = QPushButton("Kill thread")
        # Terminate (kill immediately) the thread.
        button.pressed.connect(self.thread.terminate)

        # Connect signal, so output appears on label.
        self.thread.result.connect(label.setText)

        container = QWidget()
        layout = QVBoxLayout()
        layout.addWidget(label)
        layout.addWidget(button)
        container.setLayout(layout)

        self.setCentralWidget(container)
        self.show()
```

If you run this, you'll notice that the "Thread complete" message we added after the thread's main loop is never displayed. That's because when we call .terminate() the execution just *halts* and never reaches that point in the code.

Figure 212. The thread can be terminated using the button control.

However, QThread has a *finished* signal which can be used to trigger some action after the thread completes. This is *always* fired — whether the thread terminates or shuts down cleanly.

The thread object persists after the thread has completed running & you can *usually* use this to query the thread for status. However be careful — if the thread was terminated, interacting with the thread object may cause your application to crash. The example below demonstrates this by attempting to print some information about the thread object after it is terminated.

Listing 207. concurrent/qthread_2b.py

```python
class MainWindow(QMainWindow):
    def __init__(self):
        super().__init__()

        # Create thread and start it.
        self.thread = Thread()
        self.thread.start()

        label = QLabel("Output will appear here")
        button = QPushButton("Kill thread")
        # Terminate (kill immediately) the thread.
        button.pressed.connect(self.thread.terminate)

        # Connect signal, so output appears on label.
        self.thread.result.connect(label.setText)
        self.thread.finished.connect(self.thread_has_finished)   ①

        container = QWidget()
        layout = QVBoxLayout()
        layout.addWidget(label)
        layout.addWidget(button)
        container.setLayout(layout)

        self.setCentralWidget(container)
        self.show()

    def thread_has_finished(self):
        print("Thread has finished.")
        print(
            self.thread,
            self.thread.isRunning(),
            self.thread.isFinished(),
        )   ②
```

① Connecting the *finished* signal to our custom slot.

② If you terminate the thread your application will likely crash here.

While you *can* terminate a thread from inside, it's cleaner to just return from the run() method. Once you exit the run() method the thread will be automatically ended and cleaned up safely & the finished signal will fire.

Listing 208. concurrent/qthread_2c.py

```python
class Thread(QThread):
    """
    Worker thread
    """

    result = pyqtSignal(str)

    @pyqtSlot()
    def run(self):
        """
        Your code goes in this method
        """
        print("Thread start")
        counter = 0
        while True:
            time.sleep(0.1)
            # Output the number as a formatted string.
            self.result.emit(f"The number is {counter}")
            counter += 1
            if counter > 50:
                return     ①
```

① calling return in the run() method will exit and end the thread.

When you run the above example, the counter will stop at 50 because we return from the run() method. If you try and press the terminate button *after* this has happened, notice that you don't receive the *thread finished* signal a second time — the thread has already been shut down, so it cannot be terminated.

Sending data

In the previous example our thread was running but not able to receive any data from outside. Usually when you use long-running threads you want to be able to communicate with them, either to pass them work, or to control their behavior in some other way.

We've been talking about how important it is to shut your threads down cleanly. So let's start by looking at how we can communicate with our thread that we want it to shut down. As with the QRunnable examples, we can do this by using an internal flag in the thread to control the *main loop*, with the loop continuing while our flag is True.

To shut the thread down, we change the value of this flag. Below we've implemented this using a flag named is_running and custom method .stop() on the thread. When called, this method toggles the is_running flag to False. With the flag set to False the *main loop* will end, the thread will exit the run() method and the thread will shut down.

Listing 209. concurrent/qthread_3.py

```python
class Thread(QThread):
    """
    Worker thread
    """

    result = pyqtSignal(str)

    @pyqtSlot()
    def run(self):
        """
        Your code goes in this method
        """
        self.data = None
        self.is_running = True
        print("Thread start")
        counter = 0
        while self.is_running:
            time.sleep(0.1)
            # Output the number as a formatted string.
            self.result.emit(f"The number is {counter}")
            counter += 1

    def stop(self):
        self.is_running = False
```

We can then modify our button to call the custom stop() method, rather than terminate.

Listing 210. concurrent/qthread_3.py

```
button = QPushButton("Shutdown thread")
# Shutdown the thread nicely.
button.pressed.connect(self.thread.stop)
```

Since the thread shutdown cleanly, we can access the thread object without risk of it crashing. Re-add the print statement to the thread_has_finished method.

Listing 211. concurrent/qthread_3.py

```
def thread_has_finished(self):
    print("Thread has finished.")
    print(
        self.thread,
        self.thread.isRunning(),
        self.thread.isFinished(),
    )
```

If you run this you will see the number counting up as before, but pressing the button will stop the thread dead. Notice that we are able to display the metadata about the thread after the shutdown, because the thread didn't crash.

Figure 213. The thread can now be cleanly shutdown using the button.

We can use this same general approach to send any data into the thread that we like. Below we've extended our custom Thread class to add a send_data method, which accepts a single argument, and stores it internally on the thread via self.

Using this we can send in data which is accessible within the threads run() method and use it to modify behavior.

Listing 212. concurrent/qthread_4.py

```python
import sys
import time

from PyQt6.QtCore import QThread, pyqtSignal, pyqtSlot
from PyQt6.QtWidgets import (
    QApplication,
    QLabel,
    QMainWindow,
    QPushButton,
    QSpinBox,
    QVBoxLayout,
    QWidget,
)


class Thread(QThread):
    """
    Worker thread
    """

    result = pyqtSignal(str)

    @pyqtSlot()
    def run(self):
        """
        Your code goes in this method
        """
        self.data = None
        self.is_running = True
        print("Thread start")
        counter = 0
        while self.is_running:
            while self.data is None:
                time.sleep(0.1)  # wait for data <1>.
```

```python
                # Output the number as a formatted string.
                counter += self.data
                self.result.emit(f"The cumulative total is {counter}")
                self.data = None

    def send_data(self, data):
        """
        Receive data onto internal variable.
        """
        self.data = data

    def stop(self):
        self.is_running = False


class MainWindow(QMainWindow):
    def __init__(self):
        super().__init__()

        # Create thread and start it.
        self.thread = Thread()
        self.thread.start()

        self.numeric_input = QSpinBox()
        button_input = QPushButton("Submit number")

        label = QLabel("Output will appear here")

        button_stop = QPushButton("Shutdown thread")
        # Shutdown the thread nicely.
        button_stop.pressed.connect(self.thread.stop)

        # Connect signal, so output appears on label.
        button_input.pressed.connect(self.submit_data)
        self.thread.result.connect(label.setText)
        self.thread.finished.connect(self.thread_has_finished)

        container = QWidget()
        layout = QVBoxLayout()
        layout.addWidget(self.numeric_input)
        layout.addWidget(button_input)
        layout.addWidget(label)
```

```
            layout.addWidget(button_stop)
            container.setLayout(layout)

            self.setCentralWidget(container)
            self.show()

        def submit_data(self):
            # Submit the value in the numeric_input widget to the thread.
            self.thread.send_data(self.numeric_input.value())

        def thread_has_finished(self):
            print("Thread has finished.")


app = QApplication(sys.argv)
window = MainWindow()
app.exec()
```

If you run this example you'll see the following window. Use the QSpinBox to select a number and then press the button to submit it to the thread. The thread will add the incoming number onto the current counter and return the result.

Figure 214. We can now submit data to our thread, using the QSpinBox *and button.*

If you use the *Shutdown thread* button to stop the thread you may notice something a little strange. The thread *does* shutdown, but you can submit one more number before it does so and the calculation is still performed — try it!

This is because the is_running check is performed at the top of the loop and *then* the thread waits for input.

To fix this, we need to move the check of the is_running flag into the waiting loop.

Listing 213. concurrent/qthread_4b.py

```python
@pyqtSlot()
def run(self):
    """
    Your code goes in this method
    """
    print("Thread start")
    self.data = None
    self.is_running = True
    counter = 0
    while True:
        while self.data is None:
            if not self.is_running:
                return  # Exit thread.
            time.sleep(0.1)  # wait for data <1>.

        # Output the number as a formatted string.
        counter += self.data
        self.result.emit(f"The cumulative total is {counter}")
        self.data = None
```

If you run the example now, you'll see that if the button is pressed while the thread is waiting, it will exit immediately.

 Be careful when placing thread exit control conditions in your threads, to avoid any unexpected side-effects. Try and check before performing any new tasks/calculations and before emitting any data.

Often you'll also want to pass in some *initial state* data, for example configuration options to control the subsequent running of the thread. We can pass that in just as we did for QRunnable by adding arguments to our __init__

block. The provided arguments must be stored on the `self` object to be available in the `run()` method.

Listing 214. concurrent/qthread_5.py

```python
class Thread(QThread):
    """
    Worker thread
    """

    result = pyqtSignal(str)

    def __init__(self, initial_data):
        super().__init__()
        self.data = initial_data
class MainWindow(QMainWindow):
    def __init__(self):
        super().__init__()

        # Create thread and start it.
        self.thread = Thread(500)
        self.thread.start()
        # ...
```

Using these two approaches you can provide any data you need to your thread. This pattern of *waiting* for data in the thread (using `sleep` loop), processing the data and returning it via a signal is the most common pattern when working with long-running threads in Qt applications.

Let's extend the example one more time to demonstrate passing in multiple data types. In this example we modify our thread to use an *explicit* lock, called `waiting_for_data` which we can toggle between `True` and `False`. You can use this

Listing 215. concurrent/qthread_6.py

```python
class Thread(QThread):
    """
    Worker thread
    """
```

542

```python
    result = pyqtSignal(str)

    def __init__(self, initial_counter):
        super().__init__()
        self.counter = initial_counter

    @pyqtSlot()
    def run(self):
        """
        Your code goes in this method
        """

        print("Thread start")
        self.is_running = True
        self.waiting_for_data = True
        while True:
            while self.waiting_for_data:
                if not self.is_running:
                    return  # Exit thread.
                time.sleep(0.1)  # wait for data <1>.

            # Output the number as a formatted string.
            self.counter += self.input_add
            self.counter *= self.input_multiply
            self.result.emit(f"The cumulative total is {self.counter
}")

            self.waiting_for_data = True

    def send_data(self, add, multiply):
        """
        Receive data onto internal variable.
        """

        self.input_add = add
        self.input_multiply = multiply
        self.waiting_for_data = False

    def stop(self):
        self.is_running = False


class MainWindow(QMainWindow):
    def __init__(self):
        super().__init__()
```

```python
            # Create thread and start it.
            self.thread = Thread(500)
            self.thread.start()

            self.add_input = QSpinBox()
            self.mult_input = QSpinBox()
            button_input = QPushButton("Submit number")

            label = QLabel("Output will appear here")

            button_stop = QPushButton("Shutdown thread")
            # Shutdown the thread nicely.
            button_stop.pressed.connect(self.thread.stop)

            # Connect signal, so output appears on label.
            button_input.pressed.connect(self.submit_data)
            self.thread.result.connect(label.setText)
            self.thread.finished.connect(self.thread_has_finished)

            container = QWidget()
            layout = QVBoxLayout()
            layout.addWidget(self.add_input)
            layout.addWidget(self.mult_input)
            layout.addWidget(button_input)
            layout.addWidget(label)
            layout.addWidget(button_stop)
            container.setLayout(layout)

            self.setCentralWidget(container)
            self.show()

    def submit_data(self):
        # Submit the value in the numeric_input widget to the thread.
        self.thread.send_data(
            self.add_input.value(), self.mult_input.value()
        )

    def thread_has_finished(self):
        print("Thread has finished.")
```

You *can* also split your submit data methods out into a separate method per value and implement an explicit *calculate* method which releases the lock. This approach is well suited when you don't necessarily want to update *all* values all of the time. For example, if you are reading data in from an external service or hardware.

Listing 216. concurrent/qthread_6b.py

```python
class Thread(QThread):
    def send_add(self, add):
        self.input_add = add

    def send_multiply(self, multiply):
        self.input_multiply = multiply

    def calculate(self):
        self.waiting_for_data = False  # Release the lock &
calculate.

class MainWindow(QMainWindow):
    def submit_data(self):
        # Submit the value in the numeric_input widget to the thread.
        self.thread.send_add(self.add_input.value())
        self.thread.send_multiply(self.mult_input.value())
        self.thread.calculate()
```

If you run this example you'll see exactly the same behavior as before. Which approach makes the most sense in your application will depend on what the particular thread is doing.

Don't be afraid to mix and match the various threading techniques you've learned. For example, in some applications it will make sense to run certain parts of the application using persistent threads and others using thread pools.

A Sense of Progress

When a user does something in your application, the consequences of that action should be immediately apparent — either through the result of the action itself, or through an indication that *something* is being done that will provide the result. This is particularly important for long-running tasks, such as calculations or network requests, where a lack of feedback could prompt the user to repeatedly mash buttons and see nothing in return.

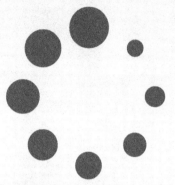

One simple approach is to disable buttons once an operation has been triggered. But with no other indicator this looks a lot like *broken*. A better alternative is to update the button with a "Working" message and an active progress indicator such as a spinner nearby.

Progress bars are a common way to address this by informing the user of what is going on — and how long it's going to take. But don't fall into the trap

Spinners or waiting icons can be used when the the duration of the task Is unknown, or very short.

of thinking progress bars are always useful! They should only be used when you they can present a linear progress towards a task

Some complex applications can have multiple concurrent tasks

Progress bars are not helpful if —
- they go backwards and forward
- they don't increase linearly with progress
- they complete too quickly

— if they don't they can be more frustrating than having no Information at all.
Any of these behaviors can give users the sense that *something isn't right* leading to frustration to confusion — "what was that dialog I missed?!" These aren't good things to make your users feel, so you should avoid it wherever possible.

Remember that your users don't know what's going on inside your application — their only insight is through the data you give them. Share data which is helpful *to your users* and keep everything else hidden. If you need debugging output, you can put it behind a menu.

DO Provide progress bars for long-running tasks.
DO Provide granular detail of sub-tasks where appropriate.
DO Estimate how long something will take, when you can.
DON'T Assume your users know which tasks are long or short.
DON'T Use progress bars that move up & down, or irregularly.

28. Running external commands & processes

So far we've looked at how to run things in separate threads, including external programs using Python `subprocess`. But in PyQt6 we can also make use of a Qt-based system for running external programs, `QProcess`. Creating and executing a job with `QProcess` is relatively straightforward.

The simplest possible example is shown below — we create a `QProcess` object and then call `.start` passing in the command to execute and a `list` of string arguments. In this case we're running our custom demo script, with Python `python dummy_script.py`.

```
p = QProcess()
p.start("python", ["dummy_script.py"])
```

 Depending on your environment, you may need to specify `python3` instead of `python`.

 You need to keep a reference to the created `QProcess` instance, either on `self` or elsewhere, while it is running.

The simple example is enough if you just want to *run* a program and don't care what happens to it. However, if you want to know more about what a program is doing, `QProcess` provides a number of signals which can be used to track the progress and state of processes.

The most useful are the `.readyReadStandardOutput` and `.readyReadStandardError` which fire whenever there is *standard output* and *standard error* ready to be read from the process. All running processes have two streams of output — *standard out* and *standard error*. The standard output returns the actual result of the execution (if any) while standard error returns any error *or* logging information.

547

```
p = QProcess()
p.readyReadStandardOutput.connect(self.handle_stdout)
p.readyReadStandardError.connect(self.handle_stderr)
p.stateChanged.connect(self.handle_state)
p.finished.connect(self.cleanup)
p.start("python", ["dummy_script.py"])
```

Additionally, there is a .finished signal which is fired when the process completes, and a .stateChanged signal which fires when the process status changes. Valid values — defined in the QProcess.ProcessState enum — are shown below.

Constant	Value	Description
QProcess.NotRunning	0	The process is not running.
QProcess.Starting	1	The process is starting, but the program has not yet been invoked.
QProcess.Running	2	The process is running and is ready for reading and writing.

In the following example we extend this basic QProcess setup to add handlers for the *standard out* and *standard err*. The signals notifying of available data connect to these handlers and trigger a request of the data from the process, using .readAllStandardError() and .readAllStandardOutput().

 The methods output raw bytes, so you need to decode it first.

In this example, our demo script dummy_script.py return a series of strings, which are parsed to provide progress information and structured data. The state of the process is also displayed on the statusbar.

The full code is shown below —

Listing 217. concurrent/qprocess.py

```python
import re
import sys

from PyQt6.QtCore import QProcess
from PyQt6.QtWidgets import (
    QApplication,
    QMainWindow,
    QPlainTextEdit,
    QProgressBar,
    QPushButton,
    QVBoxLayout,
    QWidget,
)

STATES = {
    QProcess.ProcessState.NotRunning: "Not running",
    QProcess.ProcessState.Starting: "Starting...",
    QProcess.ProcessState.Running: "Running...",
}

progress_re = re.compile("Total complete: (\d+)%")


def simple_percent_parser(output):
    """
    Matches lines using the progress_re regex,
    returning a single integer for the % progress.
    """
    m = progress_re.search(output)
    if m:
        pc_complete = m.group(1)
        return int(pc_complete)


def extract_vars(l):
    """
    Extracts variables from lines, looking for lines
    containing an equals, and splitting into key=value.
    """
    data = {}
    for s in l.splitlines():
        if "=" in s:
            name, value = s.split("=")
```

```python
            data[name] = value
    return data


class MainWindow(QMainWindow):
    def __init__(self):
        super().__init__()

        # Hold process reference.
        self.p = None

        layout = QVBoxLayout()

        self.text = QPlainTextEdit()
        layout.addWidget(self.text)

        self.progress = QProgressBar()
        layout.addWidget(self.progress)

        btn_run = QPushButton("Execute")
        btn_run.clicked.connect(self.start)

        layout.addWidget(btn_run)

        w = QWidget()
        w.setLayout(layout)
        self.setCentralWidget(w)

        self.show()

    def start(self):
        if self.p is not None:
            return

        self.p = QProcess()
        self.p.readyReadStandardOutput.connect(self.handle_stdout)
        self.p.readyReadStandardError.connect(self.handle_stderr)
        self.p.stateChanged.connect(self.handle_state)
        self.p.finished.connect(self.cleanup)
        self.p.start("python", ["dummy_script.py"])

    def handle_stderr(self):
        result = bytes(self.p.readAllStandardError()).decode("utf8")
```

```
            progress = simple_percent_parser(result)

            self.progress.setValue(progress)

    def handle_stdout(self):
        result = bytes(self.p.readAllStandardOutput()).decode("utf8")
        data = extract_vars(result)

        self.text.appendPlainText(str(data))

    def handle_state(self, state):
        self.statusBar().showMessage(STATES[state])

    def cleanup(self):
        self.p = None


app = QApplication(sys.argv)
w = MainWindow()
app.exec()
```

In this example we store a reference to the process in `self.p`, meaning we can only run a single process at once. But you are free to run as many processes as you like alongside your application. If you don't need to track information from them, you can simply store references to the processes in a `list`.

However, if you want to track progress and parse output from workers individually, you may want to consider creating a manager class to handle and track all your processes. There is an example of this in the source files with the book, named `qprocess_manager.py`.

The full source code for the example is available in the source code for the book, but below we'll look at the `JobManager` class itself.

Listing 218. concurrent/qprocess_manager.py

```
class JobManager(QAbstractListModel):
    """
    Manager to handle active jobs and stdout, stderr
```

```python
    and progress parsers.
    Also functions as a Qt data model for a view
    displaying progress for each process.
    """


    _jobs = {}
    _state = {}
    _parsers = {}

    status = pyqtSignal(str)
    result = pyqtSignal(str, object)
    progress = pyqtSignal(str, int)

    def __init__(self):
        super().__init__()

        self.status_timer = QTimer()
        self.status_timer.setInterval(100)
        self.status_timer.timeout.connect(self.notify_status)
        self.status_timer.start()

        # Internal signal, to trigger update of progress via parser.
        self.progress.connect(self.handle_progress)

    def notify_status(self):
        n_jobs = len(self._jobs)
        self.status.emit("{} jobs".format(n_jobs))

    def execute(self, command, arguments, parsers=None):
        """
        Execute a command by starting a new process.
        """

        job_id = uuid.uuid4().hex

        # By default, the signals do not have access to any
information about
        # the process that sent it. So we use this constructor to
annotate
        # each signal with a job_id.

        def fwd_signal(target):
            return lambda *args: target(job_id, *args)
```

```python
        self._parsers[job_id] = parsers or []

        # Set default status to waiting, 0 progress.
        self._state[job_id] = DEFAULT_STATE.copy()

        p = QProcess()
        p.readyReadStandardOutput.connect(
            fwd_signal(self.handle_output)
        )
        p.readyReadStandardError.connect(fwd_signal(self
.handle_output))
        p.stateChanged.connect(fwd_signal(self.handle_state))
        p.finished.connect(fwd_signal(self.done))

        self._jobs[job_id] = p

        p.start(command, arguments)

        self.layoutChanged.emit()

    def handle_output(self, job_id):
        p = self._jobs[job_id]
        stderr = bytes(p.readAllStandardError()).decode("utf8")
        stdout = bytes(p.readAllStandardOutput()).decode("utf8")
        output = stderr + stdout

        parsers = self._parsers.get(job_id)
        for parser, signal_name in parsers:
            # Parse the data using each parser in turn.
            result = parser(output)
            if result:
                # Look up the signal by name (using signal_name), and
                # emit the parsed result.
                signal = getattr(self, signal_name)
                signal.emit(job_id, result)

    def handle_progress(self, job_id, progress):
        self._state[job_id]["progress"] = progress
        self.layoutChanged.emit()

    def handle_state(self, job_id, state):
        self._state[job_id]["status"] = state
```

```
        self.layoutChanged.emit()

    def done(self, job_id, exit_code, exit_status):
        """
        Task/worker complete. Remove it from the active workers
        dictionary. We leave it in worker_state, as this is used to
        to display past/complete workers too.
        """
        del self._jobs[job_id]
        self.layoutChanged.emit()

    def cleanup(self):
        """
        Remove any complete/failed workers from worker_state.
        """
        for job_id, s in list(self._state.items()):
            if s["status"] == QProcess.ProcessState.NotRunning:
                del self._state[job_id]
        self.layoutChanged.emit()

    # Model interface
    def data(self, index, role):
        if role == Qt.ItemDataRole.DisplayRole:
            # See below for the data structure.
            job_ids = list(self._state.keys())
            job_id = job_ids[index.row()]
            return job_id, self._state[job_id]

    def rowCount(self, index):
        return len(self._state)
```

This class provides a model view interface allowing it to be used as the basis for a QListView. The custom delegate ProgressBarDelegate delegate draws a progress bar for each item, along with the job identifier. The color of the progress bar is determined by the status of the process — dark green if active, or light green if complete.

Parsing of progress information from workers is tricky in this setup, because the .readyReadStandardError and .readyReadStandardOutput signals do not pass the data, or information about the job that is ready. To work around this we define our custom jnh_id and intercept the signals to add this data to them.

Parsers for the jobs are passed in when executing the command and stored in
_parsers. Output received from each job is passed through the respective parser
and used to emit the data, or update the job's progress. We define two simple
parsers: one for extracting the current progress and one for getting the output
data.

Listing 219. concurrent/qprocess_manager.py

```python
progress_re = re.compile("Total complete: (\d+)%", re.M)


def simple_percent_parser(output):
    """
    Matches lines using the progress_re regex,
    returning a single integer for the % progress.
    """
    m = progress_re.search(output)
    if m:
        pc_complete = m.group(1)
        return int(pc_complete)


def extract_vars(l):
    """
    Extracts variables from lines, looking for lines
    containing an equals, and splitting into key=value.
    """
    data = {}
    for s in l.splitlines():
        if "=" in s:
            name, value = s.split("=")
            data[name] = value
    return data
```

The parsers are passed in as a simple list of tuple containing the function to be
used as the parser and the name of the signal to emit. The signal is looked up by
name using getattr on the JobManager. In the example we've only defined 2

signals, one for the data/result output and one for progress. But you can add as many signals and parsers as you like. Using this approach you can opt to omit certain parsers for certain tasks if you wish (for example, where no progress information is available).

Run the example code and experiment running tasks in another process. You can start multiple jobs, and watch them complete, updating their current progress as they go. Experiment with adding additional commands and parsers for your own jobs.

Figure 215. The process manager, showing active processes and progress.

Plotting

One of the major strengths of Python is in data science and visualization, using tools such as *Pandas, numpy* and *sklearn* for data analysis. Building GUI applications with PyQt6 gives you access to all these Python tools directly from within your app, allowing you to build complex data-driven apps and interactive dashboards. We've already covered the model views, which allow us to show data in lists and tables. In this chapter we'll look at the final piece of that puzzle — plotting data.

When building apps with PyQt6 you have two main choices — matplotlib (which also gives access to Pandas plots) and PyQtGraph, which creates plots with Qt-native graphics. In this chapter we'll look at how you can use these libraries to visualize data in your applications.

29. Plotting with PyQtGraph

While it is possible to embed `matplotlib` plots in PyQt6 the experience does not feel entirely *native*. For simple and highly interactive plots you may want to consider using PyQtGraph instead. PyQtGraph is built on top of PyQt6 native `QGraphicsScene` giving better drawing performance, particularly for live data, as well as providing interactivity and the ability to easily customize plots with Qt graphics widgets.

In this chapter we'll walk through the first steps of creating a plot widget with PyQtGraph and then demonstrate plot customization using line colors, line type, axis labels, background color and plotting multiple lines.

Getting started

To be able to use PyQtGraph with PyQt6 you first need to install the package to your Python environment. You can do this using `pip`.

At the time of writing PyQt6 is very new, and so you will need to use a developer install of PyQtGraph.

```
pip install git+https://github.com/pyqtgraph/pyqtgraph@master
```

Once the installation is complete you should be able to import the module as normal.

Creating a PyQtGraph widget

In PyQtGraph all plots are created using the `PlotWidget` widget. This widget provides a contained *canvas* on which plots of any type can be added and configured. Under the hood, this plot widget uses Qt native `QGraphicsScene` meaning it fast and efficient yet simple to integrate with the rest of your app. You can create a `PlotWidget` as for any other widget.

The basic template app, with a single `PlotWidget` in a `QMainWindow` is shown below.

 In the following examples we'll create the PyQtGraph widget in code. However, you can also embed PyQtGraph widgets from Qt Designer.

Listing 220. plotting/pyqtgraph_1.py

```python
import sys

from PyQt6 import QtWidgets
import pyqtgraph as pg  # import PyQtGraph after Qt


class MainWindow(QtWidgets.QMainWindow):
    def __init__(self):
        super().__init__()

        self.graphWidget = pg.PlotWidget()
        self.setCentralWidget(self.graphWidget)

        hour = [1, 2, 3, 4, 5, 6, 7, 8, 9, 10]
        temperature = [30, 32, 34, 32, 33, 31, 29, 32, 35, 45]

        # plot data: x, y values
        self.graphWidget.plot(hour, temperature)


app = QtWidgets.QApplication(sys.argv)
main = MainWindow()
main.show()
app.exec()
```

 In all our examples below we import PyQtGraph using `import pyqtgraph as pg`. This is a common convention in PyQtGraph examples to keep things tidy & reduce typing. You can import as `import pyqtgraph` if you prefer.

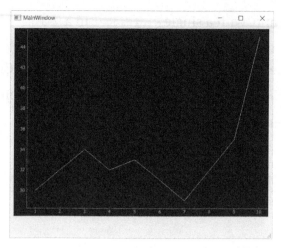

Figure 216. The custom PyQtGraph widget showing dummy data.

The default plot style of PyQtGraph is quite bare - a black background with a thin (barely visible) white line. In the next section we'll look at what options we have available to us in PyQtGraph to improve the appearance and usability of our plots.

Styling plots

PyQtGraph uses Qt's `QGraphicsScene` to render the graphs. This gives us access to all the standard Qt line and shape styling options for use in plots. However, PyQtGraph provides an API for using these to draw plots and manage the plot canvas.

Below we'll go through the most common styling features you'll need to create and customize your own plots.

Background Color

Beginning with the app skeleton above, we can change the background color by calling `.setBackground` on our `PlotWidget` instance (in `self.graphWidget`). The code below will set the background to white, by passing in the string 'w'.

```
self.graphWidget.setBackground('w')
```

You can set (and update) the background color of the plot at any time.

Listing 221. plotting/pyqtgraph_2.py

```python
import sys

from PyQt6 import QtWidgets
import pyqtgraph as pg  # import PyQtGraph after Qt


class MainWindow(QtWidgets.QMainWindow):
    def __init__(self):
        super().__init__()

        self.graphWidget = pg.PlotWidget()
        self.setCentralWidget(self.graphWidget)

        hour = [1, 2, 3, 4, 5, 6, 7, 8, 9, 10]
        temperature = [30, 32, 34, 32, 33, 31, 29, 32, 35, 45]

        self.graphWidget.setBackground("w")
        self.graphWidget.plot(hour, temperature)


app = QtWidgets.QApplication(sys.argv)
main = MainWindow()
main.show()
app.exec()
```

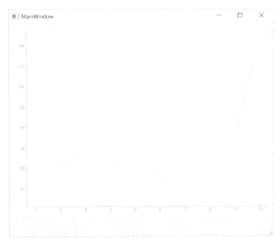

Figure 217. Changed PyQtGraph Plot Background to White.

There are a number of simple colors available using single letters, based on the standard colors used in `matplotlib`. They're pretty unsurprising, except that 'k' is used for black.

Table 7. Common color codes

Color	Letter code
blue	b
green	g
red	r
cyan (bright blue-green)	c
magenta (bright pink)	m
yellow	y
black	k
white	w

In addition to these single letter codes, you can also set colors using hex notation eg. `#672922` as a string.

```
self.graphWidget.setBackground('#bbccaa')          # hex
```

RGB and RGBA values can be passed in as a 3-tuple or 4-tuple respectively, using values 0-255.

```
self.graphWidget.setBackground((100,50,255))       # RGB each 0-255
self.graphWidget.setBackground((100,50,255,25))    # RGBA (A = alpha
opacity)
```

Lastly, you can also specify colors using Qt's `QColor` type directly.

```
self.graphWidget.setBackground(QtGui.QColor(100,50,254,25))
```

This can be useful if you're using specific QColor objects elsewhere in your application, or to set your plot background to the default GUI background color.

```
color = self.palette().color(QtGui.QPalette.Window)  # Get the
default window background,
self.graphWidget.setBackground(color)
```

Line Color, Width & Style

Lines in PyQtGraph are drawn using standard Qt QPen types. This gives you the same full control over line drawing as you would have in any other QGraphicsScene drawing. To use a pen to plot a line, you simply create a new QPen instance and pass it into the plot method.

Below we create a QPen object, passing in a 3-tuple of int values specifying an RGB value (of full red). We could also define this by passing 'r', or a QColor object. Then we pass this into plot with the *pen* parameter.

```
pen = pg.mkPen(color=(255, 0, 0))
self.graphWidget.plot(hour, temperature, pen=pen)
```

The complete code is shown below.

Listing 222. plotting/pyqtgraph_3.py

```python
import sys

from PyQt6 import QtWidgets
import pyqtgraph as pg  # import PyQtGraph after Qt


class MainWindow(QtWidgets.QMainWindow):
    def __init__(self):
        super().__init__()

        self.graphWidget = pg.PlotWidget()
        self.setCentralWidget(self.graphWidget)

        hour = [1, 2, 3, 4, 5, 6, 7, 8, 9, 10]
        temperature = [30, 32, 34, 32, 33, 31, 29, 32, 35, 45]

        self.graphWidget.setBackground("w")

        pen = pg.mkPen(color=(255, 0, 0))
        self.graphWidget.plot(hour, temperature, pen=pen)


app = QtWidgets.QApplication(sys.argv)
main = MainWindow()
main.show()
app.exec()
```

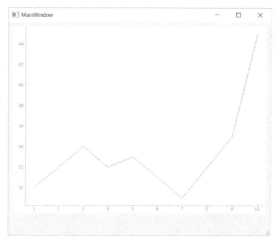

Figure 218. Changing Line Color.

By changing the QPen object we can change the appearance of the line, including both line width in pixels and style (dashed, dotted, etc.) using standard Qt line styles. For example, the following example creates a 15px width dashed line in red.

```
pen = pg.mkPen(color=(255, 0, 0), width=15, style=QtCore.Qt.PenStyle
.DashLine)
```

The result is shown below, giving a 15px dashed red line.

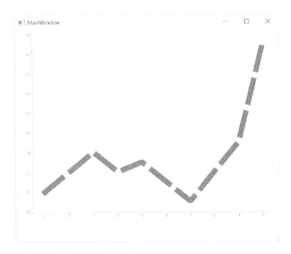

Figure 219. Changing Line Width and Style.

The standard Qt line styles can all be used, including `Qt.PenStyle.SolidLine`, `Qt.PenStyle.DashLine`, `Qt.PenStyle.DotLine`, `Qt.PenStyle.DashDotLine` and `Qt.PenStyle.DashDotDotLine`. Examples of each of these lines are shown in the image below, and you can read more in the Qt Documentation [https://doc.qt.io/qt-6/qpen.html#pen-style].

Line Markers

For many plots it can be helpful to place markers in addition or instead of lines on the plot. To draw a marker on the plot, pass the symbol to use as a marker when calling `.plot` as shown below.

```
self.graphWidget.plot(hour, temperature, symbol='+')
```

In addition to `symbol` you can also pass in `symbolSize`, `symbolBrush` and `symbolPen` parameters. The value passed as `symbolBrush` can be any color, or `QBrush` type, while `symbolPen` can be passed any color or a `QPen` instance. The *pen* is used to draw the outline of the shape, while **brush** is used for the fill.

For example the below code will give a blue cross marker of size 30, on a thick red line.

```
pen = pg.mkPen(color=(255, 0, 0), width=15, style=QtCore.Qt.PenStyle
.DashLine)
self.graphWidget.plot(hour, temperature, pen=pen, symbol='+',
symbolSize=30, symbolBrush=('b'))
```

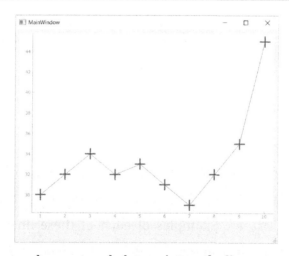

Figure 220. Symbols are shown at each data point on the line.

In addition to the + plot marker, PyQtGraph supports the following standard markers shown in the table below. These can all be used in the same way.

Variable	Marker Type
o	Circular
s	Square

Variable	Marker Type
t	Triangular
d	Diamond
+	Cross

 If you have more complex requirements you can also pass in any QPainterPath object, allowing you to draw completely custom marker shapes.

Plot Titles

Chart titles are important to provide context to what is shown on a given chart. In PyQtGraph you can add a main plot title using the setTitle() method on the PlotWidget, passing in your title string.

```
self.graphWidget.setTitle("Your Title Here")
```

You can apply text styles, including colors, font sizes and weights to your titles (and any other labels in PyQtGraph) by passing additional arguments. The available syle arguments are shown below.

Style	Type
color	(str) e.g. 'CCFF00'
size	(str) e.g. '8pt'
bold	(bool) True or False
italic	(bool) True or False

The code below sets the color to blue with a font size of 30pt.

```
self.graphWidget.setTitle("Your Title Here", color="b", size="30pt")
```

You can also style your headers with HTML tag syntax if you prefer, although it's less readable.

```
self.graphWidget.setTitle("<span style=\"color:blue;font-size:30pt
\">Your Title Here</span>")
```

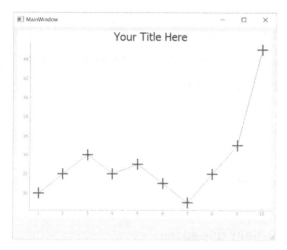

Figure 221. Plot with a styled title.

Axis Labels

Similar to titles, we can use the `setLabel()` method to create our axis titles. This requires two parameters, *position* and *text*. The *position* can be any one of `'left','right','top','bottom'` which describe the position of the axis on which the text is placed. The 2nd parameter *text* is the text you want to use for the label.

You can pass additional style parameters into the method. These differ slightly than for the title, in that they need to be valid CSS name-value pairs. For example, the size is now `font-size`. Because the name `font-size` has a hyphen in it, you cannot pass it directly as a parameter, but must use the `**dictionary` method.

```
styles = {'color':'r', 'font-size':'30pt'}
self.graphWidget.setLabel('left', 'Temperature (°C)', **styles)
self.graphWidget.setLabel('bottom', 'Hour (H)', **styles)
```

These also support HTML syntax if you prefer.

```
self.graphWidget.setLabel('left', "<span style=\"color:red;font-
size:30px\">Temperature (°C)</span>")
self.graphWidget.setLabel('bottom', "<span style=\"color:red;font-
size:30px\">Hour (H)</span>")
```

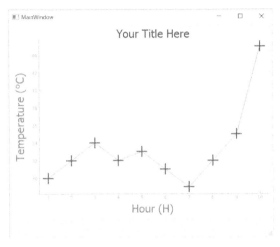

Figure 222. Axis labels with a custom style.

Legends

In addition to the axis and plot titles you will often want to show a legend identifying what a given line represents. This is particularly important when you start adding multiple lines to a plot. Adding a legend to a plot can be accomplished by calling .addLegend on the PlotWidget, however before this will work you need to provide a name for each line when calling .plot().

The example below assigns a name "Sensor 1" to the line we are plotting with .plot(). This name will be used to identify the line in the legend.

```
self.graphWidget.plot(hour, temperature, name = "Sensor 1", pen =
NewPen, symbol='+', symbolSize=30, symbolBrush=('b'))
self.graphWidget.addLegend()
```

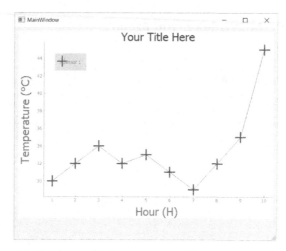

Figure 223. The plot with the legend, showing a single item.

 The legend appears in the top left by default. If you would like to move it, you can easily drag and drop the legend elsewhere. You can also specify a default offset by passing a 2-tuple to the *offset* parameter when creating the legend.

Background Grid

Adding a background grid can make your plots easier to read, particularly when trying to compare relative x & y values against each other. You can turn on a background grid for your plot by calling .showGrid on your PlotWidget. You can toggle x and y grids independently.

The following with create the grid for both the X and Y axis.

```
self.graphWidget.showGrid(x=True, y=True)
```

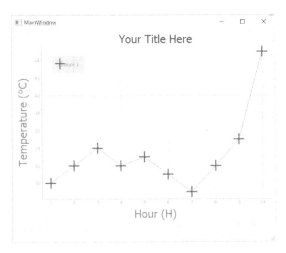

Figure 224. The plot grid.

Setting Axis Limits

Sometimes it can be useful to restrict the range of data which is visible on the plot, or to lock the axis to a consistent range regardless of the data input (e.g. a known min-max range). In PyQtGraph this can be done using the .setXRange() and .setYRange() methods. These force the plot to only show data within the specified ranges on each axis.

Below we set two ranges, one on each axis. The 1st argument is the minimum value and the 2nd is the maximum.

```
self.graphWidget.setXRange(5, 20, padding=0)
self.graphWidget.setYRange(30, 40, padding=0)
```

A optional padding argument causes the range to be set larger than specified by the specified fraction (this between 0.02 and 0.1 by default, depending on the size of the ViewBox). If you want to remove this padding entirely, pass 0.

```
self.graphWidget.setXRange(5, 20, padding=0)
self.graphWidget.setYRange(30, 40, padding=0)
```

The complete code so far is shown below:

Listing 223. plotting/pyqtgraph_4.py

```python
import sys

from PyQt6 import QtWidgets
import pyqtgraph as pg  # import PyQtGraph after Qt


class MainWindow(QtWidgets.QMainWindow):
    def __init__(self):
        super().__init__()

        self.graphWidget = pg.PlotWidget()
        self.setCentralWidget(self.graphWidget)

        hour = [1, 2, 3, 4, 5, 6, 7, 8, 9, 10]
        temperature = [30, 32, 34, 32, 33, 31, 29, 32, 35, 45]

        # Add Background color to white
        self.graphWidget.setBackground("w")
        # Add Title
        self.graphWidget.setTitle(
            "Your Title Here", color="b", size="30pt"
        )
        # Add Axis Labels
        styles = {"color": "#f00", "font-size": "20px"}
        self.graphWidget.setLabel("left", "Temperature (°C)",
 **styles)
        self.graphWidget.setLabel("bottom", "Hour (H)", **styles)
        # Add legend
        self.graphWidget.addLegend()
        # Add grid
        self.graphWidget.showGrid(x=True, y=True)
        # Set Range
        self.graphWidget.setXRange(0, 10, padding=0)
        self.graphWidget.setYRange(20, 55, padding=0)

        pen = pg.mkPen(color=(255, 0, 0))
        self.graphWidget.plot(
            hour,
            temperature,
            name="Sensor 1",
            pen=pen,
```

```
            symbol-"+",
            symbolSize=30,
            symbolBrush=("b"),
        )


app = QtWidgets.QApplication(sys.argv)
main = MainWindow()
main.show()
app.exec()
```

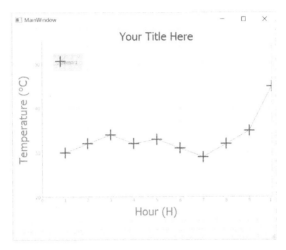

Figure 225. Limiting the range of the axis.

Plotting multiple lines

It is common for plots to involve more than one line. In PyQtGraph this is as simple as calling `.plot()` multiple times on the same `PlotWidget`. In the following example we're going to plot two lines of similar data, using the same line styles, thicknesses etc. for each, but changing the line color.

To simplify this we can create our own custom `plot` method on our `MainWindow`. This accepts `x` and `y` parameters to plot, the name of the line (for the legend) and a color. We use the color for both the line and marker color.

```
    def plot(self, x, y, plotname, color):
        pen = pg.mkPen(color=color)
        self.graphWidget.plot(x, y, name=plotname, pen=pen, symbol
='+', symbolSize=30, symbolBrush=(color))
```

To plot separate lines we'll create a new array called `temperature_2` and populate it with random numbers similar to `temperature` (now `temperature_1`). Plotting these alongside each other allows us to compare them together. Now, you can call plot function twice and this will generate 2 lines on the plot.

```
self.plot(hour, temperature_1, "Sensor1", 'r')
self.plot(hour, temperature_2, "Sensor2", 'b')
```

Listing 224. plotting/pyqtgraph_5.py

```python
import sys

from PyQt6 import QtWidgets
import pyqtgraph as pg  # import PyQtGraph after Qt


class MainWindow(QtWidgets.QMainWindow):
    def __init__(self):
        super().__init__()

        self.graphWidget = pg.PlotWidget()
        self.setCentralWidget(self.graphWidget)

        hour = [1, 2, 3, 4, 5, 6, 7, 8, 9, 10]
        temperature_1 = [30, 32, 34, 32, 33, 31, 29, 32, 35, 45]
        temperature_2 = [50, 35, 44, 22, 38, 32, 27, 38, 32, 44]

        # Add Background color to white
        self.graphWidget.setBackground("w")
        # Add Title
        self.graphWidget.setTitle(
            "Your Title Here", color="b", size="30pt"
        )
        # Add Axis Labels
```

```python
        styles = {"color": "#f00", "font-size": "20px"}
        self.graphWidget.setLabel("left", "Temperature (°C)",
**styles)
        self.graphWidget.setLabel("bottom", "Hour (H)", **styles)
        # Add legend
        self.graphWidget.addLegend()
        # Add grid
        self.graphWidget.showGrid(x=True, y=True)
        # Set Range
        self.graphWidget.setXRange(0, 10, padding=0)
        self.graphWidget.setYRange(20, 55, padding=0)

        self.plot(hour, temperature_1, "Sensor1", "r")
        self.plot(hour, temperature_2, "Sensor2", "b")

    def plot(self, x, y, plotname, color):
        pen = pg.mkPen(color=color)
        self.graphWidget.plot(
            x,
            y,
            name=plotname,
            pen=pen,
            symbol="+",
            symbolSize=30,
            symbolBrush=(color),
        )


app = QtWidgets.QApplication(sys.argv)
main = MainWindow()
main.show()
app.exec()
```

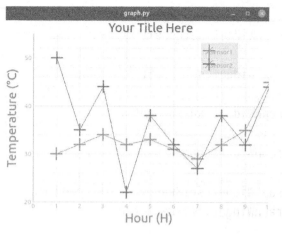

Figure 226. A plot with two lines.

 Play around with this function, customizing your markers, line widths, colors and other parameters.

Clearing the plot

Finally, sometimes you might want to clear and refresh the plot periodically. You can easily do that by calling `.clear()`.

```
self.graphWidget.clear()
```

This will remove the lines from the plot but keep all other attributes the same.

Updating the plot

While you *can* simply clear the plot and redraw all your elements again, this means Qt has to destroy and recreate all your QGraphicsScene objects. For small or simple plots this is probably not noticeable, but if you want to create high-peformance streaming plots it is much better to update the data in place. PyQtGraph takes the new data and updates the plotted line to match without affecting any other elements in the plot.

To update a line we need a reference to the line object. This reference is returned when first creating the line using `.plot` and we can simply store this in a variable. Note that this is a reference to the *line* not to the plot.

```
my_line_ref = graphWidget.plot(x, y)
```

Once we have the reference, updating the plot is simply a case of calling `.setData` on the reference to apply the new data.

Listing 225. plotting/pyqtgraph_6.py

```python
import sys
from random import randint

from PyQt6 import QtWidgets, QtCore
import pyqtgraph as pg  # import PyQtGraph after Qt


class MainWindow(QtWidgets.QMainWindow):
    def __init__(self):
        super().__init__()

        self.graphWidget = pg.PlotWidget()
        self.setCentralWidget(self.graphWidget)

        self.x = list(range(100))  # 100 time points
        self.y = [
            randint(0, 100) for _ in range(100)
        ]  # 100 data points

        self.graphWidget.setBackground("w")

        pen = pg.mkPen(color=(255, 0, 0))
        self.data_line = self.graphWidget.plot(
            self.x, self.y, pen=pen
        )  ①

        self.timer = QtCore.QTimer()
        self.timer.setInterval(50)
        self.timer.timeout.connect(self.update_plot_data)
        self.timer.start()

    def update_plot_data(self):
```

```
        self.x = self.x[1:]  # Remove the first y element.
        self.x.append(
            self.x[-1] + 1
        )  # Add a new value 1 higher than the last.

        self.y = self.y[1:]  # Remove the first
        self.y.append(randint(0, 100))  # Add a new random value.

        self.data_line.setData(self.x, self.y)  # Update the data.


app = QtWidgets.QApplication(sys.argv)
w = MainWindow()
w.show()
app.exec()
```

① Here we take a reference to the line we plotted, storing it as `self.data_line`.

We use a `QTimer` to update the data every 50ms, setting the trigger to call a custom slot method `update_plot_data` where we'll change the data. We define this timer in the `__init__` block so it is automatically started.

If you run the app you will see a plot with random data scrolling rapidly to the left, with the X values also updating and scrolling in time, as if streaming data. You can replace the random data with your own real data, taken for example from a live sensor readout or API. PyQtGraph is performant enough to support multiple plots using this method.

Conclusion

In this chapter we've discovered how to draw simple plots with PyQtGraph and customize lines, markers and labels. For a complete overview of PyQtGraph methods and capabilities see the PyQtGraph Documentation & API Reference [http://www.pyqtgraph.org/documentation/]. The PyQtGraph repository on Github [https://github.com/pyqtgraph/pyqtgraph] also has complete set of more complex example plots in Plotting.py (shown below).

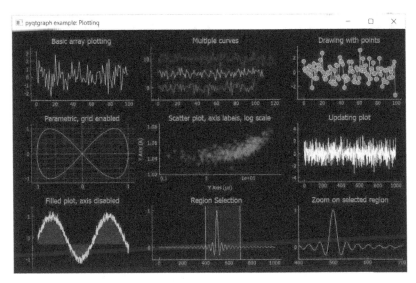

Figure 227. Example plots taken from the PyQtGraph documentation.

30. Plotting with Matplotlib

In the previous part we covered plotting in PyQt6 using PyQtGraph. That library uses the Qt vector-based QGraphicsScene to draw plots and provides a great interface for interactive and high performance plotting.

However, there is another plotting library for Python which is used far more widely, and which offers a richer assortment of plots — Matplotlib [https://www.matplotlib.org]. If you're migrating an existing data analysis tool to a PyQt6 GUI, or if you simply want to have access to the array of plot abilities that Matplotlib offers, then you'll want to know how to include Matplotlib plots within your application.

In this chapter we'll cover how to embed Matplotlib plots in your PyQt6 applications

Many other Python libraries — such as seaborn [https://github.com/mwaskom/seaborn] and pandas [https://pandas.pydata.org/pandas-docs/version/0.13/visualization.html] — make use of Matplotlib for plotting. These plots can be embedded in PyQt6 in the same way shown here, and the reference to the axes passed when plotting. There is a pandas example at the end of this chapter.

Installing Matplotlib

The following examples assume you have Matplotlib installed. If not you can install it using pip.

At the time of writing PyQt6 is very new. There is an experimental branch with [Qt6 support](https://github.com/matplotlib/matplotlib/pull/19255) which you can install with —

```
pip install git+https://github.com/anntzer/matplotlib.git@qt6
```

A simple example

The following minimal example sets up a Matplotlib canvas `FigureCanvasQTAgg` which creates the `Figure` and adds a single set of axes to it. This canvas object is also a `QWidget` and so can be embedded straight into an application as any other Qt widget.

Listing 226. plotting/matplotlib_1.py

```python
import sys

from PyQt6 import QtWidgets  # import PyQt6 before matplotlib

import matplotlib
from matplotlib.backends.backend_qtagg import FigureCanvasQTAgg
from matplotlib.figure import Figure

matplotlib.use("QtAgg")


class MplCanvas(FigureCanvasQTAgg):
    def __init__(self, parent=None, width=5, height=4, dpi=100):
        fig = Figure(figsize=(width, height), dpi=dpi)
        self.axes = fig.add_subplot(111)
        super().__init__(fig)


class MainWindow(QtWidgets.QMainWindow):
    def __init__(self):
        super().__init__()

        # Create the maptlotlib FigureCanvasQTAgg object,
        # which defines a single set of axes as self.axes.
        sc = MplCanvas(self, width=5, height=4, dpi=100)
        sc.axes.plot([0, 1, 2, 3, 4], [10, 1, 20, 3, 40])
        self.setCentralWidget(sc)

        self.show()


app = QtWidgets.QApplication(sys.argv)
w = MainWindow()
app.exec()
```

In this case we're adding our `MplCanvas` widget as the central widget on the window with `.setCentralWidget()`. This means it will take up the entirety of the window and resize together with it. The plotted data `[0,1,2,3,4]`, `[10,1,20,3,40]` is provided as two lists of numbers (x and y respectively) as required by the `.plot` method.

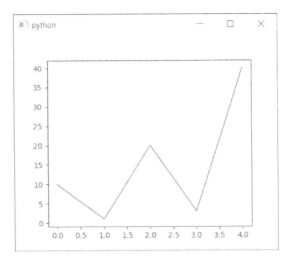

Figure 228. A simple plot.

Plot controls

Plots from Matplotlib displayed in PyQt6 are actually rendered as simple (bitmap) images by the *Agg* backend. The `FigureCanvasQTAgg` class wraps this backend and displays the resulting image on a Qt widget. The effect of this architecture is that Qt is unaware of the positions of lines and other plot elements — only the x, y coordinates of any clicks and mouse movements over the widget.

However, support for handling Qt mouse events and transforming them into interactions on the plot is built into Matplotlib. This can be controlled through a custom toolbar which can be added to your applications alongside the plot. In this section we'll look at adding these controls so we can zoom, pan and get data from embedded Matplotlib plots.

The complete code, importing the toolbar widget `NavigationToolbar2QT` and adding it to the interface within a `QVBoxLayout`, is shown below —

Listing 227. plotting/matplotlib_2.py

```
import sys
```

```python
from PyQt6 import QtWidgets  # import PyQt6 before matplotlib

import matplotlib
from matplotlib.backends.backend_qtagg import FigureCanvasQTAgg
from matplotlib.backends.backend_qtagg import (
    NavigationToolbar2QT as NavigationToolbar,
)
from matplotlib.figure import Figure


matplotlib.use("QtAgg")


class MplCanvas(FigureCanvasQTAgg):
    def __init__(self, parent=None, width=5, height=4, dpi=100):
        fig = Figure(figsize=(width, height), dpi=dpi)
        self.axes = fig.add_subplot(111)
        super().__init__(fig)


class MainWindow(QtWidgets.QMainWindow):
    def __init__(self):
        super().__init__()

        sc = MplCanvas(self, width=5, height=4, dpi=100)
        sc.axes.plot([0, 1, 2, 3, 4], [10, 1, 20, 3, 40])

        # Create toolbar, passing canvas as first parameter, parent
        (self, the MainWindow) as second.
        toolbar = NavigationToolbar(sc, self)

        layout = QtWidgets.QVBoxLayout()
        layout.addWidget(toolbar)
        layout.addWidget(sc)

        # Create a placeholder widget to hold our toolbar and canvas.
        widget = QtWidgets.QWidget()
        widget.setLayout(layout)
        self.setCentralWidget(widget)

        self.show()
```

```
app = QtWidgets.QApplication(sys.argv)
w = MainWindow()
app.exec()
```

We'll step through the changes.

First we import the toolbar widget from
`matplotlib.backends.backend_qt5agg.NavigationToolbar2QT` renaming it with the
simpler name `NavigationToolbar`. We create an instance of the toolbar by calling
`NavigationToolbar` with two parameters, first the canvas object `sc` and then the
parent for the toolbar, in this case our `MainWindow` object `self`. Passing in the
canvas links the created toolbar to it, allowing it to be controlled. The resulting
toolbar object is stored in the variable `toolbar`.

We need to add two widgets to the window, one above the other, so we use a
`QVBoxLayout`. First we add our toolbar widget `toolbar` and then the canvas widget
`sc` to this layout. Finally, we set this layout onto our simple `widget` layout
container which is set as the central widget for the window.

Running the above code will produce the following window layout, showing the
plot at the bottom and the controls on top as a toolbar.

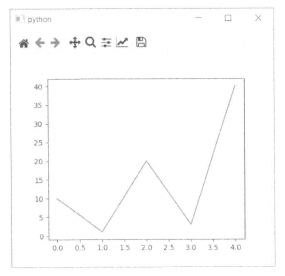

Figure 229. Matplotlib canvas with toolbar.

The buttons provided by `NavigationToolbar2QT` allow for control of the following actions —

- Home, Back/Forward, Pan & Zoom which are used to navigate through the plots. The Back/Forward buttons can step backwards and forwards through navigation steps, for example zooming in and then clicking Back will return to the previous zoom. Home returns to the initial state of the plot.

- Plot margin/position configuration which can adjust the plot within the window.

- Axis/curve style editor, where you can modify plot titles and axes scales, along with setting plot line colors and line styles. The color selection uses the platform-default color picker, allowing any available colors to be selected.

- Save, to save the resulting figure as an image (all Matplotlib supported formats).

A few of these configuration settings are shown below.

Figure 230. Matplotlib figure options.

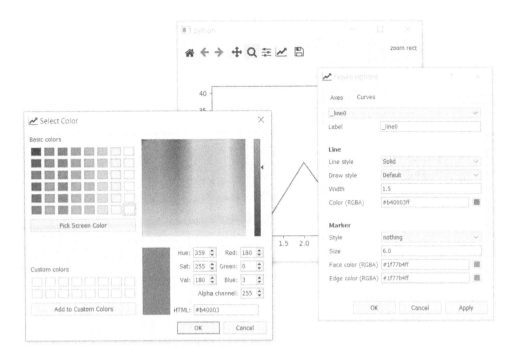

Figure 231. Matplotlib curve options.

For more information on navigating and configuring Matplotlib plots, take a look at the official Matplotlib toolbar documentation [https://matplotlib.org/3.1.1/users/navigation_toolbar.html].

Updating plots

Quite often in applications you'll want to update the data shown in plots, whether in response to input from the user or updated data from an API. There are two ways to update plots in Matplotlib, either

1. clearing and redrawing the canvas (simpler, but slower) or,

2. by keeping a reference to the plotted line and updating the data.

If performance is important to your app it is recommended you do the latter, but the first is simpler. We start with the simple clear-and-redraw method first below —

Clear and redraw

Listing 228. plotting/matplotlib_3.py

```python
import random
import sys

from PyQt6 import (
    QtCore,
    QtWidgets,
)  # import PyQt6 before matplotlib

import matplotlib
from matplotlib.backends.backend_qtagg import FigureCanvasQTAgg
from matplotlib.figure import Figure


matplotlib.use("QtAgg")


class MplCanvas(FigureCanvasQTAgg):
    def __init__(self, parent=None, width=5, height=4, dpi=100):
        fig = Figure(figsize=(width, height), dpi=dpi)
        self.axes = fig.add_subplot(111)
        super().__init__(fig)


class MainWindow(QtWidgets.QMainWindow):
    def __init__(self):
        super().__init__()

        self.canvas = MplCanvas(self, width=5, height=4, dpi=100)
        self.setCentralWidget(self.canvas)

        n_data = 50
        self.xdata = list(range(n_data))
        self.ydata = [random.randint(0, 10) for i in range(n_data)]
        self.update_plot()

        self.show()

        # Setup a timer to trigger the redraw by calling update_plot.
        self.timer = QtCore.QTimer()
```

```
        self.timer.setInterval(100)
        self.timer.timeout.connect(self.update_plot)
        self.timer.start()

    def update_plot(self):
        # Drop off the first y element, append a new one.
        self.ydata = self.ydata[1:] + [random.randint(0, 10)]
        self.canvas.axes.cla()  # Clear the canvas.
        self.canvas.axes.plot(self.xdata, self.ydata, "r")
        # Trigger the canvas to update and redraw.
        self.canvas.draw()


app = QtWidgets.QApplication(sys.argv)
w = MainWindow()
app.exec()
```

In this example we've moved the plotting to a `update_plot` method to keep it self-contained. In this method we take our `ydata` array and drop off the first value with `[1:]` then append a new random integer between 0 and 10. This has the effect of scrolling the data to the left.

To redraw we simply call `axes.cla()` to clear the axes (the entire canvas) and the `axes.plot(⋯)` to re-plot the data, including the updated values. The resulting canvas is then redrawn to the widget by calling `canvas.draw()`.

The `update_plot` method is called every 100 *msec* using a `QTimer`. The clear-and-refresh method is fast enough to keep a plot updated at this rate, but as we'll see shortly, falters as the speed increases.

In-place redraw

The changes required to update the plotted lines in-place are fairly minimal, requiring only an addition variable to store and retrieve the reference to the plotted line. The updated `MainWindow` code is shown below.

Listing 229. plotting/matplotlib_4.py

```python
class MainWindow(QtWidgets.QMainWindow):
    def __init__(self):
        super().__init__()

        self.canvas = MplCanvas(self, width=5, height=4, dpi=100)
        self.setCentralWidget(self.canvas)

        n_data = 50
        self.xdata = list(range(n_data))
        self.ydata = [random.randint(0, 10) for i in range(n_data)]

        # We need to store a reference to the plotted line
        # somewhere, so we can apply the new data to it.
        self._plot_ref = None
        self.update_plot()

        self.show()

        # Setup a timer to trigger the redraw by calling update_plot.
        self.timer = QtCore.QTimer()
        self.timer.setInterval(100)
        self.timer.timeout.connect(self.update_plot)
        self.timer.start()

    def update_plot(self):
        # Drop off the first y element, append a new one.
        self.ydata = self.ydata[1:] + [random.randint(0, 10)]

        # Note: we no longer need to clear the axis.
        if self._plot_ref is None:
            # First time we have no plot reference, so do a normal
plot.
            # .plot returns a list of line <reference>s, as we're
            # only getting one we can take the first element.
            plot_refs = self.canvas.axes.plot(
                self.xdata, self.ydata, "r"
            )
            self._plot_ref = plot_refs[0]
        else:
            # We have a reference, we can use it to update the data
for that line.
            self._plot_ref.set_ydata(self.ydata)
```

```
# Trigger the canvas to update and redraw.
self.canvas.draw()
```

First, we need a variable to hold a reference to the plotted line we want to update, which here we're calling _plot_ref. We initialize self._plot_ref with None so we can check its value later to determine if the line has already been drawn — if the value is still None we have not yet drawn the line.

 If you were drawing multiple lines you would probably want to use a list or dict data structure to store the multiple references and keep track of which is which.

Finally, we update the ydata data as we did before, rotating it to the left and appending a new random value. Then we either —

1. if self._plot_ref is None (i.e. we have not yet drawn the line) draw the line and store the reference in self._plot_ref, or

2. update the line in place by calling self._plot_ref.set_ydata(self.ydata)

We obtain a reference to the plotted line when calling .plot. However .plot returns a list (to support cases where a single .plot call can draw more than one line). In our case we're only plotting a single line, so we simply want the first element in that list – a single Line2D object. To get this single value into our variable we can assign to a temporary variable plot_refs and then assign the first element to our self._plot_ref variable.

```
plot_refs = self.canvas.axes.plot(self.xdata, self.ydata, 'r')
self._plot_ref = plot_refs[0]
```

You could also use tuple-unpacking, picking off the first (and only) element in the list with —

```
self._plot_ref, = self.canvas.axes.plot(self.xdata, self.ydata, 'r')
```

If you run the resulting code, there will be no noticeable difference in performance between this and the previous method at this speed. However if you attempt to update the plot faster (e.g. down to every 10 *msec*) you'll start to notice that clearing the plot and re-drawing takes longer, and the updates do not keep up with the timer. Whether this performance difference is enough to matter in your application depends on what you're building, and should be weighed against the added complication of keeping and managing the references to plotted lines.

Embedding plots from Pandas

Pandas is a Python package focused on working with table (data frames) and series data structures, which is particularly useful for data analysis workflows. It comes with built-in support for plotting with Matplotlib and here we'll take a quick look at how to embed these plots into PyQt6. With this you will be able to start building PyQt6 data-analysis applications built around Pandas.

Pandas plotting functions are directly accessible from the DataFrame objects. The function signature is quite complex, giving a lot of options to control how the plots will be drawn.

```
DataFrame.plot(
    x=None, y=None, kind='line', ax=None, subplots=False,
    sharex=None, sharey=False, layout=None, figsize=None,
    use_index=True, title=None, grid=None, legend=True, style=None,
    logx=False, logy=False, loglog=False, xticks=None, yticks=None,
    xlim=None, ylim=None, rot=None, fontsize=None, colormap=None,
    table=False, yerr=None, xerr=None, secondary_y=False,
    sort_columns=False, **kwargs
)
```

The parameter we're most interested in is ax which allows us to pass in our own matplotlib.Axes instance on which Pandas will plot the DataFrame.

Listing 230. plotting/matplotlib_5.py

```python
import sys

from PyQt6 import (
    QtCore,
    QtWidgets,
)  # import PyQt6 before matplotlib

import matplotlib
import pandas as pd
from matplotlib.backends.backend_qtagg import FigureCanvasQTAgg
from matplotlib.figure import Figure


matplotlib.use("QtAgg")


class MplCanvas(FigureCanvasQTAgg):
    def __init__(self, parent=None, width=5, height=4, dpi=100):
        fig = Figure(figsize=(width, height), dpi=dpi)
        self.axes = fig.add_subplot(111)
        super().__init__(fig)


class MainWindow(QtWidgets.QMainWindow):
    def __init__(self):
        super().__init__()

        # Create the maptlotlib FigureCanvasQTAgg object,
        # which defines a single set of axes as self.axes.
        sc = MplCanvas(self, width=5, height=4, dpi=100)

        # Create our pandas DataFrame with some simple
        # data and headers.
        df = pd.DataFrame(
            [
                [0, 10],
                [5, 15],
                [2, 20],
                [15, 25],
                [4, 10],
            ],
            columns=["A", "B"],
        )
```

```python
        # plot the pandas DataFrame, passing in the
        # matplotlib Canvas axes.
        df.plot(ax=sc.axes)

        self.setCentralWidget(sc)
        self.show()


app = QtWidgets.QApplication(sys.argv)
w = MainWindow()
app.exec()
```

The key step here is passing the canvas axes in when calling the plot method on the `DataFrame` on the line `df.plot(ax=sc.axes)`. You can use this same pattern to update the plot any time, although bear in mind that Pandas clears and redraws the entire canvas, meaning that it is not ideal for high performance plotting.

The resulting plot generated through Pandas is shown below —

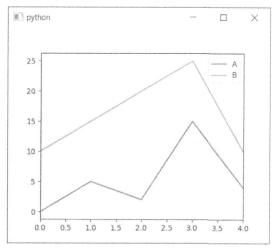

Figure 232. Pandas generated plot, in matplotlib Canvas.

Just as before, you can add the Matplotlib toolbar and control support to plots generated using Pandas, allowing you to zoom/pan and modify them live. The following code combines our earlier toolbar example with the Pandas example.

Listing 231. plotting/matplotlib_6.py

```python
import sys

from PyQt6 import (
    QtCore,
    QtWidgets,
)  # import PyQt6 before matplotlib

import matplotlib
import pandas as pd
from matplotlib.backends.backend_qtagg import FigureCanvasQTAgg
from matplotlib.backends.backend_qtagg import (
    NavigationToolbar2QT as NavigationToolbar,
)
from matplotlib.figure import Figure


matplotlib.use("QtAgg")


class MplCanvas(FigureCanvasQTAgg):
    def __init__(self, parent=None, width=5, height=4, dpi=100):
        fig = Figure(figsize=(width, height), dpi=dpi)
        self.axes = fig.add_subplot(111)
        super().__init__(fig)


class MainWindow(QtWidgets.QMainWindow):
    def __init__(self):
        super().__init__()

        # Create the maptlotlib FigureCanvasQTAgg object,
        # which defines a single set of axes as self.axes.
        sc = MplCanvas(self, width=5, height=4, dpi=100)

        # Create our pandas DataFrame with some simple
        # data and headers.
        df = pd.DataFrame(
            [
                [0, 10],
                [5, 15],
                [2, 20],
                [15, 25],
                [4, 10],
```

```
            ],
            columns=["A", "B"],
        )

        # plot the pandas DataFrame, passing in the
        # matplotlib Canvas axes.
        df.plot(ax=sc.axes)

        # Create toolbar, passing canvas as first parameter, parent
(self, the MainWindow) as second.
        toolbar = NavigationToolbar(sc, self)

        layout = QtWidgets.QVBoxLayout()
        layout.addWidget(toolbar)
        layout.addWidget(sc)

        # Create a placeholder widget to hold our toolbar and canvas.
        widget = QtWidgets.QWidget()
        widget.setLayout(layout)
        self.setCentralWidget(widget)
        self.show()


app = QtWidgets.QApplication(sys.argv)
w = MainWindow()
app.exec()
```

Running this you should see the following window, showing a Pandas plot
embedded in PyQt6 alongside the Matplotlib toolbar.

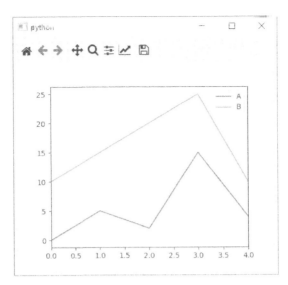

Figure 233. Pandas plot with matplotlib toolbar.

What's next

In this chapter we looked at how you can embed Matplotlib plots in your PyQt6 applications. Being able to use Matplotlib plots in your applications allows you to create custom data analysis and visualization tools from Python.

Matplotlib is a *huge* library and too big to cover in detail. If you're not familiar with Matplotlib plotting and want to give it a try, take a look at the documentation [https://matplotlib.org/] and example plots [https://matplotlib.org/3.1.1/gallery/index.html] to see what is possible.

Further PyQt6 Features

The topics we've covered so far are enough to build perfectly functional desktop applications with PyQt6. In this chapter we'll take a look at some more technical and lesser-known aspects of the Qt framework to gain a deeper understanding of how things work. For many applications the topics covered here are unnecessary, but they are good to have in your toolbox for when you need them!

31. Timers

In applications you often want to perform some tasks regularly or even just at *some point in the future*. In PyQt6 this is accomplished by using *timers*. The QTimer class gives you access to two different types of timer — *recurring* or *interval* timers, and *single shot* or *one off* timers. Both can be hooked up to functions and methods in your application to cause them to execute whenever you need. In this chapter we'll look at these two types of timer and demonstrate how you can use them to automate your apps.

Interval timers

Using the QTimer class you can create *interval* timers for any duration in *msecs*. On each specified duration, the timer will *time out*. To trigger something to happen each time this occurs, you connect the timer's timeout signal to whatever you want to do — just like you would with any other signal.

In the example below we setup up a timer, running every 100 *msecs*, which rotates a dial.

Listing 232. further/timers_1.py

```python
import sys

from PyQt6.QtCore import QTimer
from PyQt6.QtWidgets import QApplication, QDial, QMainWindow


class MainWindow(QMainWindow):
    def __init__(self):
        super().__init__()

        self.dial = QDial()
        self.dial.setRange(0, 100)
        self.dial.setValue(0)

        self.timer = QTimer()
        self.timer.setInterval(10)
        self.timer.timeout.connect(self.update_dial)
        self.timer.start()

        self.setCentralWidget(self.dial)

    def update_dial(self):
        value = self.dial.value()
        value += 1  # increment
        if value > 100:
            value = 0
        self.dial.setValue(value)


app = QApplication(sys.argv)
w = MainWindow()
w.show()

app.exec()
```

This is just a simple example — you can do *anything* you want in the connected methods. However, the standard event loop rules apply and triggered tasks should return quickly to avoid blocking the GUI. If you need to perform regular long-running tasks, you can use the timer to trigger a separate thread or process.

You **must** keep a reference to the created timer object, for the duration that the timer is running. If you don't then the timer object will be deleted and the timer will stop — without warning. If you create a timer and it doesn't seem to be working, check you've kept a reference to the object.

If the accuracy of the timer is important, you can adjust this by passing a `Qt.QTimerType` **value** to `timer.setTimerType`.

Listing 233. further/timers_1b.py

```
self.timer.setTimerType(Qt.TimerType.PreciseTimer)
```

The available options are shown below. Don't make your timers more accurate than they need to be. You may block important UI updates.

Timer type	Value	Description
Qt.TimerType.PreciseTimer	0	Precise timers try to keep millisecond accuracy
Qt.TimerType.CoarseTimer	1	Coarse timers try to keep accuracy within 5% of the desired interval
Qt.TimerType.VeryCoarseTimer	2	Very coarse timers only keep full second accuracy

Note that even the most precise timer only *tries* to keep millisecond accuracy. Anything in the GUI thread risks being blocked by UI updates and your own Python code. If accuracy is *that* important, then put the work in another thread or process you control completely.

Single shot timers

If you want to trigger something, but only have it occur once, you can use a *single shot* timer. These are constructed using *static methods* on the `QTimer` object. The simplest form just accepts a time in *msecs* and whatever *callable* you want to trigger when the timer fires — for example, the method you want to run.

In the following example we use a single shot timer to *uncheck* a toggleable push button after its pushed down.

Listing 234. further/timers_2.py

```python
import sys

from PyQt6.QtCore import QTimer
from PyQt6.QtWidgets import QApplication, QMainWindow, QPushButton


class MainWindow(QMainWindow):
    def __init__(self):
        super().__init__()

        self.button = QPushButton("Press me!")
        self.button.setCheckable(True)
        self.button.setStyleSheet(
            # Make the check state red so easier to see.
            "QPushButton:checked { background-color: red; }"
        )

        self.button.toggled.connect(self.button_checked)

        self.setCentralWidget(self.button)

    def button_checked(self):
        print("Button checked")
        QTimer.singleShot(1000, self.uncheck_button)   ①

    def uncheck_button(self):
        print("Button unchecked")
        self.button.setChecked(False)


app = QApplication(sys.argv)
w = MainWindow()
w.show()

app.exec()
```

① The `uncheck_button` method will be called after 1000 msecs.

If you run this example and press the button you'll see it become *checked* and turn red — using custom styles. Then after a second the button will revert to its *unchecked* state.

To achieve this we've chained together two custom methods using a *single shot* timer. First we connect the `toggled` signal from the button to a method `button_checked`. This fires off the *single shot* timer. When this timer times out, it calls `uncheck_button` which actually unchecks the button. This allows us to postpone the unchecking of the button by a configurable amount.

Unlike interval timers, you *don't* need to keep a reference to the created timer — the `QTimer.singleShot()` method doesn't return one.

Postponing-via the event queue

You can use zero-timed *single shot* timers to postpone operations via the event queue. When the timer is triggered the timer event goes to the back of the event queue (as it is a new event) and will only get processed once all existing events have been processed.

Remember that signals (and events) are only processed once you return control from Python to the event loop. If you trigger a series of signals in a method, and want to do something *after* they've occurred, you can't do it directly in the same method. The code there will be executed before the signals take effect.

```
def my_method(self):
    self.some_signal.emit()
    self.some_other_signal.emit()
    do_something_here()    ①
```

① This function will be executed before the two signals take effect.

By using a *single shot* timer you can push the subsequent operation to the back of the event queue & ensure it occurs last.

```
def my_method(self):
    self.some_signal.emit()
    self.some_other_signal.emit()
    QTimer.singleShot(0, do_something_here) ①
```

① This will be executed *after* the signal's effects.

 This technique only guarantees that the do_something_here function executes after the preceding signals, not any downstream effects of them. **Don't** be tempted to increase the value of *msecs* to work around this, as this makes your application dependent on system timings.

32. Extending Signals

We've seen a basic introduction to signals already, but that only scratches the surface of what you can do with them. In this chapter we'll look at how you can create your own signals and customize the data sent with them.

Custom Signals

So far we've only looked at signals that Qt itself provides on the built-in widgets. However, you can also make use of your own *custom* signals in your own code. This is a great way to *decouple* modular parts of your application, meaning parts of your app can respond to things happening elsewhere without needing to know anything about the structure of your app.

 One good indication that you need to *decouple* parts of your app is the use of .parent() to access data on other unrelated widgets. But it also applies to any place where you are referring to objects through other objects, e.g. self.my_other_window.dialog.some_method. This kind of code is prone to breaking — in multiple places — when you change or restructure your application. Avoid it wherever possible!

By putting these updates in the event queue you also help to keep your app responsive — rather than having one big *update* method, you can split the work up into multiple *slot* methods and trigger them all with a single signal.

You can define your own signals using the pyqtSignal method provided by PyQt6. Signals are defined as *class attributes* passing in the Python type (or types) that will be emitted with the signal. You can choose any valid Python variable name for the name of the signal, and any Python type for the signal type.

Listing 235. further/signals_custom.py

```python
import sys

from PyQt6.QtCore import pyqtSignal
from PyQt6.QtWidgets import QApplication, QMainWindow


class MainWindow(QMainWindow):

    message = pyqtSignal(str)   ①
    value = pyqtSignal(int, str, int)   ②
    another = pyqtSignal(list)   ③
    onemore = pyqtSignal(dict)   ④
    anything = pyqtSignal(object)   ⑤

    def __init__(self):
        super().__init__()

        self.message.connect(self.custom_slot)
        self.value.connect(self.custom_slot)
        self.another.connect(self.custom_slot)
        self.onemore.connect(self.custom_slot)
        self.anything.connect(self.custom_slot)

        self.message.emit("my message")
        self.value.emit(23, "abc", 1)
        self.another.emit([1, 2, 3, 4, 5])
        self.onemore.emit({"a": 2, "b": 7})
        self.anything.emit(1223)

    def custom_slot(self, *args):
        print(args)


app = QApplication(sys.argv)
window = MainWindow()
window.show()

app.exec()
```

① Signal emitting a string.

② Signal emitting 3 different types.

③ Signal emitting a list.

④ Signal emitting a dictionary.

⑤ Signal emitting *anything*.

As you can see the signals can be connected and emitted as normal. You can send any Python type, including multiple types, and compound types (e.g. dictionaries, lists).

If you define your signal as `pyqtSignal(object)` it will be able to transmit absolutely any Python type at all. But this isn't *usually* a good idea as receiving slots will then need to deal with all types.

 You can create signals on any class that is a subclass of `QObject`. That includes all widgets, including the main window and dialog boxes.

Modifying Signal Data

Signals are connected to *slots* which are functions (or methods) which will be run every time the signal fires. Many signals also transmit data, providing information about the state change or widget that fired them. The receiving slot can use this data to perform different actions in response to the same signal.

However, there is a limitation — the signal can only emit the data it was designed to. Take for example, the `QPushButton.clicked` signal which fires when the button is clicked. The *clicked+ signal emits a single piece of data — the _checked* state of the button after being clicked.

 For non-checkable buttons, this will always be `False`.

The slot receives this data, but nothing more. It does not know *which* widget triggered it, or anything about it. This is usually fine. You can tie a particular widget to a unique function which does precisely what that widget requires. Sometimes however you want to add additional data so your slot methods can be a little smarter. There's a neat trick to do just that.

The additional data you send could be the triggered widget itself, or some associated metadata which your slot needs to perform the intended result of the signal.

Intercepting the signal

Instead of connecting the signal directly to the target slot function, you use an intermediate function to intercept the signal, modify the signal data and forward that on to your target slot. If you define the intermediate function in a context that has access to the widget that emitted the signal, you can pass that with the signal too.

This slot function must accept the value sent by the signal (here the checked state) and then call the *real* slot, passing any additional data with the arguments.

```
def fn(checked):
    self.button_clicked(checked, <additional args>)
```

Rather than define this intermediate function like this, you can also achieve the same thing inline using a lambda function. As above, this accepts a single parameter checked and then calls the real slot.

```
lambda checked: self.button_clicked(checked, <additional args>)
```

In both examples the <additional args> can be replaced with anything you want to forward to your slot. In the example below we're forwarding the QPushButton object action to the receiving slot.

```
btn = QPushButton()
btn.clicked.connect( lambda checked: self.button_clicked(checked,
btn) )
```

Our button_clicked slot method will receive both the original checked value and the QPushButton object. Our receiving slot could look something like this —

```
# a class method.
def button_clicked(self, checked, btn):
    # do something here.
```

 You can reorder arguments in your intermediate function if you like.

The following example shows it in practice, with our button_clicked slot receiving the check state and the widget object. In this example, we hide the button in the handler so you can't click it again!

Listing 236. further/signals_extra_1.py

```python
import sys

from PyQt6.QtWidgets import QApplication, QMainWindow, QPushButton


class MainWindow(QMainWindow):
    def __init__(self):
        super().__init__()

        btn = QPushButton("Press me")
        btn.setCheckable(True)
        btn.clicked.connect(
            lambda checked: self.button_clicked(checked, btn)
        )

        self.setCentralWidget(btn)

    def button_clicked(self, checked, btn):
        print(btn, checked)
        btn.hide()


app = QApplication(sys.argv)

window = MainWindow()
window.show()
app.exec()
```

Problems with loops

A common reason for wanting to connect signals in this way is when you're building a series of widgets and connecting signals programmatically in a loop. Unfortunately, then things aren't always so simple.

If you construct intercepted signals in a loop and want to pass the loop variable to the receiving slot, you'll hit a problem. For example, in the following example, we're creating a series of buttons, and trying to pass the sequence number with the signal. Clicking a button should update the label with the value of the button.

Listing 237. further/signals_extra_2.py

```python
import sys

from PyQt6.QtWidgets import (
    QApplication,
    QHBoxLayout,
    QLabel,
    QMainWindow,
    QPushButton,
    QVBoxLayout,
    QWidget,
)


class MainWindow(QMainWindow):
    def __init__(self):
        super().__init__()

        v = QVBoxLayout()
        h = QHBoxLayout()

        for a in range(10):
            button = QPushButton(str(a))
            button.clicked.connect(
                lambda checked: self.button_clicked(a)
            )  ①
            h.addWidget(button)

        v.addLayout(h)
        self.label = QLabel("")
        v.addWidget(self.label)

        w = QWidget()
        w.setLayout(v)
        self.setCentralWidget(w)

    def button_clicked(self, n):
        self.label.setText(str(n))


app = QApplication(sys.argv)
```

```
window = MainWindow()
window.show()
app.exec()
```

① We accept the checked variable on our lambda but discard it. This button is not checkable, so it will always be False.

If you run this you'll see the problem — no matter which button you click, you get the same number (9) shown on the label. Why 9? It's the last value of the loop.

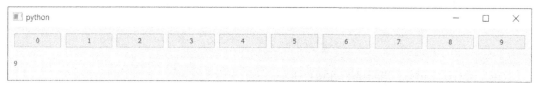

Figure 234. No matter which button you press, the label always shows 9.

The issue is here —

```
for a in range(10):
    button = QPushButton(str(a))
    button.clicked.connect(
        lambda checked: self.button_clicked(a)
    )
```

The problem is the line lambda: self.button_clicked(a) where we define the call to the final slot. Here we are passing a, but this remains bound to the loop variable. When the lambda is evaluated (when the signal fires) the value of a will be the value it had at *the end of the loop*, so clicking any of them will result in the same value being sent (here 9).

The solution is to pass the value in as a named parameter. By doing this the value is *bound* at the time the lamdba is created, and will hold value of a at *that iteration of the loop*. This ensures the correct value whenever it is called.

If this is gobbledygook, don't worry! Just remember to always used named parameters for your intermediate functions.

```
lambda checked, a=a: self.button_clicked(a) )
```

 You don't *have* to use the same variable name, you could use `lambda val=a: self.button_clicked(val)` if you prefer. The important thing is to use *named parameters*.

Putting this into our loop, it would look like this:

Listing 238. further/signals_extra_3.py

```
for a in range(10):
    button = QPushButton(str(a))
    button.clicked.connect(
        lambda checked, a=a: self.button_clicked(a)
    ) ①
    h.addWidget(button)
```

If you run this now, you'll see the expected behavior — clicking on a button will show the correct value in the label.

Figure 235. When you press a button, the number pressed is shown below.

Below are a few more examples using inline `lambda` functions to modify the data sent with the `MainWindow.windowTitleChanged` signal. They will all fire once the `.setWindowTitle` line is reached and the `my_custom_fn` slot will output what they receive.

Listing 239. further/signals_extra_4.py

```python
import sys

from PyQt6.QtWidgets import QApplication, QMainWindow


class MainWindow(QMainWindow):
    def __init__(self):
        super().__init__()

        # SIGNAL: The connected function will be called whenever the window
        # title is changed. The new title will be passed to the function.
        self.windowTitleChanged.connect(self.on_window_title_changed)

        # SIGNAL: The connected function will be called whenever the window
        # title is changed. The new title is discarded in the lambda and the
        # function is called without parameters.
        self.windowTitleChanged.connect(lambda x: self.my_custom_fn())

        # SIGNAL: The connected function will be called whenever the window
        # title is changed. The new title is passed to the function
        # and replaces the default parameter
        self.windowTitleChanged.connect(lambda x: self.my_custom_fn(x))

        # SIGNAL: The connected function will be called whenever the window
        # title is changed. The new title is passed to the function
        # and replaces the default parameter. Extra data is passed from
        # within the lambda.
        self.windowTitleChanged.connect(
            lambda x: self.my_custom_fn(x, 25)
        )

        # This sets the window title which will trigger all the above signals
        # sending the new title to the attached functions or lambdas
```

```
as the
            # first parameter.
            self.setWindowTitle("This will trigger all the signals.")

    # SLOT: This accepts a string, e.g. the window title, and prints
it
    def on_window_title_changed(self, s):
        print(s)

    # SLOT: This has default parameters and can be called without a
value
    def my_custom_fn(self, a="HELLLO!", b=5):
        print(a, b)



app = QApplication(sys.argv)

window = MainWindow()
window.show()
app.exec()
```

33. Working with Relative Paths

Paths describe the location of files in your filesystem.

When we load external data files into our applications we typically do this using paths. While straightforward in principle, there are a couple of ways this can trip you up. As your applications grow in size, maintaining the paths can get a bit unwieldly and it's worth taking a step back to implement a more reliable system.

Relative paths

There are two types of path — *absolute* and *relative*. An *absolute* path describes the path entirely from the *root* (bottom) of the filesystem, while a *relative* path describes the path from (or relative to) the current location in the filesystem.

It is not immediately obvious, but when you provide just a filename for a file, e.g. `hello.jpg`, that is a *relative* path. When the file is loaded, it is loaded relative to the *current active folder*. Confusingly, the *current active folder* is not necessarily the same folder your script is in.

In the Widgets chapter we introduced a simple approach for dealing with this problem when loading an image. We used the `__file__` built-in to get the path of the currently running script (our application) and then used `os` functions to first get the *directory* of our script and then use that to build the full path.

Listing 240. basic/widgets_2b.py

```python
import os
import sys

from PyQt6.QtGui import QPixmap
from PyQt6.QtWidgets import QApplication, QLabel, QMainWindow

basedir = os.path.dirname(__file__)
print("Current working folder:", os.getcwd())    ①
print("Paths are relative to:", basedir)    ②


class MainWindow(QMainWindow):
    def __init__(self):
        super().__init__()

        self.setWindowTitle("My App")

        widget = QLabel("Hello")
        widget.setPixmap(QPixmap(os.path.join(basedir, "otje.jpg")))

        self.setCentralWidget(widget)


app = QApplication(sys.argv)

window = MainWindow()
window.show()

app.exec()
```

This works well for simple applications where you have a single main script and load relatively few files. But having to duplicate the basedir calculation in every file you load from and use os.path.join to construct the paths everywhere quickly turns into a maintenance headache. If you ever need to restructure the files in your project, it's not going to be fun. Thankfully there is a simpler way!

Why not just use absolute paths? Because they will only work on your own filesystem, or a filesystem with exactly the same structure. If I develop an application in my own home folder and use absolute paths to refer to files, e.g. /home/martin/myapp/images/somefile.png, it will only work for other people who *also* have a home folder named martin and put the folder there. That would be a bit strange.

Using a Paths class

The data files your application needs to load are usually fairly structured — there are common *types* of file to load, or you are loading them for common *purposes*. Typically you will store related files in related folders to make managing them easier. We can make use of this existing structure to build a regular way to construct paths for our files.

To do this we can create a custom Paths class which uses a combination of attributes and methods to build folder and file paths respectively. The core of this is the same os.path.dirname(__file__) and os.path.join() approach used above, with the added benefit of being self-contained and easily modifiable.

Take the following code and add it to the root of your project, in a file named paths.py.

Listing 241. further/paths.py

```python
import os


class Paths:

    base = os.path.dirname(__file__)
    ui_files = os.path.join(base, "ui")
    images = os.path.join(base, "images")
    icons = os.path.join(images, "icons")
    data = os.path.join(base, "images")

    # File loaders.
    @classmethod
    def ui_file(cls, filename):
        return os.path.join(cls.ui_files, filename)

    @classmethod
    def icon(cls, filename):
        return os.path.join(cls.icons, filename)

    @classmethod
    def image(cls, filename):
        return os.path.join(cls.images, filename)

    @classmethod
    def data(cls, filename):
        return os.path.join(cls.data, filename)
```

To experiment with the paths module you can start up a Python
interpreter in your project root and use `from paths import Paths`

Now, anywhere in your application you can import the `Paths` class an use it
directly. The *attributes* `base`, `ui_files`, `icons`, `images`, and `data` all return the paths
to their respective folders under the base folder. Notice how the `icons` folder is
constructed from the `images` path — nesting this folder under that one.

Feel free to customize the names and structure of the paths, etc. to match the folder structure in your own project.

```
>>> from paths import Paths
>>> Paths.ui_files
'U:\\home\\martin\\books\\create-simple-gui-applications\\code
\\further\\ui'
>>> Paths.icons
'U:\\home\\martin\\books\\create-simple-gui-applications\\code
\\further\\images\\icons'
```

We **don't** create an object *instance* instance from this class — we don't call Paths() — because we don't need one. The paths are static and unchanging, so there is no internal *state* to manage by creating an object. Notice that the methods must be decorated as @classmethod to be accessible on the class itself.

The methods ui_file, icon, image and data are used to generate paths including filenames. In each case you call the method passing in the filename to add to the end of the path. These methods all depend on the folder *attributes* described above. For example, if you want to load a specific icon you can call the Paths.icon() method, passing in the name, to get the full path back.

```
>>> Paths.icon('bug.png')
'U:\\home\\martin\\books\\create-simple-gui-applications\\code
\\further\\images\\icons\\bug.png'
```

In your application code you could use this as follows to construct the path and load the icon.

```
QIcon(Paths.icon('bug.png'))
```

This keeps your code much tidier, helps ensure the paths are correct and makes it much easier if you ever want to restructure how your files are stored. For example, say you want to move icons up to the top level folder: now you only need to change the paths.py definition and all icons will work as before.

```
icons = os.path.join(images, 'icons')
# to move to top level, make icons derive from base instead
icons = os.path.join(base, 'icons')
```

34. System tray & macOS menus

System tray applications (or menu bar applications) can be useful for making common functions available in a small number of clicks. For full desktop applications they're a useful shortcut to control apps without opening up the whole window.

Qt provides a simple interface for building cross-platform system tray (Windows) or menu bar (macOS) apps. Below is a minimal working example for showing an icon in the toolbar/system tray with a menu. The action in the menu isn't connected and so doesn't do anything yet.

Listing 242. further/systray.py

```python
import os
import sys

from PyQt6.QtGui import QIcon
from PyQt6.QtWidgets import (
    QAction,
    QApplication,
    QColorDialog,
    QMenu,
    QSystemTrayIcon,
)


basedir = os.path.dirname(__file__)


app = QApplication(sys.argv)
app.setQuitOnLastWindowClosed(False)

# Create the icon
icon = QIcon(os.path.join(basedir, "icon.png"))

# Create the tray
tray = QSystemTrayIcon()
tray.setIcon(icon)
tray.setVisible(True)

# Create the menu
menu = QMenu()
action = QAction("A menu item")
menu.addAction(action)

# Add a Quit option to the menu.
quit = QAction("Quit")
quit.triggered.connect(app.quit)
menu.addAction(quit)

# Add the menu to the tray
tray.setContextMenu(menu)


app.exec()
```

You'll notice that there isn't a `QMainWindow`, simply because we don't have any window to show. You can create a window as normal without affecting the behavior of the system tray icon.

The default behavior in Qt is to close an application once all the active windows have closed. This won't affect this toy example, but will be an issue in application where you do create windows and then close them. Setting `app.setQuitOnLastWindowClosed(False)` stops this and will ensure your application keeps running.

The provided icon shows up in the toolbar (you can see it on the left hand side of the icons grouped on the right of the system tray or menubar).

Figure 236. The icon showing on the menubar.

Clicking (or right-clicking on Windows) on the icon shows the added menu.

Figure 237. The menubar app menu.

This application doesn't do anything yet, so in the next part we'll expand this example to create a mini color-picker.

Below is a more complete working example using the built in QColorDialog from Qt to give a toolbar accessible color picker. The menu lets you choose to get the picked color as HTML-format #RRGGBB, rgb(R,G,B) or hsv(H,S,V).

Listing 243. further/systray_color.py

```python
import os
import sys

from PyQt6.QtGui import QIcon
from PyQt6.QtWidgets import (
    QAction,
    QApplication,
    QColorDialog,
    QMenu,
    QSystemTrayIcon,
)

basedir = os.path.dirname(__file__)


app = QApplication(sys.argv)
app.setQuitOnLastWindowClosed(False)

# Create the icon
icon = QIcon(os.path.join(basedir, "color.png"))

clipboard = QApplication.clipboard()
dialog = QColorDialog()


def copy_color_hex():
    if dialog.exec():
        color = dialog.currentColor()
        clipboard.setText(color.name())


def copy_color_rgb():
    if dialog.exec():
        color = dialog.currentColor()
        clipboard.setText(
            "rgb(%d, %d, %d)"
```

```python
            % (color.red(), color.green(), color.blue())
        )


def copy_color_hsv():
    if dialog.exec():
        color = dialog.currentColor()
        clipboard.setText(
            "hsv(%d, %d, %d)"
            % (color.hue(), color.saturation(), color.value())
        )


# Create the tray
tray = QSystemTrayIcon()
tray.setIcon(icon)
tray.setVisible(True)

# Create the menu
menu = QMenu()
action1 = QAction("Hex")
action1.triggered.connect(copy_color_hex)
menu.addAction(action1)

action2 = QAction("RGB")
action2.triggered.connect(copy_color_rgb)
menu.addAction(action2)

action3 = QAction("HSV")
action3.triggered.connect(copy_color_hsv)
menu.addAction(action3)

quit = QAction("Quit")
quit.triggered.connect(app.quit)
menu.addAction(quit)

# Add the menu to the tray
tray.setContextMenu(menu)

app.exec()
```

As in the previous example there is no QMainWindow for this example. The menu is created as before, but adding 3 actions for the different output formats. Each action is connected to a specific handler function for the format it represents. Each handler shows a dialog and, if a color is selected, copies that color to the clipboard in the given format.

As before, the icon appears in the toolbar.

Figure 238. The Color picker on the toolbar.

Clicking the icon shows a menu, from which you can select the format of image you want to return.

Figure 239. The Color picker menu

Once you've chosen the format, you'll see the standard Qt color picker window.

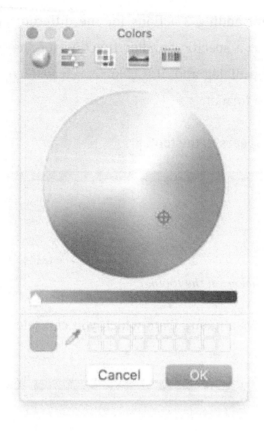

Figure 240. The system Color picker window

Select the color you want and click OK. The chosen color will be copied to the clipboard in the requested format. The formats available will product the following output:

Value	Ranges
#a2b3cc	00-FF
rgb(25, 28, 29)	0-255
hsv(14, 93, 199)	0-255

Adding a system tray icon for a full app

So far we've shown how to create a standalone system tray application with no main window. However, sometimes you may wish to have a system tray icon *as well* as a window. When this is done, typically the main window can be opened and closed (hidden) from the tray icon, without closing the application. In this section we'll look at how to build this kind of application with Qt5.

In principle it's quite straightforward — create our main window, and connect a signal from an action to the .show() method of the window.

Below is a small tray notes application called "PenguinNotes". When run, it puts a small penguin icon in your system track or macOS toolbar.

Clicking the small penguin icon in the tray will show the window. The window contains a QTextEdit editor into which you can write notes. You can close the window as normal, or by clicking again on the tray icon. The and app will remain running in the tray. To close the app you can use **File** › **Close** — closing will automatically save the notes.

Listing 244. further/systray_window.py

```python
import os
import sys

from PyQt6.QtGui import QIcon
from PyQt6.QtWidgets import (
    QAction,
    QApplication,
    QMainWindow,
    QMenu,
    QSystemTrayIcon,
    QTextEdit,
)

basedir = os.path.dirname(__file__)

app = QApplication(sys.argv)
app.setQuitOnLastWindowClosed(False)

# Create the icon
icon = QIcon(os.path.join(basedir, "animal-penguin.png"))

# Create the tray
```

```
tray = QSystemTrayIcon()
tray.setIcon(icon)
tray.setVisible(True)


class MainWindow(QMainWindow):
    def __init__(self):
        super().__init__()

        self.editor = QTextEdit()
        self.load()  # Load up the text from file.

        menu = self.menuBar()
        file_menu = menu.addMenu("&File")

        self.reset = QAction("&Reset")
        self.reset.triggered.connect(self.editor.clear)
        file_menu.addAction(self.reset)

        self.quit = QAction("&Quit")
        self.quit.triggered.connect(app.quit)
        file_menu.addAction(self.quit)

        self.setCentralWidget(self.editor)

        self.setWindowTitle("PenguinNotes")

    def load(self):
        with open("notes.txt", "r") as f:
            text = f.read()
        self.editor.setPlainText(text)

    def save(self):
        text = self.editor.toPlainText()
        with open("notes.txt", "w") as f:
            f.write(text)

    def activate(self, reason):
        if (
            reason == QSystemTrayIcon.ActivationReason.Trigger
        ):  # Icon clicked.
            self.show()
```

```
w = MainWindow()

tray.activated.connect(w.activate)
app.aboutToQuit.connect(w.save)

app.exec()
```

 On macOS the Quit action will appear in the application menu (on the far left, with the application name), not the File menu. If we didn't also add the **File** › **Reset** action, the File menu would be empty and hidden (try it!)

Below is a screenshot of the notes app with the window open.

Figure 241. The notes editor window.

The control of showing and hiding the window is handled in the `activate` method on our `QMainWindow`. This is connected to the tray icon `.activated` signal at the bottom of the code, using `tray.activated.connect(w.activate)`.

```
def activate(self, reason):
    if reason == QSystemTrayIcon.Trigger:  # Icon clicked.
        if self.isVisible():
            self.hide()
        else:
            self.show()
```

This signal is triggered under a number of different circumstances, so we must first check to ensure we are only using QSystemTrayIcon.Trigger.

Reason	Value	Description
QSystemTrayIcon.Unknown	0	Unknown reason.
QSystemTrayIcon.Context	1	Context menu requested (single click macOS, right-click Windows).
QSystemTrayIcon.DoubleClick	2	Icon double clicked. On macOS double-click only fires if no context menu is set, as the menu opens with a single click.
QSystemTrayIcon.Trigger	3	Icon clicked once.
QSystemTrayIcon.MiddleClick	4	Icon clicked with the middle mouse button.

By listening to these events you should be able to construct any type of system tray behavior you wish. However, be sure to check the behavior on all your target platforms.

35. Enums & the Qt Namespace

When you see a line like the following in your application, you might have wondered what the `Qt.ItemDataRole.DisplayRole` or `Qt.ItemDataRole.CheckStateRole` objects actually *are*.

 In earlier versions of PyQt there were also shortcut names such as `Qt.DisplayRole`, so you may still see these in code. In PyQt6 you must always use the long-form. All examples in this book use the fully-qualified names.

```
def data(self, role, index):

    if role == Qt.ItemDataRole.DisplayRole:
        # do something
```

Qt makes use of these types extensively for meaningful constants in code. Many of them are available in the Qt *namespace*, that is as `Qt.<something>`, although there are object-specific types such as `QDialogButtonBox.StandardButton.Ok` which work in exactly the same way.

But *how* do they work? In this chapter we'll take a close look at how these constants are formed and how to work with them effectively. To do that we'll need to touch on some fundamentals like binary numbers. But understanding these deeply isn't *necessary* to get something from this chapter — as always we'll focus on how we can apply things as we learn them.

It's all just numbers

If you check the `type()` of a flag you'll see the name of a class. These classes are the *group* that a given flag belongs to. For example, `Qt.ItemDataRole.DecorationRole` is of type `Qt.ItemDataRole` — you can see these groups in the Qt documentation [https://doc.qt.io/qt-6/qt.html#ItemDataRole-enum].

You can run the following code in a Python shell, just import the Qt namespace first with `from PyQt6.QtCore import Qt`.

```
>>> type(Qt.ItemDataRole.DecorationRole)
<enum 'ItemDataRole'>
```

These types are *enums* — a type which restricts its values to a set of predefined values. In PyQt6 they are defined as Python `Enum` types.

Each of these values is *actually* a simple integer number. The value of `Qt.ItemDataRole.DisplayRole` is 0, while `Qt.ItemDataRole.EditRole` has a value of 2. The integer values themselves are *meaningless* but have a meaning in the particular context in which they are used.

```
>>> int(Qt.ItemDataRole.DecorationRole)
1
```

For example, would you expect the following to evaluate to `True`?

```
>>> Qt.ItemDataRole.DecorationRole == Qt.AlignmentFlag.AlignLeft
True
```

Probably not. But both `Qt.ItemDataRole.DecorationRole` and `Qt.AlignmentFlag.AlignLeft` have an integer value of 1 and so are numerically equal. These numeric values can usually be ignored. As long as you use the constants in their appropriate context they will always work as expected.

Table 8. Values given in the documentation can be in decimal or binary.

Identifier	Value (hex)	Value (decimal)	Description
Qt.AlignmentFlag.AlignLeft	0x0001	1	Aligns with the left edge.

Identifier	Value (hex)	Value (decimal)	Description
`Qt.AlignmentFlag.AlignRight`	0x0002	2	Aligns with the right edge.
`Qt.AlignmentFlag.AlignHCenter`	0x0004	4	Centers horizontally in the available space.
`Qt.AlignmentFlag.AlignJustify`	0x0008	8	Justifies the text in the available space.
`Qt.AlignmentFlag.AlignTop`	0x0020	32	Aligns with the top.
`Qt.AlignmentFlag.AlignBottom`	0x0040	64	Aligns with the bottom.
`Qt.AlignmentFlag.AlignVCenter`	0x0080	128	Centers vertically in the available space.
`Qt.AlignmentFlag.AlignBaseline`	0x0100	256	Aligns with the baseline.

If you look at the numbers in the table above you may notice something odd. Firstly, they don't increase by 1 for each constant, but double each time. Secondly, the horizontal alignment hex numbers are all in one column, while the vertical alignment numbers are in another.

This pattern of numbers is intentional and it allows us to do something very neat — combine flags together to create compound flags. To understand this we'll need to take a quick look at how integer numbers are represented by a computer.

Binary & Hexadecimal

When we count normally we use *decimal* a base-10 number system. It has 10 digits, from 0-9 and each digit in a decimal number is worth 10x that which preceded it. In the following example, our number 1251 is made up of 1x1000, 2x100, 5x10 and 1x1.

1000	100	10	1
1	2	5	1

Computers store data in binary, a series of on and off states represented in written form as 1s and 0s. Binary is a base-2 number system. It has 2 digits, from 0-1 and each digit in a binary number is worth 2x that which preceded it. In the following example, our number 5 is made up of 1x4 and 1x1.

8	4	2	1	Decimal
0	1	0	1	5

Writing binary numbers gets cumbersome quickly — 5893 in binary is 1011100000101 — but converting back and forward to decimal is not much better. To make it easier to work with binary numbers *hexadecimal* is frequently used in computing. This is a numeric system with 16 digits (0-9A-F). Each hexadecimal digit has a value between 0-15 (0-A) equivalent to 4 binary digits. This makes it straightforward to convert between the two.

The table below shows the numbers 0-15, together with the same value in binary and hexadecimal. The value of a given binary number can be calculated by adding up the numbers at the top of each column with a 1 in them.

8	4	2	1	Hex	Dec
0	0	0	0	0	0
0	0	0	1	1	1

8	4	2	1	Hex	Dec
0	0	1	0	2	2
0	0	1	1	3	3
0	1	0	0	4	4
0	1	0	1	5	5
0	1	1	0	6	6
0	1	1	1	7	7
1	0	0	0	8	8
1	0	0	1	9	9
1	0	1	0	A	10
1	0	1	1	B	11
1	1	0	0	C	12
1	1	0	1	D	13
1	1	1	0	E	14
1	1	1	1	F	15

This pattern continues for higher numbers. For example, below is the number 25 in binary, constructed from 16 x 1, 8 x 1 and 1 x 1.

16	8	4	2	1
1	1	0	0	1

Because each digit in a binary value is either a 1 or a 0 (True or False) we can use individual binary digits as *boolean flags* — state markers which are either *on* or *off*. A single integer value can store multiple flags, using unique binary digits for each. Each of these flags would have their own *numerical value* based on the position of the binary digit they set to 1.

That is exactly how the Qt flags work. Looking at our alignment flags again, we can now see why the numbers were chosen — each flag is a unique non-overlapping bit. The *values* of the flags come from the binary digit the flag has set to 1.

`Qt.AlignmentFlag.AlignLeft`	1	00000001
`Qt.AlignmentFlag.AlignRight`	2	00000010
`Qt.AlignmentFlag.AlignHCenter`	4	00000100
`Qt.AlignmentFlag.AlignJustify`	8	00001000
`Qt.AlignmentFlag.AlignTop`	32	00100000
`Qt.AlignmentFlag.AlignBottom`	64	01000000
`Qt.AlignmentFlag.AlignVCenter`	128	10000000

When testing these flags directly with == you don't need to worry about all this. But this arrangement of values unlocks the ability to *combine* the flags together to create compound flags which represent more than one state *at the same time*. This allows you to have a single flag variable representing, for example, left & bottom aligned.

Bitwise OR (|) combination

Any two numbers, with non-overlapping binary representations can be added together while leaving their original binary digits in place. For example, below we add 1 and 2 together, to get 3 —

Table 9. Add

001	1
010	+ 2
011	= 3

The 1 digits in the original numbers are preserved in the output. In contrast, if we add together 1 and 3 to get 4, the 1 digits of the original numbers are not in the result — both are now zero.

$$
\begin{array}{ll}
001 & 1 \\
011 & + 3 \\
100 & = 4
\end{array}
$$

ℹ️ You can see the same effect in decimal — compare adding 100 and 50 to give 150 vs. adding 161 and 50 to give 211.

Since we're using 1 values in specific binary positions to *mean* something, this poses a problem. For example, if we *added* the value of an alignment flag twice, we would get something else both entirely right (mathematically) and entirely wrong (in meaning).

Table 10. Add

00000001	1	Qt.AlignmentFlag.AlignLeft
00000001	+ 1	+ Qt.AlignmentFlag.AlignLeft
00000010	= 2	= Qt.AlignmentFlag.AlignRight

```
>>> Qt.AlignmentFlag.AlignLeft + Qt.AlignmentFlag.AlignLeft == Qt
.AlignmentFlag.AlignRight
True
```

For this reason, when working with binary flags we combine them using a *bitwise OR* — which is performed in Python using the | (pipe) operator. In a *bitwise OR* you combine two numbers together by comparing them at the binary level. The result is a new number, where binary digits are set to 1 if they were 1 in *either* of the inputs. But importantly, *digits are not carried* and do not affect adjacent digits.

When you have non-overlapping digits bitwise OR is the same as add (+).

Qt.AlignmentFlag.AlignLeft	00000001
Qt.AlignmentFlag.AlignTop	00100000

Taking the two alignment constants above, we can combine their values together using a *bitwise OR* to produce the output to give align *top left*.

Table 11. Bitwise OR

00000001	1	Qt.AlignmentFlag.AlignLeft
00100000	OR 32	| Qt.AlignmentFlag.AlignTop
00100001	= 33	Qt.AlignmentFlag.AlignLeft | Qt.AlignmentFlag.AlignTop

```
>>> int(Qt.AlignmentFlag.AlignLeft | Qt.AlignmentFlag.AlignTop)
33
```

So, if we combine 32 with 1 we get 33. This should hopefully not be too surprising. But what if we accidentally add Qt.AlignmentFlag.AlignLeft multiple times?

```
>>> int(Qt.AlignmentFlag.AlignLeft | Qt.AlignmentFlag.AlignLeft | Qt
.AlignmentFlag.AlignTop)
33
```

The same result! The *bitwise OR* outputs a 1 in a binary position if there is a 1 in any of the inputs. It doesn't add them up, carry or overflow anything into other digits — meaning you can \| the same value together multiple times and you just end up with what you started with.

```
>>> int(Qt.AlignmentFlag.AlignLeft | Qt.AlignmentFlag.AlignLeft | Qt
.AlignmentFlag.AlignLeft)
1
```

Or, in binary —

Table 12. Bitwise OR

00000001	1	Qt.AlignmentFlag.AlignLeft
00000001	OR 1	| Qt.AlignmentFlag.AlignLeft
00000001	= 1	= Qt.AlignmentFlag.AlignLeft

And finally, comparing the values.

```
>>> Qt.AlignmentFlag.AlignLeft | Qt.AlignmentFlag.AlignLeft == Qt
.AlignmentFlag.AlignLeft
True

>>> Qt.AlignmentFlag.AlignLeft | Qt.AlignmentFlag.AlignLeft == Qt
.AlignmentFlag.AlignRight
False
```

Checking compound flags

We can check simple flags by comparing against the flag itself, as we've already seen —

```
>>> align = Qt.AlignmentFlag.AlignLeft
>>> align == Qt.AlignmentFlag.AlignLeft
True
```

For combined flags we can also check equality with the combination of flags —

```
>>> align = Qt.AlignmentFlag.AlignLeft | Qt.AlignmentFlag.AlignTop
>>> align == Qt.AlignmentFlag.AlignLeft | Qt.AlignmentFlag.AlignTop
True
```

But sometimes, you want to know if a given variable *contains* a specific flag. For example, perhaps we want to know if `align` has the *align left* flag set, regardless of any other alignment state.

How can we check that an element has `Qt.AlignmentFlag.AlignLeft` applied, once it's been combined with another? In this case a `==` comparison will not work, since they are not numerically equal.

```
>> alignment = Qt.AlignmentFlag.AlignLeft | Qt.AlignmentFlag.AlignTop
>> alignment == Qt.AlignmentFlag.AlignLeft  # 33 == 1
False
```

We need a way to compare the `Qt.AlignmentFlag.AlignLeft` flag against the bits of our compound flag. For this we can use a *bitwise AND*.

Bitwise AND (&) checks

In Python, *bitwise AND* operations are performed using the & operator.

In the previous step we combined together `Qt.AlignmentFlag.AlignLeft` (1) and `Qt.AlignmentFlag.AlignTop` (32) to produce "Top Left" (33). Now we want to check if the resulting combined flag has the align left flag set. To test we need to use *bitwise AND* which checks bit by bit to see if both input values are 1, returning a 1 in that place if it is true.

Table 13. Bitwise AND

00100001	33	Qt.AlignmentFlag.AlignLeft | Qt.AlignmentFlag.AlignTop
00000001	AND 1	& Qt.AlignmentFlag.AlignLeft

```
00000001                = 1            = Qt.AlignmentFlag.AlignLeft
```

This has the effect of *filtering* the bits in our input variable to only those that are set in our target flag `Qt.AlignmentFlag.AlignLeft`. If this one bit is set, the result is non-zero, if it is unset the result is 0.

```
>>> int(alignment & Qt.AlignmentFlag.AlignLeft)
1  # result is the numerical value of the flag, here 1.
```

For example, if we tested our alignment variable against `Qt.AlignmentFlag.AlignRight` the result is 0.

```
00100001        33        Qt.AlignmentFlag.AlignLeft |
                          Qt.AlignmentFlag.AlignTop

00000010        2         & Qt.AlignmentFlag.AlignRight

00000000        0         = Qt.AlignmentFlag.AlignLeft
```

```
>>> int(alignment & Qt.AlignmentFlag.AlignRight)
0
```

Because in Python 0 is equal to `False` and any other value is `True`. This means that when testing two numbers against one another with bitwise AND, if *any* bits are in common the result will be > 0, and be `True`.

With a combination of bitwise OR and AND you should be able to achieve everything you need with the Qt flags.

36. Working with command-line arguments

If you have created an application which works with specific file types — for example a video editor that opens videos, a document editor that opens document files — it can be useful to have your application open these files automatically. On all platforms, when you tell the OS to open a file with a specific application, the *filename* to open is passed to that application as a command-line *argument*.

When your application is run, the arguments passed to the application are always available in `sys.argv`. To open files automatically, you can check the value of `sys.argv` at startup and, if you find a filename in there, open it.

The following app when run will open a window with all the command line arguments received displayed.

Listing 245. further/arguments.py

```python
from PyQt6.QtWidgets import (
    QApplication,
    QWidget,
    QLabel,
    QVBoxLayout,
)

import sys


class Window(QWidget):
    def __init__(self):
        super().__init__()

        layout = QVBoxLayout()

        for arg in sys.argv:   ①
            l = QLabel(arg)
            layout.addWidget(l)

        self.setLayout(layout)
        self.setWindowTitle("Arguments")


app = QApplication(sys.argv)
w = Window()
w.show()

app.exec()
```

① `sys.argv` is a list of strings. *All* arguments are strings.

Run this app from the command line, passing in a filename (you can make anything up, we don't load it). You can pass as many, or as few, arguments as you like.

Arguments are passed to your application as a `list` of `str`. *All* arguments are strings, even numeric ones. You can access any argument you like using normal

647

list indexing—for example `sys.argv[1]` would return the 2nd argument.

Try running the script above with the following—

```
python arguments.py filename.mp4
```

This will produce the window below. Notice that when run with `python` the first argument is *actually* the Python file which is being executed.

Figure 242. The window open showing the command line arguments.

If you package your application for distribution, this may no longer be the case—the first argument may now be the file you are opening, as there is no Python file passed as an argument. This can cause problems, but a simple way around this is to use the *last* argument passed to your application as the filename, e.g.

```
if len(sys.argv) > 0:
    filename_to_open = sys.argv[-1]
```

Alternatively, you can remove the currently executing script name if it is in the list. The currently executing Python script name is always available in `__file__`.

```
if __file__ in sys.argv:
    sys.argv.remove(__file__)
```

 It will *always* be in the list, unless you have packaged your app.

Below is a further example, where we accept a filename on the command line, and then open that text file for display in a `QTextEdit`.

Listing 246. further/arguments_open.py

```python
from PyQt6.QtWidgets import QApplication, QMainWindow, QTextEdit

import sys


class MainWindow(QMainWindow):
    def __init__(self):
        super().__init__()

        self.editor = QTextEdit()

        if __file__ in sys.argv:    ①
            sys.argv.remove(__file__)

        if sys.argv:    ②
            filename = sys.argv[0]    ③
            self.open_file(filename)

        self.setCentralWidget(self.editor)
        self.setWindowTitle("Text viewer")

    def open_file(self, fn):

        with open(fn, "r") as f:
            text = f.read()

        self.editor.setPlainText(text)


app = QApplication(sys.argv)
w = MainWindow()
w.show()

app.exec()
```

① If the script name is in `sys.argv` remove it.

② If there is still something in `sys.argv` (not empty).

649

③ Take the first argument as the filename to open.

You can run this as follows, to view the passed in text file.

```
python arguments_open.py notes.txt
```

Packaging & Distribution

Design isn't finished until somebody is using it.

— Brenda Laurel, PhD

There is not much fun in creating your own application if you can't share it with other people — whether that means publishing it commercially, sharing it online or just giving it to someone you know. Sharing your apps allows other people to benefit from your hard work!

Packaging Python applications for distribution has typically been a little tricky, particularly when targeting multiple platforms (Windows, macOS and Linux). This is because of the need to bundle the source, data files, the Python runtime and all associated libraries in a way that will work reliably on the target system. Thankfully there are tools available to take care of this for you!

In this chapter we'll walk through the process of packaging up your apps to share with other people.

37. Packaging with PyInstaller

PyInstaller is a cross-platform PyQt6 packaging system which supports building desktop applications for Windows, macOS and Linux. It automatically handles packaging of your Python applications, along with any associated libraries and data files, either into a standalone one-file executable or a distributable folder you can then use to create an installer.

In this chapter we'll walk through the process using *PyInstaller* to package a PyQt6 application. The app we'll be building is deliberately simple, including just a window and a few icons, but the same process can be used to build any of your own applications. We'll cover customizing your application's name, icons and bundling data files in a reproducible way. We'll also cover some common issues which you may encounter when building your own apps.

Once we have *built* the application into a distributable executable, we'll move onto creating Windows Installers, macOS Disk Images and Linux packages which you can share with other people.

 The source downloads for this book include complete build examples for Windows, macOS and Ubuntu Linux.

 You always need to compile your app on the target system. So, if you want to build a Windows executable you'll need to do this on a Windows system.

Requirements

PyInstaller works out of the box with PyQt6 and as of writing, current versions of *PyInstaller* are compatible with Python 3.6+. Whatever project you're working on, you should be able to package your apps. This tutorial assumes you have a working installation of Python with `pip` package management working.

You can install *PyInstaller* using `pip`.

```
pip3 install PyInstaller
```

If you experience problems packaging your apps, your first step should *always* be to update your *PyInstaller* and *hooks* packages to the latest versions using:

```
pip3 install --upgrade PyInstaller pyinstaller-hooks-contrib
```

The *hooks* module contains specific packaging instructions and workarounds for common Python packages and is updated more regularly than *PyInstaller* itself.

Getting Started

It's a good idea to start packaging your application *from the very beginning* so you can confirm that packaging is still working as you develop it. This is particularly important if you add additional dependencies. If you only think about packaging at the end, it can be difficult to debug exactly *where* the problems are.

For this example we're going to start with a simple skeleton app, which doesn't do anything interesting. Once we've got the basic packaging process working, we'll start extending things, confirming the build is still working at each step.

To start with, create a new folder for your application and then add the following app in a file named app.py.

Listing 247. packaging/basic/app.py

```python
from PyQt6.QtWidgets import QMainWindow, QApplication, QPushButton

import sys


class MainWindow(QMainWindow):
    def __init__(self):
        super().__init__()

        self.setWindowTitle("Hello World")

        button = QPushButton("My simple app.")
        button.pressed.connect(self.close)

        self.setCentralWidget(button)
        self.show()


app = QApplication(sys.argv)
w = MainWindow()
app.exec()
```

This is a basic bare-bones application which creates a custom QMainWindow and adds a simple QPushButton to it. Pressing the button will close the window. You can run this app as follows:

```
python app.py
```

This should produce the following window.

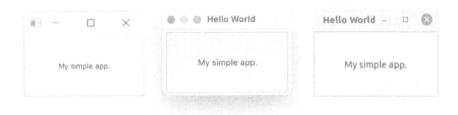

Figure 243. Simple app on Windows, macOS and Ubuntu Linux.

Building the basic app

Now that we have confirmed our simple application is working, we can create our first test build. Open your terminal (shell) and navigate to the folder containing your project. Run the following command to create a *PyInstaller* build.

```
pyinstaller --windowed app.py
```

 The `--windowed` command line option is required to build a `.app` bundle on macOS and to hide the *terminal* output on Windows. On Linux it has no effect.

You'll see a number of messages output, giving debug information about what *PyInstaller* is doing. These are useful for debugging issues in your build, but can otherwise be ignored.

Listing 248. Output running `pyinstaller` *on Windows*

```
> pyinstaller app.py
388 INFO: PyInstaller: 4.7
388 INFO: Python: 3.7.6
389 INFO: Platform: Windows-10-10.0.22000-SP0
392 INFO: wrote app.spec
394 INFO: UPX is not available.
405 INFO: Extending PYTHONPATH with paths
....etc.
```

After the build is complete, look in your folder and you'll notice you now have two new folders `dist` and `build`.

Name	Date modified	Type	Size
__pycache__	06/04/2020 17:49	File folder	
build	07/04/2020 13:49	File folder	
dist	08/04/2020 14:15	File folder	
app	03/04/2020 15:05	Python Source File	1 KB
app.spec	08/04/2020 14:15	SPEC File	1 KB

Figure 244. build & dist folders created by PyInstaller.

Below is a truncated listing of the folder structure showing the `build` and `dist` folders. The actual files will differ depending on which platform you're building on, but the general structure is always the same.

```
.
├────── app.py
├────── app.spec
├────── build
│       └────── app
│               ├────── localpycos
│               ├────── Analysis-00.toc
│               ├────── COLLECT-00.toc
│               ├────── EXE-00.toc
│               ├────── PKG-00.pkg
│               ├────── PKG-00.toc
│               ├────── PYZ-00.pyz
│               ├────── PYZ-00.toc
│               ├────── app
│               ├────── app.pkg
│               ├────── base_library.zip
│               ├────── warn-app.txt
│               └────── xref-app.html
└────── dist
        └────── app
                ├────── lib-dynload
        . . .
```

The `build` folder is used by *PyInstaller* to collect and prepare the files for bundling, it contains the results of analysis and some additional logs. For the most part, you can ignore the contents of this folder, unless you're trying to debug issues.

The `dist` (for "distribution") folder contains the files to be distributed. This includes your application, bundled as an executable file, together with any associated libraries (for example PyQt6). Everything necessary to run your application will be in this folder, meaning you can take this folder and *distribute* it to someone else to run your app.

You can try running your built app yourself now, by running the executable file named `app` from the `dist` folder. After a short delay you'll see the familiar window of your application pop up as shown below.

Figure 245. Simple app, running after being packaged.

In the same folder as your Python file, alongside the `build` and `dist` folders *PyInstaller* will have also created a `.spec` file.

The .spec file

The `.spec` file contains the build configuration and instructions that *PyInstaller* uses to package up your application. Every *PyInstaller* project has a `.spec` file, which is generated based on the command line options you pass when running `pyinstaller`.

When we ran `pyinstaller` with our script, we didn't pass in anything other than the name of our Python application file. This means our spec file currently contains only the default configuration. If you open it, you'll see something similar to what we have below.

Listing 249. packaging/basic/app.spec

```python
# -*- mode: python ; coding: utf-8 -*-


block_cipher = None


a = Analysis(['app.py'],
             pathex=[],
             binaries=[],
             datas=[],
             hiddenimports=[],
             hookspath=[],
```

```
            hooksconfig={},
            runtime_hooks=[],
            excludes=[],
            win_no_prefer_redirects=False,
            win_private_assemblies=False,
            cipher=block_cipher,
            noarchive=False)
pyz = PYZ(a.pure, a.zipped_data,
            cipher=block_cipher)

exe = EXE(pyz,
          a.scripts,
          [],
          exclude_binaries=True,
          name='app',
          debug=False,
          bootloader_ignore_signals=False,
          strip=False,
          upx=True,
          console=True,
          disable_windowed_traceback=False,
          target_arch=None,
          codesign_identity=None,
          entitlements_file=None )
coll = COLLECT(exe,
              a.binaries,
              a.zipfiles,
              a.datas,
              strip=False,
              upx=True,
              upx_exclude=[],
              name='app')
```

The first thing to notice is that this is a Python file, meaning you can edit it and use Python code to calculate values for the settings. This is mostly useful for complex builds, for example when you are targeting different platforms and want to conditionally define additional libraries or dependencies to bundle.

If you're building on macOS you'll also have an additional BUNDLE block, which is used to build the .app bundle. That section will look something like this:

```
app = BUNDLE(coll,
             name='app.app',
             icon=None,
             bundle_identifier=None)
```

If you're starting your build on another platform, but want to target macOS later you can add this to the end of your .spec file manually.

Once a .spec file has been generated, you can pass this to pyinstaller instead of your script to repeat the previous build process. Run this now to rebuild your executable.

```
pyinstaller app.spec
```

The resulting build will be identical to the build used to generate the .spec file (assuming you have made no changes to your project). For many *PyInstaller* configuration changes you have the option of passing command-line arguments, or modifying your existing .spec file. Which you choose is up to you, although I would recommend editing the .spec file for more complex builds.

Tweaking the build

We've created a very simple application and build our first executable. Now we'll look at a few things we can do to tweak the build.

Naming your app

One of the simplest changes you can make is to provide a proper "name" for your application. By default the app takes the name of your source file (minus the extension), for example main or app. This isn't usually what you want to name the executable.

You can provide a nicer name for *PyInstaller* to use for your executable file (and dist folder) by editing the .spec file and changing the name= under the EXE and

COLLECT blocks (and BUNDLE on macOS).

Listing 250. packaging/custom/hello-world.spec

```
exe = EXE(pyz,
          a.scripts,
          [],
          exclude_binaries=True,
          name='hello-world',
          debug=False,
          bootloader_ignore_signals=False,
          strip=False,
          upx=True,
          console=True,
          disable_windowed_traceback=False,
          target_arch=None,
          codesign_identity=None,
          entitlements_file=None )
coll = COLLECT(exe,
               a.binaries,
               a.zipfiles,
               a.datas,
               strip=False,
               upx=True,
               upx_exclude=[],
               name='hello-world')
```

The name under EXE is the name of the *executable file* while the name under COLLECT is the name of the output folder.

 I'd recommend you to use a name with no spaces for the executable — use hyphens or CamelCase instead.

The name specified in the BUNDLE block is used for the macOS app bundle, which is the user-visible name of the application shown in Launchpad and on the dock. In our example we've called our application executable "hello-world", but for the .app bundle you can use the more friendly "Hello World.app".

Listing 251. packaging/custom/hello-world.spec

```
app = BUNDLE(coll,
             name='Hello World.app',
             icon=None,
             bundle_identifier=None)
```

Alternatively, you can re-run the `pyinstaller` command and pass the `-n` or `--name` configuration flag along with your `app.py` script.

```
pyinstaller --windowed -n "hello-world" app.py
# or
pyinstaller --windowed --name "hello-world" app.py
```

The resulting executable file will be given the name `hello-world` and the unpacked build placed in the folder `dist\hello-world\`. The name of the `.spec` file is taken from the name passed in on the command line, so this will *also* create a new spec file for you, called `hello-world.spec` in your root folder.

 If you've created a new `.spec` delete the old one to avoid getting confused!

Name	Date modified	Type	Size
PyQt5	14/04/2022 11:42	File folder	
base_library.zip	14/04/2022 11:42	Compressed (zipp...	760 KB
d3dcompiler_47.dll	28/01/2022 12:55	Application extens...	4,077 KB
hello-world.exe	14/04/2022 11:42	Application	1,722 KB
libcrypto-1_1.dll	24/01/2022 16:57	Application extens...	3,303 KB
libEGL.dll	28/01/2022 10:48	Application extens...	25 KB

Figure 246. Application with custom name "hello-world".

Application icon

Another simple improvement we can make is to change the application icon which is shown while the application is running. We can set the icon for the application window/dock by calling `.setWindowIcon()` in the code.

Listing 252. packaging/custom/app.py

```python
from PyQt6.QtWidgets import QMainWindow, QApplication, QPushButton
from PyQt6.QtGui import QIcon

import sys


class MainWindow(QMainWindow):
    def __init__(self):
        super().__init__()

        self.setWindowTitle("Hello World")

        button = QPushButton("My simple app.")
        button.pressed.connect(self.close)

        self.setCentralWidget(button)
        self.show()


app = QApplication(sys.argv)
app.setWindowIcon(QIcon("icon.svg"))
w = MainWindow()
app.exec()
```

Here we've added the `.setWindowIcon` call to the `app` instance. This defines a *default* icon to be used for all windows of our application. You *can* override this on a per-window basis if you like, by calling `.setWindowIcon` on the window itself. Copy the icon into the same folder as your script.

If you run the above application you should now see the icon appears on the window on Windows and on the dock in macOS or Ubuntu Linux.

Figure 247. Windows showing the custom icon.

A note about icons.

In this example we're setting a single icon file, using a *Scalable Vector Graphics* (SVG) file which will appear sharp at any size. You can *instead* use bitmap images, in which case you will want to provide multiple sizes to ensure the icon always appears sharp. On Windows you can do this by building an ICO file, which is a special file containing multiple icons. On Linux you can provide multiple different PNG files during install (see the Linux packaging section). On macOS the multiple icon sizes are provided by an ICNS file included in the .app bundle.

Yes, this is confusing! But thankfully Qt supports the various icon formats across all platforms.

Even if you *don't* see the icon, keep reading!

Dealing with relative paths

There is a gotcha here, which might not be immediately apparent. Open a shell and change to the folder where your script is saved. Run it as normal:

```
python3 app.py
```

If the icons are in the correct location, you should see them. Now change to the parent folder, and try and run your script again (change <folder> to the name of the folder your script is in).

```
cd ..
python3 <folder>/app.py
```

Figure 248. Window with icon missing.

The icons *don't* appear. What's happening?

We're using *relative* paths to refer to our data files. These paths are relative to the *current working directory* — not the folder your script is in, but the folder you ran it from. If you run the script from elsewhere it won't be able to find the files.

 One common reason for icons not showing up, is running examples in an IDE which uses the project root as the current working directory.

This is a minor issue before the app is packaged, but once it's installed you don't know what the *current working directory* will be when it is run — if it's wrong your app won't be able to find it's data files. We need to fix this before we go any further, which we can do by making our paths relative to *our application folder*.

In the updated code below, we define a new variable basedir, using os.path.dirname to get the containing folder of __file__ which holds the full path of the current Python file. We then use this to build the relative paths for data files using os.path.join().

 Take a look at Working with Relative Paths for more information, and a more robust way of working with relative paths in your apps.

Since our app.py file is in the root of our folder, all other paths are relative to that.

Listing 253. packaging/custom/app_relative_paths.py

```python
import os
import sys

from PyQt6.QtGui import QIcon
from PyQt6.QtWidgets import QApplication, QMainWindow, QPushButton

basedir = os.path.dirname(__file__)


class MainWindow(QMainWindow):
    def __init__(self):
        super().__init__()

        self.setWindowTitle("Hello World")

        button = QPushButton("My simple app.")
        button.setIcon(QIcon(os.path.join(basedir, "icon.svg")))
        button.pressed.connect(self.close)

        self.setCentralWidget(button)
        self.show()


app = QApplication(sys.argv)
app.setWindowIcon(QIcon(os.path.join(basedir, "icon.svg")))
w = MainWindow()
app.exec()
```

Try and run your app again from the parent folder — you'll find that the icon now appears as expected, no matter where you launch the app from.

Taskbar Icons (Windows Only)

On Windows `.setWindowIcon()` will correctly set the icon on your windows. However, due to how Windows keeps track of windows and groups them on the taskbar, sometimes the icon will not show up on the taskbar.

666

If it does for you, great! But it may not work when you distribute your application, so follow the next steps anyway!

When you run your application, Windows looks at the executable and tries to guess what "application group" it belongs to. By default, any Python scripts (which includes your application) are grouped under the same "Python" group, and so will show the Python icon. To stop this happening, we need to provide Windows with a different application identifier for our app.

The code below does this, by calling `SetCurrentProcessExplicitAppUserModelID()` with a custom application id.

Listing 254. packaging/custom/app_windows_taskbar.py

```python
from PyQt6.QtWidgets import QMainWindow, QApplication, QPushButton
from PyQt6.QtGui import QIcon

import sys, os

basedir = os.path.dirname(__file__)

try:   ①
    from ctypes import windll  # Only exists on Windows.

    myappid = "mycompany.myproduct.subproduct.version"   ②
    windll.shell32.SetCurrentProcessExplicitAppUserModelID(myappid)
except ImportError:
    pass


class MainWindow(QMainWindow):
    def __init__(self):
        super().__init__()

        self.setWindowTitle("Hello World")

        button = QPushButton("My simple app.")
        button.setIcon(QIcon(os.path.join(basedir, "icon.svg")))
        button.pressed.connect(self.close)

        self.setCentralWidget(button)
        self.show()


app = QApplication(sys.argv)
app.setWindowIcon(QIcon(os.path.join(basedir, "icon.svg")))
w = MainWindow()
app.exec()
```

① The code is wrapped in a try/except block since the windll module is not available on non-Windows platforms. This allows your application to continue working on macOS & Linux.

② Customize the app identifier string for your own applications.

The listing above shows a generic `mycompany.myproduct.subproduct.version` string, but you *should* change this to reflect your actual application. It doesn't really matter what you put for this purpose, but the convention is to use reverse-domain notation, `com.mycompany` for the company identifier.

Add this to your script and your icon will *definitely* show on the taskbar.

Figure 249. Custom icon showing on the taskbar.

Executable icons (Windows only)

We now have the icon showing correctly while the application is running. But you may have noticed that your application *executable* still has a different icon. On Windows application executables can have icons embedded in them to make them more easily identifiable. The default icon is one provided by PyInstaller, but you can replace it with your own.

To add an icon to the Windows executable you need to provide an `.ico` format file to the `EXE` block.

Listing 255. packaging/custom/hello-world-icons.spec

```
exe = EXE(pyz,
          a.scripts,
          [],
          exclude_binaries=True,
          name='hello-world',
          icon='icon.ico',
          debug=False,
          bootloader_ignore_signals=False,
          strip=False,
          upx=True,
          console=True,
          disable_windowed_traceback=False,
          target_arch=None,
          codesign_identity=None,
          entitlements_file=None )
```

To create an .ico file, I recommend you use Greenfish Icon Editor Pro
[http://greenfishsoftware.org/gfie.php], a free and open-source tool which can also
build icons for Windows. An example .ico file is included in the downloads with
this book.

If you run the pyinstaller build with the modified .spec file, you'll see the
executable now has the custom icon.

Figure 250. Windows executable showing the default and custom icons.

You can also provide the icon by passing --icon icon.ico to
pyinstaller on the initial build. You can provide multiple icons
this way to support macOS and Windows.

macOS .app bundle icon (macOS only)

On macOS applications are distributed in .app bundles, which can have their own icons. The bundle icon is used to identify the application in the Launchpad and on the dock when the application is launched. *PyInstaller* can take care of adding the icon to the app bundle for you, you just need to pass an ICNS format file to the BUNDLE block in the .spec file. This icon will then show up on the resulting bundle, and be shown when the app is started.

Listing 256. packaging/custom/hello-world-icons.spec

```
app = BUNDLE(coll,
             name='Hello World.app',
             icon='icon.icns',
             bundle_identifier=None)
```

ICNS is the file format for icon files on macOS. You can create icon files on macOS using Icon Composer [https://github.com/lemonmojo/IconComposer2x/]. You can also create macOS icons on Windows using Greenfish Icon Editor Pro [http://greenfishsoftware.org/gfie.php].

Hello World   hello-world

Hello World   hello-world

Figure 251. macOS .app bundle showing the default and custom icons.

 You can also provide the icon by passing --icon icon.icns to pyinstaller on the initial build. You can provide multiple icons this way to support macOS and Windows.

In our example the icon set on the bundle will be replaced by the .setWindowIcon call when the application launches. However, on macOS you can skip the setWindowIcon() call entirely and just set the icon through the .app bundle if you wish.

Data files and Resources

So we now have a application working, with a custom name, custom application icon and a couple of tweaks to ensure that the icon is displayed on all platforms and wherever the application is launched from. With this in place, the final step is to ensure that this icon is correctly packaged with your application and continues to be shown when run from the dist folder.

 Try it, it wont.

The issue is that our application now has a dependency on a *external data file* (the icon file) that's not part of our source. For our application to work, we now need to distribute this data file along with it. *PyInstaller* can do this for us, but we need to tell it what we want to include, and where to put it in the output.

In the next section we'll look at the options available to you for managing data files associated with your app. This approach is not just for icon files, it can be used for any other *data* files, including Qt Designer .ui files, needed by your application.

Bundling data files with PyInstaller

Our application now has a dependency on a single icon file.

Listing 257. packaging/data-file/app.py

```
from PyQt6.QtWidgets import (
    QMainWindow,
    QApplication,
    QPushButton,
    QVBoxLayout,
    QLabel,
    QWidget,
)
```

```python
from PyQt6.QtGui import QIcon
import sys, os

basedir = os.path.dirname(__file__)

try:
    from ctypes import windll  # Only exists on Windows.

    myappid = "mycompany.myproduct.subproduct.version"
    windll.shell32.SetCurrentProcessExplicitAppUserModelID(myappid)
except ImportError:
    pass


class MainWindow(QMainWindow):
    def __init__(self):
        super().__init__()

        self.setWindowTitle("Hello World")
        layout = QVBoxLayout()
        label = QLabel("My simple app.")
        label.setMargin(10)
        layout.addWidget(label)

        button = QPushButton("Push")
        button.pressed.connect(self.close)
        layout.addWidget(button)

        container = QWidget()
        container.setLayout(layout)

        self.setCentralWidget(container)

        self.show()


app = QApplication(sys.argv)
app.setWindowIcon(QIcon(os.path.join(basedir, "icon.svg")))
w = MainWindow()
app.exec()
```

The simplest way to get this data file into the dist folder is to just tell *PyInstaller* to copy them over. *PyInstaller* accepts a list of individual file paths to copy over, together with a folder path relative to the dist/<app name> folder where it should to copy them *to*.

As with other options, this can be specified by command line arguments, --add -data which you can provide multiple times.

```
pyinstaller --add-data "icon.svg:." --name "hello-world" app.py
```

 The path separator is platform-specific, on Linux or Mac use : while on Windows use ;

Or via the datas list in the Analysis section of the spec file, as a 2-tuple of source and destination locations.

```
a = Analysis(['app.py'],
             pathex=[],
             binaries=[],
             datas=[('icon.svg', '.')],
             hiddenimports=[],
             hookspath=[],
             runtime_hooks=[],
             excludes=[],
             win_no_prefer_redirects=False,
             win_private_assemblies=False,
             cipher=block_cipher,
             noarchive=False)
```

And then execute the .spec file with:

```
pyinstaller hello-world.spec
```

In both cases we are telling *PyInstaller* to copy the specified file icon.svg to the location . which means the output folder dist. We could specify other locations here if we wanted. If you run the build, you should see your .svg file now in the output folder `dist` ready to be distributed with your application.

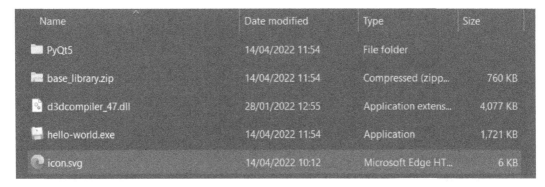

Figure 252. The icon file copied to the dist folder.

If you run your app from `dist` you should now see the icon as expected.

Figure 253. The icon showing on the window (Windows) and dock (macOS and Ubuntu)

 The file must be loaded in Qt using a *relative path*, and be in the same relative location to the EXE as it was to the `.py` file for this to work.

 If you start your build on a Windows machine, your `.spec` file may end up containing paths using double back-slashes \\. This will not work on other platforms, so you should replace these with single forward-slashes /, which work on all platforms.

Bundling data folders

Usually you will have more than one data file you want to include with your packaged file. The latest PyInstaller versions let you bundle folders just like you would files, keeping the sub-folder structure. To demonstrate bundling folders of data files, lets add a few more buttons to our app and add icons to them. We can place these icons under a folder named icons.

Listing 258. packaging/data-folder/app.py

```python
from PyQt6.QtWidgets import (
    QMainWindow,
    QApplication,
    QLabel,
    QVBoxLayout,
    QPushButton,
    QWidget,
)
from PyQt6.QtGui import QIcon
import sys, os

basedir = os.path.dirname(__file__)

try:
    from ctypes import windll  # Only exists on Windows.

    myappid = "mycompany.myproduct.subproduct.version"
    windll.shell32.SetCurrentProcessExplicitAppUserModelID(myappid)
except ImportError:
    pass


class MainWindow(QMainWindow):
    def __init__(self):
        super().__init__()

        self.setWindowTitle("Hello World")
        layout = QVBoxLayout()
        label = QLabel("My simple app.")
        label.setMargin(10)
        layout.addWidget(label)

        button_close = QPushButton("Close")
        button_close.setIcon(
            QIcon(os.path.join(basedir, "icons", "lightning.svg"))
        )
        button_close.pressed.connect(self.close)
        layout.addWidget(button_close)
```

```
        button_maximize = QPushButton("Maximize")
        button_maximize.setIcon(
            QIcon(os.path.join(basedir, "icons", "uparrow.svg"))
        )
        button_maximize.pressed.connect(self.showMaximized)
        layout.addWidget(button_maximize)

        container = QWidget()
        container.setLayout(layout)

        self.setCentralWidget(container)

        self.show()


app = QApplication(sys.argv)
app.setWindowIcon(QIcon(os.path.join(basedir, "icons", "icon.svg")))
w = MainWindow()
app.exec()
```

> ℹ️ The Windows taskbar icon fix is included in this code, you can skip it if you are not building an application for Windows.

The icons (both SVG files) are stored under a subfolder named 'icons'.

```
.
├──── app.py
└──── icons
      └──── lightning.svg
      └──── uparrow.svg
      └──── icon.svg
```

If you run this you'll see the following window, with icons on the buttons and an icon in the window or dock.

Figure 254. Window with multiple icons.

To copy the `icons` folder across to our build application, we just need to add the folder to our `.spec` file `Analysis` block. As for the single file, we add it as a tuple with the source path (from our project folder) and the destination folder under the resulting `dist` folder.

Listing 259. packaging/data-folder/hello-world.spec

```python
# -*- mode: python ; coding: utf-8 -*-


block_cipher = None


a = Analysis(['app.py'],
             pathex=[],
             binaries=[],
             datas=[('icons', 'icons')],
             hiddenimports=[],
             hookspath=[],
             hooksconfig={},
             runtime_hooks=[],
             excludes=[],
             win_no_prefer_redirects=False,
             win_private_assemblies=False,
             cipher=block_cipher,
             noarchive=False)
pyz = PYZ(a.pure, a.zipped_data,
             cipher=block_cipher)

exe = EXE(pyz,
          a.scripts,
          [],
          exclude_binaries=True,
```

```
            name='hello-world',
            icon='icons/icon.ico',
            debug=False,
            bootloader_ignore_signals=False,
            strip=False,
            upx=True,
            console=False,
            disable_windowed_traceback=False,
            target_arch=None,
            codesign_identity=None,
            entitlements_file=None )
coll = COLLECT(exe,
            a.binaries,
            a.zipfiles,
            a.datas,
            strip=False,
            upx=True,
            upx_exclude=[],
            name='hello-world')
app = BUNDLE(coll,
            name='Hello World.app',
            icon='icons/icon.icns',
            bundle_identifier=None)
```

If you run the build using this spec file you'll now see the icons folder copied across to the dist folder. If you run the application from the folder — or anywhere else — the icons will display as expected, as the relative paths remain correct in the new location.

Wrapping up

With all these changes in place, you will now be able to reproducibly build your application on across all platforms. In the next chapters we'll move onto taking our built executables and building them into working installers.

So far we've stepped through the process of building an application with PyInstaller on your own platform. Often you'll want to build your app for all platforms.

As already mentioned, you can only build for a given platform *on* that platform — i.e. if you want to build a Windows executable, you'll need to do it on Windows. However, *ideally* you want to be able to do this using the same `.spec` file, to simplify maintenance. If you want to target multiple platforms try your `.spec` file *now* on other systems to ensure the built is set up correctly. If something doesn't work, check back at the platform-specific notes throughout this chapter.

38. Creating a Windows installer with InstallForge

So far we've used *PyInstaller* to bundle applications for distribution. The output of this bundling process is a folder, named `dist` which contains all the files our application needs to run. While you *could* share this folder with your users as a ZIP file it's not the best user experience.

Windows desktop applications are normally distributed with *installers* which handle the process of putting the executable (and any other files) in the correct place and adding *Start Menu* shortcuts. Next we'll look at how we can take our `dist` folder and use it to create a functioning Windows installer.

To create our installer we'll be using a tool called InstallForge [https://installforge.net/]. InstallForge is free and can be downloaded from this page [https://installforge.net/download/]. The working InstallForge configuration is available in the downloads for this book, as `Hello World.ifp` however bear in mind that the source paths will need to be updated for your system.

 If you're impatient, you can download the Example Windows Installer [https://downloads.pythonguis.com/DemoAppInstallforge.exe] first.

We'll now walk through the basic steps of creating an installer with *InstallForge*.

General

When you first run *InstallForge* you'll be presented with this General tab. Here you can enter the basic information about your application, including the name, program version, company and website.

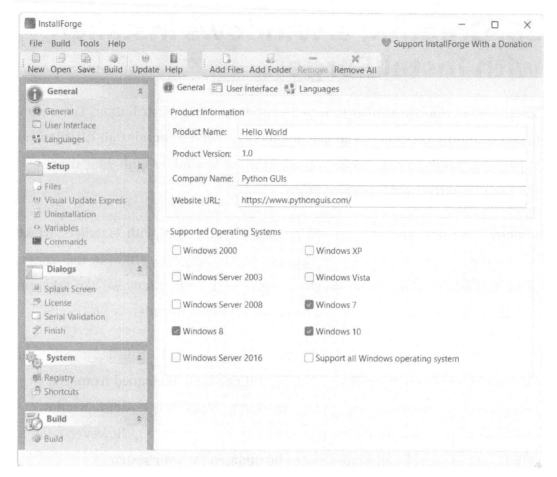

Figure 255. InstallForge initial view, showing General settings.

You can also select the target platforms for the installer, from various versions of Windows that are currently available. This ensures people can only install your application on versions of Windows which are compatible with it.

There is no magic here, selecting additional platforms in the installer won't make your application work on them! You need to check your application runs on the target versions of Windows before enabling them in the installer.

Setup

Click on the left sidebar to open the "Files" page under "Setup". Here you can specify the files to be bundled in the installer.

Use "Add Files..." on the toolbar and select *all the files* in the dist/hello-world folder produced by *PyInstaller*. The file browser that pops up allows multiple file selections, so you can add them all in a single go, however you need to add folders separately. Click "Add Folder..." and add any folders under dist/hello-world such as your icons folder and other libraries.

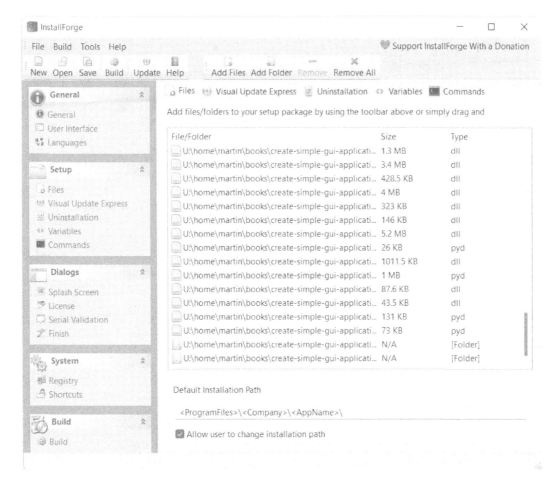

Figure 256. InstallForge Files view, add all files & folders to be packaged.

 Contents of selected folders will be included recursively, you do not need to select subfolders.

Once you're finished scroll through the list to the bottom and ensure that the folders are listed to be included. You want all files and folders *under* dist/hello-world to be present. But the folder dist/hello-world itself *should not* be listed.

The default install path can be left as-is. The values between angled brackets, e.g.

`<company>`, are variables and will be filled automatically from the configuration.

Next, it's nice to allow your users to uninstall your application. Even though it's undoubtedly awesome, they may want to remove it at some time in the future. You can do this under the "Uninstall" tab, simply by ticking the box. This will also make the application appear in Windows "Add or Remove Programs".

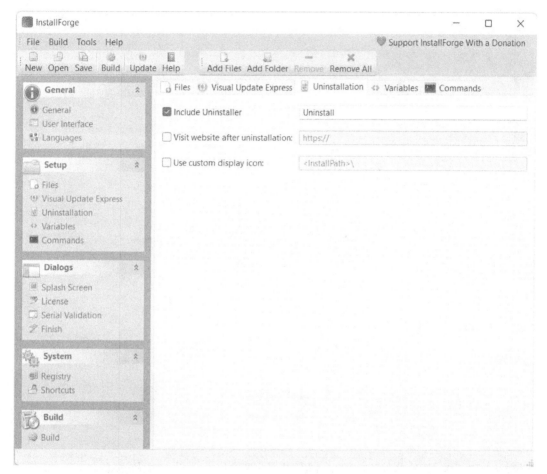

Figure 257. InstallForge add Uninstaller for your app.

Dialogs

The "Dialogs" section can be used to show custom messages, splash screens or license information to the user. The "Finish" tab lets you control what happens once the installer is complete, and it's helpful here to give the user the *option* to run your program once it's installed.

To do this you need to tick the box next to "Run program" and add your own application EXE into the box. Since `<installpath>\` is already specified, we can just add `hello-world.exe`. *Arguments* can be used to pass any arguments to the program on the first launch.

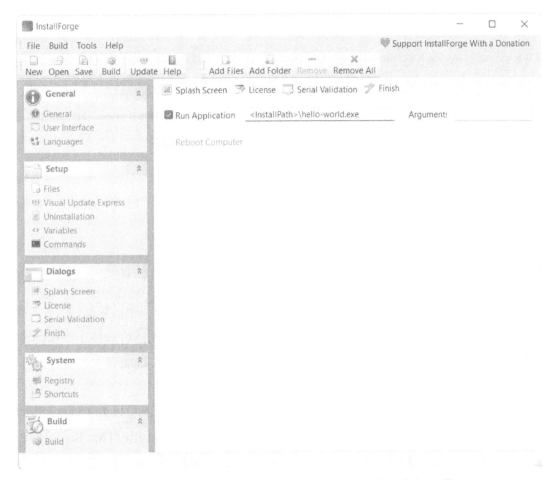

Figure 258. InstallForge configure optional run program on finish install.

System

Under "System" select "Shortcuts" to open the shortcut editor. Here you can specify shortcuts for both the Start Menu and Desktop if you like.

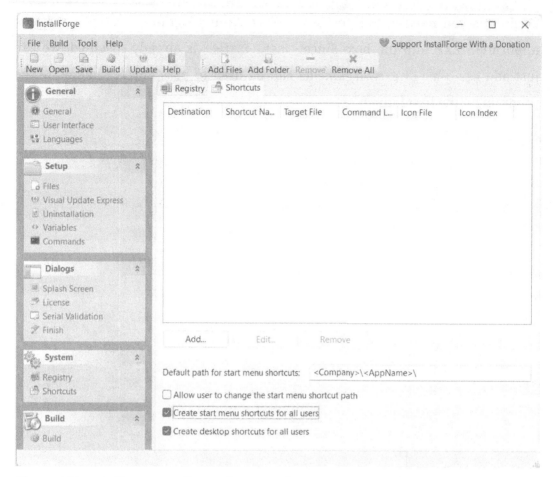

Figure 259. InstallForge configure Shortcuts, for Start Menu and Desktop.

Click "Add..." to add new shortcuts for your application. Choose between Start menu and Desktop shortcuts, and fill in the name and target file. This is the path your application EXE will end up at once installed. Since `<installpath>\` is already specified, you simply need to add your application's EXE name onto the end, here `hello-world.exe`

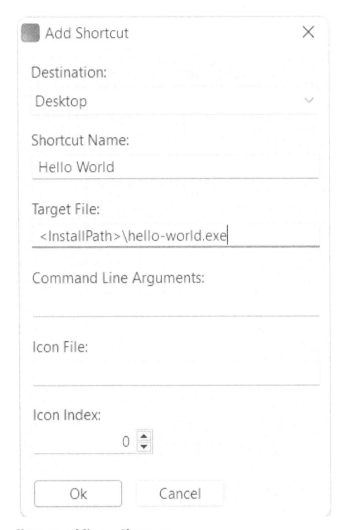

Figure 260. InstallForge, adding a Shortcut.

Build

With the basic settings in place, you can now build your installer.

 At this point you can save your *InstallForge* project so you can re-build the installer from the same settings in future.

Click on the "Build" section at the bottom to open the build panel.

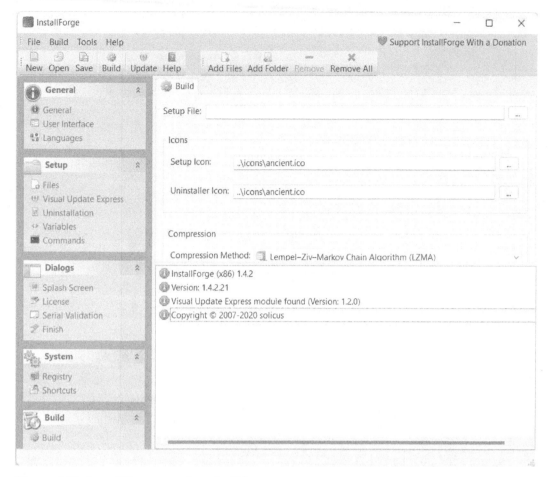

Figure 261. InstallForge, ready to build.

Click on the *Build* icon on the toolbar to start the build process. If you haven't already specified a setup file location you will be prompted for one. This is the location where you want the **completed installer** to be saved. The build process will began, collecting and compressing the files into the installer.

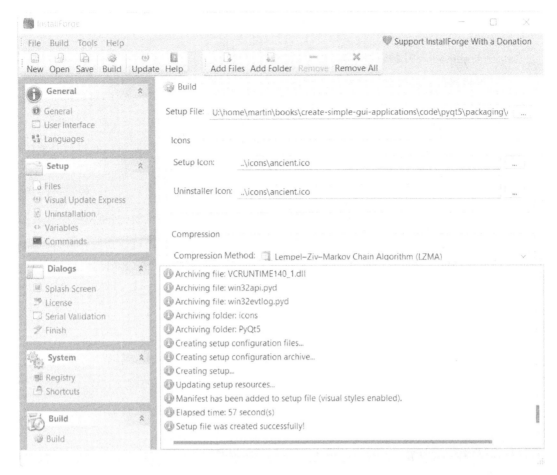

Figure 262. InstallForge, build complete.

Once complete you will be prompted to run the installer. This is entirely optional, but a handy way to find out if it works.

Running the installer

The installer itself shouldn't have any surprises, working as expected. Depending on the options selected in *InstallForge* you may have extra panels or options.

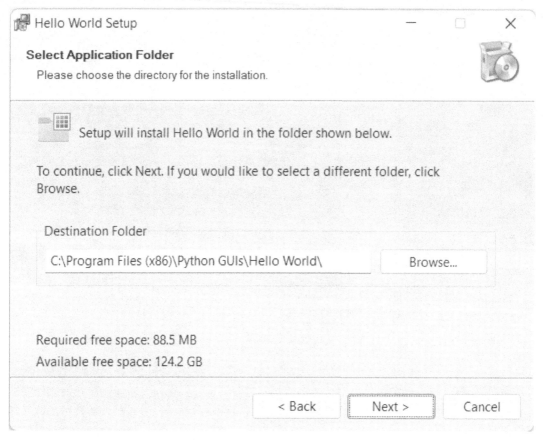

Figure 263. InstallForge, running the resulting installer.

Step through the installer until it is complete. You can optionally run the application from the last page of the installer, or you can find it in your start menu.

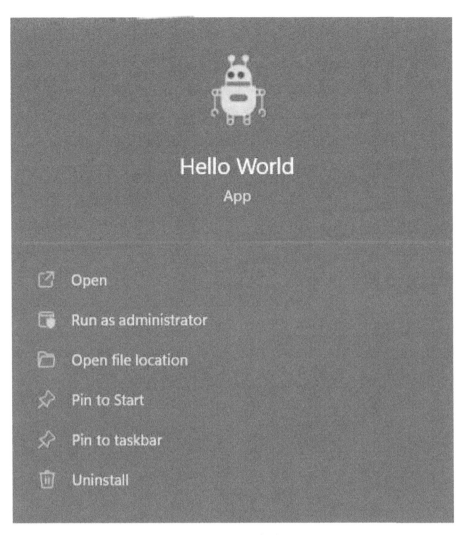

Figure 264. Hello World in the Start Menu on Windows 11.

Wrapping up

In a previous chapter we covered how to build your PyQt6 applications into a distributable executable using *PyInstaller*. In this chapter we've taken this built *PyInstaller* application and walked through the steps of using *InstallForge* to build an installer for the app. Following these steps you should be able to package up your own applications and make them available to other people on Windows.

Another popular tool for building Windows installers is NSIS [https://nsis.sourceforge.io/Main_Page] which is a *scriptable* installer, meaning you configure it's behavior by writing custom scripts. If you're going to be building your application frequently and want to automate the process, it's definitely worth a look.

39. Creating a macOS Disk Image Installer

In a previous chapter we used *PyInstaller* to build a macOS `.app` file from our application. Opening this `.app` will run your application, and you can technically distribute it to other people as it is. However, there's a catch — macOS `.app` files are actually just folders with a special extension. This means they aren't suited for sharing as they are — end users would need to download all the individual files inside the folder.

The solution is to distribute the `.app` inside a *Zip* `.zip` or *disk image* `.dmg` file. Most commercial software uses disk images since you can also include a shortcut to the user's *Applications* folder, allowing them to drag the application over in a single move. This is now so common than many users would be quite confused to be faced with anything else. Let's just stick with the convention.

 If you're impatient, you can download the Example macOS Disk Image [https://downloads.pythonguis.com/DemoAppMacOS.dmg] first.

create-dmg

It's relatively straightforward to create DMG files yourself, but I'd recommend starting by using the tool `create-dmg` which can be installed from Homebrew. This tool installs as a simple command-line tool, which you can call passing in a few parameters to generate your DMG installer.

You can install the `create-dmg` package with Homebrew.

```
brew install create-dmg
```

Once installed you have access to the `create-dmg` bash script. Below is a subset of the options, which can be displayed by running `create-dmg --help`

```
--volname <name>: set volume name (displayed in the Finder sidebar
and window title)
--volicon <icon.icns>: set volume icon
--background <pic.png>: set folder background image (provide png,
gif, jpg)
--window-pos <x> <y>: set position the folder window
--window-size <width> <height>: set size of the folder window
--text-size <text_size>: set window text size (10-16)
--icon-size <icon_size>: set window icons size (up to 128)
--icon <file_name> <x> <y>: set position of the file's icon
--hide-extension <file_name>: hide the extension of file
--app-drop-link <x> <y>: make a drop link to Applications, at
location x, y
--eula <eula_file>: attach a license file to the dmg
--no-internet-enable: disable automatic mount&copy
--format: specify the final image format (default is UDZO)
--add-file <target_name> <file|folder> <x> <y>: add additional file
or folder (can be used multiple times)
--disk-image-size <x>: set the disk image size manually to x MB
--version: show tool version number
-h, --help: display the help
```

 Volume is a technical name for a disk, so *Volume name* is the
name you want to give to the *disk image* (DMG) itself.

Together with the options given above, you need to specify the output name for
your DMG file and an input folder — the folder containing your `.app` generated
by *PyInstaller*.

Below we'll use `create-dmg` to create an installer DMG for our Hello World
application. We're only using some of the available options here — setting the
name & icon of the disk volume, positioning and sizing the window, setting the
icon for our app and adding the `/Applications` drop destination link. This is the
bare minimum you will likely want to set for your own applications, and you can
customize it further yourself if you prefer.

Since `create-dmg` copies all files in the specified folder into the DMG you'll need to ensure that your .app file is in a folder by itself. I recommend creating a folder dmg and copying the built .app bundle into it into it. Below I've created a small script to perform the packaging, including a test to check for and remove any previously-built DMG files.

Listing 260. packaging/installer/mac/makedmg.sh

```sh
#!/bin/sh
test -f "Hello World.dmg" && rm "Hello World.dmg"
test -d "dist/dmg" && rm -rf "dist/dmg"
# Make the dmg folder & copy our .app bundle in.
mkdir -p "dist/dmg"
cp -r "dist/Hello World.app" "dist/dmg"
# Create the dmg.
create-dmg \
  --volname "Hello World" \
  --volicon "icons/icon.icns" \
  --window-pos 200 120 \
  --window-size 800 400 \
  --icon-size 100 \
  --icon "Hello World.app" 200 190 \
  --hide-extension "Hello World.app" \
  --app-drop-link 600 185 \
  "Hello World.dmg" \
  "dist/dmg/"
```

Save this into the root of your project named build-dmg.sh and then make it executable with.

```
$ chmod +x build-dmg.sh
```

Then execute the script to build the package.

```
$ ./build-dmg.sh
```

The create-dmg process will run and a DMG file will be created in the current folder, matching the name you've given for the output file (the second to last argument, with the .dmg extension). You can now distribute the resulting DMG file to other macOS users!

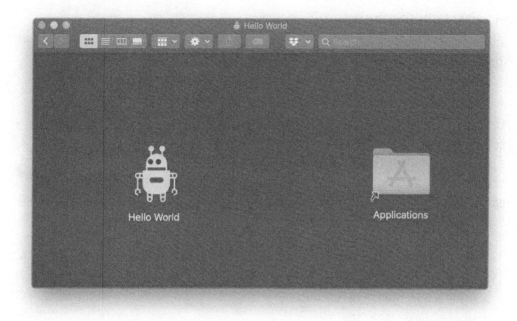

Figure 265. The resulting Disk Image showing our .app *bundle and the Applications shortcut. Drag the app across to install.*

 For more information on create-dmg see the documentation on Github [https://github.com/create-dmg/create-dmg].

40. Creating a Linux Package with fpm

In an previous chapter we used *PyInstaller* to bundle the application into a Linux executable, along with the associated data files. The output of this bundling process is a folder which can be shared with other users. However, in order to make it easy for them to *install* it on their system, we need to create a Linux *package*.

Packages are distributable files which allow users to install software on their Linux system. They automatically handle putting files in the correct places, as well as setting up application entries in the dock/menu to make it easier to launch the app.

On Ubuntu (and Debian) packages are named .deb files, on Redhat .rpm and on Arch Linux .pacman. These files are all different formats, but thankfully the process for building them is the same using a tool named *fpm*. fpm [https://github.com/jordansissel/] is a packaging system by Jordan Issel, which takes a folder (or list of files) and assembles them into a Linux package.

 In this chapter we'll work through the steps for creating a Linux package, using an Ubuntu .deb file as an example. However, thanks to the magic of *fpm*, you will be able to use the same approach for other Linux systems.

hello-world.deb

Figure 266. Ubuntu Package, for our "Hello World" application

If you're impatient, you can download the Example Ubuntu Package [https://downloads.pythonguis.com/hello-world.deb] first.

Installing fpm

The `fpm` tool is written in *ruby* and requires *ruby* to be installed to use it. Install *ruby* using your systems package manager, for example.

```
$ sudo apt-get install ruby
```

Once *ruby* is installed, you can install `fpm` using the `gem` tool.

```
$ gem install fpm --user-install
```

 If you see a warning that you don't have `~/.local/share/gem/ruby/2.7.0/bin` in your `PATH` you will need to add that to your path [https://askubuntu.com/a/60219] in your `.bashrc` file.

Once the installation is complete, you're ready to use `fpm`. You can check it is installed and working by running:

```
$ fpm --version
1.14.2
```

Checking your build

In a terminal, change to the folder containing your application source files & run a *PyInstaller* build to generate the `dist` folder. Test that the generated build runs as expected (it works, and icons appear) by opening the `dist` folder in the file manager, and double-clicking on the application executable.

If everything works, you're ready to package the application — if not, go back and double check everything.

 It's *always* a good idea to test your built application before packaging it. That way, if anything goes wrong, you know where the problem is!

Now let's package our folder using `fpm`.

Structuring your package

Linux packages are used to install all sorts of applications, including system tools. Because of this they are set up to allow you to place files anywhere in the Linux filesystem — and there are specific *correct* places to put different files. For a GUI application like ours, we can put our executable and associated data files all under the same folder (in `/opt`). However, to have our application show up in the menus/search we'll also need to install a `.desktop` file under `/usr/share/applications`.

The simplest way to ensure things end up in the correct location is to recreate the target file structure in a folder & then tell `fpm` to package using that folder as the root. This process is also easily automatable using a script (see later).

In your projects root folder, create a new folder called `package` and subfolders which map to the target filesystem — `/opt` will hold our application *folder* `hello-world`, and `/usr/share/applications` will hold our `.desktop` file, while `/usr/share/icons`··· will hold our application icon.

```
$ mkdir -p package/opt
$ mkdir -p package/usr/share/applications
$ mkdir -p package/usr/share/icons/hicolor/scalable/apps
```

Next copy (recursively, with `-r` to include subfolders) the contents of `dist/app` to `package/opt/hello-world` — the `/opt/hello-world` path is the destination of our application folder after installation.

```
$ cp -r dist/hello-world package/opt/hello-world
```

 We're copying the dist/hello-world folder. The name of this folder will depend on the name configured in *PyInstaller*.

The icons

We've already set an icon for our application while it's running, using the penguin.svg file. However, we want our application to show it's icon in the dock/menus. To do this correctly, we need to copy our application icons into a specific location, under /usr/share/icons.

This folder contains all the icon *themes* installed on the system, but default icons for applications are always placed in the *fallback* hicolor theme, at /usr/share/icons/hicolor. Inside this folder, there are various folders for different sizes of icons.

```
$ ls /usr/share/icons/hicolor/
128x128/         256x256/         64x64/            scalable/
16x16/           32x32/           72x72/            symbolic/
192x192/         36x36/           96x96/
22x22/           48x48/           icon-theme.cache
24x24/           512x512/         index.theme
```

We're using a *Scalable Vector Graphics* (SVG) file so our icon belongs under the scalable folder. If you're using a specifically sized PNG file, place it in the correct location — and feel free to add multiple different sizes, to ensure your application icon looks good when scaled. Application icons go in the subfolder apps.

```
$ cp icons/penguin.svg
package/usr/share/icons/hicolor/scalable/apps/hello-world.svg
```

 Name the destination filename of the icon after your application to avoid it clashing with any others! Here we're calling it hello-world.svg.

The .desktop file

The .desktop file is a text configuration file which tells the Linux desktop about a desktop application — for example, where to fine the executable, the name and which icon to display. You should include a .desktop file for your apps to make them easy to use. An example .desktop file is shown below — add this to the root folder of your project — with the name hello-world.desktop, and make any changes you like.

Listing 261. packaging/installer/linux/hello-world.desktop

```
[Desktop Entry]

# The type of the thing this desktop file refers to (e.g. can be
Link)
Type=Application

# The application name.
Name=Hello World

# Tooltip comment to show in menus.
Comment=A simple Hello World application.

# The path (folder) in which the executable is run
Path=/opt/hello-world

# The executable (can include arguments)
Exec=/opt/hello-world/hello-world

# The icon for the entry, use the target filesystem path.
Icon=hello-world
```

Now the `hello-world.desktop` file is ready, we can copy it into our install package with.

```
$ cp hello-world.desktop package/usr/share/applications
```

Permissions

Packages retain the permissions of installed files from when they were packaged, but will be installed by `root`. In order for ordinary users to be able to run the application, you need to change the permissions of the files created.

We can recursively apply the correct permissions *755 - owner can read/write/execute, group/others can read/execute.* to our executable and folders, and *644, owner can read/write, group/others can read* to all our other library and icons/desktop files.

702

```
$ find package/opt/hello-world -type f -exec chmod 644 -- {} +
$ find package/opt/hello-world -type d -exec chmod 755 -- {} +
$ find package/usr/share -type f -exec chmod 644 -- {} +
$ chmod +x package/opt/hello-world/hello-world
```

Building your package

Now everything is where it should be in our package "filesystem", we're ready to start building the package itself.

Enter the following into your shell.

```
fpm -C package -s dir -t deb -n "hello-world" -v 0.1.0 -p hello-world.deb
```

The arguments in order are:

- -C the folder to change to before searching for files: our package folder

- -s the type of source(s) to package: in our case dir, a folder

- -t the type of package to build: a deb Debian/Ubuntu package

- -n the name of the application: "hello-world"

- -v the version of the application: 0.1.0

- -p the package name to output: hello-world-deb

 You can create other package types (for other Linux distributions) by changing the -t argument. For more command line arguments, see the fpm documentation [https://fpm.readthedocs.io/en/latest/getting-started.html#using-it-to-package-an-executable].

After a few seconds, you should see a message to indicate that the package has been created.

```
$ fpm -C package -s dir -t deb -n "hello-world" -v 0.1.0 -p hello-
world.deb
Created package {:path=>"hello-world.deb"}
```

Installation

The package is ready! Let's install it.

```
$ sudo dpkg -i hello-world.deb
```

You'll see some output as the install completes.

```
Selecting previously unselected package hello-world.
(Reading database ... 172208 files and directories currently
installed.)
Preparing to unpack hello-world.deb ...
Unpacking hello-world (0.1.0) ...
Setting up hello-world (0.1.0) ...
```

Once installation has completed, you can check the files are where you expect,
under /opt/hello-world

```
$ ls /opt/hello-world
app                        libpcre2-8.so.0
base_library.zip           libpcre.so.3
icons                      libpixman-1.so.0
libatk-1.0.so.0            libpng16.so.16
libatk-bridge-2.0.so.0     libpython3.9.so.1.0
etc.
```

Next try and run the application from the menu/dock—you can search for
"Hello World" and the application will be found (thanks to the .desktop file).

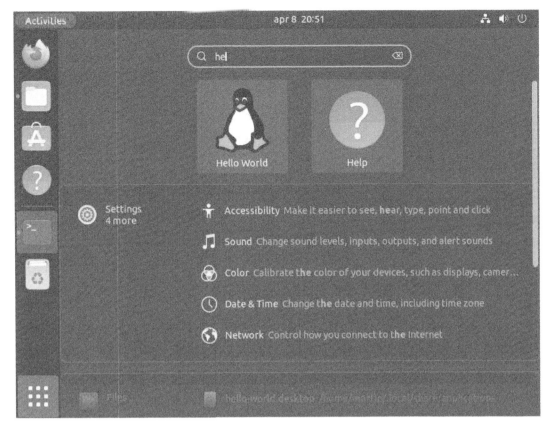

Figure 267. Application shows up in the Ubuntu search panel, and will also appear in menus on other environments.

If you run the application, the icons will show up as expected.

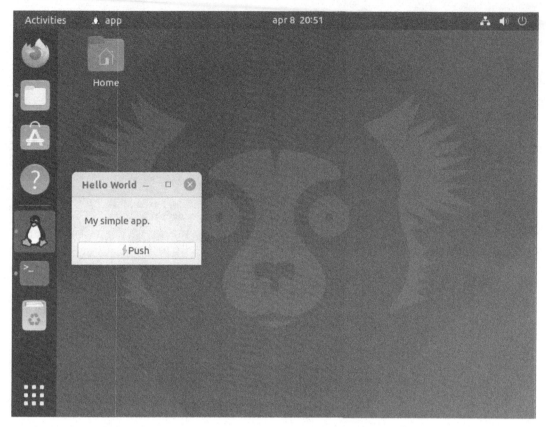

Figure 268. Application runs and all icons show up as expected.

Scripting the build

We've walked through the steps required to build an installable Ubuntu .deb package from a PyQt6 application. While it's relatively straightforward once you know what you're doing, if you need to do it regularly it can get quite tedious and prone to mistakes.

To avoid problems, I recommend scripting this with a simple bash script & fpm's own automation tool.

package.sh

Save in your project root and chmod +x to make it executable.

Listing 262. packaging/installer/linux/package.sh

```sh
#!/bin/sh
# Create folders.
[ -e package ] && rm -r package
mkdir -p package/opt
mkdir -p package/usr/share/applications
mkdir -p package/usr/share/icons/hicolor/scalable/apps

# Copy files (change icon names, add lines for non-scaled icons)
cp -r dist/hello-world package/opt/hello-world
cp icons/penguin.svg
package/usr/share/icons/hicolor/scalable/apps/hello-world.svg
cp hello-world.desktop package/usr/share/applications

# Change permissions
find package/opt/hello-world -type f -exec chmod 644 -- {} +
find package/opt/hello-world -type d -exec chmod 755 -- {} +
find package/usr/share -type f -exec chmod 644 -- {} +
chmod +x package/opt/hello-world/hello-world
```

.fpm **file**

`fpm` allows you to store the configuration for the packaging in a configuration file. The file name must be `.fpm` and it must be in the folder you run the `fpm` tool. Our configuration is as follows.

Listing 263. packaging/installer/linux/.fpm

```
-C package
-s dir
-t deb
-n "hello-world"
-v 0.1.0
-p hello-world.deb
```

 You can override any of the options you like when executing fpm by passing command line arguments as normal.

Executing the build

With these scripts in place our application can be packaged reproducibly with the commands:

```
pyinstaller hello-world.spec
./package.sh
fpm
```

Feel free to customize these build scripts further yourself to suit your own project!

In this chapter we've stepped through the process of taking a working build from *PyInstaller* and using fpm to bundle this up into a distributable Linux package for Ubuntu. Following these steps you should be able to package up your own applications and make them available to other people.

Example applications

By now you should have a firm grasp of how to go about building simple applications with PyQt6. To show how you can put what you've learnt into practice, I've included a couple of example applications in this chapter. These applications are functional, simple and in some ways *incomplete*. Use them for inspiration, to pull apart and as an opportunity to improve. Read on for a walkthrough of each app's most interesting parts.

The full source for both applications is available for download, along with 13 other applications in my 15 Minute Apps [https://github.com/pythonguis/15-minute-apps] repository on Github. Have fun!

There are also other examples of miniature apps throughout this book — for example the *Paint* and *Todo* apps — I encourage you to extend these too, it's the best way to learn.

41. Mozzarella Ashbadger

Mozzarella Ashbadger is the latest revolution in web browsing! Go back and forward! Print! Save files! Get help! (you'll need it). Any similarity to other browsers is entirely coincidental.

Figure 269. Mozzarella Ashbadger.

 This application makes use of features covered in Signals & Slots, Extending Signals and Widgets.

The source code for Mozzarella Ashbadger is provided in two forms, one with tabbed browsing and one without. Adding tabs complicates the signal handling a little bit, so the tab-less version is covered first.

To create the browser we need to install an additional PyQt6 component — *PyQtWebEngine*. You can do this with `pip` from the command line as follows.

```
pip3 install pyqt6-webengine
```

Source code

The full source for the tab-less browser is included in the downloads for this book. The browser code has the name `browser.py`.

```
python3 browser.py
```

🚀 **Run it!** Explore the *Mozzarella Ashbadger* interface and features before moving onto the code.

The browser widget

The core of our browser is the QWebEngineView which we import from QtWebEngineWidgets. This provides a complete browser window, which handles the rendering of the downloaded pages. Below is the bare-minimum of code required to use web browser widget in PyQt6.

Listing 264. app/browser_skeleton.py

```python
import sys

from PyQt6.QtCore import QUrl
from PyQt6.QtWebEngineWidgets import QWebEngineView
from PyQt6.QtWidgets import QApplication, QMainWindow


class MainWindow(QMainWindow):
    def __init__(self):
        super().__init__()

        self.browser = QWebEngineView()
        self.browser.setUrl(QUrl("https://www.google.com"))

        self.setCentralWidget(self.browser)

        self.show()


app = QApplication(sys.argv)
window = MainWindow()

app.exec()
```

If you click around a bit you'll discover that the browser behaves as expected — links work correctly, and you can interact with the pages. However, you'll also notice things you take for granted are missing — like an URL bar, controls or any sort of interface whatsoever. This makes it a little tricky to use.

Let's convert this bare-bones browser into something a little more usable!

Paths

To make working with interface icons easier, we can start by defining a Working with Relative Paths. It defines a single folder location for data files icons and a method icon for creating paths for icons. This allows us to using Paths.icon() to load our icons for the browser interface.

Listing 265. app/paths.py

```
import os


class Paths:

    base = os.path.dirname(__file__)
    icons = os.path.join(base, "icons")

    # File loaders.
    @classmethod
    def icon(cls, filename):
        return os.path.join(cls.icons, filename)
```

Saved in the same folder as our browser, it can be imported as:

Listing 266. app/browser.py

```
from paths import Paths
```

Navigation

Now that is in place we can add some interface controls, using a series of QActions on a QToolbar. We add these definitions to the __init__ block of the QMainWindow. We use our Paths.icon() method to load up the file using relative paths.

Listing 267. app/browser.py

```python
navtb = QToolBar("Navigation")
navtb.setIconSize(QSize(16, 16))
self.addToolBar(navtb)

back_btn = QAction(
    QIcon(Paths.icon("arrow-180.png")), "Back", self
)
back_btn.setStatusTip("Back to previous page")
back_btn.triggered.connect(self.browser.back)
navtb.addAction(back_btn)
```

The QWebEngineView includes slots for forward, back and reload navigation, which we can connect to directly to our action's .triggered signals.

We use the same QAction structure for the remaining controls.

Listing 268. app/browser.py

```python
        next_btn = QAction(
            QIcon(Paths.icon("arrow-000.png")), "Forward", self
        )
        next_btn.setStatusTip("Forward to next page")
        next_btn.triggered.connect(self.browser.forward)
        navtb.addAction(next_btn)

        reload_btn = QAction(
            QIcon(Paths.icon("arrow-circle-315.png")),
            "Reload",
            self,
        )
        reload_btn.setStatusTip("Reload page")
        reload_btn.triggered.connect(self.browser.reload)
        navtb.addAction(reload_btn)

        home_btn = QAction(QIcon(Paths.icon("home.png")), "Home",
  self)
        home_btn.setStatusTip("Go home")
        home_btn.triggered.connect(self.navigate_home)
        navtb.addAction(home_btn)
```

Notice that while forward, back and reload can use built-in slots, the navigate home button requires a custom slot function. The slot function is defined on our QMainWindow class, and simply sets the URL of the browser to the Google homepage. Note that the URL must be passed as a QUrl object.

Listing 269. app/browser.py

```python
    def navigate_home(self):
        self.browser.setUrl(QUrl("http://www.google.com"))
```

Challenge

Try making the home navigation location configurable. You could create a Preferences QDialog with an input field.

Any decent web browser also needs an URL bar, and some way to stop the navigation — either when it's by mistake, or the page is taking too long.

Listing 270. app/browser.py

```
        self.httpsicon = QLabel()  # Yes, really!
        self.httpsicon.setPixmap(QPixmap(Paths.icon("lock-
nossl.png")))
        navtb.addWidget(self.httpsicon)

        self.urlbar = QLineEdit()
        self.urlbar.returnPressed.connect(self.navigate_to_url)
        navtb.addWidget(self.urlbar)

        stop_btn = QAction(
            QIcon(Paths.icon("cross-circle.png")), "Stop", self
        )
        stop_btn.setStatusTip("Stop loading current page")
        stop_btn.triggered.connect(self.browser.stop)
        navtb.addAction(stop_btn)
```

As before the 'stop' functionality is available on the QWebEngineView, and we can simply connect the .triggered signal from the stop button to the existing slot. However, other features of the URL bar we must handle independently.

First we add a QLabel to hold our SSL or non-SSL icon to indicate whether the page is secure. Next, we add the URL bar which is simply a QLineEdit. To trigger the loading of the URL in the bar when entered (return key pressed) we connect to the .returnPressed signal on the widget to drive a custom slot function to trigger navigation to the specified URL.

Listing 271. app/browser.py

```python
def navigate_to_url(self):  # Does not receive the Url
    q = QUrl(self.urlbar.text())
    if q.scheme() == "":
        q.setScheme("http")

    self.browser.setUrl(q)
```

We also want the URL bar to update in response to page changes. To do this we can use the .urlChanged and .loadFinished signals from the QWebEngineView. We set up the connections from the signals in the __init__ block as follows:

Listing 272. app/browser.py

```python
self.browser.urlChanged.connect(self.update_urlbar)
self.browser.loadFinished.connect(self.update_title)
```

Then we define the target slot functions which for these signals. The first, to update the URL bar accepts a QUrl object and determines whether this is a http or https URL, using this to set the SSL icon.

 This is a terrible way to test if a connection is 'secure'. To be correct we should perform a certificate validation.

The QUrl is converted to a string and the URL bar is updated with the value. Note that we also set the cursor position back to the beginning of the line to prevent the QLineEdit widget scrolling to the end.

Listing 273. app/browser.py

```python
    def update_urlbar(self, q):

        if q.scheme() == "https":
            # Secure padlock icon
            self.httpsicon.setPixmap(
                QPixmap(Paths.icon("lock-ssl.png"))
            )

        else:
            # Insecure padlock icon
            self.httpsicon.setPixmap(
                QPixmap(Paths.icon("lock-nossl.png"))
            )

        self.urlbar.setText(q.toString())
        self.urlbar.setCursorPosition(0)
```

It's also a nice touch to update the title of the application window with the title of the current page. We can get this via `browser.page().title()` which returns the contents of the `<title></title>` tag in the currently loaded web page.

Listing 274. app/browser.py

```python
    def update_title(self):
        title = self.browser.page().title()
        self.setWindowTitle("%s - Mozzarella Ashbadger" % title)
```

File operations

A standard File menu with `self.menuBar().addMenu("&File")` is created assigning the `F` key as a Alt-shortcut (as normal). Once we have the menu object, we can can assign `QAction` objects to create the entries. We create two basic entries here, for opening and saving HTML files (from a local disk). These both require custom slot functions.

Listing 275. app/browser.py

```python
file_menu = self.menuBar().addMenu("&File")

open_file_action = QAction(
    QIcon(Paths.icon("disk--arrow.png")),
    "Open file...",
    self,
)
open_file_action.setStatusTip("Open from file")
open_file_action.triggered.connect(self.open_file)
file_menu.addAction(open_file_action)

save_file_action = QAction(
    QIcon(Paths.icon("disk--pencil.png")),
    "Save Page As...",
    self,
)
save_file_action.setStatusTip("Save current page to file")
save_file_action.triggered.connect(self.save_file)
file_menu.addAction(save_file_action)
```

The slot function for opening a file uses the built-in `QFileDialog.getOpenFileName()` function to create a file-open dialog and get a name. We restrict the names by default to files matching *.htm or *.html.

We read the file into a variable `html` using standard Python functions, then use `.setHtml()` to load the HTML into the browser.

Listing 276. app/browser.py

```python
def open_file(self):
    filename, _ = QFileDialog.getOpenFileName(
        self,
        "Open file",
        "",
        "Hypertext Markup Language (*.htm *.html);;"
        "All files (*.*)",
    )

    if filename:
        with open(filename, "r") as f:
            html = f.read()

        self.browser.setHtml(html)
        self.urlbar.setText(filename)
```

Similarly to save the HTML from the current page, we use the built-in `QFileDialog.getSaveFileName()` to get a filename. However, this time we get the HTML using `self.browser.page().toHtml()`.

This is an *asynchronous* method, meaning that we do not receive the HTML immediately. Instead we must pass in a *callback* method which will receive the HTML once it is prepared. Here we create a simple `writer` function that handles it for us, using the filename from the local scope.

Listing 277. app/browser.py

```python
    def save_file(self):
        filename, _ = QFileDialog.getSaveFileName(
            self,
            "Save Page As",
            "",
            "Hypertext Markup Language (*.htm *html);;"
            "All files (*.*)",
        )

        if filename:
            # Define callback method to handle the write.
            def writer(html):
                with open(filename, "w") as f:
                    f.write(html)

            self.browser.page().toHtml(writer)
```

Printing

We can add a print option to the File menu using the same approach we used earlier. Again this needs a custom slot function to perform the print action.

Listing 278. app/browser.py

```python
        print_action = QAction(
            QIcon(Paths.icon("printer.png")), "Print...", self
        )
        print_action.setStatusTip("Print current page")
        print_action.triggered.connect(self.print_page)
        file_menu.addAction(print_action)

        # Create our system printer instance.
        self.printer = QPrinter()
```

Qt provides a complete print framework which is based around QPrinter objects, on which you *paint* the pages to be printed. To start the process we open a QPrintDialog for the user. This allows them to choose the target printer and configure the print.

We created the QPrinter object in our __init__ and stored it as self.printer. In our print handler method we pass this printer to the QPrintDialog so it can be configured. If the dialog is accepted we pass the (now configured) printer object to self.browser.page().print to trigger the print.

Listing 279. app/browser.py

```
def print_page(self):
    page = self.browser.page()

    def callback(*args):
        pass

    dlg = QPrintDialog(self.printer)
    dlg.accepted.connect(callback)
    if dlg.exec() == QDialog.DialogCode.Accepted:
        page.print(self.printer, callback)
```

Notice that .print also accepts a second parameter — a callback function which receives the result of the print. This allows you to show a notification that the print has completed, but here we're just swallowing the callback silently.

Help

Finally, to complete the standard interface we can add a Help menu. This is defined as before, two two custom slot functions to handle the display of a About dialog, and to load the 'browser page' with more information.

Listing 280. app/browser.py

```python
help_menu = self.menuBar().addMenu("&Help")

about_action = QAction(
    QIcon(Paths.icon("question.png")),
    "About Mozzarella Ashbadger",
    self,
)
about_action.setStatusTip(
    "Find out more about Mozzarella Ashbadger"
)   # Hungry!
about_action.triggered.connect(self.about)
help_menu.addAction(about_action)

navigate_mozzarella_action = QAction(
    QIcon(Paths.icon("lifebuoy.png")),
    "Mozzarella Ashbadger Homepage",
    self,
)
navigate_mozzarella_action.setStatusTip(
    "Go to Mozzarella Ashbadger Homepage"
)
navigate_mozzarella_action.triggered.connect(
    self.navigate_mozzarella
)
help_menu.addAction(navigate_mozzarella_action)
```

We define two methods to be used as slots for the Help menu signals. The first navigate_mozzarella opens up a page with more information on the browser (or in this case, this book). The second creates and executes a custom QDialog class AboutDialog which we will define next.

Listing 281. app/browser.py

```
    def navigate_mozzarella(self):
        self.browser.setUrl(QUrl("https://www.pythonguis.com/"))

    def about(self):
        dlg = AboutDialog()
        dlg.exec()
```

The definition for the about dialog is given below. The structure follows that seen earlier in the book, with a QDialogButtonBox and associated signals to handle user input, and a series of QLabels to display the application information and a logo.

The only trick here is adding all the elements to the layout, then iterate over them to set the alignment to the center in a single loop. This saves duplication for the individual sections.

Listing 282. app/browser.py

```python
class AboutDialog(QDialog):
    def __init__(self):
        super().__init__()

        QBtn = QDialogButtonBox.StandardButton.Ok  # No cancel
        self.buttonBox = QDialogButtonBox(QBtn)
        self.buttonBox.accepted.connect(self.accept)
        self.buttonBox.rejected.connect(self.reject)

        layout = QVBoxLayout()

        title = QLabel("Mozzarella Ashbadger")
        font = title.font()
        font.setPointSize(20)
        title.setFont(font)

        layout.addWidget(title)

        logo = QLabel()
        logo.setPixmap(QPixmap(Paths.icon("ma-icon-128.png")))
        layout.addWidget(logo)

        layout.addWidget(QLabel("Version 23.35.211.233232"))
        layout.addWidget(QLabel("Copyright 2015 Mozzarella Inc."))

        for i in range(0, layout.count()):
            layout.itemAt(i).setAlignment(Qt.AlignmentFlag
.AlignHCenter)

        layout.addWidget(self.buttonBox)

        self.setLayout(layout)
```

Tabbed Browsing

Figure 270. Mozzarella Ashbadger (Tabbed).

Source code

The full source for the tabbed browser is included in the downloads for this book. The browser code has the name `browser_tabs.py`.

🚀 **Run it!** Explore the Mozzarella Ashbadger *Tabbed Edition* before moving onto the code.

Creating a `QTabWidget`

Adding a tabbed interface to our browser is simple using a `QTabWidget`. This provides a simple container for multiple widgets (in our case `QWebEngineView` widgets) with a built-in tabbed interface for switching between them.

Two customizations we use here are `.setDocumentMode(True)` which provides a Safari-like interface on macOS, and `.setTabsClosable(True)` which allows the user to close the tabs in the application.

We also connect `QTabWidget` signals `tabBarDoubleClicked`, `currentChanged` and `tabCloseRequested` to custom slot methods to handle these behaviors.

Listing 283. app/browser_tabs.py

```python
        self.tabs = QTabWidget()
        self.tabs.setDocumentMode(True)
        self.tabs.tabBarDoubleClicked.connect(self
.tab_open_doubleclick)
        self.tabs.currentChanged.connect(self.current_tab_changed)
        self.tabs.setTabsClosable(True)
        self.tabs.tabCloseRequested.connect(self.close_current_tab)

        self.setCentralWidget(self.tabs)
```

The three slot methods accept an `i` (index) parameter which indicates which tab the signal resulted from (in order).

We use a double-click on an empty space in the tab bar (represented by an index of -1 to trigger creation of a new tab. For removing a tab, we use the index directly to remove the widget (and so the tab), with a simple check to ensure there are at least 2 tabs — closing the last tab would leave you unable to open a new one.

The `current_tab_changed` handler uses a `self.tabs.currentWidget()` construct to access the widget (`QWebEngineView` browser) of the currently active tab, and then uses this to get the URL of the current page. This same construct is used throughout the source for the tabbed browser, as a simple way to interact with the current browser view.

Listing 284. app/browser_tabs.py

```python
    def tab_open_doubleclick(self, i):
        if i == -1:  # No tab under the click
            self.add_new_tab()

    def current_tab_changed(self, i):
        qurl = self.tabs.currentWidget().url()
        self.update_urlbar(qurl, self.tabs.currentWidget())
        self.update_title(self.tabs.currentWidget())

    def close_current_tab(self, i):
        if self.tabs.count() < 2:
            return

        self.tabs.removeTab(i)
```

Listing 285. app/browser_tabs.py

```python
    def add_new_tab(self, qurl=None, label="Blank"):

        if qurl is None:
            qurl = QUrl("")

        browser = QWebEngineView()
        browser.setUrl(qurl)
        i = self.tabs.addTab(browser, label)

        self.tabs.setCurrentIndex(i)
```

Signal & Slot changes

While the setup of the QTabWidget and associated signals is simple, things get a little trickier in the browser slot methods.

Whereas before we had a single QWebEngineView now there are multiple views, all with their own signals. If signals for hidden tabs are handled things will get all mixed up. For example, the slot handling a loadCompleted signal must check that the source view is in a visible tab.

We can do this using our trick for sending additional data with signals. In the tabbed browser we're using the lambda style syntax to do this.

Below is an example of doing this when creating a new QWebEngineView in the add_new_tab function.

Listing 286. app/browser_tabs.py

```
        # More difficult! We only want to update the url when it's
from the
        # correct tab
        browser.urlChanged.connect(
            lambda qurl, browser=browser: self.update_urlbar(
                qurl, browser
            )
        )

        browser.loadFinished.connect(
            lambda _, i=i, browser=browser: self.tabs.setTabText(
                i, browser.page().title()
            )
        )
```

As you can see, we set a lambda as the slot for the urlChanged signal, accepting the qurl parameter that is sent by this signal. We add the recently created browser object to pass into the update_urlbar function.

The result is, whenever this urlChanged signal fires update_urlbar will receive both the new URL and the browser it came from. In the slot method we can then check to ensure that the source of the signal matches the currently visible browser — if not, we simply discard the signal.

Listing 287. app/browser_tabs.py

```python
def update_urlbar(self, q, browser=None):

    if browser != self.tabs.currentWidget():
        # If this signal is not from the current tab, ignore
        return

    if q.scheme() == "https":
        # Secure padlock icon
        self.httpsicon.setPixmap(
            QPixmap(Paths.icon("lock-ssl.png"))
        )

    else:
        # Insecure padlock icon
        self.httpsicon.setPixmap(
            QPixmap(Paths.icon("lock-nossl.png"))
        )

    self.urlbar.setText(q.toString())
    self.urlbar.setCursorPosition(0)
```

Going further

Explore the rest of the source code for the tabbed version of the browser paying particular attention to the user of `self.tabs.currentWidget()` and passing additional data with signals. This a good practical use case for what you've learnt, so experiment and see if you can break/improve it in interesting ways.

Challenges

You might like to try adding some additional features —

- Bookmarks (or Favorites) — you could store these in a simple text file, and show them in a menu.

- Favicons — those little website icons, would look great on the tabs.

- View source code — add a menu option to see the source code for the page.

- Open in New Tab — add a right-click context menu, or keyboard shortcut, to open a link in a new tab.

42. Moonsweeper

Explore the mysterious moon of Q'tee without getting too close to the alien natives!

Moonsweeper is a single-player puzzle video game. The objective of the game is to explore the area around your landed space rocket, without coming too close to the deadly B'ug aliens. Your trusty tricounter will tell you the number of B'ugs in the vicinity.

Suggested reading

This application makes use of features covered in Signals & Slots, and Events.

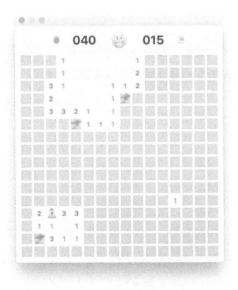

Figure 271. Moonsweeper.

This a simple single-player exploration game modelled on *Minesweeper* where you must reveal all the tiles without hitting hidden mines. This implementation uses custom `QWidget` objects for the tiles, which individually hold their state as mines, status and the adjacent count of mines. In this version, the mines are replaced with alien bugs (B'ug) but they could just as easily be anything else.

In many **Minesweeper** variants the initial turn is considered a free go — if you hit a mine on the first click, it is moved somewhere else. Here we cheat a little bit by taking the first go for the player, ensuring that it is on a non-mine spot. This allows us not to worry about the bad first move which would require us to recalculate the adjacencies. We can explain this away as the "initial exploration around the rocket" and make it sound completely sensible.

Challenge!

If you want to implement this, you can catch the first click on a position and at that point generate mines/adjacencies, excluding your location, before handling the click. You will need to give your custom widgets access to the parent window object.

Source code

The full source for the *Moonsweeper* game is included in the downloads for this book. The game file is saved with the name `minesweeper.py`.

```
python3 minesweeper.py
```

Paths

To make working with interface icons easier, we can start by defining a `Paths` class as described in Working with Relative Paths. It defines a single folder location for data files `icons` and a method `icon` for creating paths for icons. This allows us to using `Paths.icon()` to load our icons for the game interface.

Listing 288. app/paths.py

```python
import os


class Paths:

    base = os.path.dirname(__file__)
    icons = os.path.join(base, "icons")

    # File loaders.
    @classmethod
    def icon(cls, filename):
        return os.path.join(cls.icons, filename)
```

Saved in the same folder as our Moonsweeper app, it can be imported as:

Listing 289. app/moonsweeper.py

```python
from paths import Paths
```

Icons & Colors

Now the paths are defined, we can use them to load some icons for use in our game — a *bug*, a *flag*, a *rocket* and a *clock*. We also define a set of colors for the interface states, a series of *status* flags to track how the game is progressing — each with an associated smiley-face icon.

Listing 290. app/moonsweeper.py

```
IMG_BOMB = QImage(Paths.icon("bug.png"))
IMG_FLAG = QImage(Paths.icon("flag.png"))
IMG_START = QImage(Paths.icon("rocket.png"))
IMG_CLOCK = QImage(Paths.icon("clock-select.png"))

NUM_COLORS = {
    1: QColor("#f44336"),
    2: QColor("#9C27B0"),
    3: QColor("#3F51B5"),
    4: QColor("#03A9F4"),
    5: QColor("#00BCD4"),
    6: QColor("#4CAF50"),
    7: QColor("#E91E63"),
    8: QColor("#FF9800"),
}

STATUS_READY = 0
STATUS_PLAYING = 1
STATUS_FAILED = 2
STATUS_SUCCESS = 3

STATUS_ICONS = {
    STATUS_READY: Paths.icon("plus.png"),
    STATUS_PLAYING: Paths.icon("smiley.png"),
    STATUS_FAILED: Paths.icon("cross.png"),
    STATUS_SUCCESS: Paths.icon("smiley-lol.png"),
}
```

Playing Field

The playing area for Moonsweeper is a NxN grid, containing a set number of mines. The dimensions and mine counts we'll use are taken from the default values for the Windows version of Minesweeper. The values used are shown in the table below:

Table 14. Table Dimensions and mine counts

Level	Dimensions	Number of Mines

Easy	8 x 8	10
Medium	16 x 16	40
Hard	24 x 24	99

We store these values as a constant LEVELS defined at the top of the file. Since all the playing fields are square we only need to store the value once (8, 16 or 24).

Listing 291. app/minesweeper.py

```
LEVELS = [("Easy", 8, 10), ("Medium", 16, 40), ("Hard", 24, 99)]
```

The playing grid could be represented in a number of ways, including for example a 2D 'list of lists' representing the different states of the playing positions (mine, revealed, flagged).

However, in our implementation we'll be using an object-orientated approach, where individual positions on the map hold all relevant data about themselves. Taking this a step further, we can make these objects individually responsible for drawing themselves. In Qt we can do this simply by subclassing from QWidget and then implementing a custom paint function.

We'll cover the construction and behavior of these custom widgets before moving onto it's appearance. Since our tile objects are subclassing from QWidget we can lay them out like any other widget. We do this, by setting up a QGridLayout.

Listing 292. app/minesweeper.py

```
        self.grid = QGridLayout()
        self.grid.setSpacing(5)
        self.grid.setSizeConstraint(QLayout.SizeConstraint
    .SetFixedSize)
```

Next we need to set up the playing field, creating our position tile widgets and adding them our grid. The initial setup for the level is defined in custom method, which reads from LEVELS and assigns a number of variables to the window. The window title and mine counter are updated, and then the setup of the grid is begun.

Listing 293. app/minesweeper.py

```python
def set_level(self, level):
    self.level_name, self.b_size, self.n_mines = LEVELS[level]

    self.setWindowTitle("Moonsweeper - %s" % (self.level_name))
    self.mines.setText("%03d" % self.n_mines)

    self.clear_map()
    self.init_map()
    self.reset_map()
```

The setup functions will be covered next.

We're using a custom Pos class here, which we'll look at in detail later. For now you just need to know that this holds all the relevant information for the relevant position in the map — including, for example, whether it's a mine, revealed, flagged and the number of mines in the immediate vicinity.

Each Pos object also has 3 custom signals *clicked*, *revealed* and *expandable* which we connect to custom slot methods. Finally, we call resize to adjust the size of the window to the new contents. Note that this is actually only necessary when the window *shrinks* — it will grow automatically.

Listing 294. app/minesweeper.py

```
def init_map(self):
    # Add positions to the map
    for x in range(0, self.b_size):
        for y in range(0, self.b_size):
            w = Pos(x, y)
            self.grid.addWidget(w, y, x)
            # Connect signal to handle expansion.
            w.clicked.connect(self.trigger_start)
            w.revealed.connect(self.on_reveal)
            w.expandable.connect(self.expand_reveal)

    # Place resize on the event queue, giving control back to Qt
before.
    QTimer.singleShot(0, lambda: self.resize(1, 1))   ①
```

① The `singleShot` timer is required to ensure the resize runs after Qt is aware of the new contents. By using a timer we guarantee control will return to Qt *before* the resize occurs.

We also need to implement the inverse of the `init_map` function to remove tile objects from the map. Removing tiles will be necessary when moving from a higher to a lower level. It would be possible to be a little smarter here and adding/removing only those tiles that are necessary to get to the correct size. But, since we already have the function to add all up to the right size, we can cheat a bit.

Challenge

Update this code to add/remove the neccessary tiles to size the new level dimensions.

Notice that we both remove the item from the grid with `self.grid.removeItem(c)` and clear the parent `c.widget().setParent(None)`. This second step is necessary, since adding the items assigning them the parent window as a parent. Just removing them leaves them floating in the window outside the layout.

Listing 295. app/minesweeper.py

```python
def clear_map(self):
    # Remove all positions from the map, up to maximum size.
    for x in range(0, LEVELS[-1][1]):     ①
        for y in range(0, LEVELS[-1][1]):
            c = self.grid.itemAtPosition(y, x)
            if c:     ②
                c.widget().close()
                self.grid.removeItem(c)
```

① To ensure we clear all sizes of maps we take the dimension of the highest level.

② If there isn't anything in the grid at this location, we can skip it.

Now we have our grid of positional tile objects in place, we can begin creating the initial conditions of the playing board. This process is rather complex, so it's broken down into a number of functions. We name them _reset (the leading underscore is a convention to indicate a private function, not intended for external use). The main function reset_map calls these functions in turn to set it up.

The process is as follows —

1. Remove all mines (and reset data) from the field.

2. Add new mines to the field.

3. Calculate the number of mines adjacent to each position.

4. Add a starting marker (the rocket) and trigger initial exploration.

5. Reset the timer.

Listing 296. app/minesweeper.py

```
def reset_map(self):
    self._reset_position_data()
    self._reset_add_mines()
    self._reset_calculate_adjacency()
    self._reset_add_starting_marker()
    self.update_timer()
```

The separate steps from 1-5 are described in detail in turn below, with the code for each step.

The first step is to reset the data for each position on the map. We iterate through every position on the board, calling .reset() on the widget at each point. The code for the .reset() function is defined on our custom Pos class, we'll explore in detail later. For now it's enough to know it clears mines, flags and sets the position back to being unrevealed.

Listing 297. app/minesweeper.py

```
def _reset_position_data(self):
    # Clear all mine positions
    for x in range(0, self.b_size):
        for y in range(0, self.b_size):
            w = self.grid.itemAtPosition(y, x).widget()
            w.reset()
```

Now all the positions are blank, we can begin the process of adding mines to the map. The maximum number of mines n_mines is defined by the level settings, described earlier.

Listing 298. app/minesweeper.py

```python
def _reset_add_mines(self):
    # Add mine positions
    positions = []
    while len(positions) < self.n_mines:
        x, y = (
            random.randint(0, self.b_size - 1),
            random.randint(0, self.b_size - 1),
        )
        if (x, y) not in positions:
            w = self.grid.itemAtPosition(y, x).widget()
            w.is_mine = True
            positions.append((x, y))

    # Calculate end-game condition
    self.end_game_n = (self.b_size * self.b_size) - (
        self.n_mines + 1
    )
    return positions
```

With mines in position, we can now calculate the 'adjacency' number for each position — simply the number of mines in the immediate vicinity, using a 3x3 grid around the given point. The custom function get_surrounding simply returns those positions around a given x and y location. We count the number of these that is a mine is_mine == True and store.

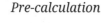

Pre-calculation

Pre-calculating the adjacent counts in this way helps simplify the reveal logic later.

Listing 299. app/minesweeper.py

```python
def _reset_calculate_adjacency(self):
    def get_adjacency_n(x, y):
        positions = self.get_surrounding(x, y)
        return sum(1 for w in positions if w.is_mine)

    # Add adjacencies to the positions
    for x in range(0, self.b_size):
        for y in range(0, self.b_size):
            w = self.grid.itemAtPosition(y, x).widget()
            w.adjacent_n = get_adjacency_n(x, y)
```

A starting marker is used to ensure that the first move is *always* valid. This is implemented as a *brute force* search through the grid space, effectively trying random positions until we find a position which is not a mine. Since we don't know how many attempts this will take, we need to wrap it in an continuous loop.

Once that location is found, we mark it as the start location and then trigger the exploration of all surrounding positions. We break out of the loop, and reset the ready status.

Listing 300. app/minesweeper.py

```python
    def _reset_add_starting_marker(self):
        # Place starting marker.

        # Set initial status (needed for .click to function)
        self.update_status(STATUS_READY)

        while True:
            x, y = (
                random.randint(0, self.b_size - 1),
                random.randint(0, self.b_size - 1),
            )
            w = self.grid.itemAtPosition(y, x).widget()
            # We don't want to start on a mine.
            if not w.is_mine:
                w.is_start = True
                w.is_revealed = True
                w.update()

                # Reveal all positions around this, if they are not
mines either.
                for w in self.get_surrounding(x, y):
                    if not w.is_mine:
                        w.click()
                break

        # Reset status to ready following initial clicks.
        self.update_status(STATUS_READY)
```

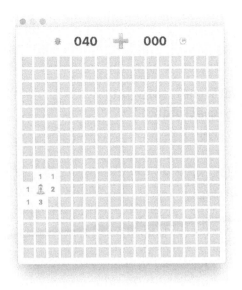

Figure 272. Initial exploration around rocket.

Position Tiles

As previously described, we've structured the game so that individual tile positions hold their own state information. This means that Pos objects are ideally positioned to handle game logic which reacts to interactions that relate to their own state — in other words, this is where the magic is.

Since the Pos class is relatively complex, it is broken down here in to main themes, which are discussed in turn. The initial setup `__init__` block is simple, accepting an x and y position and storing it on the object. Pos positions never change once created.

To complete setup the `.reset()` function is called which resets all object attributes back to default, zero values. This flags the mine as *not the start position, not a mine, not revealed* and *not flagged.* We also reset the adjacent count.

Listing 301. app/minesweeper.py

```python
class Pos(QWidget):

    expandable = pyqtSignal(int, int)
    revealed = pyqtSignal(object)
    clicked = pyqtSignal()

    def __init__(self, x, y):
        super().__init__()

        self.setFixedSize(QSize(20, 20))
        self.x = x
        self.y = y
        self.reset()

    def reset(self):
        self.is_start = False
        self.is_mine = False
        self.adjacent_n = 0
        self.is_revealed = False
        self.is_flagged = False

        self.update()
```

Gameplay is centered around mouse interactions with the tiles in the playfield, so detecting and reacting to mouse clicks is central. In Qt we catch mouse clicks by detecting the mouseReleaseEvent. To do this for our custom Pos widget we define a handler on the class. This receives QMouseEvent with the information containing what happened. In this case we are only interested in whether the mouse release occurred from the left or the right mouse button.

For a left mouse click we check whether the tile is flagged or already revealed. If it is either, we ignore the click — making flagged tiles 'safe', unable to be click by accident. If the tile is not flagged we simply initiation the .click() method (see later).

For a right mouse click, on tiles which are *not* revealed, we call our

`.toggle_flag()` method to toggle a flag on and off.

Listing 302. app/minesweeper.py

```python
def mouseReleaseEvent(self, e):
    if (
        e.button() == Qt.MouseButton.RightButton
        and not self.is_revealed
    ):
        self.toggle_flag()

    elif e.button() == Qt.MouseButton.LeftButton:
        # Block clicking on flagged mines.
        if not self.is_flagged and not self.is_revealed:
            self.click()
```

The methods called by the `mouseReleaseEvent` handler are defined below.

The `.toggle_flag` handler simply sets `.is_flagged` to the inverse of itself (`True` becomes `False`, `False` becomes `True`) having the effect of toggling it on and off. Note that we have to call `.update()` to force a redraw having changed the state. We also emit our custom `.clicked` signal, which is used to start the timer — because placing a flag should also count as starting, not just revealing a square.

The `.click()` method handles a left mouse click, and in turn triggers the reveal of the square. If the number of adjacent mines to this `Pos` is zero, we trigger the `.expandable` signal to begin the process of auto-expanding the region explored (see later). Finally, we again emit `.clicked` to signal the start of the game.

Finally, the `.reveal()` method checks whether the tile is already revealed, and if not sets `.is_revealed` to `True`. Again we call `.update()` to trigger a repaint of the widget.

The optional emit of the `.revealed` signal is used only for the endgame full-map reveal. Because each reveal triggers a further lookup to find what tiles are also revealable, revealing the entire map would create a large number of redundant callbacks. By suppressing the signal here we avoid that.

Listing 303. app/minesweeper.py

```
def toggle_flag(self):
    self.is_flagged = not self.is_flagged
    self.update()

    self.clicked.emit()

def click(self):
    self.reveal()
    if self.adjacent_n == 0:
        self.expandable.emit(self.x, self.y)

    self.clicked.emit()

def reveal(self, emit=True):
    if not self.is_revealed:
        self.is_revealed = True
        self.update()

        if emit:
            self.revealed.emit(self)
```

Finally, we define a custom `paintEvent` method for our `Pos` widget to handle the display of the current position state. As described in [chapter] to perform custom paint over a widget canvas we take a `QPainter` and the `event.rect()` which provides the boundaries in which we are to draw — in this case the outer border of the `Pos` widget.

Revealed tiles are drawn differently depending on whether the tile is a *start position, bomb* or *empty space*. The first two are represented by icons of a rocket and bomb respectively. These are drawn into the tile `QRect` using `.drawPixmap`. Note we need to convert the `QImage` constants to pixmaps, by passing through `QPixmap` by passing.

custom function for that purpose. It simple iterates across a 3x3 grid around the point, with a check to ensure we do not go out of bounds on the grid edges ($0 \geq$ x $\leq$ self.b_size). The returned list contains a Pos widget from each surrounding location.

Listing 305. app/minesweeper.py

```
def get_surrounding(self, x, y):
    positions = []

    for xi in range(max(0, x - 1), min(x + 2, self.b_size)):
        for yi in range(max(0, y - 1), min(y + 2, self.b_size)):
            if not (xi == x and yi == y):
                positions.append(
                    self.grid.itemAtPosition(yi, xi).widget()
                )

    return positions
```

The expand_reveal method is triggered in response to a click on a tile with zero adjacent mines. In this case we want to expand the area around the click to any spaces which also have zero adjacent mines, and also reveal any squares around the border of that expanded area (which aren't mines).

This *can* be achieved by looking at all squares around the clicked square, and triggering a .click() on any that do not have .n_adjacent == 0. The normal game logic takes over and expands the area automatically. However, this is a bit inefficient, resulting in a large number of redundant signals (each square triggers up to 9 signals for each surrounding square).

Instead we use a self-contained method to determine the area to be revealed, and then trigger the reveal (using .reveal() to avoid the .clicked signals.

We start with a list to_expand containing the positions to check on the next iteration, a list to_reveal containing the tile widgets to reveal, and a flag any_added to determine when to exit the loop. The loop stops the first time no new widgets are added to to_reveal.

Inside the loop we reset `any_added` to `False`, and empty the `to_expand` list, keeping a temporary store in `l` for iterating over.

For each `x` and `y` location we get the 8 surrounding widgets. If any of these widgets is not a mine, and is not already in the `to_reveal` list we add it. This ensures that the edges of the expanded area are all revealed. If the position has no adjacent mines, we append the coordinates onto `to_expand` to be checked on the next iteration.

By adding any non-mine tiles to `to_reveal`, and only expanding tiles that are not already in `to_reveal`, we ensure that we won't visit a tile more than once.

Listing 306. app/minesweeper.py

```
    def expand_reveal(self, x, y):
        """
        Iterate outwards from the initial point, adding new locations
    to the
        queue. This allows us to expand all in a single go, rather
    than
        relying on multiple callbacks.
        """
        to_expand = [(x, y)]
        to_reveal = []
        any_added = True

        while any_added:
            any_added = False
            to_expand, l = [], to_expand

            for x, y in l:
                positions = self.get_surrounding(x, y)
                for w in positions:
                    if not w.is_mine and w not in to_reveal:
                        to_reveal.append(w)
                        if w.adjacent_n == 0:
                            to_expand.append((w.x, w.y))
                            any_added = True

        # Iterate an reveal all the positions we have found.
        for w in to_reveal:
            w.reveal()
```

Endgames

Endgame states are detected during the reveal process following a click on a title. There are two possible outcomes —

1. Tile is a mine, game over.

2. Tile is not a mine, decrement the `self.end_game_n`.

This continues until `self.end_game_n` reaches zero, which triggers the win game process by calling either `game_over` or `game_won`. Success/failure is triggered by revealing the map and setting the relevant status, in both cases.

Listing 307. app/minesweeper.py

```python
def on_reveal(self, w):
    if w.is_mine:
        self.game_over()

    else:
        self.end_game_n -= 1  # decrement remaining empty spaces

        if self.end_game_n == 0:
            self.game_won()

def game_over(self):
    self.reveal_map()
    self.update_status(STATUS_FAILED)

def game_won(self):
    self.reveal_map()
    self.update_status(STATUS_SUCCESS)
```

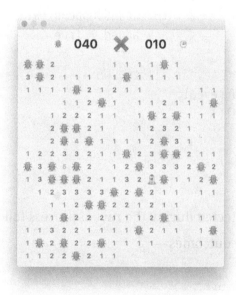

Figure 273. Oh no. Eaten by a B'ug.

Status

The user interface for Moonsweeper is pretty simple: one display showing the number of mines, one showing the amount of time elapsed, and a button to start/restart the game.

Both the labels are defined as QLabel objects with the with the same QFont size and color. These are defined on the QMainWindow object so we can access and update them at a later time. Two additional icons (a clock and a mine) are also defined as QLabel objects.

The button is a QPushButton with a defined icon, which is updated in set_status in response to status changes. The .pressed signal is connected to a custom slot method button_pressed which handles the signal differently depending on the game state.

Listing 308. app/minesweeper.py

```python
        self.mines = QLabel()
        self.mines.setAlignment(
            Qt.AlignmentFlag.AlignHCenter
            | Qt.AlignmentFlag.AlignVCenter
        )

        self.clock = QLabel()
        self.clock.setAlignment(
            Qt.AlignmentFlag.AlignHCenter
            | Qt.AlignmentFlag.AlignVCenter
        )

        f = self.mines.font()
        f.setPointSize(24)
        f.setWeight(QFont.Weight.Bold)
        self.mines.setFont(f)
        self.clock.setFont(f)

        self.clock.setText("000")

        self.button = QPushButton()
```

```
        self.button.setFixedSize(QSize(32, 32))
        self.button.setIconSize(QSize(32, 32))
        self.button.setIcon(QIcon(Paths.icon("smiley.png")))
        self.button.setFlat(True)

        self.button.pressed.connect(self.button_pressed)

        self.statusBar()

        l = QLabel()
        l.setPixmap(QPixmap.fromImage(IMG_BOMB))
        l.setAlignment(
            Qt.AlignmentFlag.AlignRight | Qt.AlignmentFlag
.AlignVCenter
        )
        hb.addWidget(l)

        hb.addWidget(self.mines)
        hb.addWidget(self.button)
        hb.addWidget(self.clock)

        l = QLabel()
        l.setPixmap(QPixmap.fromImage(IMG_CLOCK))
        l.setAlignment(
            Qt.AlignmentFlag.AlignLeft | Qt.AlignmentFlag
.AlignVCenter
        )
        hb.addWidget(l)

        vb = QVBoxLayout()
        vb.setSizeConstraint(QLayout.SizeConstraint.SetFixedSize)
        vb.addLayout(hb)
```

If the game is currently in progress self.status == STATUS_PLAYING a button press is interpreted as "I give up" and the game_over state is triggered.

If the game is currently won self.status == STATUS_SUCCESS or lost self.status == STATUS_FAILED the press is taken to mean "Try again" and the game map is reset.

Listing 309. app/minesweeper.py

```python
def button_pressed(self):
    if self.status == STATUS_PLAYING:
        self.game_over()

    elif (
        self.status == STATUS_FAILED
        or self.status == STATUS_SUCCESS
    ):
        self.reset_map()
```

Menus

There is only a single menu for Moonsweeper which holds the game controls. We create a `QMenu` by calling `.addMenu()` on the `QMainWindow.menuBar()` as normal.

The first menu item is a standard `QAction` for "New game" wit the `.triggered` action connected to the `.reset_map` function, which performs the entire map setup process. For new games we keep the existing board size & layout so do not need to re-init the map.

In addition we add a submenu "Levels" which contains a `QAction` for each level defined in `LEVELS`. The level name is taken from the same constant, and custom status message is built from the stored dimensions. We connect the action `.triggered` signal to `.set_level`, using the `lambda` method to discard the default signal data and instead pass along the level number.

Listing 310. app/minesweeper.py

```python
game_menu = self.menuBar().addMenu("&Game")

new_game_action = QAction("New game", self)
new_game_action.setStatusTip(
    "Start a new game (your current game will be lost)"
)
new_game_action.triggered.connect(self.reset_map)
game_menu.addAction(new_game_action)

levels = game_menu.addMenu("Levels")
for n, level in enumerate(LEVELS):
    level_action = QAction(level[0], self)
    level_action.setStatusTip(
        "{1}x{1} grid, with {2} mines".format(*level)
    )
    level_action.triggered.connect(
        lambda checked=None, n=n: self.set_level(n)
    )
    levels.addAction(level_action)
```

Going further

Take a look through the rest of the source code we've not covered.

Challenge

You might like to try make the following changes —

- Try changing the graphics to make you're own themed version of Minesweeper.

- Add support for non-square playing fields. Rectangular? Try a circle!

- Change the timer to count down — explore the Moon against the clock!

- Add power-ups: squares give bonuses, extra time, invincibility.

Appendix A: Installing PyQt6

Before you start coding you will first need to have a working installation of PyQt6 on your system. If you don't have PyQt6 set up yet, the following sections will guide you through how to do this on Windows, macOS and Linux.

 Note that the following instructions are **only** for installation of the **GPL licensed** version of PyQt. If you need to use PyQt in a non-GPL project you will need to purchase an alternative license from Riverbank Computing [https://www.riverbankcomputing.com] to release your software.

Installation on Windows

PyQt6 for Windows can be installed as for any other application or library. As of Qt 5.6 installers are available to install via PyPi, the Python Package archive. To install PyQt6 from Python3 simply run —

```
pip3 install pyqt6
```

After install is finished, you should be able to run python and import PyQt6.

Note that if you want access to Qt Designer or Qt Creator you will need to download this from the Qt downloads site [https://qt.io/download].

Installation on macOS

If you already have a working installation of Python 3 on macOS, you can go ahead and install PyQt6 as for any other Python package, using the following —

```
pip3 install pyqt6
```

If you *don't* have an installation of Python 3, you will need to install one first. You can download macOS installers for Python 3 from the Python homepage [https://www.python.org/]. Once installed, you should be able to use the `pip3 install` command above to install PyQt6.

Another alternative is to use Homebrew [http://brew.sh/]. Homebrew is a package manager for command-line software on macOS. Homebrew has both Python 3 and PyQt6 available in their repositories.

Figure 274. Homebrew — the missing package manager for macOS.

To install homebrew run the following from the command line —

```
ruby -e "$(curl -fsSL
https://raw.githubusercontent.com/Homebrew/install/master/install)"
```

 This is also available to copy and paste from the Homebrew homepage.

Once Homebrew is installed you can then install Python with —

```
brew install python3
```

With Python installed, you can then install PyQt6 as normal, using `pip3 install pyqt6`, or alternatively choose to install it using Homebrew with —

```
brew install pyqt6
```

Installation on Linux

The simplest way to install PyQt6 on Linux is to use Python's `pip` packaging tool, just as for other packages. For Python3 installations this is usually called `pip3`.

```
pip3 install pyqt6
```

Once the installation is finished, you should be able to run `python3` (or `python` depending on your system) and `import PyQt6`.

Appendix B: Translating C++ Examples to Python

When writing applications with PyQt6 we are really writing applications with Qt.

PyQt6 acts as a wrapper around the Qt libraries, translating Python method calls to C++, handling type conversions and transparently creating Python objects to represent Qt objects in your applications. The result of all this cleverness is that you can use Qt from Python while writing *mostly* Pythonic code — if we ignore the *camelCase*.

While there is a lot of PyQt6 example code out there, there are far more Qt C++ examples. The core documentation is written for C++. The library is written in C++. This means that sometimes, when you're looking how to do something, the only resource you'll find is a C++ tutorial or some C++ code.

Can you use it? Yes! If you have no experience with C++ (or C-like languages) then the code can look like gibberish. But before you were familiar with Python, Python probably looked a bit like gibberish too. You don't need to be able to *write* C++ to be able to *read* it. Understanding and decoding is easier than writing.

With a little bit of effort you'll be able to take any C++ example code and translate it into fully-functional Python & PyQt6. In this chapter we'll take a snippet of Qt5 code and step-by-step convert it into fully-working Python code.

The example code

We'll start with the following example block of code creating a simple window with a `QPushButton` and a `QLineEdit`. Pressing on the button will clear the line edit. Pretty exciting stuff, but this includes a few key parts of translating Qt examples to PyQt6 — namely, widgets, layouts and signals.

```
#include <QtWidgets>

int main(int argc, char *argv[])
{
    QApplication app(argc, argv);
    QWidget window;
    QLineEdit *lineEdit = new QLineEdit();
    QPushButton *button = new QPushButton("Clear");
    QHBoxLayout *layout = new QHBoxLayout();
    layout->addWidget(lineEdit);
    layout->addWidget(button);

    QObject::connect(&button,    &QPushButton::pressed,
                     &lineEdit, &QLineEdit::clear);

    window.setLayout(layout);
    window.setWindowTitle("Why?");
    window.show();
    return app.exec();
}
```

 Remember that a Qt widget without a parent is always a separate window. Here we have a single window created as a QWidget.

Below we'll step through the process of converting this code to Python.

Imports

In C++ *imports* are called *includes*. They're found at the top of the file, just as in Python (though only by convention) and look like this —

```
#include <QtWidgets>
```

In C-like languages the # indicates that include is a *pre-processor directive* not a comment. The value between <> is the name of the module to import. Note that unlike Python, importing a module makes all contents of that module available

in the global namespace. This is the equivalent of doing the following in
Python —

```python
from PyQt6.QtWidgets import *
```

Global imports like this are generally frowned upon in Python, and you should
instead either —

1. only import the objects you need, or

2. import the module itself and use it to reference it's children

```python
from PyQt6.QtWidgets import QApplication, QWidget, QLineEdit,
QPushButton, QHBoxLayout
```

Or, alternatively...

```python
from PyQt6 import QtWidgets
```

...and then reference as QtWidgets.QApplication(). Which you choose for your
own code is entirely up to you, however in this example we're going to follow the
first style. Applying that to the code gives us the following result so far.

```
from PyQt6.QtWidgets import (
    QApplication, QWidget, QLineEdit, QPushButton, QHBoxLayout
)

int main(int argc, char *argv[])
{
    QApplication app(argc, argv);
    QWidget window;
    QLineEdit *lineEdit = new QLineEdit();
    QPushButton *button = new QPushButton("Clear");
    QHBoxLayout *layout = new QHBoxLayout();
    layout->addWidget(lineEdit);
    layout->addWidget(button);

    QObject::connect(&button,   &QPushButton::pressed,
                     &lineEdit, &QLineEdit::clear);

    window.setLayout(layout);
    window.setWindowTitle("Why?");
    window.show();
    return app.exec();
}
```

 Since we're making changes iteratively, the code won't work until the very end.

int main(int argc, char *argv[])

Every C++ program needs a main(){} block which contains the first code to be run when the application is executed. In Python *any* code at the top-level of the module (i.e. not indented inside a function, class or methods) will be run when the script is executed.

```
from PyQt6.QtWidgets import (
    QApplication, QWidget, QLineEdit, QPushButton, QHBoxLayout
)

QApplication app(argc, argv);
QWidget window;
QLineEdit *lineEdit = new QLineEdit();
QPushButton *button = new QPushButton("Clear");
QHBoxLayout *layout = new QHBoxLayout();
layout->addWidget(lineEdit);
layout->addWidget(button);

QObject::connect(&button,   &QPushButton::pressed,
                 &lineEdit, &QLineEdit::clear);

window.setLayout(layout);
window.setWindowTitle("Why?");
window.show();
app.exec();
```

You may have seen the following code block in Python application code, which is also often referred to as the __main__ block.

```
if __name__ == '__main__':
    ...your code here...
```

However, this works in a subtly different way. While this block *will* be run when a script is executed, so would any code that is not indented. The purpose of this block is actually to *prevent* this code executing when the module is imported, rather than executed as a script.

You can nest your code inside this block if you wish, although unless your file is going to be imported as a module it isn't strictly necessary.

C++ types

Python is a *dynamically typed* language, meaning you can change the type of a variable after it has been defined. For example, the following is perfectly valid Python.

```
a = 1
a = 'my string'
a = [1,2,3]
```

Many other languages, C++ included, are *statically typed*, meaning that once you define the type of a variable it cannot be changed. For example, the following is very definitely *not* valid C++.

```
int a = 1;
a = 'my string';
```

The above highlights an immediate consequence of static typing in languages: you define the type of a variable *when you create it*.

In C++ this is done explicitly by providing a type decorator on the line when the variable is defined, above int.

In lines like the following the first name is the name of type (class) that is being created by the remainder of the line.

```
QApplication app(argc, argv);
QWidget window;

QLineEdit *lineEdit = new QLineEdit();
QPushButton *button = new QPushButton("Clear");
QHBoxLayout *layout = new QHBoxLayout();
```

In Python we do not need these type definitions, so we can just delete them.

```
lineEdit = new QLineEdit();
button = new QPushButton("Clear");
layout = new QHBoxLayout();
```

For `application` and `window` it's exactly the same principle. However, if you're not familiar with C++ it might not be obvious those lines are creating an variable at all.

There are differences between creating objects with `new` and without in C++ but you don't need to concern yourself with that in Python and can consider them both equivalent.

```
QWidget *window = new QWidget();
QWidget window;

QApplication *app = new QApplication(argc, argv);
QApplication app;
```

To convert to Python, take the class name (e.g. `QApplication`) from the left, and place it in front of open and closing brackets `()`, adding them if they aren't already there. Then move the name of the *variable* to the left, with an `=`. For `window` that gives us —

```
window = QWidget()
```

In Python `QApplication` only accepts a single parameter, a list of arguments from `sys.argv` (equivalent to `argv`). This gives us the code —

```
import sys

app = QApplication(sys.argv);
```

So far our complete code block is looking like the following.

```
from PyQt6.QtWidgets import (
    QApplication, QWidget, QLineEdit, QPushButton, QHBoxLayout
)

import sys

app = QApplication(argc, argv);
window = QWidget()
lineEdit = QLineEdit();
button = QPushButton("Clear");
layout = QHBoxLayout();
layout->addWidget(lineEdit);
layout->addWidget(button);

QObject::connect(&button,   &QPushButton::pressed,
                 &lineEdit, &QLineEdit::clear);

window.setLayout(layout);
window.setWindowTitle("Why?");
window.show();
app.exec();
```

Signals

Signals are key to making the example work, and unfortunately the C++ syntax
for Qt signals is a little tricky. The example signal we're working with is shown
below.

```
QObject::connect(&button,   &QPushButton::pressed,
                 &lineEdit, &QLineEdit::clear);
```

If you're not familiar with C++ this will be quite difficult to parse. But if we
remove all the syntax it will get much clearer.

```
connect(button, QPushButton.pressed, lineEdit, QLineEdit.clear)
// or...
connect(<from object>, <from signal>, <to object>, <to slot>>)
```

Working from left to right we have, the *object* we're connecting from, the *signal* we're connecting from on that object, then the *object* we're connecting to, then finally the *slot* (or function) we're connecting to on that object. This is the equivalent of writing the following in PyQt6 —

```
button.pressed.connect(lineedit.clear)
```

Making that change gives us the following in progress code.

```
from PyQt6.QtWidgets import (
    QApplication, QWidget, QLineEdit, QPushButton, QHBoxLayout
)

app = QApplication(sys.argv)
window = QWidget()
lineEdit = QLineEdit()
button = QPushButton("Clear")
layout = QHBoxLayout()
layout->addWidget(lineEdit);
layout->addWidget(button);

button.pressed.connect(lineEdit.clear)

window.setLayout(layout);
window.setWindowTitle("Why?");
window.show();
app.exec();
```

Syntax

By now we've converted all the really troublesome parts, so we can do a final syntax-correction pass. These are a simple search-replace.

First search for all instances of -> or :: and replace with .. You'll notice that the C++ code also uses . in some places — this comes back to how those variables were created earlier (new vs. not). Again, you can ignore that here and simply use . everywhere.

```
layout.addWidget(lineEdit);
layout.addWidget(button);
```

Finally, remove all line-ending semi-colon ; marks.

```
layout.addWidget(lineEdit)
layout.addWidget(button)
```

 You technically don't *have* to do this, as ; is a valid line-terminator in Python. It's just not necessary.

The following code is now working Python.

```python
import sys

from PyQt6.QtWidgets import (
    QApplication,
    QHBoxLayout,
    QLineEdit,
    QPushButton,
    QWidget,
)

app = QApplication(sys.argv)
window = QWidget()
lineEdit = QLineEdit()
button = QPushButton("Clear")
layout = QHBoxLayout()
layout.addWidget(lineEdit)
layout.addWidget(button)

button.pressed.connect(lineEdit.clear)

window.setLayout(layout)
window.setWindowTitle("Why?")
window.show()
app.exec()
```

In Python code it is normal (though not *required*) to subclass the window class so the initialization code can be self-contained within the __init__ block. The code below has been reworked into that structure, moving all except the creation of the window object (now MyWindow) and app, and app.exec() call into the __init__ block.

```python
import sys

from PyQt6.QtWidgets import (
    QApplication,
    QHBoxLayout,
    QLineEdit,
    QPushButton,
    QWidget,
)


class MyWindow(QWidget):
    def __init__(self, *args, **kwargs):
        super().__init__(*args, **kwargs)

        lineEdit = QLineEdit()
        button = QPushButton("Clear")
        layout = QHBoxLayout()
        layout.addWidget(lineEdit)
        layout.addWidget(button)

        button.pressed.connect(lineEdit.clear)

        self.setLayout(layout)
        self.setWindowTitle("Why?")
        self.show()


app = QApplication(sys.argv)
window = MyWindow()
app.exec()
```

Applying the process to your own code

This is a very simple example, however if you follow the same process you can reliably convert any C++ Qt code over to it's Python equivalent. When converting your own sample of code try and stick to this stepwise approach to minimize the risk of missing something or inadvertently breaking it. If you end up with Python code that runs but is subtly different it can be hard to debug.

 If you have a code example you would like help with translating, you can always get in touch and I'll try and help you out.

Appendix C: PyQt6 and PySide6 — What's the difference?

If you start building Python application with Qt6 you'll soon discover that there are in fact two packages which you can use to do this — PyQt6 and PySide6.

In this short chapter I'll run through why exactly this is, whether you need to care (spoiler: you really don't), what the (few) differences are and how to work around them. By the end you should be comfortable re-using code examples from both PyQt6 and PySide6 tutorials to build your apps, regardless of which package you're using yourself.

Background

Why are there two libraries?

PyQt is developed by Phil Thompson of Riverbank Computing Ltd. [https://www.riverbankcomputing.com/software/pyqt/intro] and has existed for a very long time — supporting versions of Qt going back to 2.x. In 2009 Nokia, who owned Qt toolkit at the time, wanted to make the Python bindings for Qt available in a more permissive LGPL license. Unable to come to agreement with Riverbank (who would lose money from this, so fair enough) they then released their own *bindings as _PySide.*

 It's called *PySide* because "side" is Finnish for "binder".

The two interfaces were basically equivalent, but over time development of PySide lagged behind PyQt. This was particularly noticeable following the release of Qt 5 — the Qt5 version of PyQt (PyQt5) has been available since mid-2016, while the first stable release of PySide2 was 2 years later. With that in mind, it is unsurprising that many Qt5 on Python examples use PyQt5 — if only because it was *available.*

However, the Qt project has recently adopted PySide as the official Qt for Python release [https://www.qt.io/qt-for-python] which should ensure its viability going forward. When Qt6 was released, both Python bindings were available shortly after.

	PyQt6	PySide6
First stable release	Jan 2021	Dec 2020
Developed by	Riverbank Computing Ltd.	Qt
License	GPL or commercial	LGPL
Platforms	Python 3	Python 3

Which should you use? Well, honestly, it doesn't really matter.

Both packages are wrapping the same library — Qt6 — and so have 99.9% identical APIs (see below for the few differences). Anything you learn with one library will be easily applied to a project using the other. Also, no matter with one you choose to use, it's worth familiarizing yourself with the other so you can make the best use of all available online resources — using PyQt6 tutorials to build your PySide6 applications for example, and *vice versa*.

In this short chapter I'll run through the few notable differences between the two packages and explain how to write code which works seamlessly with both. After reading this you should be able to take any PyQt6 example online and convert it to work with PySide6.

Licensing

The main notable difference between the two versions is licensing — with PyQt6 being available under a GPL or commercial license, and PySide6 under a LGPL license.

If you are planning to release your software itself under the GPL, or you are developing software which will not be *distributed*, the GPL requirement of PyQt6 is unlikely to be an issue. However, if you want to distribute your software but not share your source code you will need to purchase a commercial license from Riverbank for PyQt6 or use PySide6.

 Qt itself is available under a *Qt Commercial License*, GPL 2.0, GPL 3.0 and LGPL 3.0 licenses.

Namespaces & Enums

One of the major changes introduced for PyQt6 is the need to use fully qualified names for enums and flags. Previously, in both PyQt5 and PySide2 you could make use of shortcuts — for example `Qt.DecorationRole`, `Qt.AlignLeft`. In PyQt6 these are now `Qt.ItemDataRole.DisplayRole` and `Qt.Alignment.AlignLeft` respectively. This change affects all enums and flag groups in Qt. In PySide6 both long and short names remain supported.

UI files

Another major difference between the two libraries is in their handling of loading `.ui` files exported from Qt Creator/Designer. PyQt6 provides the `uic` submodule which can be used to load UI files directly, to produce an object. This feels pretty Pythonic (if you ignore the camelCase).

```
import sys
from PyQt6 import QtWidgets, uic

app = QtWidgets.QApplication(sys.argv)

window = uic.loadUi("mainwindow.ui")
window.show()
app.exec()
```

The equivalent with PySide6 is one line longer, since you need to create a `QUILoader` object first. Unfortunately the API of these two interfaces is different too (`.load` vs `.loadUI`).

```
import sys
from PySide6 import QtCore, QtGui, QtWidgets
from PySide6.QtUiTools import QUiLoader

loader = QUiLoader()

app = QtWidgets.QApplication(sys.argv)
window = loader.load("mainwindow.ui", None)
window.show()
app.exec()
```

To load a UI onto an existing object in PyQt6, for example in your
QMainWindow.init you can call uic.loadUI passing in self(the existing widget) as
the second parameter.

```
import sys
from PyQt6 import QtCore, QtGui, QtWidgets
from PyQt6 import uic


class MainWindow(QtWidgets.QMainWindow):

    def __init__(self, *args, **kwargs):
        super().__init__(*args, **kwargs)
        uic.loadUi("mainwindow.ui", self)


app = QtWidgets.QApplication(sys.argv)
window = MainWindow()
window.show()
app.exec()
```

The PySide6 loader does not support this — the second parameter to .load is the
parent widget of the widget you're creating. This prevents you adding custom
code to the __init__ block of the widget, but you can work around this with a
separate function.

```
import sys
from PySide6 import QtWidgets
from PySide6.QtUiTools import QUiLoader

loader = QUiLoader()

def mainwindow_setup(w):
    w.setWindowTitle("MainWindow Title")

app = QtWidgets.QApplication(sys.argv)

window = loader.load("mainwindow.ui", None)
mainwindow_setup(window)
window.show()
app.exec()
```

Converting UI files to Python

Both libraries provide identical scripts to generate Python importable modules from Qt Designer .ui files. For PyQt6 the script is named pyuic5 —

```
pyuic6 mainwindow.ui -o MainWindow.py
```

You can then import the UI_MainWindow object, subclass using multiple inheritance from the base class you're using (e.g. QMainWIndow) and then call self.setupUI(self) to set the UI up.

```
import sys
from PyQt6 import QtWidgets
from MainWindow import Ui_MainWindow

class MainWindow(QtWidgets.QMainWindow, Ui_MainWindow):

    def __init__(self, *args, **kwargs):
        super().__init__(*args, **kwargs)
        self.setupUi(self)


app = QtWidgets.QApplication(sys.argv)
window = MainWindow()
window.show()
app.exec()
```

For PySide6 it is named `pyside6-uic` —

```
pyside6-uic mainwindow.ui -o MainWindow.py
```

The subsequent setup is identical.

```
import sys
from PySide6 import QtWidgets
from MainWindow import Ui_MainWindow

class MainWindow(QtWidgets.QMainWindow, Ui_MainWindow):

    def __init__(self, *args, **kwargs):
        super().__init__(*args, **kwargs)
        self.setupUi(self)


app = QtWidgets.QApplication(sys.argv)
window = MainWindow()
window.show()
app.exec_()
```

For more information in using Qt Designer with either PyQt6 or PySide6 see the Qt Creator chapter.

exec() or exec_()

The `.exec()` method is used in Qt to start the event loop of your `QApplication` or dialog boxes. In Python 2.7 `exec` was a keyword, meaning it could not be used for variable, function or method names. The solution used in both PyQt4 and PySide was to rename uses of `.exec` to `.exec_()` to avoid this conflict.

Python 3 removed the `exec` keyword, freeing the name up to be used. As a result from Qt6 all `.exec()` calls are named just as in Qt itself. However, PySide6 still supports `.exec_()` so don't be surprised if you see this in some code.

Slots and Signals

Defining custom slots and signals uses slightly different syntax between the two libraries. PySide6 provides this interface under the names `Signal` and `Slot` while PyQt6 provides these as `pyqtSignal` and `pyqtSlot` respectively. The behavior of them both is identical for defining and slots and signals.

The following PyQt6 and PySide6 examples are identical —

```
my_custom_signal = pyqtSignal()  # PyQt6
my_custom_signal = Signal()  # PySide6

my_other_signal = pyqtSignal(int)  # PyQt6
my_other_signal = Signal(int)  # PySide6
```

Or for a slot —

```
@pyqtslot
def my_custom_slot():
    pass

@Slot
def my_custom_slot():
    pass
```

If you want to ensure consistency across PyQt6 and PySide6 you can use the following import pattern for PyQt6 to use the Signal and @Slot style there too.

```
from PyQt6.QtCore import pyqtSignal as Signal, pyqtSlot as Slot
```

 You could of course do the reverse from PySide6.QtCore import Signal as pyqtSignal, Slot as pyqtSlot although that's a bit confusing.

QMouseEvent

In PyQt6 QMouseEvent objects no longer have the .pos(), .x() or .y() shorthand property methods for accessing the position of the event. You must use the .position() property to get a QPoint object and access the .x() or .y() methods on that. The .position() method is also available in PySide6.

Features in PySide6 but not in PyQt6

As of Qt 6 PySide supports two Python feature flags to help make code more *Pythonic* with snake_case variable names and the ability to assign and access properties directly, rather than using getter/setter functions. The example below shows the impact of these changes on code —

Listing 311. Standard PySide6 code.

```
table = QTableWidget()
table.setColumnCount(2)

button = QPushButton("Add")
button.setEnabled(False)

layout = QVBoxLayout()
layout.addWidget(table)
layout.addWidget(button)
```

The same code, but with `snake_case` and `true_property` enabled.

Listing 312. PySide6 code with Snake case & properties.

```
from __feature__ import snake_case, true_property

table = QTableWidget()
table.column_count = 2

button = QPushButton("Add")
button.enabled = False

layout = QVBoxLayout()
layout.add_widget(table)
layout.add_widget(button)
```

These feature flags are a nice improvement for code readability, however as they are not supported in PyQt6 it makes migration between the libraries more difficult.

Supporting both in libraries

 You don't need to worry about this if you're writing a standalone app, just use whichever API you prefer.

If you're writing a library, widget or other tool you want to be compatible with both PyQt6 and PySide6 you can do so easily by adding both sets of imports.

```
import sys

if 'PyQt6' in sys.modules:
    # PyQt6
    from PyQt6 import QtGui, QtWidgets, QtCore
    from PyQt6.QtCore import pyqtSignal as Signal, pyqtSlot as Slot

else:
    # PySide6
    from PySide6 import QtGui, QtWidgets, QtCore
    from PySide6.QtCore import Signal, Slot
```

This is the approach used in our custom widgets library, where we support for PyQt6 and PySide6 with a single library import. The only caveat is that you must ensure PyQt6 is imported before (as in on the line above or earlier) when importing this library, to ensure it is in sys.modules.

To account for the lack of shorthand enum and flags in PyQt6 you can generate these yourself. For example, the following code will copy references for each of the enum objects elements up to their parent object, making them accessible as in PyQt5, PySide2 & PySide6. The code would only need to be run under PyQt6.

```
enums = [
    (QtCore.Qt, 'Alignment'),
    (QtCore.Qt, 'ApplicationAttribute'),
    (QtCore.Qt, 'CheckState'),
    (QtCore.Qt, 'CursorShape'),
    (QtWidgets.QSizePolicy, 'Policy'),
]

# Look up using the long name (e.g. QtCore.Qt.CheckState.Checked,
used
# in PyQt6) and store under the short name (e.g. QtCore.Checked, used
# in PyQt5, PySide2 & accepted by PySide6).
for module, enum_name in enums:
    for entry in getattr(module, enum_name):
        setattr(module, entry.name, entry)
```

Alternatively, you can define a custom function to handle the namespace lookup.

```
def _enum(obj, name):
    parent, child = name.split('.')
    result = getattr(obj, child, False)
    if result:  # Found using short name only.
        return result

    obj = getattr(obj, parent)  # Get parent, then child.
    return getattr(obj, child)
```

When passed an object and a PyQt6 compatible long-form name, this function will return the correct enum or flag on both PyQt6 and PySide6.

```
>>> _enum(PySide6.QtCore.Qt, 'Alignment.AlignLeft')
PySide6.QtCore.Qt.AlignmentFlag.AlignLeft
>>> _enum(PyQt6.QtCore.Qt, 'Alignment.AlignLeft')
<Alignment.AlignLeft: 1>
```

If you're doing this in multiple files it can get a bit cumbersome. A nice solution to this is to move the import logic and custom shim methods to their own file, e.g.

named `qt.py` in your project root. This module imports the Qt modules (`QtCore`, `QtGui`, `QtWidgets`, etc.) from one of the two libraries, and then you import into your application from there.

The contents of the `qt.py` are the same as we used earlier —

```python
import sys

if 'PyQt6' in sys.modules:
    # PyQt6
    from PyQt6 import QtGui, QtWidgets, QtCore
    from PyQt6.QtCore import pyqtSignal as Signal, pyqtSlot as Slot


else:
    # PySide6
    from PySide6 import QtGui, QtWidgets, QtCore
    from PySide6.QtCore import Signal, Slot


def _enum(obj, name):
    parent, child = name.split('.')
    result = getattr(obj, child, False)
    if result:  # Found using short name only.
        return result

    obj = getattr(obj, parent)  # Get parent, then child.
    return getattr(obj, child)
```

You must remember to add any other PyQt6 modules you use (browser, multimedia, etc.) in both branches of the if block. You can then import **Qt6** into your own application as follows —

```python
from .qt import QtGui, QtWidgets, QtCore, _enum
```

...and it will work seamlessly across either library.

784

That's really it

There's not much more to say — the two libraries really are that similar. However, if you do stumble across any other PyQt6/PySide6 examples or features which you can't easily convert, drop me a note.

Appendix D: What next?

This book covers the key things you need to know to start creating GUI applications with Python. If you've made it here you should be well on your way to create your own apps!

But there is still a lot to discover while you build your applications. To help with this I post regular tips, tutorials and code snippets on the accompanying website [https://www.pythonguis.com/]. Like this book all samples are MIT licensed and free to mix into your own apps. You may also be interested in joining the Python GUI Academy [https://academy.pythonguis.com/] where there are video tutorials covering the topics in this book & beyond.

Thanks for reading, and if you have any feedback or suggestions please let me know [mailto:martin@pythonguis.com]!

Get access to updates

If you bought this book direct from me, you will receive automatic updates to this book. If you bought this book elsewhere, you can email your receipt to me [mailto:register@pythonguis.com] to get access future updates.

Documentation

Resource
Qt6 Documentation [https://doc.qt.io/qt-6/]
PyQt6 Library documentation [http://pyqt.sourceforge.net/Docs/PyQt6/]
PySide "Qt for Python" Library documentation [https://doc.qt.io/qtforpython/]

Copyright

This book is ©2022 Martin Fitzpatrick. All code examples in this book are free to use in your own programming projects without license.

43. Thank you

This book continues to be expanded and updated in response to reader feedback. Thankyou to the following readers for their contributions, which helped make this edition what it is!

- James Battat

- Alex Bender

- Andries Broekema

- Juan Cabanela

- Max Fritzler

- Olivier Girard

- Richard Hohlfield

- Cody Jackson

- John E Kadwell

- Jeffrey R Kennedy

- Gajendra Khanna

- Bing Xiao Liu

- Alex Lombardi

- Juan Pablo Donayre Quintana

- Rodrigo de Salvo Braz

- Guido Tognan

If you have feedback or suggestions for future editions, please get in touch [mailto:martin@pythonguis.com].

Index

Made in the USA
Las Vegas, NV
02 January 2024

83774165R00437

Listing 304. app/minesweeper.py

```python
def paintEvent(self, event):
    p = QPainter(self)
    p.setRenderHint(QPainter.RenderHint.Antialiasing)

    r = event.rect()

    if self.is_revealed:
        if self.is_start:
            p.drawPixmap(r, QPixmap(IMG_START))

        elif self.is_mine:
            p.drawPixmap(r, QPixmap(IMG_BOMB))

        elif self.adjacent_n > 0:
            pen = QPen(NUM_COLORS[self.adjacent_n])
            p.setPen(pen)
            f = p.font()
            f.setBold(True)
            p.setFont(f)
            p.drawText(
                r,
                Qt.AlignmentFlag.AlignHCenter
                | Qt.AlignmentFlag.AlignVCenter,
                str(self.adjacent_n),
            )

    else:
        p.fillRect(r, QBrush(Qt.GlobalColor.lightGray))
        pen = QPen(Qt.GlobalColor.gray)
        pen.setWidth(1)
        p.setPen(pen)
        p.drawRect(r)

        if self.is_flagged:
            p.drawPixmap(r, QPixmap(IMG_FLAG))
```

Mechanics

We commonly need to get all tiles surrounding a given point, so we have a

QPixmap vs. QImages

You might think "why not just store these as `QPixmap` objects since that's what we're using? We can't do this and store them in constants because you can't create `QPixmap` objects before your `QApplication` is up and running.

For empty positions (not rockets, not bombs) we optionally show the adjacency number if it is larger than zero. To draw text onto our `QPainter` we use `.drawText()` passing in the `QRect`, alignment flags and the number to draw as a string. We've defined a standard color for each number (stored in `NUM_COLORS`) for usability.

For tiles that are *not* revealed we draw a tile, by filling a rectangle with light gray and draw a 1 pixel border of darker grey. If `.is_flagged` is set, we also draw a flag icon over the top of the tile using `drawPixmap` and the tile `QRect`.